Cold War Europe

Cold War Europe

The Politics of a Contested Continent

Mark Gilbert

ROWMAN & LITTLEFIELD
Lanham • Boulder • New York • London

Published by Rowman & Littlefield
A wholly owned subsidiary of
The Rowman & Littlefield Publishing Group, Inc.
4501 Forbes Boulevard, Suite 200, Lanham, Maryland 20706
www.rowman.com

Unit A, Whitacre Mews, 26-34 Stannary Street, London SE11 4AB,
United Kingdom

British Library Cataloguing in Publication Information Available

Library of Congress Cataloging-in-Publication Data
Gilbert, Mark, 1961–
Cold War Europe : the politics of a contested continent / Mark Gilbert.
pages cm
Includes bibliographical references and index.
ISBN 978-1-4422-1984-7 (cloth : alk. paper) — ISBN 978-1-4422-1985-4 (pbk. : alk. paper) —
ISBN 978-1-4422-1986-1 (electronic)
1. Europe—Politics and government—1945- 2. Cold War. I. Title.
D1053.G48 2014
940.55—dc23
2014034723

∞ ™ The paper used in this publication meets the minimum requirements of American
National Standard for Information Sciences Permanence of Paper for Printed Library
Materials, ANSI/NISO Z39.48-1992.

Printed in the United States of America

Contents

Acronyms Used in the Text

ACP	Communist Party (Albania)
AMAG	American Mission to Greece
AVH	State Security Police (Hungary)
BCP	Communist Party (Bulgaria)
BSP	Socialist Party (Bulgaria)
CCP	Communist Party (China)
CDU	Christian Democrats (West Germany)
CFM	Council of Foreign Ministers
CGIL	General Workers' Confederation (Italy)
CIA	Central Intelligence Agency
CIS	Commonwealth of Independent States
CMEA	Council for Mutual Economic Assistance
CND	Campaign for Nuclear Disarmament
CPSU	Communist Party (Soviet Union)
CSCE	Conference on Security and Cooperation in Europe
CSU	Christian Social Union (Bavaria)
CWHP	Cold War History Project
DC	Christian Democracy (Italy)
DM	Deutsche Mark
DP	Democratic Party (Albania)

EAM	National Liberation Front (Greece)
ECA	European Cooperation Agency
ECSC	European Coal and Steel Community
ECU	European Currency Unit
EDC	European Defense Community
EEC	European Economic Community
ELAS	National Liberation Army (Greece)
EMS	European Monetary System
END	European Nuclear Disarmament
EPC	European Political Community
ERP	European Recovery Plan
EU	European Union
FDP	Free Democrat Party (West Germany)
FIDESz	Alliance of Young Democrats (Hungary)
FRG	Federal Republic of Germany
FRUS	Foreign Relations of the United States
FTU	Free Trade Union Movement (Poland)
GDA	Greek Democratic Army
GDP	Gross Domestic Product
GDR	German Democratic Republic
GNP	Gross National Product
HDZ	Democratic Union (Croatia)
ICBM	intercontinental ballistic missile
ICFTU	International Confederation of Free Trade Unions
IGC	intergovernmental conference
IISS	International Institute for Strategic Studies
IKV	Interdenominational Peace Council (Netherlands)
IMF	International Monetary Fund
KČE	Communist Party (Czechoslovakia)
KdA	Campaign Against Nuclear Death (West Germany)
KGB	State Security Police (Soviet Union)
KKE	Communist Party (Greece)

KOR	Committee for the Defense of the Workers (Poland)
KPD	Communist Party (Germany)
MDF	Democratic Forum (Hungary)
MDP	Democrat Movement (Portugal)
MDS	Movement for a Democratic Slovakia
MFA	Armed Forces Movement (Portugal)
MLF	multilateral force
NATO	North Atlantic Treaty Organization
NDF	National Democratic Front (Romania)
NEP	New Economic Policy (Soviet Union)
NSC	National Security Council
NSF	National Salvation Front (Romania)
NVA	People's Army (GDR)
OAS	Secret Organized Army (French Algeria)
OEEC	Organisation for European Economic Co-operation
PASOK	Pan-Hellenic Socialist Party (Greece)
PCE	Communist Party (Spain)
PCF	Communist Party (France)
PCI	Communist Party (Italy)
PCP	Communist Party (Portugal)
PDS	Democratic Party of the Left (Italy)
PDS	Party of Democratic Socialism (Germany)
PLA	Party of Labor (Albania)
PNW	Prevention of Nuclear War
PPD	Popular Democrats (Portugal)
PRI	Republican Party (Italy)
PSF	Socialist Party (France)
PSI	Socialist Party (Italy)
PSLI	Socialist Party of the Italian Workers
PSOE	Socialist Party (Spain)
RFE	Radio Free Europe
SACEUR	Supreme Allied Commander in Europe

SALT	Strategic Arms Limitations Talks
SDI	Strategic Defense Initiative
SEATO	South East Asia Treaty Organization
SED	Socialist Unity Party (GDR)
SHAPE	Supreme Headquarters Allied Powers Europe
SKDL	Finnish People's Democratic League
SNGP	Siberian Natural Gas Pipeline
SPA	Socialist Party (Albania)
SPD	Social Democrats (West Germany)
SSR	Soviet Socialist Republic
SzDSz	Alliance of Free Democrats (Hungary)
UNO	United Nations Organization
U.S.	United States
USSR	Union of Soviet Socialist Republics
WEU	Western European Union
WTO	Warsaw Treaty Organization

Acknowledgments

This book is a companion volume to my *European Integration: A Concise History*, which was published by Rowman & Littlefield in November 2011. Like its predecessor, this book is a general narrative of a major aspect of postwar European political history.

Publisher Susan McEachern was supportive and encouraging and almost excessively willing to turn a blind eye to the numerous false starts caused by my fluctuating research interests and general restlessness. We have now published four books together, and I can only salute her infallible courtesy and endless patience, and express my thanks for her confidence in my work.

Since September 2012 I have been resident professor of history and international relations at SAIS Europe, the Bologna Center of the Paul H. Nitze School of Advanced International Studies of the Johns Hopkins University. This remarkable institution, which for sixty years has provided an agora where American students of international affairs and their European (and, increasingly, non-European) counterparts can meet, learn, and debate, offers a unique interdisciplinary environment for a historian with interests outside his field. I probably would not have written this book had I not been invited by SAIS to teach, as an adjunct professor, a course entitled "Europe in the Cold War" back in 2009. In different iterations, I have now taught the course five times, and I can here only dimly convey how much my students' insights and enthusiasm have contributed to making this book possible. In academic year 2012–2013, Martha Simms was both a student in the class and my research assistant. She was particularly helpful in the preparation of chapters 3 through 6.

Erik Jones, the head of the European Studies Program at SAIS, first invited me to teach in Bologna, and he has remained a constant stimulus. My colleagues Marco Cesa, David Ellwood, John Harper, Masha Hedberg, and

David Unger have all discussed some of the issues raised in the book with me, and many other things, too. SAIS librarians Ludovica Barozzi, Gail Martin, and John Williams deserve a special thanks for their friendly efficiency and dedication. Above all, working with Ken Keller, the director of the Bologna Center for the past eight years, has been a revelation. I used to wonder what the somewhat nebulous phrase "academic leadership" really meant: I now know.

Anne Deighton of Oxford University, Federico Romero of the European University Institute, Christopher Hill of Cambridge University, and Antonio Varsori of Padua University have had to read a lot of my work in recent years: I can only thank them for their kindness and positive judgments. I hope they will read this book, too.

Chapter 2 is based upon a chapter I originally published in *A Companion to Europe since 1945* (Oxford: Blackwell, 2009). I would like to thank the book's editor, Klaus Larres, and Tessa Harvey of Wiley Blackwell for allowing me to reissue my work here. Parts of chapter 10 originally appeared (in Italian) in *Le crisi transatlantiche. Continuità e trasformazioni*, (Roma: Edizioni di storia e letteratura, 2007). I am indebted to Mario Del Pero and Federico Romero, the book's editors, for their willingness to allow me to reproduce (in English) some of my words.

As always, my biggest debt is to Luciana and Francisco, for putting up with me at home and for dealing so well with my repeated absences during the academic year. I would like to dedicate the book, however, to five teachers: Howard Davies, Hilary Sheffield, David Manning, A. J. M. Milne, and Charles Reynolds. The first two named taught me, respectively, English literature and history at school; the latter three led brilliant, challenging seminars in political thought and international relations when I was an undergraduate at Durham University. Thirty years on, I realize just how much I owe them all.

Chapter One

Introduction

The American diplomatic historian John Lewis Gaddis categorized the Cold War as a "long peace."[1] Gaddis's argument was that the essential characteristic of the Cold War was precisely that it was not a war at all, at any rate one between the superpowers. Fear of nuclear destruction ensured that the United States and the Soviet Union refrained from furthering their interests and defending their prestige by using war as an instrument of policy. This argument is valid, of course, only if one ignores proxy wars and wars in the developing world; Afghanistan, Korea, Southeast Asia, Central America, and Sub-Saharan Africa were ravaged by hot wars that were of Cold War provenance.[2]

It remains true that in Europe the struggle between the two giants that had emerged victorious at the end of World War II did not culminate in a major military conflict. This is not to imply that Europe's Cold War was peaceful, at any rate in the Soviet bloc. Between 1947 and 1953, spurred by Soviet leader Joseph Stalin, the national communist parties of Central Europe reconstructed their countries along the same lines as the Soviet Union, which communists the world over regarded as the society advancing most rapidly toward social justice. The human consequences of this act of political compulsion were vast. Although economic growth was spurred and social modernization took place, hundreds of thousands of Czechs, Romanians, Hungarians, and other peoples saw their traditional ways of life smashed to pieces. Tens of thousands lost their lives in the postwar terror, and millions were persecuted, while patterns of land ownership, social structures, and rival political identities were destroyed ruthlessly.

The only test that the Stalinist communism recognized was History—with a capital H. By using terror, collectivization, and the crash industrialization of an agricultural society, the USSR had become a great power and had been

able to defeat the Nazi invasion. An omelet had been made, albeit at the cost of millions of eggs.[3] As the British political thinker Sir Isaiah Berlin commented at the conclusion of a visit to the USSR in 1945, in Russia the Soviet leadership had inherited an "Athenian society" in which a "small elite"—the Russian aristocracy and intelligentsia—was "supported" by a "dark mass of idle, feckless, semi-barbarous helots." If there was "one single continuing strain in the Leninist policy," Berlin argued, it was "the desire to make of these dark people full human beings." Berlin warned that the ideological outlook of Stalin and his closest collaborators was such that "no cost" in human or civil liberties was regarded as too high a price to pay for the "organized material progress" of the masses.[4]

Had communist society provided the peoples of Eastern and Central Europe with a higher standard of living and more significant cultural achievements than the West, then the human costs associated with its imposition would have been unflinchingly proclaimed as acceptable by communists and "fellow travelers" across Europe. But the central fact about the Cold War in Europe—the fact from which everything else stemmed—is that communism flunked the test it had set itself. After an initial surge in production, as rural societies were transformed into industrial civilizations producing coal, steel, ships, tractors, and cement, and in which entire new cities were built to house (dismally) the flood of workers being directed from agriculture to industry, communist societies began to display the defects of a command economy. The goods they produced were mostly inferior to western products and could only be sold to other communist states; innovation was snuffed out by ideological conformity and the lack of competition; hours of work were long and workplace conditions were often dreadful—worse, certainly, than was permitted in most of the capitalist states of Europe.

The official propaganda of the communist states continued to claim, however, that their citizens were living in "really existing socialism," which was depicted as a higher form of social organization than the bourgeois capitalism of Western Europe. There was hence a radical disjuncture between rhetoric and reality. To use a phrase made famous by Czech playwright and political activist Václav Havel, citizens of a communist state had to learn to "live within the lie." That is to say, they had to constantly act as if they believed that an obsolete steelworks belching poisonous smoke was a triumph of socialist prosperity, or that Soviet leader Leonid Brezhnev's turgid memoirs were a literary masterpiece, or even that the secret police were guardians of the achievements of the revolution. After Stalin's death, outright terror ceased to be communist society's organizing principle, but the doublethink required of the citizens remained, and so did a watchful secret police. Moreover, when the people rebelled, as they did in Hungary in 1956, Czechoslovakia in 1968, and Poland in 1981, military force was employed to restore "socialist legality."

The history of the Cold War, when depicted from a European perspective, has to be largely about the process by which communist ideology and the pervasive dictatorships erected in its name were discredited and fell apart. Having said this, one should not make the error—typical of much early Cold War political science in the United States—of characterizing the communist bloc as monolithic. The communist parties of Europe were not invariably faithful executors of Moscow's "line" (though usually they were). Stalin broke with Yugoslavia in 1948 because Belgrade was a potential troublemaker; Yugoslav leader Josip Broz Tito certainly showed his mettle in the ensuing clash between his country and the rest of the Soviet bloc. Poland's leader Władisław Gomułka bluntly told the USSR to stay out of his country's internal affairs in 1956. The Albanians deviated from Moscow's line in the early 1960s in order to pursue Chairman Mao's purist brand of Marxism-Leninism (and then judged Mao's own heirs wanting). Italian party chief Palmiro Togliatti ticked off Soviet leader Nikita Khrushchev for his overbearing attitude toward the Chinese deviationists (and by implication toward all those, including the more moderate Italians, who wanted to find their own way to socialism). Most strikingly of all, in 1968, Czechoslovakia's leadership encouraged innovations in the ideological sphere that were designed to lead to political pluralism and then evaded repeated demands from its neighbors to stifle the liberal and inquiring society that bubbled to the surface in Prague as soon as ideological controls were relaxed. Soviet tanks were needed to re-store normality, which of course was really abnormality. All these "devia-tions," or nuances, have to be brushed meticulously into the picture.

While the rise and fall of European communism inevitably occupies the center of the canvas, the relationship between the western democracies and the United States is an important part of this book's composition. I have drawn a picture of a litigious alliance. In the West, contestation with the dominant local superpower was largely conducted by elites, who clamored for a U.S. military commitment to Europe but who were anything but quies-cent allies. It was not easy for proud nations like Great Britain or France to acknowledge that they were no longer able to defend themselves without U.S. aid or to bend their foreign policy concerns to wider U.S. strategic interests. The Suez crisis in 1956, when Britain and France invaded Egypt against Washington's wishes, was an emblematic moment in this regard.

Still, there was no case during the Cold War of a West European people rising up in desperate anguish against the institutions of representative de-mocracy and the socio-economic order established after 1945. Even the stu-dent protests of 1968 were, if one thinks about it, essentially an elite demon-stration rather than a popular insurrection. In the early 1980s, millions of ordinary British, Dutch, German, and Italian citizens protested against the siting of U.S. intermediate range missiles on their territory, and their protest was backed by most of Western Europe's left-wing parties. But the protest was nonviolent and did not aim at the overthrow of these countries' regimes.

Certainly no people in Western Europe, Italy alone excepted, showed the slightest interest in experimenting with communist rule (France was gov-erned by a coalition of socialists and communists between 1981 and 1984, but the Socialist Party [PSF] was the dominant partner and also held the presidency). Not by chance, Italy possessed both a communist party whose commitment to democratic norms was by the 1970s firm (though not beyond reproach) and ruling political elites whose commitment to the liberal values espoused by the West at times seemed rather tenuous.

The task that this book has set itself, therefore, is to paint a picture in which Europeans (statesmen and peoples) were protagonists in the Cold War from its origins to its end. Europeans imposed "really existing socialism" and also resisted and theorized it. They contributed to the construction of the West and disputed U.S. hegemony (though even French president Charles de Gaulle did not challenge American leadership). They certainly played a cru-cial role in bringing the conflict to an end, superpower diplomacy notwith-standing. Mikhail S. Gorbachev's "new thinking," President Ronald Rea-gan's broadness of vision, President George Bush's diplomatic deftness all contributed to terminating the Cold War, but the peoples and leaders of Europe were the protagonists. In this respect, the book has taken its lead from a remarkable work of contemporary history, Gale Stokes's *The Walls Came*

Tumbling Down, whose depiction of the enormous transformation in the politics and society of Central and Eastern Europe wrought by people power between 1968 and 1989 is wholly convincing in interpretation.[5] The year 1989 was indeed a second 1848, a vast revolt across most of Europe against an oppressive order that thankfully has so far not been the prelude to repression and reaction—which is what usually happens in Europe's great transformative moments.

The book is organized in thematic chapters that are also in approximate chronological order: that is to say, it is a narrative history. Chapter 2, "From War to Cold War," deals with the "outbreak" of the Cold War, which is another way of saying that it charts the decisions, mistakes, and strategic considerations that led to a breakdown in relations between the USSR and its western allies between 1945 and the summer of 1947, when the United States launched the Marshall Plan as a "soft power" adjunct to the uncompromising anti-communism of the March 1947 declaration of the Truman Doctrine. In response, the USSR created the Communist Information Bureau, or Cominform, to act as a clearinghouse in the struggle against so-called capitalist imperialism, and began the Stalinization of the peoples and territories in its sphere of interest.

Chapter 3 is concerned precisely with the imposition of a totalitarian form of society on Central Europe in the wake of the formation of the Cominform. "Totalitarian" is a word that many scholars find too redolent of western Cold War propaganda, but it is, in my view, a necessary descriptor for the Stalinist phase in postwar European history.[6] The atmosphere that prevailed in the communist bloc states—but also within the communist parties of the West—can realistically be characterized in no other way.

Chapter 4, by contrast, deals with the United States' fragile relationship with its *imperium* in Western and Southern Europe. Between 1947 and 1958, the United States took the lead in establishing the North Atlantic Treaty Organization (NATO), in promoting a security dimension to European integration, and in consolidating its position in Europe's problematic southern flank. In all these endeavors, the United States met opposition, or principled disagreement, from its European allies and had to rely on European politicians—some of whom were distinctly unsavory—to achieve a reasonable approximation of its goals. Any metaphorical suggestion that the United States was somehow the architect of the Cold War order should be accepted only with a sense of realism as to how architects actually work: they change their plans constantly in response to their clients, to officials from town hall, and to the builders who have to turn their blueprints into livable edifices. Certainly, that is how American policy makers dealt with the Europeans in the 1950s. They did not just tell the Europeans what to do, and the Europeans did not necessarily listen to their advice.

Maintaining communist control of Central Europe was even messier. Chapter 5 deals with the "turmoil" that beset the Soviet bloc—indeed, the whole world communist movement—as a result of de-Stalinization and the secret speech denouncing Stalin's crimes made by the Soviet leader, Nikita S. Khrushchev, in February 1956. Khrushchev's speech was a watershed in Europe's long peace, not least because its smashing of ideological idols gave world communism a body blow from which it never really recovered. If communism was inevitably the future, and if the Soviet party was the infallible interpreter of history's direction, how was it possible that it had been led down the wrong road by a criminal maniac who had murdered millions? When the disillusioned Poles and Hungarians demanded to be allowed to choose their own path toward socialist development in 1956, or even to abandon socialism altogether, they were repressed brutally. But the underlying, nagging problem of legitimacy unveiled by Khrushchev's revelations could not be dispelled by tanks. The year 1956, which also experienced the Suez crisis, was as a result the most important single year in the European Cold War until 1989.

Chapter 6 deals with the question of Germany, its division in 1949, and its political and economic development in the 1950s in two separate states—the Federal Republic of Germany (FRG) and the German Democratic Republic (GDR), as the communist half of the country was euphemistically known. The German question was crucial in the early Cold War since it was there that conflict was most likely to break out. Any such war would have been nuclear from day one: NATO planning assumed the use of tactical weapons—most of which were more powerful than the bombs dropped on Hiroshima and Nagasaki—to stop advancing Soviet tanks. Nevertheless, between 1958 and 1961, Soviet leader Khrushchev tried to force the West to accept a settlement for Germany that would have led to its unification, neutralization, and perhaps communization. When Khrushchev's bluff was called, the GDR built the Berlin Wall in August 1961 and the European Cold War acquired its most notorious (and ugly) icon.

Chapters 7 and 8 look at European dissent toward the superpowers in both the Soviet bloc and in the West. The 1960s was a decade of contestation, and not just because of the massive student protests that swept the continent. The USSR's role as the leader of the world socialist movement and as the interpreter of the politically correct line (the origin of this phrase) was contested by both Chinese and European communists in the face of the failure of Khrushchev's foreign policy in Berlin and Cuba, and in the face of growing evidence that the communist bloc, far from superseding the West in production and living standards, as Khrushchev had frequently boasted, was falling behind both economically and culturally. The most powerful internal critique of Soviet practice was mounted by the Czechs, whose attempt, under party leader Alexander Dubček, to construct "socialism with a human face" was crushed by Soviet tanks.

In the West, French president Charles de Gaulle tried—in vain—to persuade his fellow democratic leaders in Europe that the United States' security and economic policies were demeaning and that Western Europe needed to forge its own destiny, with its own strong institutions of governance, its own *force de frappe*, and its own policy of détente with the communist world. France left NATO's command structure in 1966. Between de Gaulle, radicalized Maoist students afraid of being *cocacolonisé*, the neo-Stalinist French Communist Party, and liberal intellectuals alarmed by the scale of the "American challenge" to Europe's industrial base and economic future, France was hostile terrain for the United States in the 1960s (as was Sweden).[7]

In the 1970s and early 1980s, West European leaders, above all FRG chancellor Willy Brandt, sought to establish a working relationship with the countries of the Soviet bloc and to diminish tensions by recognizing the GDR, accepting the inviolability of the frontiers of Poland, and extending human contacts with the benighted citizens of East Germany. This so-called *Ostpolitik* was reinforced by a broader effort by democratic Europe to negotiate with the Soviet bloc in the Conference on Security and Cooperation in Europe (CSCE) between 1972 and August 1975, when the so-called Helsinki Accords were signed. At Helsinki, the USSR and its satellites signed up to a document that guaranteed the liberal freedoms of speech, assembly, worship, and political organization. They even published the fact of their signature in their party newspapers. Human rights activists across the communist bloc, most notably the Charter 77 movement in Czechoslovakia, seized the opportunity to point out abuses of the Helsinki principles. Of course, such "dissident" voices soon found themselves behind bars, or working in menial jobs under constant harassment from the authorities' paid snoopers. But by their actions they punctured the communist version of reality.[8] In 1980, the shipyard workers of Poland, by launching what amounted to a proletarian revolution against the communist bourgeoisie of their country, completed the job of showing that the communist system was bankrupt both economically and intellectually—though this did not prevent the regime from launching a coup d'état to restore its power. Chapter 9 discusses these developments in detail.

In Chapter 10, the focus shifts back to the transatlantic relationship. The frustrations expressed by Charles de Gaulle in the 1960s became a commonplace in the 1970s. The United States and its Western European allies squabbled over monetary policy, over the EEC's desire to conduct an independent foreign policy, over the Mediterranean, where U.S. policy was suspicious of the process of democratization, over the U.S. defense posture in Europe, and, after the election of Ronald Reagan, over the president's anti-Soviet rhetoric and arms buildup. The transatlantic relationship arguably touched its Cold

War nadir between 1968 and 1984, although it retained enough cohesion to site intermediate nuclear missiles in response to prior Soviet deployments of similar weapons and to face down mass campaigns against the missiles' presence.

Strange as it may seem today, few thought that communism was on the verge of disintegrating in the mid-1980s. The Polish workers' movement, Solidarity, had been crushed by the state, the United States was distrusted and unpopular in much of Western and Southern Europe, and in January 1985, the USSR chose a new leader, Mikhail S. Gorbachev, whose style and policy of perestroika (restructuring) charmed even the stoniest European opponents of communism—Britain's prime minister Margaret Thatcher, for instance. Yet Gorbachev's attempts at reform were in fact a desperate last throw for the communist system, which was falling hopelessly behind the West in economic terms—further, probably, than the West's most sophisticated analysts realized. Chapter 11 deals with the unraveling of the communist system of power across Europe between 1985 and 1989. By the end of 1989, the Berlin Wall had been breached; a former dissident, Václav Havel, had become president of Czechoslovakia; free elections had been held in Poland; and a bloody coup d'état had overthrown the regime in Romania. The Hungarian communists were themselves prudently democratizing their nation. Romania apart, these tumultuous events took place without loss of life. Only the USSR, the GDR (nominally), and still-Stalinist Albania remained communist.

The giant earthquake that took place in 1989 was followed by huge aftershocks that reshaped the map of Europe. Germany was improbably united as early as October 1990, less than a year after the fall of the Berlin Wall, an event that propelled a parallel intensification in the process of European unification and the signature of the Treaty on European Union in February 1992. The USSR broke up under the triple effect of its international humiliation, its economic and ideological failure, and the demand for national sovereignty by its constituent peoples; Czechoslovakia followed suit in 1992, while the end of the Cold War also precipitated Yugoslavia into interethnic strife between 1989 and 1992. Albania lapsed into anarchy; on the other side of the Adriatic, Italy's seemingly perennial political system lost its rationale when the Cold War ended. Its communist party jettisoned its Marxist-Leninist baggage in 1988 through 1989, and the governing Christian Democrats and Socialists were robbed of the bogeyman with which they had retained their hold over the Italian middle class. Major political upheaval ensued. The book's concluding chapter deals both with this redrawing of Europe's political geography and the smashing of its last Cold War icons.

This overview will have clarified for the reader that the book's main subject matter is political history. There is little, alas, on the cultural Cold War, and little too on the purely military aspects of the conflict. Anybody wishing to find insight into the Cold War novel in German prose, or the role of the American foundations in financing European culture, or the maneuverability and deployment of battle tanks, has chosen the wrong volume.

This narrative choice was deliberate. The book has no pretension to be a definitive, all-encompassing account, but is—like any general history—an essay that tries to isolate and emphasize what is central to the story. In a passage I never tire of quoting, the Polish-British historian Lewis Namier said that "the function of the historian is akin to that of the painter and not of the photographic camera; to discover and set forth, to single out and stress that which is the nature of the thing, and not to reproduce indiscriminately all that meets the eye."[9] I think politics *is* the "nature of the thing" in Europe's long peace, but I am aware that that has meant leaving a great deal out.

It has also meant putting a great deal in. Writing this book has required me to read widely in the contemporary histories of the numerous European countries whose political development was deeply influenced by the Cold War. Albania, Greece, Portugal, and Romania are all painted into the portrayal of the Cold War given by this book, although Czechoslovakia, Germany, Hungary, Italy, and Poland are naturally given an even more prominent place in the book's composition. The superpowers are integrated into the picture, but I have tried not to let them crowd the canvas. Stalin, Khrushchev, and Gorbachev, however, more than any U.S. president, really mattered to the lives, politics, and indeed existence of the European peoples. Their actions are thus central to the portrait of Europe's long peace depicted here and, without overloading the volume with Kremlinology, I have given substantial narrative space to how certain key political changes occurred in Moscow. The story would not have made sense otherwise.

I have often thought that only a polymath who read (at least) Russian, French, Polish, Czech, Italian, and German could possibly attempt this volume, but since such paragons have not written a book like this one in English, I thought I would try. The book is a textbook, not a work for specialists, and as such I hope that its intended readers—university students and their instructors—will find it a useful survey of a vast topic.

NOTES

1. John Lewis Gaddis, *The Long Peace: Inquiries into the History of the Cold War* (Oxford: Oxford University Press, 1987), 215–45.

2. Odd Arne Westad's brilliant *The Global Cold War* (Cambridge: Cambridge University Press, 2006) powerfully argues that the Cold War was, in effect, a continuation (indeed, in many ways an exacerbation) of European imperialism by two superpowers whose worldviews and political cultures were paradoxically strongly anticolonial. The Cold War, in Westad's depiction, was a bloody worldwide struggle for mastery between two messianic ideologies, not a prolonged tense standoff between two great powers.

3. Timothy Snyder, *Bloodlands: Europe between Hitler and Stalin* (London: Random House, 2011), 53, estimates that about 3.3 million people starved as a result of the collectiviza-

tion of agriculture and its associated repression in Ukraine alone in the early 1930s. The Soviet census of 1937 found eight million fewer citizens than expected, most of whom were certainly victims of Stalin's policies, or else the children they did not have. The demographers responsible for the census were shot. During the "Great Terror" (1934–1939), at least three-quarters of a million "kulaks" (peasants), army officers, and party members were executed as "class enemies" as Stalin wiped out all groups that might constitute an alternative regime. Millions more unfortunates were sentenced to long terms in the labor camps of Siberia and Kazakhstan, where many froze or were worked to death. The point is that this bloodbath was regarded as a model of successful modernization by the communists who took power in Central Europe after 1947.

4. Quoted in Anne Deighton, "Don and Diplomat: Isaiah Berlin and Britain's Early Cold War," *Cold War History* 13 (2013): 533. The telegram is reprinted in full in Berlin, *The Soviet Mind: Russian Culture under Communism*, ed. Henry Hardy (Washington, DC: The Brookings Institution, 2011), 1–27.

5. Gale Stokes, *The Walls Came Tumbling Down* (Oxford: Oxford University Press, 1993). I am citing the first edition, since it is the one that made such a lasting impression on me. A second edition was published in 2008.

6. See Abbott Gleason, *Totalitarianism: The Inner History of the Cold War* (Oxford: Oxford University Press, 1997), especially chapter 7, 121–42, for a discussion of the word's abuse during the Cold War.

7. See Jean-Jacques Servan-Schreiber, *The American Challenge* (London: Pelican, 1968) for an analysis of how U.S. technical knowledge, financial strength, organizational skill, political cohesion, and flexibility were turning Europe into a second-rate civilization.

8. Two outstanding books that stress this point are Federico Romero, *Storia della guerra fredda: L'ultimo conflitto per L'Europa* (Turin: Einaudi, 2009), which is one of the most thoughtful general histories of the Cold War currently available, and Daniel C. Thomas, *The Helsinki Effect* (Princeton, NJ: Princeton University Press, 2001), which is the most able application of constructivist international relations theory to contemporary history that I know.

9. Lewis Namier, "History and Political Culture," in *The Varieties of History: From Voltaire to the Present*, ed. Fritz Stern (London: Macmillan 1970), 379.

Chapter Two

From War to Cold War

By late summer 1944, the Red Army was fighting its way into Poland and Romania and would shortly occupy Bulgaria. American and British troops had invaded France in June 1944 and, with the assistance of Charles de Gaulle's Free French forces, liberated Paris at the end of August. The Greek capital, Athens, was seized by the British in October 1944; Italy, meanwhile, had been freed as far north as Florence. In short, it was clear that the Third Reich was doomed. Germany's casualties were totaled in the millions, and its armies were outgunned, outnumbered, and overstretched.

In Czechoslovakia, Poland, Italy, Norway, Yugoslavia, and France, the Nazis were fighting savage wars of repression against partisans. Villages such as Lidice in Czechoslovakia, Oradour in France, and Marzabotto in Italy, whose inhabitants were exterminated in reprisal for partisan attacks, remain evocative *lieux de mémoire* to this day. In Poland, massacres of civilians were daily events. In August 1944, as Russian troops neared Warsaw, partisans of the Polish Home Army raised a heroic insurrection against the Germans. Ominously, the advancing Soviet forces halted their forward drive and waited while SS units crushed the uprising. The USSR, whose forces had already met armed opposition and sabotage as they pushed into territory that had belonged to Poland prior to the August 1939 Nazi-Soviet Pact, no more wanted patriotic guerrilla units operating within their territory than did the Germans. [1]

As the Nazis retreated, the machinery of the Final Solution was wound down. Europe would soon discover the damage done by the Nazis' ideological madness. Between five and six million Jews had been killed by the *Einsatzgruppen* (death squads) or in the extermination camps located in eastern Poland. Hundreds of thousands of other "undesirables"—political opponents, the Roma, the mentally and physically handicapped, homosexuals—had also been murdered.

The Allies themselves were waging war with terrible brutality. Dresden, Hamburg, and the Ruhr were victims of "obliteration raids" during the last months of the war. In the east, advancing Soviet forces treated the enemy with the same callous indifference to human life that the Nazis themselves had applied in Russia. Captured German soldiers were either shot or sent eastward to windswept labor camps behind the lines. Many never returned.

The central question facing the Allies was whether they would continue their wartime cooperation to revive a morally and physically devastated continent. As the war drew to an end, there was still optimism on this score. President Franklin Delano Roosevelt and Premier Winston Churchill believed that they had a good working relationship with Soviet leader Joseph Stalin and could reach a settlement with him. This optimism was shattered by events. The Allies found it harder to make peace than war. As a result, Germany was partitioned economically and politically by 1947, although the formal creation of the two Germanies only occurred in the summer of 1949. In Eastern Europe, Soviet-backed regimes gradually eliminated all political opposition.

At the end of the war, Stalin told the Yugoslav intellectual Milovan Djilas that every victorious army inevitably imposed its own social system on the territory it had conquered.[2] It was a principle that the United States and Britain regarded as admissible only in part.

THE HIGH TIDE OF COOPERATION

Great Britain and the United States tried to satisfy Stalin's territorial ambitions and security fears between the fall of 1944 and the summer of 1945. Over Poland, in particular, the western Allies followed a conciliatory policy. The Soviet Union absorbed large tracts of prewar Poland and constructed a provisional government in Warsaw that was dominated by pro-Moscow communists and socialists. Even though Churchill and Roosevelt had committed themselves in the Atlantic Charter (August 1941) to making no territorial changes that did not accord with the wishes of the affected populations, London and Washington yielded to Stalin's principal demands. The Red Army dominated Poland, and Soviet cooperation was essential both for the war against Japan and in countries like Greece and Italy, where Churchill's policy of backing conservative, preferably monarchist, governments would have run into difficulty if Stalin had given covert support to the well-armed communist parties of those countries. Above all, good relations between the Allies were essential if the United Nations, the international security organization that was Roosevelt's brainchild, was to survive and prosper.

The process of accommodation with Stalin's ambitions began as early as 9 October 1944, when Premier Churchill and Foreign Secretary Anthony Eden met Stalin and Foreign Minister Vyacheslav Molotov in Moscow. During this summit, Churchill presented the Soviet leader with a "naughty document" that shared out influence in the Balkans and Eastern Europe according to percentages. In Romania, the USSR would have 90 percent influence; in Bulgaria, 75 percent (which was amended to 80 percent by the two foreign ministers in subsequent negotiations). Hungary and Yugoslavia would be shared 50:50, while Britain would have 90 percent influence in Greece. Stalin scrawled a large tick on the document, which had an immediate effect on the political development of the region.

Stalin stayed quiet in December 1944 and January 1945 when British troops in Greece crushed an uprising by the communist-controlled National Liberation Front (EAM) and forced its military wing, the National People's Liberation Army (ELAS), to disarm. Churchill was unable to restore the exiled monarch, since King George II of the Hellenes' association with the prewar Metaxas dictatorship made him unacceptable to most public opinion, but the British government, including its Labour Party ministers, remained determined to exclude the EAM from the provisional government. Churchill, who theatrically flew to Athens on 26 December 1944, persuaded the king to accept Archbishop Damaskinos of Athens as regent and installed a new government that was initially led by a soldier with a colorful past as a coup leader, Nikolaos Plastiris. In November 1945, a government of centrists headed by a liberal worthy, Themistoklis Sophoulis, was backed by the British, but it commanded the loyalty of neither the far left nor the far right. Persistent violence marred Greece politics between January 1945 and March 1946, when national elections supervised by American, British, and French observers took place.[3]

Romania also suffered the consequences of the Moscow agreement. On 27 February 1945, the provisional government, which was headed by an antifascist general, Nicolae Rădescu, was subverted when Stalin intervened directly to compel King Michael of Romania, the head of state, to appoint Petru Groza, the leader of the so-called Ploughman's Front, the Romanian Communist Party's rural front organization, as premier. In August 1944, there had not been a thousand communists in the entire country, and this empowering of Moscow's stooges within the country was a democratic travesty.[4]

Stalin's power grab in Romania came within days of the conclusion of the Crimea conference at Yalta (4–11 February 1945) and it disturbed Roosevelt, but Churchill explained priorities clearly: "In order to have the freedom to save Greece, Eden and I at Moscow in October recognized that Russia should have a largely preponderant voice in Roumania [*sic*] and Bulgaria. . . . Stalin adhered very strictly to this understanding during the thirty days fighting against the communists and ELAS in the city of Athens."[5] Romania, like it or not, had to be sacrificed to keep Greece in the western camp. Nevertheless, neither Britain nor the United States gave formal recognition to the Groza government until February 1946.

Churchill and Roosevelt hoped against hope that Stalin would allow at least a façade of democracy in the countries falling into the Soviet orbit. At Yalta the three leaders approved a "Declaration on Liberated Europe" that committed them to assist the peoples "liberated from the dominion of Nazi Germany" (including the peoples of the former Axis regimes) to "solve by democratic means their pressing political and economic problems." The declaration committed the three Allies to forming "interim governmental authorities broadly representative of all democratic elements in the population," and facilitating the holding of "free elections."

Nevertheless, the policy of accommodating Stalin was continued at Yalta. Churchill and Roosevelt made the arduous journey to Russia at Stalin's behest and made several key concessions to the Soviet tyrant when they got there.

In Europe, Roosevelt sided with Stalin over the German question. A Carthaginian peace was to be imposed upon defeated Germany. The USSR was determined to exact retribution for the gigantic damage done to the Russian people by the Nazi invaders. U.S. policy makers did not go so far, but certainly favored a punitive peace. In August 1944, Secretary of the Treasury Henry Morgenthau had envisaged the "pastoralization" of Germany. The Ruhr valley, Germany's industrial heartland, "should not only be stripped of all presently existing industries, but so weakened and so controlled that it cannot in the foreseeable future become an industrial area."[6] Morgenthau believed that Germany should lose territory to Poland and France and that the rest of the country should be divided into a north German state and a south German state based on Bavaria, with the Ruhr being kept under international jurisdiction.

At Yalta, the Big Three indeed contemplated "dismemberment" as a permanent solution for the German question. In the meantime, Germany and Austria were to be divided into four administrative "control zones," with the Russians occupying the east of Germany and Britain occupying the north of the country and the Ruhr. The United States would occupy Bavaria and the south, while France would control the Saarland and the German southwest. French Premier Charles de Gaulle made no secret of his view that "certain western regions of the Reich" should be "permanently removed" from German sovereignty.[7]

The three leaders agreed that harsh reparations should be imposed. The USSR demanded the astronomical figure of $20 billion, with half at least going to the USSR and Poland. The British, mindful of the lessons of 1919, did not want to name a figure until it was clear how much, if anything,

Germany could afford to pay. Britain, whose highly industrialized occupation zone needed massive food imports to survive, wanted Germany to be able to pay for its own imports from industrial production before any industrial plant with war potential was taken in reparations. In Finance Minister Sir John Anderson's words, "our policy ought to be to draw the fangs while leaving some of the teeth." The Russians, by contrast, wanted a "Morgenthau plus" policy, both to get compensation for its own vast losses and in order to ensure that Germany could never make war again. In the end, it was agreed to take the $20 billion figure as a basis for further discussions.[8]

The other major issue upon which the western Allies sought to accommodate Stalin's wishes was the question of Poland, which everyone at Yalta knew was a test case for future cooperation between the three Allies. Poland had been ravaged by the Nazis and had lost 18 percent of its population in the war. Polish soldiers, sailors, and airmen had fought with British forces and taken heavy casualties, especially in the Italian campaign. The resistance of the Polish Home Army to the Nazis had been brave almost beyond belief. If any country deserved to decide its own destiny, Poland did. On the other hand, how could Stalin, mindful of the aggressive war fought by Poland against the USSR in 1919–1920, and of Poland's strategic position as a cushion between Russia and Germany, possibly permit an unfriendly regime in Warsaw?

The Poles, moreover, had no reason to feel friendly to Moscow. Stalin had colluded with Hitler in August 1939 to partition Poland and had treated the populations of the territories it subsequently occupied with appalling brutality. Hundreds of thousands of Poles had been transported to Siberia after the Red Army invaded Poland in October 1939. Tens of thousands had been shot.[9] The culmination of this campaign of terror was the mass murder, in April and May 1940, of approximately fifteen thousand captured Polish officers at Katyn Wood near Smolensk.

This terrible crime caused an irrevocable breach between the USSR and the Polish government in exile in London. When the Germans discovered and publicized the mass graves of the slaughtered soldiers in April 1943, the USSR claimed that the Nazis were trying to hide their own responsibility for the deed. The London Poles, against British advice, asked for an impartial investigation of the officers' deaths by the International Red Cross. In response, the USSR branded the London Poles as "fascist collaborators" and established a rival government, the Polish "Committee of National Liberation," in the town of Lublin. When Soviet troops entered Poland, Stalin recognized the Lublin Poles as the government. The task for Churchill and Roosevelt at Yalta was to persuade Stalin to attenuate this decision. Poland's legitimate political forces expected no less.

At Yalta, however, the two western Allies yielded to both of Stalin's main demands on the Polish question. First, they confirmed that Poland's eastern frontier would be, with some slight modifications in Poland's favor, based upon a line drawn in July 1920 by Lord Curzon, the then British foreign secretary. The Curzon line proposal restored to the Soviet Union almost all the territory acquired as a result of the Nazi-Soviet pact. Churchill and Roosevelt, however, felt constrained to go along with the Soviets' demands. At the Tehran Conference in November 1943, when the USSR was still doing most of the fighting, the two leaders had informally promised Stalin, with the aid of three matchsticks symbolizing the borders of Poland, the USSR, and Germany, supremacy over the territories in question. They knew there was no possibility of reneging on their bargain at Yalta. The Red Army was in situ.[10] Poland was therefore to be compensated in the west with German territory at the peace conference that would conclude the conflict.

The second concession made by Roosevelt and Churchill was equally grave. The western Allies acknowledged that the Committee of National Liberation, rather than the legal government in London, should provide the nucleus of the provisional government. The conference communiqué did recognize, however, that the committee should be "reorganized on a broader democratic basis with the inclusion of democratic leaders from Poland itself and from Poles abroad." Stalin agreed, too, that "free and unfettered" elections would be held in Poland in which "all democratic and anti-Nazi parties shall have the right to take part," though events would soon show that the Soviet leader's interpretation of what constituted a free election did not coincide with any reasonable definition of the term, and that the opportunity to "take part" would be honored more in the breach than in the observance.

Given the situation, it is hard to see what more could have been extracted from Stalin, but the USSR's failure to permit political pluralism in Poland would prove to be one of the chief causes of the friction that eroded trust between the Big Three at war's end. Stalin, in fact, from the outset obstructed the reorganization of the Polish government on a broader basis. The Soviets initially objected to the inclusion of Stanisław Mikołajczyk, the leader of the Peasant Party, and of other representative Polish politicians. Access to all the countries under Soviet occupation, especially Poland, was sporadic and subject to rigid controls. In mid-March, Churchill anxiously wrote to Roosevelt to say that "we are in the presence of a great failure and an utter breakdown of what was settled at Yalta."[11] In May 1945, a delegation of sixteen Polish socialists to Moscow was arrested and put on trial for sedition when it tried to discuss the implementation of the Yalta protocol's provisions for Poland. As George Orwell pithily commented: "The forcing of Quisling governments upon unwilling peoples is undesirable whoever does it."[12] Unfortunately, Orwell's dictum was one that Stalin was unwilling to heed.

Nevertheless, the new Truman administration (Harry S. Truman had become president in April 1945 upon the death of Roosevelt), conscious that the Soviet Union then had in the United States "a deposit of goodwill as great, if not greater than any other country," sought tenaciously for a compromise. [13] At the end of May, presidential aide Harry S. Hopkins was sent as special envoy to Moscow. Stalin persuaded Hopkins (who returned from Moscow enthusiastic about doing business with Stalin) to accept that the Polish government should be supplemented merely by Mikołajczyk, as deputy premier, and by four other non-communist ministers. Stalin even promised Hopkins that Poland would eventually establish a democracy like Holland's. [14] Even by Stalin's standards this pledge was mendacious, but it served to enhance American goodwill toward the USSR.

The British government went along with Hopkins's solution, even though there was a striking contrast between Stalin's behavior in Poland and Britain's own behavior in Italy, where a provisional government led by a resistance hero, Ferruccio Parri, that contained several communists or pro-Moscow socialists in key positions was contemporaneously formed under British auspices. British diplomats were genuinely alarmed about the threat represented by the Italian Communist Party (PCI), but concluded that there was no alternative to the Italians' learning democracy through its practice.

Equally important, Mikołajczyk himself agreed to return to Poland, despite the opposition of most of the London Poles. His view was that it was necessary to "create a provisional government which would attempt to prepare democratic elections as the first step towards reestablishing a free and sovereign state." [15] Mikołajczyk's decision was an act of good faith in the Soviets' promise to allow "free and unfettered" elections in his war-battered country. It did at least provide Poland with the prospect of pluralism, and in fact, the Peasant Party rapidly became the most popular political formation in the country. It boasted six hundred thousand members by the end of 1945.

The deal over Poland opened the way to a solution for the most important postwar question: how to arrange the political and economic organization of Germany. This was the principal topic of the conference between the Big Three held in Potsdam near Berlin between 17 July and 2 August 1945. By the end of the conference, Stalin was the only one of the three nations' leaders who had been in post at Yalta. Truman had replaced Roosevelt in April 1945 and Churchill was evicted from office at the end of July by a Labour landslide in the British general election (the conference was briefly interrupted to allow Churchill to go home).

Churchill's place as premier devolved upon the prim figure of Clement Attlee, while Britain's voice in foreign affairs took on the belligerent tones of Ernest Bevin, a former trade union leader who had been minister of labor during the war. A proletarian who detested communism, Bevin was skeptical from the first that the USSR would negotiate in good faith and was determined to take a tougher line with Stalin than Churchill and Foreign Minister Anthony Eden had done.

The Potsdam Conference established a conference of foreign ministers (CFM), composed of representatives from Britain, the United States, and the USSR (France and China, the other two members of the Security Council of the UNO, were subsequently admitted). The CFM's task was to draw up treaties of peace with Italy, Bulgaria, Romania, Hungary, and Finland—Germany's allies—and to prepare a peace treaty that could be presented to Germany at such time as it had "a government adequate for the purpose." Until then, the conference agreed that Germany was to be administered by a "Control Council" of the military commanders in charge of the four zones established at Yalta.

The Control Council's main job was to dismantle Germany's war-making potential, to "convince the Germans that they have suffered a total military defeat and that they cannot escape responsibility for what they have brought upon themselves," and to "prepare the ground" for democracy in Germany and for the reintegration of a democratic Germany into international society. Germany was not to be broken up into separate states, but the federal principle was to be encouraged and local government on "democratic principles" was to be introduced as soon as possible.

Germany, in short, was to be a kind of mandate administered by the wartime Allies. It was to be treated as an economic unit and common policies were to be developed by the Control Council to establish a functioning economy. Somewhat in contradiction to this ambition, however, it was decided at Potsdam that each country could take reparations from its own zone, while the USSR would meet Poland's claims against Germany from its own share. The western Allies would moreover transfer from their zones 15 percent of any capital stock "unnecessary for the German peace economy" to the Russians in exchange for food and raw materials of equal value from the Soviet zone (which was more agricultural in character). A further 10 percent was to be transferred without any return payment at all.

The Potsdam conference, though it issued an agreed communiqué and a clear plan of action, was marked in its early stages by some sharp exchanges between Stalin and Churchill, who accused the Soviet leader of having failed to implement the Yalta accords. Britain and the United States refused to recognize the governments constructed in Romania, Bulgaria, and Hungary and further protested against the elimination of political rivals by the Yugoslav Communist Party. It should be said that Churchill's complaints would have carried greater moral weight had he acknowledged the democracies' own failings. The regime imposed on Greece was hardly a triumph for democratic values; General Franco's Spain was a standing reproach to the principles that Britain and the United States ostensibly espoused;[16] the postwar French government slaughtered thousands after riots in Sétif, Algeria, in May 1945 and shelled Damascus in the same month. Britain was still an empire that did not pay even lip service to democracy throughout most of its colonial "possessions."

The United States, moreover, was no more willing to allow Soviet interference in territories that it regarded as strategically important than the USSR was willing to allow western influence in Poland. After the successful testing (in July) and use (on 6 and 9 August 1945) of the atomic bomb on Japan, Washington brusquely intimated to the USSR that it had no intention of allowing Soviet forces of occupation into Hokkaido, the northernmost island in Japan, as Stalin had requested. The argument used by U.S. diplomacy was that American forces had borne the brunt of the conflict with Japan, whereas the USSR had entered the war against Japan literally as the atomic bombs were bringing the war to an end. But Great Britain was not made an occupying power either, and Britain had expended huge amounts of blood and treasure in the war against Japan. To Stalin, it must have looked as if Washington was intent on reducing Soviet influence in Eastern Europe, but was setting up a new Monroe Doctrine for East Asia.

Yet despite the growing tensions between Washington, London, and Moscow, the year 1945 still represented the high tide of wartime cooperation. Deals over reparations, over the composition of the Polish government, and over the formation of the CFM were struck. The Nuremburg trials of twenty-four leading Nazis, including Hermann Göring, Rudolf Hess, Joachim Von Ribbentrop, and Julius Streicher, began on 20 November 1945, and British, American, and Russian lawyers cooperated in their prosecution for war crimes. Twelve death sentences were eventually pronounced.

The CFM, despite verbal clashes between Bevin and Molotov, did eventually reach agreement on treaties of peace with Germany's former allies. These treaties were signed on 10 February 1947 in Paris. Italy, in particular, regarded its settlement as a national humiliation. Italy lost the province of Trieste to Yugoslavia, the Dodecanese islands to Greece, and all its colonies. The city of Trieste became an international territory. Italy had to pay substantial reparations to Albania, Ethiopia, Greece, the USSR, and, above all, Yugoslavia. On the day that the treaty was signed, flags were lowered to half-mast, a symbolic ten-minute silence was held, and the Parliament stopped its debates for half an hour. The newspaper *Il Popolo* proclaimed that "the people of Rome are united in dignified protest while at Paris Italy is being mutilated."[17]

Italians' anger at the peace treaty derived from the fact that they regarded themselves as victims of fascism, not as supporters. Italians believed that they had redeemed themselves by fighting courageously for the liberation of their country after the German occupation in September 1943. The nations surrounding Italy were less charitable. For them, the Italian people had been largely complicit in Mussolini's crimes. Britain and the United States tended to the latter view, but the harsh treaty with Italy was also dictated by the desire to maintain good relations with the USSR, which regarded a severe peace with Italy as a test case of Britain and the United States' goodwill.

THE IRON CURTAIN

The success of the peace treaty negotiations notwithstanding, 1946 was characterized by growing exasperation by U.S. and British policy makers with the USSR's methods. President Truman famously expostulated to Secretary of State Byrnes on 5 January 1946 that Soviet behavior in Romania, Poland, and Iran was a "high-handed outrage." He was "tired of babying the Soviets," he added.[18] Historian John Lewis Gaddis confirms that the "period of late February and early March, 1946, marked a decisive turning point in American foreign policy towards the Soviet Union."[19] Instead of pursuing conciliation—which was increasingly decried as appeasement by public opinion—the United States began to treat the USSR as an opponent, not as a partner and ally.

The chief reason for this shift of policy was that the communist parties of Central Europe were subverting the principles enunciated by the Yalta "Declaration on Liberated Europe." Elections were held in Hungary in November 1945, and the Communists scored just 17 percent of the vote, far less than the Smallholders' Party's 58 percent and slightly behind the Social Democrats. The Smallholders were prevented from forming a government, however, by a pre-electoral deal whereby all the principal political parties pledged themselves to cooperate after the poll in a government of national unity. Following their defeat, the Hungarian communist leader Mátyás Rákosi was called to Moscow to receive instructions. Subsequently, the Hungarian communists intensified their aggressiveness toward the other political forces.

In Bulgaria, the communists' "purge" of their political competitors "started very early, was particularly violent, and was especially comprehensive."[20] Elections in November 1945 were rigged, with the "Fatherland Front" (a communist-dominated coalition of parties) grabbing 88 percent of the vote. After Potsdam, Romanian politics was characterized by intimidation of all forces opposing the communists and their clients. King Michael of Romania went on strike against the government's democratic illegitimacy, by refusing to sign the Groza government's legislation into law. He was simply ignored.

Nevertheless, in December 1945, at a Moscow summit with his Soviet counterparts, Secretary of State James F. Byrnes acknowledged that a Polish-style solution, with governments built upon a central core of communist ministers, was the most appropriate one for both Romania and Bulgaria. This may have been yet another surrender to the inevitable, but given that Mikołajczyk's Peasant Party, despite being easily the most popular party in

Poland, was being harassed relentlessly by the communist-controlled police, Byrnes's concessions in effect gave a "free hand" to the USSR in the Balkans.[21]

The consequences of Byrnes's deal were obvious to everybody within months. In Bulgaria, the communists strengthened their grip on the "Fatherland Front," ended the monarchy, and won elections held on 27 October 1946. The opposition Agrarian Party, courageously led by Nikola Petkov, nevertheless obtained 30 percent of the vote: in reality, the Agrarians' support was probably far higher. In Romania, the National Democratic Front (NDF), composed of the Communists, the "Ploughman's Front," and pro-Moscow Socialists, consolidated its grip over the country. In November 1946, the NDF obtained a two-thirds majority in general elections that were, to put it charitably, less than "free and unfettered." Only in Czechoslovakia, where the Communist Party managed to get 38 percent of a genuinely free vote in May 1946, did a Soviet-backed party command popular legitimacy. But even in Czechoslovakia, the communists governed as if they were a conspiracy.

In the Soviet zone of Germany, political parties were allowed to organize under the supervision of the Soviet authorities. From the beginning, however, the Communist Party (KPD), despite committing itself to a gradualist "German road to socialism," was tarred by its association with the USSR's occupation policies. It was also outflanked on the left, among antifascist working-class voters, by the Social Democrats (SPD), whose national leader, the concentration camp survivor Kurt Schumacher, was an articulate critic of Stalinism. Schumacher's "intransigent and bellicose anti-Soviet socialism posed a particularly sharp threat to Soviet authority in Germany."[22] The USSR dealt with the threat posed by the SPD by exerting pressure on the party's leader in the Soviet zone, Otto Grotewohl, to endorse unity with the KPD. The *Sozialistische Einheitspartei Deutschlands* (Socialist Unity Party: SED) held its first unification congress on 21–22 April 1946. The new party boasted 1.3 million members by the fall of 1946, but it nevertheless lacked support among the people. In provincial elections in October 1946, the SED could not achieve majorities even in the Soviet zone and was thrashed by the SPD in elections to an all-Berlin city assembly. Free elections were never held again in what subsequently became East Germany.

Stalin had told Polish communist leader Władisław Gomułka in November 1945 that a small and well-organized force of approximately two hundred thousand committed members could hold a country in thrall provided that it had "instructions as to what to say and how to say it." Such cynicism was the mainspring of the party line in country after country after Potsdam.[23]

The monopolization of power in Eastern Europe by the communists was prominently reported in the U.S. media, notably the *New York Times*, and became a major political issue. Republican spokesmen on foreign affairs, such as Senator Arthur H. Vandenberg of Michigan and future Secretary of State John Foster Dulles, were vocal in attacking the Truman administration's low-key response toward Soviet demands.[24] Stalin, moreover, seemed to be throwing down the gauntlet. On 9 February 1946, the Soviet leader made a radio broadcast that boasted of the USSR's "vitality" and affirmed that the war had proved that the "Soviet social system is better than any other social system." The rightness of Soviet policy in the 1930s, above all the decision to leap from an agricultural economy to an industrial one in one dramatic decade, had been amply vindicated by events. The USSR now possessed an army that was second to none (indeed, Stalin ominously averred, it "could teach others quite a lot"). Russia's scientists, moreover, would soon be able "not only to overtake but also in the near future to surpass the achievements of science outside our country." This remark, obviously, was a veiled warning that Moscow was working on the atomic bomb.[25]

On 22 February 1946, George F. Kennan, a diplomat in the U.S. embassy in Moscow, circulated his "Long Telegram." By arguing that world communism, with its base in the USSR, was "a political force committed fanatically to the belief that with the U.S. there can be no permanent modus vivendi" and that possessed "an elaborate and far-flung apparatus for the exertion of its influence in other countries," Kennan's eight-thousand-word analysis provided policy makers with a conceptual justification for taking a tougher line with the USSR. His lengthy document was rapidly diffused throughout the administration and became the intellectual rationale for the policy of "containment."[26] It was a European, however, who stated the growing alienation from the USSR most eloquently. In March 1946, at Fulton, Missouri, with President Truman in approving attendance, Winston Churchill put the new mood into words in a remarkable speech from which, usually, only a single phrase is remembered:

> From Stettin in the Baltic to Trieste in the Adriatic an iron curtain has descended across the continent. Behind that line lie all the capitals of the ancient states of central and eastern Europe. Warsaw, Berlin, Prague, Vienna, Budapest, Belgrade, Bucharest and Sofia, all of these famous cities and their populations around them lie in what I must call the Soviet sphere, and all are subject in one form or other, not only to Soviet influence but to a very high and, in some cases, increasing measure of control from Moscow. Athens alone—Greece with its immortal glories—is free to decide its future at an election under British, American and French observation. The Russian-dominated Polish government has been encouraged to make enormous and wrongful inroads upon Germany, and mass expulsions of Germans on a scale grievous and undreamed-of are now taking place. The Communist parties, which were very small in all these eastern states of Europe, have been raised to preeminence and power far beyond their numbers and are seeking everywhere

to obtain totalitarian control. Police governments are prevailing in nearly every case, and, so far, except in Czechoslovakia, there is no true democracy.[27]

Churchill had been complicit in the creation of this situation and so, even more egregiously, had the Roosevelt and Truman administrations. Marc Trachtenberg has convincingly contended that U.S. policy toward Europe in 1945 was based upon tacit mutual recognition of the two superpowers' respective spheres of interest. Washington was willing to go along with the "new political order the Soviets had set up in eastern Europe," Trachtenberg affirms, in return for the Soviet passiveness in Japan and Western Europe, especially Italy. This policy, of course, could never be openly acknowledged, since "it would have come across as callous" with American public opinion.[28]

Certainly, in the second semester of 1945 the USSR distinguished between the Americans, whose policy was given broad approval, and the British, whose "reactionary" democratic socialist government and residual imperialism became the target of a "concerted attack" by the Soviet press.[29] Bevin himself was afraid that Byrnes aspired to a settlement with the Soviet Union that would "allow the Americans to withdraw from Europe and in effect leave the British to get on with the Russians as best they could."[30]

By the spring of 1946, however, Western policy makers were concluding that they had backed the wrong horse when they pursued a policy of engagement with Stalin. Churchill's Fulton speech was an act of penitence for a serious lapse of judgment. The United States and Britain increasingly perceived themselves to be facing a remorseless foe that presented a threat to their way of life. Precisely this argument was made from inside Russia itself by Maxim Litvinov, Molotov's predecessor as foreign minister, who at great personal risk warned the British ambassador to Moscow, Frank Roberts, that the USSR, like Nazi Germany, would only be deterred by a policy of bluntly saying no.[31] Churchill in effect was arguing at Fulton that conciliation of the western powers' wartime ally had gone too far and that "there should no longer be any pretense that the leading members of the United Nations stood in an equally close relationship with each other."[32] His conclusion was that the British Commonwealth and the United States needed to cooperate to provide "an overwhelming assurance of security" against the USSR. They should put their trust in the UNO, but also keep their powder dry.

The West's new resolve was first demonstrated during the Iran crisis in March 1946, when the USSR refused to withdraw, in accordance with its wartime treaty with Iran, from the northern territories that it had occupied. Britain and the United States brought the issue before the UNO Security Council, and the USSR backed down in the face of international opinion. The Iran showdown convinced Bevin and Byrnes that Stalin would be reasonable if he were faced with firmness.

In Europe, the place where the West's leaders resolved to flex their muscles with the USSR was Germany. The USSR had despoiled Germany after May 1945. The plight of German women in the Soviet zone in 1945 and through 1946 is one of the worst human rights tragedies of the twentieth century. Hundreds of thousands of German women were raped by Russian soldiers; many of these victims contracted venereal diseases or were forced to seek backstreet abortions. Thousands more killed themselves or were shot out of hand, often with their menfolk.[33] The Red Army's commanders did little to keep their troops under control, especially in the first months of the occupation.

The Soviet forces also plundered their zone of its productive plant and equipment. East Prussia was incorporated into Russia, Silesia given to Poland, and both territories were de-Germanized ruthlessly. Soviet and Polish troops drove millions from their land and homes. Vehicles, workshops, and equipment belonging to the "displaced persons," to use the English euphemism for refugees employed at the time, were then sequestered as reparations by the Soviet authorities or stolen as booty by Russian troops. In their zone of conquered Germany, the USSR interpreted the Yalta and Potsdam commitments to the payment of heavy reparations by defeated Germany as a license to strip the territory of its industrial base and to commandeer its current production as payment in kind. Pierre de Senarclen's comment that the Russians "spread over Germany and its satellites like the locusts of biblical Egypt, grabbing an enormous war booty haphazardly and without consulting their allies," is a touch lurid, but is not inaccurate.[34] Norman Naimark estimates that "one third of the productive capacity of industry in the Soviet zone was removed altogether from the hands of the Germans" in the aftermath of the war. He adds that the "Russian appetite for German factories and goods was insatiable."[35]

The Soviets had excellent reasons for seizing as much as they could. Rebuilding the Soviet economy was Stalin's priority. The USSR needed German rolling stock, lathes, trucks, and machine tools to survive the winter: Stalin did not feel squeamish about imposing hardship upon a people whose army had murdered so many citizens of the USSR.

Nevertheless, Soviet policy took a toll on innocent German citizens, not just former Nazis. The Russian zone was essentially robbed of its ability to earn a living for its own people and for the millions of *Umsiedler* ("evacuees") who had been driven out of their homes in the East. Living standards fell precipitously as the zone's output fell, while its population grew. The Soviet zone, moreover, contrary to the letter of the Potsdam accords, remained sealed off from the rest of Germany. Trade links, individual travel, press reporting, and postal services were all obstructed by the Soviet zone's administration. The USSR, moreover, pressed relentlessly in the CFM for a definition of "capital stock" that would enable it to claim a larger share of the industrial plant of Western Germany as reparations, even if that meant drastically lowering living standards for Germans in the other zones. Nor did the Russians honor their promise at Potsdam to barter agricultural commodities for industrial plant. The worst fears of British officials before Yalta came true: the Germans in the British zone were all but starving and the British had to curtail their own rations in order to feed them.

The issue was not purely economic, however. Senior officials in the British Foreign Office, notably the permanent secretary, Sir Orme Sargent, were convinced that treating Germany as a single entity would only facilitate Soviet predominance. By April 1946, Bevin had adopted their analysis: Britain, Bevin believed, had to strengthen its zone's economic and political autonomy even if this meant dismemberment of Germany and a standoff with the Soviets. In a key cabinet paper circulated on 3 May 1946, the foreign secretary argued that the time had come to stop thinking of the German question "solely in terms of Germany itself" and of trying to "devise the best means of preventing the revival of a strong, aggressive Germany." The "danger of Russia," Bevin averred, was "certainly as great as, and possibly greater than, that of a revived Germany." Bevin's position was criticized by Chancellor of the Exchequer Hugh Dalton and by Aneurin Bevan, the left-wing health minister, but it received Premier Attlee's steadfast support, both then and later.[36]

By May 1946, when General Lucius Clay, commander of the U.S. zone, suspended reparations payments to the USSR, Washington was also coming to the conclusion that as much of Germany as possible should be united economically whether the Russians liked it or not. In July 1946, at the end of the Paris meeting of the CFM, Byrnes announced Washington's intention to merge the American zone with "any other" zone, a proposal that the British applauded and the USSR attacked. So-called Bizonia came into being on 1 January 1947. The Paris CFM was characterized by frank exchanges between the foreign ministers: Bevin had a stress-induced heart attack upon his return to London.

Secretary of State Byrnes outlined the thinking that lay behind this decision in a speech delivered in Stuttgart on 6 September 1946.[37] According to Byrnes, it was the U.S. government's intention to achieve the "maximum possible unification" of the German economy and to allow Germany to produce enough to stimulate economic recovery elsewhere in Europe, for "recovery in Europe . . . will be slow indeed if Germany with her great resources of iron and coal is turned into a poorhouse." The message was clear. Since the USSR had been blocking unification of the German economy, the United States was ready to form what would today be called "a coalition of the willing."

Byrnes spelled out the implications of the creation of Bizonia by adding that the United States did not want Germany to become the "satellite" of any power, or "to live under a dictatorship, foreign or domestic." Its destiny was to become a "free and independent country" like Austria (which had held free elections across its four zones on 25 November 1945, in which the Communists had obtained only 5 percent and won a mere four seats in the legislative assembly). To aid in this process, Byrnes asserted that Washington would not "shirk" its duty to keep troops in Germany for as long as necessary—a commitment that delighted the British. Byrnes noted, moreover, that although Königsberg was to be transferred to the USSR and the Saarland ceded to France, the United States would not back "any encroachment on territory which is indisputably German or any division of Germany which is not desired by the people concerned." This principle would regulate the issue of Germany's eastern border with Poland, a question which Byrnes effectively reopened in his speech.[38]

THE MARSHALL PLAN AND THE COMINFORM

The case of Germany illustrates how the tensions that were the origins of the Cold War sprang from the objective situation of European countries. The British and the Americans did not want the Germans to starve, and Britain, at any rate, could not afford to feed them. The decision to spur Germany's productive capacity originated in this generous, though self-interested impulse. But for the USSR such softness presaged betrayal and persuaded Soviet observers of the United States, such as Ambassador Nikolai Novikov, to write on 27 September 1946 that Washington's ambition was "war against the Soviet Union, which in the eyes of the American imperialists is the main obstacle in the path of the United States."[39] Suspicion that the "imperialists" intended Germany to join a capitalist crusade against the USSR ran deep among the Soviet leadership.

It was an accusation that Ernest Bevin resented. The British had not forgotten that in 1940 and 1941 they had fought the Nazis on their own, while Stalin had been Hitler's de facto ally. If Britain had been stronger, it could have provided leadership for the malnourished populations living in the region. The Labour government certainly represented a beacon of hope for millions of Europeans hoping for a better future—this was one reason why the Kremlin detested it. The European masses wanted a new metamorphosis of the European state that would make the provision of mass welfare its main priority, and British Labour was a bold democratic experiment in this direction.

Reconstructing Western Europe, on top of building Jerusalem in Britain, maintaining (most of) the empire, and being an occupation force in the Indian Ocean was, however, a mission far beyond the strength of Britain's war-torn economy. In December 1945, Britain had experienced a "financial Dunkirk" when the United States had given Britain a loan of $3.75 billion. The respite was temporary. Throughout 1946, Britain's reserves leached away at frightening speed as defense commitments and imports took their inevitable toll.[40] Far from being a regional hegemon, indeed, Britain was in the same fix as its neighbors. Everybody in Europe was desperate for the dollars necessary to finance reconstruction. In 1946, Britain had a trade deficit of $764 million with the United States; France's deficit was $650 million. In 1947, Western Europe had a collective trade deficit of $4.75 billion.[41] European countries desperately needed American raw materials and capital goods. According to Milward, the "deterioration of Western Europe's balance of trade with the United States was largely caused by very high and increasing levels of imports of machinery, steel and transport equipment."[42] Paying for such goods was difficult, however. It required a lot of Scotch whisky or French perfume to pay for ships, tractors, and airplanes. Long before the Marshall Plan, Washington was already lending the Europeans the money necessary to buy American industry's own products.

The balance of payments' problems of the West European states had direct political consequences. They were a major reason why London sought in February 1947 to unload its responsibilities in Greece onto the United States. After the March 1946 elections, of which Churchill had boasted in the Fulton speech, the Greek situation deteriorated. Only 49 percent of the Greeks voted in the elections, which were marred by fraud and intimidation of the left-wing parties. The Communist Party (KKE) boycotted the poll altogether. As a result, the elections produced an "overwhelmingly royalist parliament, far to the right of much of the country."[43] The Populist Party, led by Konstantinos Tsaldaris, formed a government and proceeded to free wartime collaborators and to suspend habeas corpus. A reign of terror against the parties of the left followed. On 1 September 1946, a referendum on the monarchy, which was also boycotted by the KKE, authorized the return of King George by a large margin. Civil war broke out, and the British found themselves embroiled in a conflict that an alarmed Truman administration characterized as a Soviet push into the Middle East.

Along with Palestine, where Bevin was opposing the creation of a Jewish state, Greece was the single issue that most angered backbench opinion in the Labour Party; the foreign secretary could hence buy credit for his broader foreign policy by withdrawal from Athens. Chancellor of the Exchequer Hugh Dalton showed an "almost fanatical determination to force the abandonment of Greece."[44] Accordingly, on 21 February 1947, Britain informed Washington that it would have to bear the financial burden of supporting the Greeks from 31 March 1947. Britain's démarche, which came out of the blue for the Truman administration, led directly to the president's decision on 12 March 1947 to ask Congress for $400 million to "support free peoples who are resisting attempted subjugation by armed minorities and outside pressures," and specifically for the governments of Greece and Turkey.

Britain's withdrawal from Greece was, in short, the catalyst for what became known as the "Truman Doctrine," namely the commitment of the United States to resist "totalitarian regimes," the seeds of which the president believed to be "nurtured by misery and want." The Greek crisis came to a head, moreover, just weeks after elections in Poland had been held in a climate of "escalating terror."[45] Peasant Party candidates had been excluded from the ballot in large swathes of the country and subjected to wholesale beatings and arrests. Ballot fraud was rampant. Officially, the pro-Soviet "Democratic Bloc" won 80 percent of the vote and the Peasant Party just over 10 percent; in reality, Mikołajczyk would probably have won a majority in a "free and unfettered" poll. The Truman Doctrine drew the conclusion that it was America's task to provide "hope" for all those peoples, starting with the Greeks and Turks, who did not want to share the fate of the Poles and the other peoples under communist rule. Truman's speech is the most generally accepted starting date for the Cold War.

Truman's speech, which was greeted with outrage by Soviet propaganda, threw a somber shadow over the CFM's meeting in Moscow between 10 March and 24 April 1947. In Moscow, Britain and the United States (now represented by George C. Marshall) rejected Soviet demands for the creation of a centralized German government and a voice in the management of the Ruhr's industrial output. Bevin brusquely denied a Soviet claim for $10 billion in reparations, arguing that the USSR, having stripped its own occupation zone of all its assets, seemingly wanted now to rehabilitate it at the expense of British and American taxpayers. Molotov, in his turn, refused to consider an American plan for a four-power treaty to keep Germany disarmed for 25 years. By mid-April 1947, in short, relations had broken down.

The CFM debacle was followed by the exclusion of the communist parties of France and Italy from the governments of their countries. In France, this event occurred on 1 May when the French Communist Party (PCF) refused to back the government in a vote of confidence of its handling of a wages policy (the communist-dominated unions had instigated strikes over the winter of 1946–1947 for higher pay). Premier Paul Ramadier seized the chance to win kudos in Washington by excluding the PCF's ministers. France, which had hitherto been suspicious of plans to rehabilitate even part of Germany, subsequently moved toward "open acceptance" of Anglo-U.S. strategy on Germany and even of the establishment of a West German state.[46]

In Italy, tensions had been high since the election of a Constituent Assembly in June 1946. The government of Alcide De Gasperi had followed deflationary policies designed to boost exports since June 1946. These policies caused social unrest, which the PCI, nominally part of the government, ably exploited. In January 1947, De Gasperi visited Washington and obtained a $100 million loan by playing on American fears that yet another European country might turn "red." In May 1947, after De Gasperi had obtained the PCI's agreement to include the *Concordat* negotiated by Mussolini in 1929 with the Catholic Church into the new Italian Constitution, the Italian Christian Democrat suddenly resigned and formed a new government without the PCI. De Gasperi's move brought increased American aid, though research suggests that exclusion of the PCI was not a quid pro quo for loans, but a strategic decision taken by the Italian leader himself.[47]

Events in Poland, Greece, France, and Italy, together with the CFM's inability to find a solution for the German question, convinced the Americans that the Truman Doctrine's fine words about eliminating "misery and want" needed to become deeds. On his return from Moscow, Marshall publicly worried that "the patient is sinking while the doctors deliberate." Echoing views from inside the State Department, authoritative American commentators, notably Walter Lippmann, warned in May 1947 that unless the United States launched a program of political and economic aid, conditional upon the Europeans themselves taking steps toward greater European political unity, Europe might succumb to communism.[48]

Such voices were unnecessarily alarmist: Western Europe's problem was not that it was "a Lazarus in need of revival," but that it was an "athlete who was running out of breath."[49] They nevertheless provided the rhetorical background to Secretary of State Marshall's address at Harvard University on 5 June 1947 in which he expressed his alarm that "Europe's requirements for the next three or four years of foreign food and other essential products—principally from America—are so much greater than her present ability to pay that she must have substantial additional help or face economic, social, and political deterioration of a very grave character." Marshall added that while it would be "neither fitting nor efficacious" for the Truman administration to "draw up unilaterally a program designed to place Europe on its feet economically," the role of the United States should "consist of friendly aid in the drafting of a European program" and of later "support" for such a program "so far as it may be practical for us to do so." The program, the secretary of state underlined, should be "agreed to by a number, if not all European nations."

Foreign Minister Bevin grasped at once that the Americans were making a great and generous, albeit vaguely worded, offer. At Bevin's initiative, a meeting was hastily called in Paris to which all European countries, including those behind the iron curtain, were invited. Several states in Eastern Europe, notably Czechoslovakia, would not have turned up their noses at the Yankee dollar. At Paris, however, Molotov, on Stalin's orders, circled the communist wagons rather than allow the states under Soviet control to participate. By so doing, Stalin "fell into the trap that the Marshall Plan laid for him, which was to get him to build the wall that would divide Europe."[50]

To ensure discipline, Stalin intensified the ideological struggle. The communist parties of Europe, including the French and the Italians, were summoned in September 1947 to the Polish town of Szklarska Poręba for the foundation of the Communist Information Bureau (Cominform): in effect, to an indoctrination session by Stalin's henchman, Andrei Zhdanov. The new party line was made clear by Zhdanov in a lengthy report, "On the International Situation," on 25 September. In synthesis, the Soviet ideologue asserted that the Marshall Plan was to be interpreted as a cynical plot to exploit the peoples of Europe; via economic aid, Washington was pursuing the "broad aim of enslaving Europe to American capital." There could be no collaboration with this devious plan: communists had to choose which camp they were in and follow the example of the USSR, even if they were on the imperialist side of the iron curtain. Zhdanov, the highly intelligent Yugoslav intellectuals Milovan Djilas and Edvard Kardelj, and the somewhat mechanical Hungarian ideologue Mihály Farkas lashed the Italian and French communists, accusing them of "parliamentary cretinism." Zhdanov interrupted a speech by the chief PCI delegate, Luigi Longo, with a derisive attack on the PCI's expulsion from the De Gasperi government—"This is a coup d'état! What does the Party intend to do? . . . How long does the Party intend to go on retreating?" Kardelj asked why the French and Italian parties were "letting their countries be transformed . . . into vassals and bases for war against Socialism and Democracy."[51] Longo and the French leader Jacques Duclos must have wondered at times whether they would be going home.

The Italian and French delegations made abject self-criticism for their errors. They understood the logic of the party line. Stalin had been against revolutionary policies in Western Europe; now he was in favor. Those who had not divined his changing thinking in time could either admit *they* were wrong, or else fall foul of Big Brother. The following year, the PCI and the PCF were able to repay the Yugoslavs with interest for Belgrade's own deviations from the Moscow line.

When one reads the minutes of the Cominform meetings, one sees why the USSR was an impossible partner in the complicated postwar world. The United States, by brusquely shifting its policy from tacit accommodation to somewhat messianic opposition to "totalitarianism," surely deserves much of the blame for the Cold War's breaking out in 1947. The U.S. journalist Walter Lippmann argued precisely this in the series of articles that gave the conflict its name. Yet the nature of the Soviet system was such that conflict would surely have broken out anyway. Stalin would not permit more than a façade of political pluralism in the countries under his sway—especially Poland. Britain and the United States could not concede a unified Germany so long as there was a risk it would follow the Polish or Romanian pattern.

The Cold War "broke out" (by which we mean that human agents took decisions that worsened relations to the point that "war" becomes a reasonable descriptor) because a bankrupt, a cynic, and a moralist had to revive a continent whose demons had left it for dead. It is hardly surprising that they fell out over what to do and how to do it.

NOTES

1. Irina Mukhina, "New Revelations from the Former Soviet Archives: The Kremlin, the Warsaw Uprising, and the Coming of the Cold War," *Cold War History* 6 (2006): 397–411.

2. Milovan Djilas, *Conversations with Stalin* (New York: Harcourt, Brace, Jovanovich, 1962), 114.

3. Richard Clogg, *A Concise History of Greece* (Cambridge: Cambridge University Press, 1995), 136–41.

4. George Schöpflin, *Politics in Eastern Europe 1945–1992* (Oxford: Blackwell, 1996), 65.

5. Warren F. Kimball, *Churchill and Roosevelt, The Complete Correspondence*, vol. 3 (Princeton, NJ: Princeton University Press, 1984), 547.

6. Henry Morgenthau, *Germany is Our Problem* (New York: Harper and Brothers, 1945), 4.

7. Jean Lacouture, *De Gaulle: The Ruler 1945–1970* (London: Collins Harvill, 1991), 95.

8. For an in-depth discussion, see J. E. Farquharson, "Anglo-American Policy on Reparations from Yalta to Potsdam," *English Historical Review* 112 (1997): 905.

9. See Timothy Snyder, *Bloodlands: Europe between Stalin and Hitler* (London: Random House, 2011), 119–54, for the consequences for Poland of the Molotov-Ribbentrop pact.

10. Michael Charlton, *The Eagle and the Small Birds: Crisis in the Soviet Empire: From Yalta to Solidarity* (Chicago: Chicago University Press, 1984), 15–30.

11. Kimball, *Churchill and Roosevelt*, 565.

12. George Orwell, "As I Please," *Tribune*, 26 January 1945, in *The Collected Essays, Journalism, and Letters, Vol. 3*, ed. Sonia Orwell and Ian Angus (New York, Harcourt, Brace & World, 1968).

13. James Byrnes, *Speaking Frankly* (New York: Harper & Row, 1947), 71.

14. Stalin-Hopkins meeting, 27 May 1945, Foreign Relations of the United States (FRUS), Potsdam 1, 38–39.

15. Joanna Hanson, "Stanisław Mikołajczyk: November 1944–June 1945," *European History Quarterly* 21 (1991): 62.

16. Enrique Moradiellos, "The Potsdam Conference and the Spanish Problem," *Contemporary European History* 10 (2001): 73–90.

17. Sara Lorenzini, *L'Italia e il trattato di pace* (Bologna: Il Mulino, 2007), 107.

18. Harry S. Truman, *Year of Decisions* (London: Hodder & Stoughton, 1955), 492.

19. John Lewis Gaddis, *The United States and the Origins of the Cold War, 1941–1947*, 2nd ed. (New York: Columbia University Press, 2000), 312.

20. Joseph Rothschild and Nancy M. Wingfield, *Return to Diversity: A Political History of East Central Europe since World War II* (Oxford: Oxford University Press, 2000), 114.

21. Marc Trachtenberg, "The United States and Eastern Europe in 1945: A Reassessment," in Trachtenberg, *The Cold War and After: History, Theory and the Logic of International Politics* (Princeton, NJ: Princeton University Press, 2012), 89.

22. Norman Naimark, *The Russians in Germany: A History of the Soviet Zone of Occupation 1945–1949* (Cambridge, MA: Harvard University Press, 1995), 276.

23. Gomułka's Memorandum of a Conversation with Stalin, 14 November 1945, *Cold War History Project Bulletin*, no. 11 (Winter 1998): 135.

24. Gaddis, *United States and the Origins of the Cold War*, 295.

25. Joseph Stalin, "New Five-Year Plan for Russia," *Vital Speeches of the Day* (March 1946): 300–304.

26. George Kennan, "The Long Telegram," http://www.trumanlibrary.org.

27. Winston Churchill, "The Sinews of Peace," http://www.winstonchurchill.org.

28. Marc Trachtenberg, "The United States and Eastern Europe in 1945," 107 and 109.

29. Alan Bullock, *Ernest Bevin: Foreign Secretary* (Oxford: Oxford University Press, 1983), 217.

30. Bullock, *Ernest Bevin*, 216.

31. Jonathan Haslam, *Russia's Cold War: From the October Revolution to the Fall of the Wall* (New Haven, CT: Yale University Press, 2011), 72.

32. Roy Jenkins, *Churchill* (London, Macmillan, 2001), 811.

33. Naimark, *The Russians in Germany*, chapter 2 passim.

34. Pierre de Senarclens, *From Yalta to the Iron Curtain: The Great Powers and the Origin of the Cold War* (Oxford: Berg, 1995), 57.

35. Naimark, *The Russians in Germany*, 169.

36. See Anne Deighton, *The Impossible Peace, Britain, the Division of Germany and the Origins of the Cold War* (Oxford: Clarendon Press, 1994), 72–80 for the debate.

37. The speech was largely written by two New Deal liberals, Benjamin V. Cohen and the economist John Kenneth Galbraith. See Arthur Schlesinger, *A Life in the Twentieth Century* (Boston: Houghton Mifflin, 2000), 199.

38. James F. Byrnes, *Department of State Bulletin* (September 1946): 496–501.

39. The Novikov Telegram, 27 September 1946, http://academic.brooklyn.cuny.edu/history/johnson/novikov.htm.

40. For Britain's economic situation, see Robert Skidelsky, *John Maynard Keynes: Fighting for Britain 1937–1946* (London: Macmillan, 2001), 375–458. Keynes was Britain's chief negotiator for the loan.

41. For statistics, see Alan S. Milward, *The Reconstruction of Western Europe 1945–1951* (London: Routledge, 1984), 26–27.

42. Milward, *The Reconstruction of Western Europe*, 36.

43. Lawrence S. Wittner, *American Intervention in Greece, 1943–1949* (New York: Columbia University Press, 1982), 41–42.

44. Robert Frazier, "Did Britain Start the Cold War: Bevin and the Truman Doctrine," *Historical Journal* 27 (1984): 723.

45. Rothschild and Wingfield, *Return to Diversity*, 81–83.

46. Michael Creswell and Mark Trachtenberg, "France and the German Question, 1945–1955," *Journal of Cold War Studies* 5, no. 3 (2003): 14.

47. This paragraph is based on John Lamberton Harper, *America and the Reconstruction of Italy, 1945–1948* (Cambridge: Cambridge University Press, 2002), 137–58.

48. Ronald Steel, *Walter Lippmann and the American Century* (New York: Atlantic, Little Brown, 1980), 440–42.

49. John Lamberton Harper, *The Cold War* (Oxford: Oxford University Press, 2012), 69.

50. John Lewis Gaddis, *The Cold War: A New History* (New York: Penguin, 2004), 32.

51. Giuliano Procacci, ed., *The Cominform: Minutes of the Three Conferences, 1947/1948/1949* (Milan: Fondazione Feltrinelli, 1994); quotes, in order of appearance, from 235, 309, 195, 301.

Chapter Three

Stalinization

The previous chapter showed how tensions between the wartime allies led to a breakdown in their relations. By the summer of 1947, Washington believed that it was necessary to save the economies of Western Europe as a way of preserving democracy from the totalitarian peril—where the word "totalitarian" was a synonym for communist and "democracy" very often a euphemism for friendly to the United States. The USSR, in response, was rallying the communist parties of Europe to repel the new threat—as fearsome as that of Hitler's, or so the propaganda alleged—from "capitalist imperialism."

Expressed in this abstract way, the postwar division of Europe might appear a parallel process that was essentially the same on both sides of the divide: in both cases, it might seem, European peoples were brought under the hegemonic rule of non-European superpowers. We should not let language cheat reality. Unlike the nations of Western Europe, between 1947 and 1953 the nations of Central and Eastern Europe were dragooned into adopting the Soviet model of society. Police states were established and the worst features of the Stalinist regime were slavishly reproduced in one state after another. In war-blasted East Central Europe, the first decade after the end of the war was one of militarization, terror, and the imposition of a dreadful uniformity in politics and the economy. It *was* a decade of totalitarianism, if this word has any meaning at all.

SALAMI TACTICS

When the Cold War broke out, communist regimes had already crushed their main political opponents in three countries: Yugoslavia, Poland, and Bulgaria. The first of these cases is discussed at greater length later in this chapter. In Poland, as we saw in chapter 2, the communists established their predominance at the expense of the Peasant Party of Stanisław Mikołajczyk in the rigged elections of January 1947. In Bulgaria, the Agrarian Party leader Nikola Petkov was hanged by the regime in September 1947, an act of brutality that met with only formal protest from a West anxious, because of the internal situation in Greece, to demarcate spheres of influence in the Balkans. Communist control of Bulgaria by then was anyway already absolute.

Elsewhere in Central and Eastern Europe, however, a façade—and, in some countries, more than a façade—of non-communist participation in government lingered on until the worsening geopolitical climate led to an intensification of communist political control. Mátyás Rákosi, the leader of the Hungarian communists, notoriously boasted of using "salami tactics" to slice away the power of the other political forces in his country. In 1948, the Hungarian party leadership, like their peers elsewhere in the region, began chopping larger and larger slices off its rivals' residual influence. By the end of that crucial year, the "people's democracies" of Central and Eastern Europe were democracies only in name.

In Hungary, in fact, the communists had been originally compelled to cede considerable space to their opponents. As we saw in chapter 2, they came third in the free elections held in November 1945, with only 17 percent of the vote. The first postwar president of the Hungarian Republic, Zoltán Tildy, was an exponent of the Peasant Party, as was Ferenc Nagy, the first premier. The USSR insisted, however, that the communists be represented in government and that communist ministers should control the Interior Ministry. In February 1947, the communist-directed police implicated Nagy, the premier, in a shadowy conspiracy against the republic. Nagy, who was in Switzerland at the time, chose exile rather than return to certain arrest on trumped-up charges.[1] A campaign of intimidation was then waged against the Peasant Party and the Social Democrats, Hungary's second party.

Despite this campaign, the communists garnered only just over a fifth of the vote in new elections held on 31 August 1947. They eclipsed the Peasant Party and the Social Democrats within the governing "Fatherland Front" coalition, but several new parties contested the election and two of them, the Democratic People's Party (Christian Democrats), which obtained 16.5 percent of the vote, and the nationalist Independence Party, scored well. There was simply no mandate for outright communist rule in Hungary. In November 1947, however, the government first compelled parliament to suspend its powers for a year, then suppressed the Independence Party, and then, in June 1948, dissolved the Social Democrats into the Hungarian Workers' Party, where Rákosi called the shots. President Tildy was forced to step down the following month. New "elections" were held in May 1949: a list of government-approved candidates was voted for by 95.6 percent of the electorate. Voting against the list was a public act, which meant that casting a "no" ballot stamped one as an enemy of the people. In Mátyás Rákosi's Hungary, that was not a good reputation to have.

In Romania, events took a similar turn. Although King Michael remained on the throne until 30 December 1947, he reigned over a state in which the non-communist political forces were increasingly robbed of all political power. Fraudulent elections in November 1946, at which the Communist Party and its allies took three-quarters of the seats in parliament, prompted the opposition National Peasant and Liberal parties to refuse to take their seats in protest. Repressive measures swiftly followed, and throughout 1947 key opposition leaders were arrested and tried on charges of conspiracy with foreign intelligence services. Elections in March 1948 were "won" by the Romanian Workers' Party (i.e., the Communists and Social Democrats in forcible alliance), and the "Ploughman's Front," the communists' allies in the countryside. Within the ruling party, power was increasingly concentrated in the hands of a strongman, Georghe Gheorghiu-Dej, who sided with the "Muscovite" wing of the Romanian party (i.e., those leaders who had spent the war in the USSR and who arrived together with the Red Army) to overthrow his local rival Lucreţiu Pătrăşcanu, the justice minister since August 1944.[2]

It was in Czechoslovakia, however, that communist tactics had greatest international repercussions. As we have seen, the Communist Party had come to power in Prague through the ballot box, after emerging as the largest party in free elections held on 26 May 1946. The Czech communists had governed in the company of a coalition of agrarian and democratic socialist parties and had even initially responded positively to General George C. Marshall's offer of American aid. Stalin had reversed the party line rather than allow the states of Central Europe to be thus drawn into the capitalist embrace, and from September 1947, Czech communist leader Klement Gottwald knew that the ideologues of the Cominform were watching him for further signs of deviation from orthodoxy. He had to grab power to show his loyalty.

His opportunity came in February 1948. Public opinion was becoming increasingly dissatisfied with the Communist Party's occupation of the state. Key ministries were being taken over by placemen, and communist officials were abusing their powers to commandeer scarce apartments, cars, and other privileges. In Slovakia, the communists caused disgruntlement by subordinating the Slovak nation to Prague. Communist ministers were administering the economy and bore the brunt of public exhaustion and frustration with low living standards. Above all, the interior minister, Vaclav Nosek, was packing the police with party members. Elections were due in May 1948, and none of the communists' partners in government wanted to face a communist monopoly of domestic force. The democratic parties in the government—the Czech People's Party, the Social Democrats, the unfortunately named National Socialists, and the Slovak Democrats—accordingly demanded on 12 February 1948 that Nosek's partisan policy should cease. Backed by Gottwald, Nosek refused to give way. Ministers from all these parties except the Social Democrats accordingly resigned—nearly half the government.

The resignations provoked a major political crisis. The Communist Party filled the streets with paramilitary toughs in a show of strength. Ministries were seized by militants. The Social Democrat Party was taken over by its pro-communist wing. President Edvard Beneš, who had been forced to yield Czechoslovak sovereignty at Munich in October 1938 and who was now old and sick, was "determined to avoid a second national disaster" by breaking with Russia (or risking Soviet intervention). Accordingly, on 25 February 1948, Beneš allowed the Communists, with Social Democrat support, to form a government composed of card-carrying members or fellow travelers of the Party.[3] The only independent minister of any weight who remained was the foreign minister, Jan Masaryk, the son of the Czechoslovakia's founder, Thomas Masaryk. On 10 March 1948, Jan Masaryk's dead body was found in the courtyard of the Foreign Ministry. He had either jumped in anguish or had been shoved with hate.

In May 1948, a Soviet-inspired constitution was approved. In stark contrast with the Italian elections of the previous month, the subsequent election featured a single slate of approved candidates, which the voters could merely accept or decline. After the elections, president Beneš resigned (and died shortly afterward). Klement Gottwald became president of the republic, and the Social Democrats fused with the Communists into a single party. The best hope for political pluralism in Soviet-dominated Europe had become a one-party state.

Only one country in Eastern Europe broke the pattern of total communist domination: Finland. During World War II, the Finns had fought with Nazi Germany in a bid to regain the territory lost to the USSR during the Winter War of December 1939 through March 1940. Finnish troops, under the command of the legendary soldier Carl Gustaf Mannerheim, fought fiercely against the Red Army until September 1944, when an armistice was declared. The USSR subsequently followed a policy of limited interference in Finnish politics, contenting itself with exercising a de facto veto over Finnish foreign and defense policy and a watching brief over domestic Finnish politics. The January 1947 Treaty of Peace ceded the Karelian peninsula, north of Leningrad, to the USSR; gave the USSR a border with Norway by the cession of Petsamo in the far north; and allowed the Soviets to construct a naval base at Porkkala, in the outskirts of the Finnish capital of Helsinki. Finland regained its sovereignty in September 1947.

Following a policy of "national realism," Finnish president Juho Kusti Paasikivi, a veteran conservative who had been ambassador to Moscow and was a fluent Russian speaker, acquiesced to the Soviet demands. He had little choice. The largest political party in Finland in the immediate postwar period was the communist-dominated Finnish People's Democratic League

(SKDL); its leader, Mauno Pekkala, was premier between March 1946 and July 1948. Under Soviet pressure, a number of nationalist leaders closely associated with the war against the USSR were tried and imprisoned, though Mannerheim was spared this indignity. In April 1948 Finland was compelled to sign a treaty of Friendship, Cooperation and Mutual Assistance with the USSR. Under the terms of this pact, Finland committed itself to fighting with all its might to "repel" any armed attack on the USSR by Germany (or any ally of Germany) attacking via Finnish soil.

Seemingly satisfied with this pledge, the USSR restricted itself merely to diatribes and threats when, in July 1948, the Social Democrats (dubbed the "American" party by Russian propaganda) formed a government without the SKDL. In 1950, the USSR openly sided with Pekkala's candidacy for president, but did not intervene when Paasikivi was triumphantly reelected. Helsinki was free to host the Olympic Games in the summer of 1952. One can only wonder what the course of European and world history would have been had the USSR shown similar forbearance to non-communist politicians and parties elsewhere in its sphere of interest.[4]

REPLICA STATES

The establishment of what was called "People's Democracy" in Central and Eastern Europe was accompanied by the forcible introduction of the Stalinist state. Stalin's "short course" of Soviet history, a manual that was obligatory reading for the leaders of all Europe's communist parties, outlined to all true believers the path that communists should take for the achievement of socialism: concentration of political power, industrialization, collectivization of the land, expropriation of the wealthier peasants or "kulaks," and purges of class enemies and of comrades who deviated from the party line. Stalin's disciples in the nations of Central and Eastern Europe, keenly aware that they would be regarded as traitors to the cause themselves if they showed insufficient zeal, followed Stalin's prescriptions to the letter. In Tony Judt's felicitous phrase, in the late 1940s and early 1950s, the nations of the Soviet bloc were transformed into "geographically contiguous replica states" of the USSR.[5]

The years 1948–1953 were a period of reconstruction, hardship, and hope in Western Europe; in the Soviet bloc, by contrast, they were characterized by state terror and by the forcible uprooting of traditional social and economic structures. The nations of Central and Eastern Europe were transformed from being industrially backward, agricultural, and socially conservative societies, to being ones with a veneer of modernization. An industrial base was built at breakneck speed; entire cities were constructed from scratch to house the peasants flooding in from the countryside; traditional peasant society was disrupted and, in places, destroyed. As in the USSR, a Stalinist "revolution from above" was imposed upon the region, with awful human costs and only dubious gains in economic efficiency.

The imposition of the Stalinist model of the economy on to the states of Central and Eastern Europe was unreasonable—even irrational—for two main reasons. First, the countries' economies were very different among themselves; second, almost all of them were different from the USSR. The western parts of Czechoslovakia, Bohemia, and Moravia, with their advanced engineering firms and highly diversified economy, were more akin to the Rhineland or Lombardy than to the USSR: there can be no doubt that cities like Prague and Pilsen would have reproduced the "economic miracles" experienced by Dortmund and Milan had they had the good fortune to be occupied by American rather than Soviet troops after the war. Hungary, with its rich farmland, well-educated urban population, and densely populated territory, logically ought to have followed the same pattern of postwar economic development as neighboring Austria or Denmark. That is to say, it should have concentrated on producing high-value agricultural products for export and then invested the profits in light engineering and the development of a service economy.

Instead, between 1949 and 1951, all the new communist states announced ambitious plans to increase the output of coal, iron, electricity, and steel. But industrial expansion on the scale envisaged (increases, relative to 1949, of 200 to 300 percent in output by the end of the plans), compelled a radical restructuring of the labor market, and hence of society as a whole. The numbers of people engaged in food production had to be reduced by compelling the peasants to join larger, more highly mechanized "collective" farms. Nominally cooperatives, with a management subject to the democratic control of their peasant members, collective farms were in fact run like Orwell's "Animal Farm," with political commissars dictating operations. As the *Economist* pointed out in a perceptive contemporary article:

> In order that the enormous targets of the industrial plans may be achieved, despite shortage of skilled workers and machines, great masses of peasant sons and daughters must be mobilized and directed to the factories, mines and public works. . . . The men and women must be brought from the villages and they must be fed by those who remain on the land. The collective farm is above all a means of administrative—and political—centralization. Its purpose is to extract from the peasants increased food supplies and a more rapid flow of labor recruits.[6]

The peasants, however, resisted collectivization almost everywhere—in Poland, in particular, their resistance was so vehement as to make it obvious that there was no hope of maintaining political stability if the policy was pursued. Elsewhere, only part of the land was taken into collective ownership in the early 1950s.

Hungary provides an interesting case study. Collectives were first established in early 1949. After a slow start, the campaign to socialize agriculture picked up pace in 1951–1952. By 1953, nearly 20 percent of all agricultural workers (370,000 people) were employed by state-managed farms. Even though this was still only a fraction of the agricultural workforce, the damage done by collectivization was immense. Peasants were reluctant to expand production in a political climate in which they risked being denounced as "kulaks" and having their land taken away from them if they were too successful. Accordingly, they let land go fallow and sold off their animals. Crop yields soon fell well below prewar levels, as did livestock quality. Consumption of meat and dairy products fell substantially by comparison with prewar levels, along with exports of agricultural produce.[7]

In addition, the "People's Democracies" imposed a policy of "compulsory delivery" upon peasant households. In 1952, the worst year, Hungarian peasants had to hand over half of their production of wheat to the state for nominal prices. Not much was left for them to eat, still less to sell on the open market, while farm incomes slumped to just a third of those in 1949, reducing employment in the host of ancillary trades that depended upon a buoyant agricultural economy. As one authoritative study has argued: "The Hungarian regime . . . which conspicuously adopted the most radical heavy industrial program, succeeded only in reducing the standard of living and increasing unemployment."[8] The Hungarian historian Miklós Molnár made the same point even more pithily: "Shortage was one thing there was plenty of."[9]

In raw output terms, Stalinization did lead to startling increases in industrial production across the Soviet bloc. Like the USSR in the 1930s, the communist states were briefly "dizzy with success." The percentage of workers employed in industry increased markedly. All the communist states nationalized enterprises with more than a handful of employees. In the case of Bulgaria, where compensation was paid only to those who had not "helped or served" the Nazis or the royalist government, nationalization amounted to the expropriation of the entire middle class.[10] National income per head nevertheless surged. Large new towns, such as Nowa Huta (the "new Steel Mill") near Krakow in Poland, were constructed in the socialist realist architectural style around giant steel or cement works by tens of thousands of transplanted workers. *Man of Marble*, a film by the great Polish director Andrzej Wadja set in Nowa Huta, is a dramatic source for an understanding of the propaganda-laden climate that surrounded the building of socialism in the People's Democracies in the early 1950s.[11]

Foreign trade, after the January 1949 creation of the CMEA (Council for Mutual Economic Assistance; a customs union between the economies of the Soviet bloc), became dominated by the USSR. Before the CMEA, the Soviet share of these nations' trade was falling and trade between them was on the increase, which was probably why the USSR established the trade organization: greater trade cooperation might have led to closer political ties, anathema in the communist world. The CMEA nevertheless ensured that the USSR, which had pillaged its neighbors' industrial plant following the war (extracting a "flow of resources" roughly equivalent to the amount that the United States had invested in Western Europe through the Marshall Plan), would provide an outlet for manufactures produced in the satellites.[12] Unlike the equivalent exercises in economic cooperation in Western Europe, however, the trade regime established was essentially autarchic. The rebuilt or newly constructed industries of Czechoslovakia, the GDR, and Hungary were spared from having to compete with their peers in the West. In the short term, that meant guaranteed sales and higher incomes. In the long term, it led to the besetting sins of any autarchy: lack of innovation and economic stagnation.

The regimes' propaganda nevertheless broadcast the social benefits that were a concomitant of economic growth in the People's Democracies. A lavishly illustrated pamphlet about life in Czechoslovakia distributed in 1950 by the PCI, for instance, gloated over the living standards that Czech workers had acquired just five years after the end of the war. The fact that everybody worked, the pamphlet stressed, meant that a typical family's take-home pay amounted to a "neat little sum." The family's son was able to buy a motorcycle with "a mere year's savings" and take his young bride to the cinema or theatre at subsidized rates. When she became pregnant, she would receive treatment in state-owned clinics and receive the equivalent of 20,000 Italian lire to offset the costs of the first months of maternity.[13] Given the hardship of daily life in Italy when this pamphlet was published, it is small wonder that many manual workers were ardent supporters of the PCI.

It was not possible to deprive the peasants of their land, or to transform workers' production quotas, or to build entire cities within a couple of years, without compulsion. Stalinization and terror went hand in hand, just as they had in the USSR in the 1930s. The propaganda pamphlet produced for Italian workers did not mention that their Czech peers could be charged and imprisoned for "defamation of prominent officials," "slandering a foreign country" (i.e., the USSR), or "hindering the fulfillment of the five-year plan." In effect, workers who failed to meet production quotas, or grumbled about the workplace commissar, could find themselves in front of a tribunal and lose their job. Once unemployed, they could be arrested for shirking work ("parasitism"). During the period of high Stalinism, repression in Czechoslovakia was not restricted to political opponents among the bourgeoisie or to wealthy peasants: tens of thousands of ordinary workers were among the victims of the new state.[14]

Hungary and Romania, whose rural populations were greater, were even more subject to mass illegality than Czechoslovakia. Securitate (the Romanian secret police) files released since 1989 clarify that the numbers of arrests carried out by the secret police peaked in the two-year period 1951–1952, when more than forty thousand took place. Priests, landowners, professionals, members of the fascist wartime "Iron Guard," but also members of postwar democratic parties, were seized indiscriminately and, in thousands of cases, suffered inhuman tortures in the name of "reeducation": Piteşti prison, about seventy miles northwest of Bucharest, was an experimental laboratory for sadists.

To real or imagined political opponents of the Romanian regime were added other categories of people. "Kulaks," as instinctive opponents of collectivization, were likely to find themselves in a camp. Tens of thousands of people were summarily deported from the border regions with Yugoslavia in June 1951, at the height of Stalin's quarrel with Yugoslav leader Tito (see below); tens of thousands more labored after April 1950 on a canal linking the Danube to the Black Sea. Thousands of the slaves thus employed died on the job. The true number of Romanians subjected to persecution during the Stalinist period is not known, but it was certainly in the hundreds of thousands—and in Romania, the use of terror was scarcely relaxed even after Stalin's death in March 1953.[15]

In Hungary, 1.3 million people were brought before a court between 1948 and 1953, most of them on political charges.[16] Nearly 700,000 of these unfortunates were punished, with penalties ranging from death to a fine or the loss of a job. To put this figure in perspective, it is worth underlining that the population of Hungary at this time was less than ten million. Like the Nazis in 1933–1934, after Hitler's seizure of power—the comparison is a perfectly fair one—the Rákosi regime was intent on eliminating all political opposition and was unscrupulous in the methods it used to achieve this goal. The Hungarian secret police, the AVH (State Security Department), headed by the fearsome Gábor Péter, was a "vast, inflated bureaucracy of terror" that subjected those convicted of political offences to appalling tortures.[17] No one was exempt from "bell fright"—the ring of the doorbell by the men in dark raincoats at two in the morning—and individuals from all social classes fell into the AVH's clutches.

The most famous case of political persecution, which became an international cause célèbre, was of Cardinal József Mindszenty, the primate of Hungary, who had been jailed by the Nazis in 1945 for advocating withdrawal from the war. Mindszenty vocally resisted the communist takeover of power, objected to attempts to suppress Catholic schools, and condemned the foundations of Marxist doctrine. In a totalitarian state, such behavior was intolerable. In the fall of 1948, a campaign was launched in the party press to "annihilate Mindszentyism."[18] The cardinal was arrested, tortured like any other enemy of the people, and placed on trial in January 1949. At the trial, a browbeaten Mindszenty admitted to financial speculation and having plotted with the Americans to restore the Habsburg empire. The Hungarian regime seemingly did not care how bizarre the show trial appeared in the eyes of the rest of the world. Mindszenty was given a life sentence.

In the meantime, Catholic monastic orders were suppressed and schools were nationalized. In Poland, where Cardinal Stefan Wyszyński sought to find "common ground" with the regime, a deeply controversial concordat was reached in April 1950. Many Polish Catholics thought that this agreement, which instructed priests to use their pastoral work to "foster respect for the laws and prerogatives of the state," was a surrender to atheism and to the terror tactics of the ruling party, which had arrested priests "in almost arbitrary waves."[19] The concordat did, however, allow the Polish church to emerge from Stalinism "relatively intact."[20] The Hungarian church, by contrast, was obliged in August 1950 to sign a concordat of its own that gave its explicit imprimatur to the regime's economic, social, and geopolitical stance: priests even had to urge their congregations to help fulfill the five-year plan.

Similar tales could be told of Albania, Bulgaria, and Yugoslavia, where Tito imposed a rigidly Stalinist model on society. A special mention, however, is due to the three Baltic states, Estonia, Latvia, and Lithuania, which were Stalinized by Stalin himself, not by his imitators.

The Baltic states had endured unimaginable oppression already in the 1940s. In June 1940 their territories were occupied by the Red Army: the three nations had been assigned to the USSR in a secret protocol to the August 1939 Nazi-Soviet Pact. Like the Poles before them, the three nations' political and military elites were promptly subjected to "pro-active repression," that is, they were deported or murdered out of hand.[21] Latvia, Lithuania, and Estonia accordingly treated the Nazis as liberators when Hitler's forces invaded the USSR in the summer of 1941 (shamefully, volunteers from all three states were found to assist the extermination of local Jewish communities). After the Nazis' defeat, partisan groups did not accept the reimposition of Moscow's rule, but waged an underground struggle against the occupying Russians and against local communists and collaborators. The methods used by the Soviet forces to reestablish control over the Baltic states were ruthless: thousands perished as the USSR installed what the London *Times* called a "relentless system of colonization."[22] Nevertheless, bands of guerrilla fighters, supported by American intelligence, were active in the forests until the early 1950s.

The three Baltic nations were literally fighting for their existence as separate peoples. After the war, Russification began, and by Stalin's death in March 1953, tens of thousands of migrants from Russia and Belarus had been imported to work in the shipyards and new industrial plants, and to staff the party and official bureaucracies. The national cultures of the three states were persecuted, as were priests of the three principal churches: Catholic, Lutheran, and Orthodox. Church lands were nationalized. Marxist-Leninist orthodoxy dominated the countries' schools and universities.

Above all, the process of collectivization and industrialization led, even more than elsewhere in Eastern Europe, to catastrophic human losses. The Baltic states were primarily agricultural in population, with a large class of relatively well-off peasants who possessed smallholdings and livestock. In 1948–1949, such "kulaks" were "liquidated as a class" with exceptional brutality. In militarized operations, the richer peasants and their extended families—grandparents and small children included—were seized by the police and deported to the wastes of Siberia and Kazakhstan. If they objected, or tried to escape, they were "hunted like animals" and shot down in cold blood.[23]

Lithuania's worst year for deportations occurred in 1948; Latvia and Estonia bore the brunt in 1949. In the spring of 1949, Operation *Priboi* (Coastal Surf), a meticulously planned operation involving thousands of heavily armed secret police troops, led to the deportation of more than ninety thousand citizens from the three Baltic nations. Over 3 percent of the Estonian population (approximately twenty thousand people) was deported between 25 and 28 March 1949. Seventy percent of the deportees were women and children. The deportees—at any rate, those who survived a journey of thousands of miles and several weeks in unsanitary and overcrowded cattle trucks—were obliged to sign a document renouncing their right to return to their homeland: they could be punished with twenty years' imprisonment in a labor camp (in effect, a death sentence) if they broke their pledge.

In a sense, the repression was successful. Terror on this scale frightened peasants of all ranks into adhering to the collective farms, and by 1950, small allotments aside, the land was almost entirely out of private hands. Agricultural yields naturally plummeted, but from the point of view of the Kremlin that did not matter so much. The Baltic states' population had been atomized, its traditional structures and community leaders smashed, and its armed resistance had been broken. Only an indomitable sense of national identity remained— and in some ways was even strengthened.

COMMUNISM ON TRIAL

The previous two sections of this chapter have shown the communist parties of Central and Eastern Europe using "salami tactics" to seize power and ruthlessly employing the power of the state against individuals or categories of people that they reputed to be opposed to the building of a socialist society. But this does not mean that the communist regimes were monolithic political forces remorselessly concentrating on the fight against their perceived political rivals. To the contrary, their leaderships contained individuals who thought that their countries' national circumstances were ill-suited to collectivization and over-rapid industrialization, or who wanted to take a more conciliatory line with the church. Purely personal rivalries were intense, moreover, and led to vicious factionalism. As in Arthur Koestler's classic novel *Darkness at Noon*, the individuals who found themselves on the wrong (i.e., losing) side of conflicts over the correct party line were punished in the only way the communist movement possessed to resolve disputes: arbitrary arrest, public slander, torture, and usually death. Stalinism in the replica states would not have been complete without the evocation of the same nightmare atmosphere that had predominated in Moscow in the 1930s, or without the Marxist equivalent of witchcraft trials.

The catalyst for the purges within the USSR's satellites was the sudden breach of relations between Stalin and Josip Broz Tito of Yugoslavia in the first half of 1948. The Yugoslav leader had passed straight to the Staliniza-tion phase of socialist development after 1945. In Yugoslavia, the communists, the winners of the civil war and the ousters of the Axis armies, had no need to pay lip service to the idea that they were sharing power. Quite autonomously, the Yugoslav regime eliminated rivals, notably the Serb nationalist leader General Draža Mihailović; attempted (against fierce opposition) to collectivize the land; and directed investment to heavy industry. Indeed, the "Yugoslav comrades pursued the 'construction of Socialism' more fanatically than did their comrades in the other European states."[24] For Stalin, Tito's problem was not his policies, but his personality and ambitions. The "Stalin of the Balkans," as he was styled, could not but arouse the enmity of the despot in the Kremlin.

In particular, Tito was an expansionist. Independently of Stalin, and against the Kremlin's wishes, he was arming the Greek communist guerrillas in a civil war against the American-backed regime in Athens. On 2 August 1947, moreover, Tito and the Bulgarian leader Georgi Dimitrov agreed to discuss the creation of a South Slav People's Republic, which the two communist leaders hoped would extend to encompass Slavs in other countries, notably Albania. Later in the fall of 1948, Dimitrov envisaged the federation being extended to Romania. Stalin, his paranoia aroused, saw these speculations as the prelude to "a socialist bloc independent of the Soviet Union."[25]

On 29 January 1948, the mouthpiece of the Soviet leadership, *Pravda*, disowned the plan for a wider Slav federation. Top Yugoslav and Bulgarian leaders, though not Tito, were already in Moscow. At a tense meeting on 10 February 1948, Stalin demanded immediate unification of Bulgaria with Yugoslavia, while ridiculing the idea of incorporating Romania. Dimitrov, a wily survivor of the communist movement's infighting, accepted at once, but the Yugoslav leaders, grasping that Stalin intended the would-be federation to be "a snare into which no idealist would put his neck" sought to evade his diktat, arguing that Yugoslavia had the duty (and right) to find its own national road to socialism.[26] The issue was ultimately a personal conflict. Stalin had decreed that the states of Central and Eastern Europe should be replica states of the USSR under his control; Tito was too strong a character to yield to such a request unconditionally and began to demand the removal of Soviet military advisers from the country and to monitor Yugoslav politicians linked to the USSR.

The Yugoslavs' refusal to bow the knee—which was possible, of course, because Tito's regime had liberated its own territory mostly without the help of the Red Army—led to an exchange of rancorous diplomatic letters until, on 28 June 1948, at the second meeting of the Cominform in the Romanian capital, Bucharest, the conflict burst into the open with a public denunciation by the other European communist parties of the "incorrect line" being followed by Belgrade. The Cominform appealed for "healthy elements" in Yugoslavia to remove Tito and certain other key individuals in the leadership.[27] Tito became a pariah. A boycott was imposed on Yugoslavia's economy by the rest of the communist bloc. A state of high tension was created between the Balkan state and its neighbors, with thousands of border incidents being recorded over the next few years. By the fall of 1949, the "Tito clique" was being accused by the Cominform of having betrayed the workers of Yugoslavia on behalf of "the Anglo-American imperialists" and having "transformed Belgrade into an American center for espionage and anticommunist propaganda."[28]

Stalin was convinced that he could topple Tito without difficulty. He seriously underestimated his opponent. Tito responded to the Soviet threats by conducting a ruthless purge to remove pro-Soviet elements from the Yugoslav party and leadership. In all, more than thirty thousand such unfortunates were sent to a concentration camp on the island of Goli Otok. More than three thousand of them perished there.[29]

The Yugoslav communist (and later, dissident) Milovan Djilas wrote that in Stalin was joined the "criminal senselessness of a Caligula, with the refinement of a Borgia and the brutality of an Ivan the Terrible."[30] Stalin, and his security chief, the serial rapist and psychopath Lavrenti Beria, now gave ample proof of the exactness of Djilas's description by orchestrating a giant purge of all those leaders within the communist parties of Central and Eastern Europe who were regarded as being potential deviants from the Moscow line.[31] Would-be "Titoists" were identified in every communist party east of the Elbe and brought to trial on fabricated charges.

The bloodletting began in Albania, where Koçi Xoxe, the minister of the interior, lost a struggle for power with Enver Hoxha, a (then) pro-Soviet figure. Xoxe was arrested in November 1948 and tried in camera on 12 May 1949. Xoxe, who had been tortured for months, admitted to being a monarchist spy and an informer for the English and American intelligence services. On 8 July 1949, Xoxe was sentenced to death and was hanged a few days later. Leading figures in his faction were sentenced to long prison sentences. Mass purges followed. "Within a year, the whole Yugoslav wing of the Albanian party was in prison or in concentration camps."[32]

The logical victim of the purge in Bulgaria was Georgi Dimitrov. He had colluded with Tito, after all. Dimitrov, however, was an icon of the international communist movement. In 1933, he had defied Hermann Göring in a courtroom during the show trial organized by the Nazis after the burning of the Reichstag. Suspicion thus fell on Traicho Kostov, Dimitrov's long-standing deputy, whose main sin was that he was personally unpopular with Stalin and stood in the way of the rise of Vulko Chervenkov, the protégé of security chief Beria. The Soviets removed the risk that Dimitrov would object to his right-hand man's arrest by ordering him to Moscow, where he was feted publicly but monitored night and day. Dimitrov died in July 1949, but by then Kostov was in a prison cell. At the end of March 1949, following a meeting of the central committee of the Bulgarian Communist Party (BCP), Kostov was removed from the Politburo and from his position as deputy premier. In June 1949, he was arrested, along with 200 of his supporters, and subjected to protracted torture for months by a Soviet-Bulgarian interrogation team.

Kostov's trial began on 7 December 1949 and concluded a week later. During the trial, Kostov and his "accomplices"—all of whom were high-ranking party members—were portrayed as spies of the monarchist police who had also plotted on behalf of the British and U.S. intelligence services before moving into the service of Yugoslavia and planning Bulgaria's annexation by Belgrade. With remarkable courage, Kostov ruined the staged proceedings by retracting his prepared testimony. Persuaded by Chervenkov that his life would be spared only if he pleaded for clemency, Kostov, in his death cell, then went back on his plea of innocence. He was hanged anyway. His "gang" of supposed saboteurs and spies received long prison sentences.

In Poland, the power struggles among the leadership were less bloody. Władysław Gomułka was the Polish leader most feared by Stalin. Tough-minded, shrewd, and popular within the party, which he had led with courage during the war, Gomułka was probably closest in character to Tito of all the communist bloc's principal leaders. Like Kostov, moreover, Gomułka had had difficult relations with Stalin in the past: he was no sycophant. Most important of all, he was opposed to proceeding with collectivization too quickly and took an ambiguous line on the question of the Yugoslav party's right to decide its own future. After the June 1948 meeting of the Cominform, which he did not attend, Gomułka was accused of "right-nationalist deviationism" and spent the summer struggling to retain his position—and for all he knew his life. At the September 1948 meeting of the party's central committee, Gomułka was formally denounced by the party leadership.

Gomułka was removed as party secretary, though he nominally remained in the government and the Politburo for several more months. Bolesław Bierut, a Moscow-trained functionary of dubious antecedents unknown within Poland until his arrival in the wake of the Red Army in 1944, emerged as the Polish regime's new strongman. The Workers' Party liquidated the last remnant of political pluralism in December 1948 by merging with the Socialist Party to form the Polish United Workers' Party. In 1949, suspicion was cast on Gomułka's wartime role, with strong hints being dropped by party spokesmen that he had been a secret collaborator of the Nazis. Yet, while Gomułka's equivalents elsewhere in the bloc were being tortured into making confessions of espionage on behalf of the Titoist conspiracy, Bierut limited his punishment, in 1951, to house arrest. In 1954, after Stalin's death, Gomułka could be rehabilitated politically, not posthumously, which was the fate of most of his peers. [33]

Until the mid-1950s, Hungary was the most brutal of all the "People's Democracies" and the campaign against Titoists took especially vicious form there. The "Muscovites" occupied the highest ranks of the party. Party Secretary Mátyás Rákosi regarded himself as the Stalin of Hungary, and he and his chief collaborators, Ernő Gerő, Mihály Farkas, and chief ideologist Jozsef Révai, were devoted followers of every twist and turn in Soviet policy.

The purge victim settled upon in Hungary was László Rajk, a handsome, charismatic figure who was popular with the party membership, not least because he had fought in the Spanish Civil War and led resistance within the country to the Nazi-backed regime of Admiral Horthy. In Hungary, where anti-Semitism was rife, religious origin also played a part in his popularity: Rajk was the only one of the inner core of the party's leadership who had not been born a Jew. Rajk had also shown his independence from Stalin after the war by pressing for a more rapid shift to the dictatorship of the party: Rothschild says dryly that whereas "Gomułka's heresies were nationalism and caution, Rajk's (if any) were internationalism and radicalism." [34]

Rajk was arrested on 30 May 1949 along with a disparate group of party members who were charged with the crime of being the agents of a Yugoslav-American plot orchestrated by an American spymaster called Noel Field. An American progressive who had directed the Unitarian Church's European mission in Geneva, Switzerland, and had worked for the League of Nations until 1940, Field did exist. He was a sincere antifascist who had done much to help European communists during World War II and during the Spanish Civil War. He was also a communist sympathizer with ties to the Soviet security services who feared that he had no future back in the United States. [35] Field was kidnapped by Soviet agents in Prague in May 1949 and taken to Budapest, where he was kept in solitary confinement. His wife and brother were also kidnapped in August 1949. Meanwhile, the "Rajkists" were tortured savagely until they confessed to being Field's instruments in a plot to subvert the Hungarian revolution and to murder Rákosi.

Rajk and his group's show trial, which aroused international interest because of the bizarre nature of the charges, took place in September 1949 and their executions followed on 15 October 1949. A ruthless purge of Rajk's supporters followed; his wife, Julia, was sent to jail for the grave crime of having married her husband. The "liquidation" of Rajk's faction was only the beginning. In the summer of 1950, former Social Democrats were purged, as were the senior ranks of the army. In the spring of 1951, a group of top party functionaries, headed by János Kádár, a former minister of the interior who had fallen out of Rákosi's favor, were convicted of anti-Soviet activities. Kádár was no political innocent. He had undertaken the dirty job of persuading Rajk, a personal friend, that his confession was a necessary act of political sacrifice that would not lead to his execution.[36] Kádár nevertheless fell victim.

By 1952, terror for the sake of terror was the defining feature of Rákosi's Hungary. The regime was both creating and exorcising its own demons in a climate of artificially induced hysteria. It ended by devouring some of its own perpetrators. At the end of 1952, when the so-called doctors' plot against Stalin's life seemed to presage a pogrom against Jews in the party hierarchy, the Hungarian party leaders knew that their heads were on the block. To show zeal, Rákosi initiated a purge of alleged Zionist agents on his own account. The scapegoat chosen was the head of the AVH, Gábor Péter, who now fell victim to the methods he had used on thousands of others. Arrested on New Year's Day 1953, Péter was accused of being the organizer of a Zionist conspiracy. His wife, Jolán Simon, was "broken on a wheel" to make her confess to her husband's misdeeds.[37]

Anti-Semitism was also a prominent in the purge in Czechoslovakia by which party leader Klement Gottwald exterminated his nearest rivals. The purge began in January 1951, with the arrest by the "organs" of the foreign minister, Vladimir Klementis, and Artur London, the foreign trade minister. On 23 November 1951, Rudolf Slánský, the regime's number two man and a noted Gottwald supporter, was also arrested. Soon practically every man of "Jewish origin" in the higher ranks of the Czech party was in jail. Between 20 and 27 November 1952, Slánský and thirteen others were tried. According to their indictment:

> As traitors, Trotskyists-Titoists-Zionists, bourgeois nationalists and enemies of the Czech people, of the people's democratic regime and of socialism, they created, in the service of the American imperialists . . . a conspiracy against the state . . . in order to liquidate the people's democratic regime in Czechoslovakia, restore capitalism, drag our Republic into the imperialist camp and destroy its sovereignty and national independence.[38]

In the indictment and cross-examination, "Jew baiting became an integral part of the trial procedure."[39] During the trial, the defendants were even asked if they understood Czech—despite their having been until recently esteemed members of the regime. The trial followed a familiar pattern, with the defendants admitting their deviationism, and the prosecution accusing them of fantastic acts of espionage on no basis other than the confessions that had been bashed out of them.

On 3 December 1952, eleven of the fourteen defendants, including Slánský and Klementis, were hanged, with the remaining prisoners receiving life imprisonment. Thousands of relatives, friends, and colleagues of the tried men suffered persecution both before and after the trial.[40] The world's communist press celebrated the "liquidation" of yet another imperialist plot, but behind the scenes foreign communists were well aware that Slánský's group had died because Stalin and Beria had chosen to eliminate Jews from the communist leadership, and because Gottwald had wanted to get rid of a key rival.[41] Gottwald, incidentally, died nine days after Stalin on 14 March 1953 and never answered for his crimes.

In Czechoslovakia, trials and oppression of opponents continued even after Stalin's death in March 1953, as Gottwald's unscrupulous successor Antonin Zápotocký followed a policy of eliminating all would-be opponents and consolidating the centrality of the party's Czech leadership. Leading communists of Slovak origin, such as Gustáv Husák and Ludvík Svoboda, were purged and imprisoned, although Husák recanted his confession in court.

Romania followed an essentially similar path to Czechoslovakia. In Bucharest, as in Prague, the campaign against bourgeois nationalism and Titoism was interwoven with anti-Semitism. Party leader Gheorghiu-Dej, who greatly strengthened his position in the early 1950s, had faced two main rivals within the party leadership: Lucreţiu Pătrăşcanu, who, as we have seen, was purged in 1948, and Ana Pauker, a "Muscovite" of "Jewish origin" who was the world's first female foreign minister and a figure of some prominence within the international communist movement. Pauker was demoted from the Politburo in May 1952 and together with two other senior party members, Vasile Luca and Teohari Georgescu, was accused of right-wing deviationism and espionage. A purge of prominent intellectuals and party leaders followed. Pauker was arrested in February 1953 and was further accused of passing secrets to the United States via her brother, Zalman Rabinsohn, who was an Israeli citizen and who admitted under torture to having passed on confidential information received from his sister to the Israeli government. Pauker herself was tortured after her incarceration.

The Pauker affair has often been portrayed as a mere settling of scores between factions, but Pauker's biographer, Robert Levy, has made a plausible case for seeing her arrest as a genuine case of ideological divergence.

Pauker seemingly did resist the acceleration of Stalinist orthodoxy after 1948. She consistently argued for a gradualist approach to collectivization and had actively striven to mitigate the worst rigors of the policy. She had supported Georgescu's insistence that Pătrășcanu should have a trial based upon evidence, not a Rajk- or Kostov-style show trial, and as a result, at the time of her arrest Pătrășcanu was still a living reproach to Gheorghiu-Dej's imperfect zeal in liquidating internal enemies. She had also facilitated Jewish migration from Romania to Israel. Fifty percent of Romania's Jews had survived the Holocaust, and, the Soviet Union apart, it possessed Europe's largest Jewish community. Pauker, within the limits of her power, ensured that the restrictive quotas on Jewish migration imposed by Gheorghiu-Dej to prevent skilled Jewish professionals and artisans from leaving the country were circumvented.

Above all, Pauker had fallen foul of Stalin. By 1952, the Soviet leader's anti-Semitism was rampant. As a politically unorthodox woman of Jewish birth, she was an obvious target for his paranoia. In April 1952, on a visit to Moscow, Gheorghiu-Dej was derided by Stalin, Molotov, and other members of the Politburo for having done so little against the "rightists" in the Romanian leadership. Summoned at two in the morning to eat dinner with the Soviet tyrant, Gheorghiu-Dej was pilloried by Stalin for his weakness. Speaking of Pauker, Stalin said crudely that if he had been in the Romanian leader's place, he would "have shot her in the head a long time ago." Ominously, Stalin accused Gheorghiu-Dej of having "petit-bourgeois blood" flowing through his veins; of being, in short, too squeamish to be a good communist. Such words amounted to an ultimatum: purge her, or be purged alongside her.[42]

In all probability, Pauker and Pătrășcanu were envisaged as the star defendants in a giant show trial against both Zionism and bourgeois nationalism later in 1953.[43] By the time of Pauker's arrest, preparations were well in hand for mass trials of leading Soviet Jews and for the mass resettlement of Soviet Jewry to the wastes of Siberia. The satellite states would have been expected to follow suit with pogroms of their own. Stalin died, however, before his mad plans came to fruition.

After Stalin's death, Pauker was released—she still had friends in the Kremlin—and lived for seven years as an unperson in Bucharest. She succumbed to cancer on 3 June 1960. Her fellow "conspirators" lingered in jail. Vasile Luca died in prison in 1963 and Teohari Georgescu served a three-year sentence. Lucrețiu Pătrășcanu was placed on trial and executed in April 1954, though not before he had the satisfaction of renouncing the confessions his torturers had beaten out of him and of calling his judges assassins. He was shot in the back of the head in his prison cell.

TOTALITARIANISM

It has been fashionable for decades to decry the term "totalitarianism." The word undoubtedly was exploited during the early Cold War to rally public opinion behind American foreign policy. Yet, it is hard to know what other word to use when one is faced with the task of characterizing the regimes established on the wrong side of the iron curtain during late or "high" Stalinism. A polity where one's guilt or innocence, right to own property, to worship, or to join a club of like-minded individuals is entirely dependent upon the shifting whims of political power needs a descriptor: "authoritarianism" or "despotism" will not do. As Anne Applebaum has written: "Totalitarianism remains a useful and necessary empirical description. It is long overdue for a revival."[44]

This is why this chapter has given so much space to the show trials. They throw a pitiless spotlight on the nature of the political system imposed upon the satellite states between 1948 and 1953. One of the three survivors of the Slánský trial left posterity with the most graphic account of the mental atmosphere of late Stalinism. This was Artur London, whose book *The Confession* is a primary source of great importance. London had fought in the International Brigade during the Spanish Civil War, had joined the French resistance, and had survived Mauthausen concentration camp. During the war he had recuperated from tuberculosis in a hospital in Geneva at the expense of Noel Field's Unitarian Church. This record, far from being meritorious, made him a prime candidate for a prison cell. *Someone* had to be tried, and personal acquaintance with Noel Field, and a "cosmopolitan" past, were the wrong things to have on one's curriculum vitae.

George Orwell's famous novel *1984* appeared concurrently with the trials of Rajk and Slánský. Its account of how Winston Smith, the protagonist, was tortured and eventually intellectually convinced to admit that 2+2=5, and hence to recognize that the truth is no more nor less than what the holders of political power say it is, is uncannily similar to London's account of how he was driven after months of appalling beatings, sleep deprivation, sprayings with freezing water, near starvation, and continuous interrogation, to go along with a confession of guilt that implicated him and his closest friends and colleagues in a demented plot on behalf of Tito and Zionist imperialism. As London put it, for the men who interrogated him:

> There was no more objective truth. No more facts. For them a politician was simply someone who knew how to lie and say what the Party needed, who distorted facts, a man's life, ideas and convictions, in *their* way, the way which suited *them* one day, one month, one year.[45]

This total disrespect for the truth, this conviction that the party, if it applied power ruthlessly enough, and in sufficient quantities, could make reality correspond to the world depicted by propaganda, is exactly the hubristic quality that distinguishes totalitarian regimes from the merely authoritarian. Other types of regimes have charismatic leaders, are one-party states, or have terrifying secret police forces. Only a handful of regimes in the twentieth century have attempted to suspend the real world and make it subordinate to ideology.

It was this vaulting *intellectual* ambition that attracted so many western progressives to the Stalinist experiment. It would be improper to conclude this chapter without mentioning that the events discussed in these pages were excused or even applauded by some of the most prominent writers and thinkers in Western Europe, especially in France. The French Communist Party was a totalitarian party, whose idolatry of Stalin's personality (in 1949 the PCF distributed a Soviet pamphlet entitled "Stalin: The Man We Love Most") was religious in its intensity. The PCF was perfectly integrated into the wider communist movement: "The PCF and the USSR were no more than two component parts of a greater whole: the world communist system, at that time under Stalin's leadership."[46] The willingness of the intellectuals and scholars who wrote for PCF magazines and newspapers to write propaganda for Stalin is therefore unsurprising, though one remains astounded that so many men and women of proven literary talent were prepared to demean themselves in this way. What is surprising is that the purges, trials, and massacres carried out by the Soviet bloc regimes seemingly did not shake the belief of world-famous philosophers such as Jean-Paul Sartre and Maurice Merleau-Ponty, or the progressive Catholic thinker Emmanuel Mounier, that the USSR and the Stalinist model represented Europe's best hope for progress: certainly, that they were a much better model to follow than the tawdry, materialistic capitalism of the United States. These intellectuals broadly believed that history possessed a discernible narrative: the triumph of human equality, the working class, and the collectivist state. Marxism, amended to suit Parisian tastes, was the key to historical understanding, they considered. This, Tony Judt argues, is why they explained away or outright denied the human costs of Stalinism:

> For a certain class of western intellectuals, the victim of the Rajk or Slánský trials, of labor camps, anti-Semitic purges, and daily terror, was not some obscure local Communist politician, much less unknown thousands of workers, peasants, shopkeepers, and non-Communist writers and politicians. It was, or might become, Marxism itself. There was a widely articulated fear that the essential core of communism, the pure and timeless truth at the heart of the political system, would prove vulnerable to the inadequacies and faults of the contingent historical forms that it had taken.[47]

Their fear was surely a real one. Unlike Sartre, ordinary people could grasp that there was something fundamentally rotten in a system whose leaders were cynical tyrants like Beria, Gheorghiu-Dej, Gottwald, or Rákosi and that required regular blood sacrifices from entire categories of the population. The intellectuals saw communism as the end of history; in fact, there was something savagely medieval about high Stalinism's witchcraft trials and its crude repression of the peasantry.

The totalitarian phase of the communist revolution in Eastern Europe ended, however, on 5 March 1953, when Stalin died, after four days of coma. The Soviet Politburo, which had waited by his sick bed in a mood that fluctuated between servile anxiety and suppressed joy, divided the leadership between the fearsome Beria; acting party chief Georgi Malenkov, who became premier; the wartime political commissar Nikita Khrushchev; and the veteran foreign minister, Vyacheslav Molotov. Despite the solemn rhetoric of the official communiqué announcing Stalin's demise (which asserted that Stalin's name was "boundlessly dear" to the workers of the world and would "live for ever in the hearts of the Soviet people and all progressive mankind"), the regime began shifting away from his legacy almost at once.[48]

There was indeed a deep insecurity about Stalin's heirs as they began a new epoch in the construction of socialism. The very communiqué announcing Stalin's death, by proclaiming that the "Soviet people . . . are permeated with deep love for their Communist Party, for they know that the supreme law governing all the activity of the party is service in the interests of the people," might be said to have protested a little too much. Within months of Stalin's death, the Czech authorities had to crush serious unrest and political dissent among workers at the Skoda car plant.[49] In East Berlin, Soviet tanks had to be used to quell a popular revolt against communist rule (see chapter 6). The new Soviet leadership, whatever the official propaganda proclaimed, was aware that it had inherited an empire whose subject peoples had been driven to the breaking point and beyond.

NOTES

1. Nagy subsequently published an intriguing biographical account of his experiences, *The Struggle behind the Iron Curtain* (New York: Macmillan, 1948).

2. For a detailed discussion of this power struggle, see Dennis Deletant, "New Light on Gheorghiu-Dej's Struggle for Dominance in the Romanian Communist Party, 1944–49," *Slavonic and East European Review* 73 (1995): 659–90.

3. See Hugh Seton-Watson, *The East European Revolution* (London: Methuen, 1952), 187–90, for a still relevant discussion of the Prague coup.

4. This survey of Finnish politics 1944–1950 is greatly indebted to Roy Allison, *Finland's Relations with the Soviet Union, 1944–1984* (New York: St. Martin's Press, 1985), especially 127–56.

5. Tony Judt, *Postwar: A History of Europe since 1945* (New York: Penguin, 2005), 167.

6. "Stalinism and the Peasant," *Economist*, 31 March 1951, 725.

7. Bela A. Belassa, "Collectivization in Hungarian Agriculture," *Journal of Farm Economics* 42 (1960): 35–51.

8. Derek H. Aldcroft and Stephen Morewood, *Economic Change in Eastern Europe since 1918* (Aldershot, UK: Edward Elgar, 1995), 110.

9. Miklós Molnár, *A Concise History of Hungary* (Cambridge: Cambridge University Press, 2001), 304.

10. "Bulgaria—Kingdom of Dimitrov," *Economist*, 27 March 1948, 507.

11. Czlowiek z marmuru (" Man of Marble," 1977), directed by Andrzej Wadja.

12. Paul Marer, "Has Eastern Europe Become a Liability to the Soviet Union? (III)—The Economic Aspect," in *The International Politics of Eastern Europe*, ed. Charles Gati (New York: Praeger, 1976), 61.

13. *Cecoslovacchia Popolare* (Roma: Edizioni di Cultura Sociale, 1950?), 31–32.

14. Robert Evanson, "Political Repression in Czechoslovakia, 1948–1984," *Canadian Slavonic Papers* 28 (1986): 1–21.

15. This paragraph is based upon Romulus Rusan, "Il sistema repressivo comunista in Romania," in *Il libro nero del comunismo europeo,* ed. Stéphane Courteois (Milan: Mondadori, 2007), 295–352.

16. Molnár, *A Concise History of Hungary*, 303.

17. Victor Sebestyen, *Twelve Days: Revolution 1956* (London: Weidenfeld & Nicolson, 2006), 32.

18. Anne Applebaum, *Iron Curtain: The Crushing of Eastern Europe 1944–1956* (London: Allen Lane, 2012), 283.

19. Applebaum, *Iron Curtain*, 279.

20. Applebaum, *Iron Curtain*, 284–85.

21. Aldis Purs, "Soviet in Form, Local in Content: Elite Repression and Mass Terror in the Baltic States, 1940–1943," in *Stalinist Terror in Eastern Europe: Elite Purges and Mass Repression,* ed. K. McDermott and M. Stibbe (Manchester: Manchester University Press, 2010), 22.

22. *The Times*, 23 February 1949, 5.

23. Rein Taagepera, "Soviet Collectivization of Estonian Agriculture: The Deportation Phase," *Soviet Studies* 32 (1980): 384.

24. Jeronim Perović, "The Tito-Stalin Split: A Reassessment in the Light of New Evidence," *Journal of Cold War Studies* 9, no. 4 (2007): 37.

25. George H. Hodos, *Show Trials: Stalinist Purges in Eastern Europe, 1948–1954* (New York: Praeger, 1987), 14.

26. Milovan Djilas, *Conversations with Stalin* (London: Penguin, 1962), 143.

27. For the text of the 28 June 1948 Cominform Declaration, see Stephen Clissold, ed., *Yugoslavia and the Soviet Union, 1939–1973* (London: Royal Institute of International Affairs, 1975), 202–7.

28. Clissold, *Yugoslavia and the Soviet Union*, 225.

29. Svetozar Rajak, "The Cold War in the Balkans, 1945–1956," in *The Cambridge History of the Cold War, Vol. 1*, ed. Melvyn P. Leffler and Odd Arne Westad (Cambridge: Cambridge University Press, 2010), 211–12.

30. Djilas, *Conversations*, 145.

31. For confirmation of these attacks on Beria's character, see Simon S. Montefiore, *Stalin: The Court of the Red Tsar* (London: Weidenfeld & Nicolson, 2003), especially chapter 45.

32. Hodos, *Show Trials*, 11.

33. See Anthony Kemp-Walsh, *Poland under Communism: A Cold War History* (Cambridge: Cambridge University Press, 2008), 20–48, for greater detail.

34. Joseph Rothschild, *Return to Diversity* (New York: Oxford University Press, 2007), 137.

35. Applebaum, *Iron Curtain*, 305–6.

36. François Fejto, *Ungheria 1945–1957* (Turin: Einaudi, 1957), 224.

37. Hodos, *Show Trials*, 66.

38. Artur London, *The Confession* (New York: Morrow, 1970), 267.

39. Hodos, *Show Trials*, 85.

40. For a particularly vivid example of what such persecution implied, see Heda Margolius-Kovály, *Under a Cruel Star: A Life in Prague 1941–1968* (Cambridge, MA: Plunkett Lake Press, 1986). Her husband, Rudolf Margolius, was tried and executed alongside Slánský, whom he hardly knew and did not like.

41. Renato Mieli, *Deserto rosso: un decennio da comunista* (Bologna, Italy: Il Mulino, 1996), 72–73, recounts a private conversation with Ottaviano Pastore, a journalist who had reported the Slánský trial for the PCI newspaper, *L'Unità*. "What a bloodbath . . . It can be borne no longer," Pastore told him. He nevertheless maintained the party line in his reports and vilified the traitors on trial.

42. Quoted in Robert Levy, *Ana Pauker: The Rise and Fall of a Jewish Communist* (Berkeley, : University of California Press, 2001), 203.

43. Levy, *Ana Pauker*, 151.

44. Applebaum, *Iron Curtain*, xxvi.

45. London, *Confession*, 214.

46. Philippe Bouton, "Le Parti communiste français et le stalinisme au lendemain de la Seconde Guerre mondiale," *Journal of Modern European History* 2 (2004): 80.

47. Tony Judt, *Past Imperfect: French Intellectuals 1944–1956* (Berkeley: University of California Press, 1992), 130–31.

48. *Current History*, April 1953, 247–48.

49. See Johann Smula, "The Party and the Proletariat: Škoda 1948–1953," *Cold War History* 6 (2006): 153–75, for background to the Czech workers' uprising.

Chapter Four

Creating the West

American textbooks of international history often assume that the United States dominated early Cold War Europe. Stephen Ambrose and Douglas Brinkley's famous *Rise to Globalism* says the "Marshall Plan, followed by NATO, began in earnest an era of American military, political and economic dominance in Europe."[1] Equally briskly, Robert D. Schulzinger affirms that the United States "used its wealth and military might to gain influence. It entered the two world wars, revived the economies of Europe with the Marshall Plan, created the·North Atlantic Treaty Organization, and looked with approval on the formation of the EEC as a sort of embryonic United States of Europe."[2] Such formulations—which unconsciously depict the Europeans as passive instruments of the American master plan—underestimate the role played by the European nations themselves in shaping the institutions and policies that characterized the "West" during the Cold War.

In an influential article, the Norwegian historian Geir Lundestad argued that Washington became an "empire by invitation" in the 1940s and early 1950s. Its European allies implored it to take a dominant military and economic role in partnership with the non-communist European nations.[3] Lundestad was making essentially the same point as the French intellectual Raymond Aron, whose long essay *The Imperial Republic* (1973) argued—in criticism of the so-called revisionist school of Cold War historians—that in the late 1940s the Europeans "begged" Washington to intervene in Europe before it was too late and insisted that "it was at the request of the Europeans that the North Atlantic Treaty was signed." Aron thought that both traditionalist American historiography and the revisionists, who contended that the United States was an expansionist power that bore primary responsibility for the onset of the Cold War, tended to subscribe "to the myth of American national omnipotence."[4] This chapter will amplify Aron's insight while jettisoning the imperial metaphor that he and Lundestad employ. Such metaphors are well and good provided we treat them as narrative ornaments rather than precise descriptors. If by "empire" we imply that Washington dictated high policy and its satellites hastened to obey, the "West" was in fact anything but imperial in the 1940s and 1950s. The United States did not impose its social-economic model and values on European nations, nor—usually—did it insist upon obedience to its foreign policy preferences. European nations could and did say no to American presidents. Even in those countries where American political influence was most palpable—Germany, Greece, and Italy—the extent to which Washington was able to micromanage domestic politics should not be exaggerated. This chapter will survey the transatlantic relationship in the first decade of the Cold War and show how the complexities of European politics shaped the construction of the western democracies' response to the communist challenge.

AN ATTACK AGAINST THEM ALL

Great Britain, not the United States, took the first steps to create a West European security order. On 22 January 1948, after the failure of the Council of Foreign Ministers in London in December 1947, Ernest Bevin made his famous "Western Unity" speech to the House of Commons. The foreign secretary attacked the Soviet Union for its lack of cooperation and abusive propaganda, lauded the "great heart" of the American people, and proposed a common security agreement between Britain, France, and the Benelux countries. This "important nucleus" of countries, with their huge empires, was to be the springboard for further steps toward European unity, which Bevin insisted should be a "spiritual union" based upon shared values. Bevin condemned Germany's role in recent world history, but made clear that a united *democratic* Germany would be accepted into the fellowship of European nations.[5] Bevin's speech led in March 1948 to the signature by Britain, France, Belgium, Luxembourg, and the Netherlands of the Treaty of Brussels, which committed the five nations to mutual defense and emphasized the "necessity of uniting" for the purposes of economic reconstruction.[6]

The Brussels Treaty was important, since the United States was looking for concrete signs that Marshall Plan aid would lead to greater European political unity. When in April 1948, Congress passed the European Recovery Plan (ERP), as the Marshall Plan was officially known, and appropriated the first $5 billion of spending (in all, the United States would give more than $13 billion between 1948 and 1952), the cash came with elaborate strings attached. Washington was not prepared to hand out money to European states on a bilateral basis, but insisted that a new intergovernmental body, the Organization for European Economic Cooperation (OEEC), composed of a ministerial council of the governments participating in the plan, should distribute the funds and act collectively to liberalize Western Europe's economy. A permanent secretariat was established to facilitate this task and a European Cooperation Agency (ECA), headed by the prominent American banker and diplomat Averell Harriman, was established to monitor the OEEC's work and to press the member states toward greater integration.

The Americans' plans met resistance. Michael Hogan has written that "Europeans . . . sought a recovery program that would limit the scope of collective action, meet their separate requirements and preserve the greatest degree of national self-sufficiency and autonomy. Americans, on the other hand, wanted to refashion Western Europe in the image of the United States."[7] Britain, France, and the Scandinavians were adamant, however, that they would not surrender national sovereignty to a supranational body and their views eventually prevailed.

The establishment of the OEEC was accompanied by the decision to include the western regions of Germany among the beneficiaries of ERP money, and the introduction of the Deutsche Mark (DM) for the three zones of Germany occupied by the western powers. These decisions, which in effect signaled the resolve to divide Germany rather than risk the communization of a unitary German state, provoked a major crisis in relations with the USSR. Determined to keep the option of a united Germany alive, Stalin blockaded Berlin. On 24 June 1948, land and river transport links between Berlin and the western zones of Germany's capital were cut. Two million Berliners were left with no source for the basic necessities of life except the Soviet zone—though few emigrated east.

The Berlin blockade ratcheted up tensions in Washington to a new peak of intensity. In the fall of 1948, Truman authorized contingency planning for a nuclear counteroffensive in the event of a Soviet attack on Western Europe. National Security Council (NSC) document 20/4 asserted in November 1948 that "communist ideology and Soviet behavior clearly demonstrate that the ultimate objective of the leaders of the USSR is the domination of the world." While the United States itself was for the moment unlikely to be attacked, the NSC concluded that the USSR's armed forces possessed "the capability of over-running in about six months all of Continental Europe and the Near East as far as Cairo, while simultaneously occupying important continental points in the Far East." Meanwhile, the United States' strategists feared, "Great Britain could be subjected to severe air and missile bombardment."[8]

The Soviet blockade of Berlin thus presented the West with a conundrum. Berlin had to be saved for reasons of prestige. But how was the German capital to be saved without provoking a war that destitute Europe was bound to lose? The solution was a logistically miraculous airlift. From June 1948, British and American aircraft flying from the western zones of Germany landed every few minutes on the airfields of West Berlin, unloaded, and flew back to stock up again. By mid-May 1949, when Stalin lifted the siege, more than 278,000 flights had delivered nearly two and half million tons of cargo to the beleaguered Berliners, whose courage in the face of adversity earned them worldwide admiration—remarkable so soon after the end of Hitler's war.

The Berlin blockade thus turned into a propaganda disaster for the USSR. The West—specifically, the British and Americans—had shown that it would not be intimidated and had consolidated its grip on the political loyalties of the Germans (including those in the Soviet zone of Berlin, who could not but contrast the West's generosity with the ruthless exploitation of their economy practiced by the Russian occupation forces).

The blockade also convinced the nations of Western Europe that it was time for them to shelter behind Washington's shield. The Brussels Pact had been warmly welcomed in Washington, where prominent legislator and Cold War hawk Arthur Vandenberg introduced a resolution in the U.S. Senate urging "the association of the United States by constitutional process, with such regional and other collective arrangements as are based on continuous and effective self-help and mutual aid, and as affect its national security." Vandenberg's resolution was passed overwhelmingly on 11 June 1948. As the Berlin crisis intensified, transatlantic talks involving Canada as well as the United States began on superseding the Brussels Pact with a wider transatlantic security arrangement. At the end of October 1948, the Brussels Pact foreign ministers agreed in principle that a defensive pact for the North Atlantic area was a necessary step. The Brussels Pact countries began formal negotiations with Canada and the United States in mid-December 1948.

As the talks progressed, other countries were invited to join the seven pioneers. Norway faced an abrupt choice in February 1949 when the Soviet Union demanded that it follow the example of Finland and declare its neutrality. Oslo refused, although it did guarantee Russia that foreign troops would not be stationed on Norwegian soil. On 15 March 1949, the original seven states invited Norway, together with Denmark, Iceland, Italy, and Portugal, to adhere to the North Atlantic Treaty. Italy, a Mediterranean nation, was included on French insistence and against the vocal opposition of the British Foreign Office. The text of the treaty was made public on 18 March 1949 and signed in Washington on 4 April 1949.[9]

Article Five of the North Atlantic Treaty was crucial:

> The Parties agree that an armed attack against one or more of them in Europe or North America shall be considered an attack against them all; and consequently they agree that, if such an armed attack occurs, each of them, in exercise of the right of individual or collective self-defense recognized by Article 51 of the Charter of the United Nations, will assist the Party or Parties

so attacked by taking forthwith, individually and in concert with the other
Parties, such action as it deems necessary, including the use of armed force, to
restore and maintain the security of the North Atlantic area.

In effect, this meant that the United States was pledging, albeit with a proviso
("such action as it deems necessary"), that it would come to its allies' aid in
the event of communist attack—a commitment that was given special significance in September 1949 when the USSR exploded its first atomic bomb.
Washington, moreover, immediately put its wallet to work. On 5 April 1949,
the European powers asked Washington for military and financial assistance.
By October 1949, Congress had passed the Mutual Aid Assistance Act,
which made a billion dollars available for military spending to protect the
North Atlantic area.

The USSR mobilized the communist parties of Western Europe against
the North Atlantic Treaty. In Italy and France, in particular, the campaign
against the "Atlantic Pact" was massive. Several of Italy's leading liberal
politicians opposed ratification of the treaty on constitutional grounds (the
newly adopted Italian Constitution committed Italy to a pacifist foreign policy), and so did many progressive Catholics anxious to find a modus vivendi
with the PCI. Nevertheless, communists were the North Atlantic Treaty's
main opponent. "Peace partisans" carried out strikes, protest meetings, and
acts of sabotage to block the arrival of American arms in both France and
Italy.[10]

On 15 March 1950, the Moscow-controlled World Peace Council issued
the "Stockholm Appeal" demanding the abolition of nuclear weapons as
"instruments of intimidation and mass murder of peoples" and denouncing
all those who made first use of nuclear weapons as "war criminals." Tens of
millions of Western Europeans (plus the entire adult population of the
USSR) signed the appeal, which was fronted by the French scientist (and
communist sympathizer) Frédéric Joliet-Curie, but which attracted the support of many prominent intellectuals. Pablo Picasso's famous image of the
"dove of peace," with an olive branch in its beak, was sketched for the World
Peace Council's campaigns. Once again, Italy and France led the struggle
against the American "warmongers" and their arsenal of nuclear destruction.[11]

The success of the World Peace Council among intellectuals was so strik-
ing that two communist apostates, the novelists Arthur Koestler and Ignazio
Silone, took the lead in organizing a western counterpart, the Congress on
Cultural Freedom, which held its inaugural assembly in West Berlin on 25
June 1950.[12] The congress soon became a major undertaking, sponsoring
concert tours, art exhibitions, and intellectual reviews, the most famous of
which were the London-based *Encounter*, *Preuves* in Paris, *Der Monat* in
Berlin, and *Tempo presente* in Rome. The congress, naturally, was financed

behind-the-scenes by the CIA, a fact which scandalized many when it became public knowledge in 1967 and continues to offend some to this day.[13]

SECURING THE SOUTHERN FLANK

The role of the PCI in opposing the North Atlantic Treaty and the volubility
of the antinuclear campaign in Italy are a reminder of the importance of
Europe's southern flank in the early Cold War years. During the negotiations
for the North Atlantic Treaty, both Italy and Greece had been hovering between the western and Soviet camps. The United States intervened in the
domestic politics of both countries to ensure that they chose wisely. Washington, needing military bases from which to wage war against a northern
Europe fallen under communist sway, in the early 1950s also shored up the
authoritarian regime of the Spanish Caudillo, Francisco Franco. In southern
Europe, the early Cold War was a war against communism first, and for
democracy second. The end arguably justified the means, but the means were
not always pretty.

Italy was a pivotal state in the early Cold War, second in importance for
U.S. policy makers only to Germany. By the spring of 1947, the PCI had two
million members and governed several important cities. Allied to the pro-
Moscow Socialist Party (PSI), which possessed deep roots in the organized
working class of northern Italy, PCI leader Palmiro Togliatti advocated taking power by constitutional methods, in the face of strong internal pressure
for outright insurrectionary tactics.

Togliatti's strategy made sense. Had the Italian communists heeded the
strictures of their Yugoslav comrades at the first meeting of the Cominform
in September 1947, and adopted a revolutionary strategy, the PCI would
have been suppressed by the government.[14] The PCI nevertheless became
more confrontational after the hazing that they had received at the Cominform meeting. Street clashes, strikes, and other "political muscle-flexing"
increased in intensity in the fall of 1947.[15] Allied troops were scheduled to
leave Italy on 14 December 1947, and the Italian government feared that a
communist coup might follow their removal from Italian soil.

No coup occurred, but the "Garibaldi Front" between the PCI and the PSI
still presented Washington with the specter of the most populous country in
the Mediterranean passing into the Moscow camp. The victory of Alcide De
Gasperi's Christian Democracy (DC) seemed uncertain as Italy approved its
Constitution in December 1947 and prepared for elections in April 1948.
NSC document 1/2, dated 10 February 1948, warned that the De Gasperi
government was under "strong and persistent Communist attack aimed ultimately at the creation of a Communist dictatorship subservient to Moscow."[16] The document recommended U.S. occupation of Sicily and Sardinia

if an "illegal Communist-dominated government will control all of the peninsula of Italy."[17] The communist coup d'état in Prague in February 1948, which the PCI newspaper *Unità* welcomed with the banner headline "Victory in Prague," seemed a harbinger of what might happen if the "Garibaldi Front" secured a majority, or even a substantial minority, at the polls.

One good indicator of the alarm in top U.S. government circles over a PCI victory was provided by George F. Kennan, the chief of policy planning in the State Department and the architect of the doctrine of "containment." On 15 March 1948, Kennan questioned whether it might not be "preferable" for the Italian government to "outlaw" the PCI before the April poll. Such an action might mean civil war, Kennan acknowledged, but that, too, would be "preferable" to "a bloodless election victory, unopposed by ourselves, which would . . . send waves of panic to all surrounding areas."[18]

The 18 April poll hence became "a referendum for and against Communism, the Marshall Plan and collaboration with the Western World."[19] The referendum was won by the West. The DC took 48.5 percent of the vote and won an absolute majority in both the Chamber of Deputies and the Senate. For the first time in Italy's history as a unified nation, a party of Catholic inspiration was dominant in parliament—a fact often forgotten, and which may not have occurred without the Cold War's polarizing effect on the electorate. The left alliance was reduced to blaming ballot fraud. The only silver lining for Togliatti was that the PSI fared much worse at the polls than the PCI, which enabled the PCI to become the main party of opposition.

The reasons for the DC's triumph are not hard to find. De Gasperi's personal "unexpected strength and assurance" impressed foreign observers, and undoubtedly contributed to the DC's victory.[20] The DC's vivid propaganda, with its depictions of the communist threat to the traditional family, land ownership, and Christian values, rallied voters to its shield and cross symbol. The Church hierarchy campaigned tirelessly from the nation's pulpits. Last but not least, the right-wing cartoonist and journalist Giovanni Guareschi contributed memorably to the campaign by drawing a flyer that showed a workman deliberating over his vote. The caption read: "Italian worker! Remember that in the secrecy of voting booth, Stalin can't see you but God can."

However, another important reason for the outcome of the election was the fact that the United States "took the gloves off for the first time."[21] In March 1948, the NSC authorized covert funding of both the DC and of the Socialist Party of the Italian Workers (PSLI), whose leading lights were the anti-Moscow socialists Giuseppe Saragat and Ignazio Silone. From mid-March 1948, moreover, U.S. officials from Secretary of State Marshall downward left Italians in no doubt that voting for the PCI meant exclusion from Marshall Plan aid. President Truman hastened the ERP bill through Congress in order to be able to sign it into law before the Italian elections. In the weeks preceding the election, American citizens of Italian origin took part in a letter writing campaign urging their relatives to imitate the American way of life. U.S. cash enabled the DC to afford its lavish spending on posters and propaganda. The Truman administration in effect bought the April 1948 poll in Italy by "reducing" the issues to "a series of simple choices: Democracy or totalitarianism, Christianity or atheism, America or the Soviet Union, abundance or starvation."[22]

There were excellent reasons for this interference in the democratic process. The PCI objectively did represent a danger for Italy's nascent democracy. Its links to Moscow and its hundreds of thousands of revolutionary militants meant that the PCI could not be trusted by its political rivals. As a contemporary Italian thinker argued, it was "impossible to think that once the communists had reached the 40 percent threshold, that this 40 percent would not seek to seize power, or accept being excluded from the government."[23] It was also true that neither would anti-communists accept the PCI's right to rule, even if it possessed a plurality of votes. This polarization of politics would become the bane of postwar Italy. However, in 1948 there was no reason for the DC and the Truman administration to believe that Togliatti would behave any differently from Tito, Gomułka, or Gottwald had the PCI become the largest party in the Italian parliament.

Desperate times, in short, justified desperate measures. Nevertheless, American involvement in the 1948 elections was just the beginning of a lengthy period of meddling in Italian democracy—interference whose worst effects were only mitigated by the restraint shown by De Gasperi and the leading Christian Democrats, and to a certain extent by the leaders of the PCI.

The Italian scholar Mario Del Pero has identified three phases of U.S. intervention in Italy between 1948 and 1955. The first, which he calls "Positive Containment," prevailed in 1948–1950, when Washington incorporated Italy into the North Atlantic Treaty and strove to persuade De Gasperi to modernize its economy and become a full member in good standing of the Atlantic *communitas*. Underlying U.S. thinking was the view that the poverty and injustice endemic in Italian society was the root cause of the PCI's attraction. If Italy modernized, the communist challenge would wither away. De Gasperi, however, opted for an "ambiguous economic policy" that kept inflation low, protected Italy's domestic market, and left largely intact the unwieldy corporate state constructed by fascism. It was a strategy, in short, that avoided a transformation of the economic circumstances of the party's middle-class electorate.[24]

The American hegemon could not budge De Gasperi, try as it might. The Italian premier knew that so long as the PCI followed a hard-line strategy that demonized the U.S. for "acting today in the same way that Hitler acted in his day," the United States had no choice but to cling to the DC nurse, for fear of worse.[25] Moreover, the United States had no credible alternative to the DC to call upon. Many in the Truman administration preferred the Atlanticist moderates of the Republican Party (PRI), or even the Social Democrats (as the PSLI renamed itself), to a confessional party like the DC. But these two parties combined commanded less than 10 percent of the national vote.

After 1950, the Truman administration followed a policy of "Negative Containment." Washington pressured Rome to withdraw American-funded contracts from firms that permitted communist trade unions, and put forward illiberal plans for the expulsion of card-carrying communists from administrative positions in the schools, universities, and public administration. Some companies, notably the car manufacturer FIAT, did draw up blacklists of workers and sack or transfer them. De Gasperi mostly ignored this pressure, which intensified in 1953 after the arrival of a new American ambassador, Clare Boothe Luce, a former congresswoman who was a close friend of Eisenhower and the wife of the anti-communist publisher of *Time* magazine, Henry Luce.

Boothe Luce was nevertheless a staunch supporter in Washington of the Italian cause. In the fall of 1953, during the Trieste crisis, Boothe Luce's personal connection to Eisenhower proved to be of decisive importance. The Adriatic port city, possession of which had been contested by Yugoslavia after the war, had been divided into two zones: Zone A, the city itself, which had a largely Italian population, was under Allied military occupation and was governed by Italian civilians; Zone B, the city's hinterland in the peninsula of Istria, which had a mixed population of Slovenes, Croats, and Italians, was under Belgrade's administration—though not yet under its sovereign rule. Since the Korean War had broken out in June 1950, Yugoslavia—regarded by most U.S. war planners as the most likely European target of communist invasion—had, like Italy, become an important part of Washington's strategic plans for the Mediterranean. Tito had received considerable economic and military aid ($156 million in fiscal year 1952; more than $400 million was appropriated for 1953) from Washington. London and Washington had encouraged Tito to form a Balkan Pact with Greece and Turkey. The French had even wanted to include Yugoslavia in NATO, since statements by U.S. spokesmen had left no doubt that Belgrade would be supported by NATO in the event of an attack by the USSR's satellite states.[26]

Boothe Luce argued from Rome that Italy was more important even than Yugoslavia. There would be a catastrophic loss of confidence in the DC if Italy were not allowed to regain sovereignty over the city of Trieste. Eisenhower concurred. On 8 October 1953, the NATO allies announced that their presence in the city was at an end, and Italian troops occupied Zone A. When Tito responded aggressively, U.S. warships were anchored offshore and weapons deliveries to Belgrade were suspended. Tito backed down: he had no superpower protector. Relations between the West and Yugoslavia soured, although U.S. arms shipments continued for several more years. In October 1954, the territorial division was accepted by Belgrade after a few minor adjustments to the border were made in its favor.[27]

Even overt U.S. support during the Trieste crisis did not give Boothe Luce enough leverage over the DC to persuade its leaders to clamp down on the PCI. Though De Gasperi's political star waned after the June 1953 elections, his successors continued to treat the PCI as a "legitimate enemy to be defeated, rather than eliminated as the United States would have wished."[28] To Boothe Luce, and to the coterie of upper-class Italian journalists and industrialists who advised and manipulated her, this policy seemed like appeasement. When the ambassador put forward radical plans to curb "Red" influence in Italy in January 1954, De Gasperi, in one of his last public interventions before his death, acidly described them as "international McCarthyism"—which, of course, is exactly what they were.[29]

The DC, whose rising star from 1954 onward was the diminutive but shrewd Amintore Fanfani, was determined to fight communism by using public investment to accelerate Italy's already impressive rate of economic growth. The party's 1955 congress at Naples approved an ambitious ten-year plan to create four million jobs and increase real growth by 5 percent per year. The U.S. embassy worried about the political significance of the DC's "socialist" turn, but could do nothing about it.

Boothe Luce's association with the most reactionary elements of Italian society was reproduced elsewhere in the Mediterranean. In Greece, the United States sustained the Greek state in its war against the insurrection of the communist-controlled Greek Democratic Army (GDA). The Greek civil war, which lasted until August 1949, when the GDA suffered major casualties in the Gramnos mountains, transformed Greece into a de facto protectorate of the United States. The head of AMAG (American Mission to Greece), Dwight P. Griswold, enjoyed near-plenipotentiary powers over the Greek government, its foreign policy, and the conduct of the civil war. American money fed and armed the Greek Army, kept the air force's Spitfires and Harvard fighter bombers airborne, and prevented a bankrupt economy from imploding. The Greek military became a reliable fighting force thanks to General James Van Fleet, who arrived in Greece in January 1948 and improved the training of its top soldiers. In particular, the United States backed the ascent of General Alexandros Papagos, a methodical and competent staff officer with good diplomatic skills.

The GDA admittedly contributed greatly to its own defeat: the Greek Communist Party (KKE) leader, Nikos Zahariadis, was a pro-Moscow ideologue and took Stalin's side in the clash with Tito after June 1948. Since the GDA's guerrillas were using Yugoslavia as a safe haven to rest and replenish themselves, and largely depended upon Yugoslavia for arms and ammunition, this act of ritual conformity to Moscow was self-defeating. Tito, pressed by the British and the Americans, who extended significant credits to the beleaguered Yugoslav government in 1949, enabling it to trade with the West and circumvent the Soviet embargo, closed the border and the GDA was forced to slug it out with the Greek Army in the mountains of northern Greece until its final defeat.[30] Nevertheless, it is clear that U.S. dollars and know-how were decisive in enabling Athens to survive and win the civil war.

Greece in 1949 was a case study of a country that required what we would today call "nation building." Approximately one hundred thousand people, out of a population of seven million, had perished during the civil war. Coming on top of the Nazi occupation, in which hundreds of thousands of houses and public buildings had been destroyed, along with some 7 percent of the population, the civil war had delivered a second body blow to the Greek people.[31]

Plenty of people in Greece had done very well out of the war. The Athens elite, which had profited from speculation, corruption, and black marketeering, lived luxuriously amid their destitute fellow citizens. Yet, as Richard Clogg has written, it "soon became apparent that the primary objective of post-civil war governments was the containment of communism, rather than any serious effort to reform or restructure society."[32] The U.S. government did press Greek governments to liberalize its economy—a forlorn hope. But economics played second fiddle to geopolitical concerns and the Greek elites knew it. The U.S. military-political establishment was fearful of a communist takeover in Athens long after the crushing of the GDA. NSC 103/1, a document approved by President Truman on 15 February 1951, worried that communist domination of Greece might "serve as a springboard for communist penetration, political and military, into the Eastern Mediterranean and Near East area." Except for conjectures about the likelihood of Soviet-backed Bulgarian aggression against Greece, adorned with ominous references to Bulgaria's hundreds of heavy T-34 tanks, no proof was offered that Greece was at any risk of shifting political camp.

The intellectual patrimony of NSC 68, the April 1950 report on grand strategy written by Paul H. Nitze for President Truman, was explicit in every line of NSC 103/1. As John Harper has written, NSC 68 was the "purest expression of Hobbesian fatalism in the annals of American statecraft."[33] Its underlying logic was that if American vigilance and power faltered, even for a moment, the Soviet Union would strike unmercifully at the West's weak points—as it had done in North Korea. Greece was one of the West's weak points, and its disintegration, NSC 103/1 assumed, would lead to dominoes dropping across the Middle East and Mediterranean. Turkey, Iran, Italy: none would be safe. Greek entry into the North Atlantic Treaty, which Truman agreed to sponsor in May 1951, was justified by this exercise in hypothesis.

Possessing such a perception of Greek fragility, the United States, which was providing Athens with $200 million per year in aid, naturally became embroiled in the labyrinth of domestic Greek politics. The U.S. ambassador from 1950 to 1953, James Peurifoy, intrigued with the king, with senior politicians and military men, and indicated Washington's views on policy choices and ministerial nominations. Yet it is also evident that Peurifoy, far from being Greek politics' deus ex machina (which is what most Greeks believe), soon became just another actor in the endless plot twists of the Greek political melodrama.[34]

Nevertheless, Peurifoy did overtly intervene prior to general elections in November 1952 to compel the replacement of the highly proportional electoral law with a majoritarian system. The beneficiary of this change was Alexandros Papagos, whose "Greek Rally" movement took 82 percent of the seats in parliament with only 49 percent of the vote. Papagos was a stopgap solution, voted into power by dint of his personal prestige, but after his death in 1955, his legacy was strengthened by his successor, Konstantinos Karamanlis, who also enjoyed Washington's open blessing. Karamanlis brought Greece the broadly pro-western orientation that the Americans craved. In the meantime, however, a lid was placed over demands for significant social reforms.

Spain, ruled by the fascist dictatorship of Francisco Franco, was a third Mediterranean country in which Washington put anti-communist zeal ahead of democratic principles. Spain had remained neutral during World War II, though it sent a legion of soldiers to help the Nazis on the Russian front. Spanish wartime propaganda had also been contemptuous of the social order prevailing in the United States: as late as the early 1950s, "signs of hostility toward North Americans were a constant theme in the press outlets of the three great pillars upon which the regime relied for support—the army, the church and the Falange."[35]

Franco had been treated like a pariah after the war. On 12 December 1946 the General Assembly of the UNO recommended that Spain be debarred from membership of the organization until such time as a "new and acceptable government is formed." The General Assembly added the further recommendation that member states should withdraw their ambassadors from Madrid. President Harry S. Truman backed this boycott. Truman compared the Caudillo to Hitler and Mussolini and detested the Franco regime's persecution of Protestants and freemasons (Truman was both).

Truman's position was initially popular with the voters. In 1946, the Spanish Civil War, which Franco had won with military support from Hitler and Mussolini, was interpreted as the first battle against the fascist attempt at world domination. With the advent of the Cold War, the same conflict was redepicted by America's influential "Spain lobby" as the "first battle against international communism."[36] Powerful congressmen—including Joe McCarthy—and business interests wanted to restore links with Spain and bring Franco's regime into the western camp as a member of the North

Atlantic Treaty. So too did the military, which saw Spain as a bastion from which to rally the defense of Europe, once Russian tanks had overrun Germany and France. The fact that the United States maintained ambassadors in such countries as Hungary, where political repression was even more brutal than Spain, was just one more proof, anti-communist crusaders proclaimed, that the State Department was "soft on communism." Already under fire for having "lost" China, Secretary of State Dean Acheson yielded to the "Spain lobby's" pressure after the outbreak of war in Korea.

In November 1950, the ban on diplomatic relations with Madrid was rescinded by the UNO itself. Truman acquiesced to sending an ambassador and "over the next three years, the Spain lobby's full agenda would become a reality."[37]

Or almost a reality. Great Britain and especially France blocked Spanish membership in NATO.[38] In September 1953, therefore, after protracted negotiations, Spain and the United States concluded a bilateral treaty. Washington promised economic aid, military training for Spanish officers, and access to arms on favorable terms; in return, Spain, while retaining sovereign rights, provided access to Spanish naval and air bases and allowed the United States to develop them—Rota naval base near Cadiz remains one of the largest military installations in Europe to this day. The United States provided $1.5 billion in aid over the first ten years of the treaty.

The justification for this accommodation with the Caudillo was expressed entirely in realpolitik terms. U.S. policy toward Spain was defined in June 1954 by NSC 5418/1. Stressing that Spain's "strategic geographic location is extremely important to the immediate defense of Western Europe and the Middle East and to the security of the NATO area and of the United States," this document emphasized that Spain was an "authoritarian" regime whose current leadership provided "stability." Nowhere was it suggested that American policy might encourage Spanish democratization. Indeed, the NSC agreed that:

> U.S. relations with Spain must be guided by the fact that the United States will have to cooperate closely with the government of Franco in order to insure effective implementation of military arrangements of great value to U.S. security. . . . While continuing to use its influence to persuade Spain to follow policies consonant with U.S. interests, it is important that the United States avoid steps that could be interpreted as an attempt to interfere in Spanish internal affairs.[39]

Spain, with American backing, joined the UNO in 1955. For Franco, the September 1953 accord, and the influx of American aid, were a huge propaganda success that gave his regime fresh credibility.

Overall, U.S. policy choices in the Mediterranean in the early Cold War years prized anti-communist zealotry over democratization. This choice was not necessarily unpopular with the peoples of these countries. Many Italians or Spaniards or Greeks were as hostile to communism as the Americans themselves. But many, especially among the young, subsequently identified the United States with the defense of privilege, hierarchy, and, in the case of Spain, outright political oppression. This fact was one that would have great political significance in the 1960s and 1970s.

INTEGRATING WEST GERMANY

The first secretary general of NATO was a senior British soldier, Lord Ismay. He defined the new organization's mission as being to keep "the Americans in, the Russians out and the Germans down."[40] NATO was certainly perceived by many West Europeans as being primarily a reinforcement of the Brussels Pact, and hence as a security guarantee against both Soviet invasion *and* a resurgent Germany. In April 1949 the Russians were still less feared than the Germans. The war, after all, had been over for less than five years, and its scars were still visible in every big city.

For this reason, the emergence in May 1949 of an independent West German state was an important development. In August 1949, West Germany held democratic elections that were narrowly won by the Christian Democrats (CDU), which obtained 31 percent of the vote together with its Bavarian allies, the Christian Social Union (CSU). The Social Democrats (SPD) came second with 29 percent, eclipsing the Communists, who achieved a dismal 5 percent (and in subsequent years vanished entirely). With the support of the third-placed Free Democrats (FDP), the CDU's leader Konrad Adenauer, a Rhineland conservative with impeccable anti-Nazi credentials, was elected chancellor by a single vote in the Bundestag. In order to achieve a broader parliamentary majority, many members of the chancellor's own party wanted to form a "great coalition" with the SPD, whose leader Kurt Schumacher was a staunch believer in the planned economy who nevertheless detested Stalinism. Adenauer, however, rejected any compromise with socialistic forms of economic management—which is one reason why, despite his advanced age, he rapidly became indispensable to the Americans.

Adenauer was aware that he had to persuade fellow Europeans that the new Germany could be trusted. Indeed, in his first Bundestag speech upon becoming chancellor, Adenauer affirmed that the new Germany was part of the "West," wanted good relations with its neighbors, and desired, above all else, to "eliminate" the perennial rivalry with France that had produced so much bloodshed and so many wars.[41]

On 22 November 1949, the new government signed the so-called Petersberg Agreement with Britain, France, and the United States. The agreement indicated that West Germany's "primary objective" was to achieve membership in the "international bodies" established in Western Europe since 1945; in practice, this meant the Council of Europe, an organization that had been established, with much fanfare, in May 1949 as a first step toward a federal Western Europe.[42] The agreement did not terminate the state of war between West Germany and the allies, however, which meant that the allies' high commissioners (in effect, their ambassadors) retained the right to intervene in domestic politics for security reasons and could annul laws. In short, although West Germany had held free elections and chosen its government, it remained a semi-sovereign state, not an independent nation. It possessed no army and relied for its security on the goodwill of its military occupiers.

Adenauer's policy was controversial within West Germany. Kurt Schumacher of the SPD was not alone in believing that it verged on a betrayal of the Germans stuck behind the iron curtain in the German Democratic Republic (GDR), the communist state that was born from the Soviet zone on 7 October 1949 in response to the establishment of the Federal Republic. Schumacher openly deplored Adenauer's role as the "chancellor of the allies" in a parliamentary debate over the Petersberg Agreement on 25 November 1949.

What nobody doubted was Adenauer's anti-communism. Adenauer was as fanatically anti-Soviet as even the most hawkish members of the U.S. Congress. His speeches in the early 1950s are full of references to communism as "Christianity's deadliest and most terrible enemy." Adenauer's great fear was that in pursuit of détente with the Soviets, the West might one day agree to unify Germany as a neutral state in the heart of Europe. Schumacher was prepared to take this risk; Adenauer was not. In the German chancellor's view, any such policy would lead to catastrophe: the Soviets would not rest until they had subverted German democracy from within. Once Germany had fallen, dominoes would fall across Europe: "All of us, all of Europe and finally England as well, would fall into the Russian sphere. That would mean the end of the Christian West."[43]

In order to avert this scenario, Adenauer urged that it was necessary to unite Western Europe politically and economically in a tight military alliance with the United States. The economic prosperity and democratic freedoms generated by such an arrangement, he thought, would eventually act like a magnet upon the East Germans and cause the communist state to implode. German unification would be achieved by *Westpolitik*, Adenauer considered, not by offering its neutrality in the Cold War.

Crucially, Adenauer backed his rhetoric in favor of European unity with deeds. In May 1950 the German chancellor supported the bold proposal of French foreign minister Robert Schuman to place the "whole of Franco-German coal and steel production" under a "High Authority" of civil servants whose central task would be to secure "the supply of coal and steel on identical terms to the French and German markets, as well as the markets of other member countries." As Schuman noted, "the pooling of coal and steel production" would ensure that future war between France and Germany was "not merely unthinkable, but materially impossible."[44] Adenauer's constructive role in the negotiations that turned the Schuman Plan into the European Coal and Steel Community (ECSC) treaty by April 1951 did more than words to convince Germany's neighbors that it had turned over a new leaf.

This account of the political circumstances arising from the birth of West Germany in 1949 is necessary background to understand the tensions that arose in Western Europe after the outbreak of the Korean War in June 1950. The immediate reaction of U.S. and European policy makers was that events in Korea might be a prelude to a similar strike in Europe. The 15–18 September meeting of the North Atlantic Council decided to create an integrated military force under centralized command. At the same meeting, the British, French, and U.S. foreign ministers made clear that they would regard an attack on West Germany as an attack on them all: in effect, the United States extended its security guarantee to Bonn.[45] Subsequently, a consolidated command structure, Supreme Headquarters Allied Powers Europe (SHAPE) was set up, and the Truman administration sent four U.S. divisions to reinforce its European allies' armies. General Dwight D. Eisenhower, the victorious World War II general, was nominated Supreme Allied Commander in Europe (SACEUR) in December 1950.

In return, Washington asked for accelerated German rearmament and the political normalization of West Germany. Paris responded with dismay. In October 1950, French Premier René Pleven, after consultations with the French government's éminence grise, Jean Monnet, countered by suggesting a military dimension to the ongoing negotiations on coal and steel between West Germany, France, Italy, the Netherlands, Belgium, and Luxembourg. Pleven stated that German rearmament was possible on two conditions only: first, supranational institutions to administer the defense sector; second, restrictions on German troop levels. Member states, Pleven argued, should contribute military units to the common European defense, which would then be *integrated* with contingents of German troops of no more than battalion strength. Pleven added, moreover, that British participation should be solicited. Washington responded with frustration to the French scheme. Eisenhower moaned that the Pleven Plan contained "every kind of obstacle, difficulty, and fantastic notion that misguided humanity could put into one package."[46]

The United States nevertheless had to take the French proposals seriously. After months of stall, the good personal relations of Jean Monnet with Eisenhower enabled Paris to persuade Truman that German rearmament was possible only as part of a wider process of Europeanization. A prolonged negotiation issued in the signature of the European Defense Community (EDC) Treaty in Paris on 27 May 1952 by France, West Germany, Italy, and the three low countries.

Four important points emerged from this negotiation. First, Italian premier Alcide De Gasperi inserted into the treaty an article that stated that defense cooperation should be the "prelude" to the establishment of a political union between the EDC Treaty's signatories. Second, the British, who had stayed out of the ECSC, remained equally aloof during the EDC talks. The Conservative government of Winston Churchill, elected in the fall of 1951, took the view that joining a European federation was "something which we know, in our bones, we cannot do."[47] Third, the United States, by patient diplomacy and the sheer indispensability of American aid for a French government overstretched by its commitments in Europe, North Africa, and Indochina, persuaded Paris to yield on the crucial question of the size of German military contingents. In February 1952 in Lisbon, NATO formalized plans for a seventy-five-division army by 1953 to which West Germany would provide twelve "national groupings" (or divisions) of approximately thirteen thousand men. The European Army, moreover, would be under the command of the Supreme Commander of NATO—General Eisenhower, or his successor. Fourth, Adenauer skillfully used the EDC negotiation to improve West Germany's position. If the Federal Republic was to be expected to fight for Europe, Adenauer argued, it should have its full sovereignty restored and its status as an occupied territory revoked.

This demand was accepted. The EDC Treaty was accompanied by parallel accords (the so-called Bonn conventions) between the Federal Republic and Britain, France, and the United States that, conditional upon the ratification of the EDC Treaty, ended the three allies' residual powers to intervene in domestic policy, while retaining their power of the last instance over any future peace treaty that reunified the country, defined its borders, or altered the status of Berlin. They further committed themselves to working with Bonn to achieve a united democratic Germany integrated into European institutions.

By the time it was signed, therefore, the EDC was in everybody's interests: "The EDC was seen as the panacea that assured a continued double containment of the Soviet Union and of Germany. In the long run it promised the founding of a European Federal Union closely allied with the United States."[48] From the German point of view, it was a fortuitous passport back to national sovereignty, although that did not prevent ratification of the so-called Western treaties from providing the Federal Republic with its first constitutional crisis.[49]

The EDC also rattled the Soviets' cage. In March 1952, on the eve of the treaty's signature, Stalin dramatically proposed that Germany should be unified on the basis of the frontiers agreed at Potsdam (and hence without the territory transferred to Poland), and on condition that it should remain both neutral and non-nuclear. "Free activity of democratic parties and organizations" was to be permitted, and unified Germany would be allowed limited

military forces for the purpose of self-defense.[50] Adenauer suspected—
rightly—that this maneuver was a last-ditch attempt by Moscow to sabotage
the EDC by whipping up German public opinion. The government in Bonn
told the British, French, and U.S. governments that it rejected neutralization
and could not accept any four-power deal on Germany without the participation of a freely elected all-German government at the conference table. The
western allies accordingly insisted upon the need for free elections throughout Germany before any negotiation took place. Stalin was not prepared to go
so far. In Caroline Kennedy-Pipe's words: "There was a readiness to sacrifice East Germany in exchange for a neutral Germany, but not a democratic
Germany."[51]

The USSR's response was to launch a major propaganda offensive
against ratification of the EDC across Europe. Communist newspapers, posters, and cartoons portrayed the EDC, with zero subtlety, as an American
conspiracy with pro-Nazi elements in Germany to "transform West Germany
into an American war base," and to use "the rebuilding of German militarism
and Hitlerite Wehrmacht as the American gendarme in Europe and as an
army of invasion on the countries of socialism."[52]

U.S. rhetoric went to the opposite extreme. Secretary of State Dean Acheson hailed the EDC Treaty as "one of the most important and far-reaching
events of our lifetime." His deputy, David Bruce, proclaimed the EDC to be
"the most significant thing that has happened in western civilization . . . for a
period of hundreds of years."[53] The November 1952 presidential elections
reinforced this starry-eyed enthusiasm. Both President Eisenhower and Secretary of State John Foster Dulles were ardent European federalists and
pressed for ratification of the EDC Treaty with scary zeal. Dulles, in fact, had
long implied in his speeches and writings that it was the United States'
historic duty to compel Europe to unite:

> Recurrent efforts have been made to unite Europe by violence. Napoleon tried
> it; so did the Kaiser; so did Hitler; so, now, does Stalin. . . . The United States
> now has the opportunity to bring about peacefully what every western leader,
> without regard to nation or party, recognizes ought to be done, but will not be
> done unless there is friendly but firm outside pressure. The United States can
> and should take that opportunity and exert that pressure.[54]

The problem for the Americans was that the French had now acquired
doubts. The EDC policy had been heralded by the so-called Third Force, a
loose coalition of Christian Democrats, Socialists, Radicals, and Indepen-
dents that stood precariously between the Gaullists and the Communists in
France's dysfunctional party system. After the first semester of 1952, when
the "Third Force" fell apart, the majority for the EDC gradually eroded.
Especially after Robert Schuman was replaced as foreign minister by
Georges Bidault, a conservative former premier, successive French govern-

ments lost enthusiasm for the treaty—and yet did not want to offend the United States, which was paying for France's ongoing colonial war in Vietnam (see below), by renegotiating the treaty or rejecting it outright.[55]

This situation dragged on through 1953, causing growing frustration in Washington. John Foster Dulles blustered on 14 December 1953 that the United States would carry out an "agonizing reappraisal" of its foreign and defense strategy if the EDC Treaty were not ratified. This was interpreted as a threat to make a defensive commitment to the European periphery (the United Kingdom, Greece, Italy, Spain, and Turkey) and to leave France to defend itself on the Rhine and Germany to shift for itself.

Washington's determination to get EDC through was surely reinforced by Moscow's evident fear of German remilitarization. Stalin's immediate heir, the secret police boss Lavrenti Beria, revived the alternative plan of a neutral Germany in 1953—and was even willing to contemplate a "bourgeois democratic" Germany, not a socialist one, so long as the new Germany stayed demilitarized. Even after Beria's fall (see below, chapter 5), the USSR's foreign policy priority was stopping the EDC, even at the cost of major concessions. At a conference of foreign ministers held in Berlin between 25 January and 18 February 1954, the Kremlin reiterated its commitment to a united, neutral Germany and pushed for the establishment of a general security agreement for Europe as an alternative to the "policy of blocs."[56] In the spring of 1954, Foreign Minister Molotov even reflected that the USSR should explore the possibility of offering to join NATO, though this move was presumably intended more as a propaganda gesture than anything else.[57]

Dulles ran out of patience with the French in the summer of 1954. The humiliation of the French army at Dien Bien Phu in North Vietnam in May forced a change of government in Paris. An independent leftist, Pierre Mendès France, acceded to the premiership. Dulles bluntly told the new premier that the U.S. Congress would not "appropriate another cent" for France if Paris continued to delay ratification of the EDC.[58]

Mendès France was no pushover, however. Proving conclusively that insouciance is a French word, Paris now sought to repudiate key clauses of the EDC Treaty by asking its partners to allow France to retain a national veto over measures proposed by the EDC "Commissariat," or de facto supranational defense ministry, and by eliminating the commitment to political union. This move infuriated Mendès France's peers, especially Adenauer, and Paris's requests for treaty revision were duly rebuffed. At the end of August, Mendès France placed the EDC Treaty before the National Assembly for ratification: as one contemporary noted, he was "more referee than advocate," during the ratification debate.[59]

Such lackluster leadership was inadequate for what was described as "the Dreyfus affair of the Fourth Republic." Gaullists, Communists, and a majority of the Socialists wrapped themselves in the French flag. The treaty's supporters, by contrast, pushed the case for European unity with religious zeal. The debate verged on the hysterical, with speakers proclaiming that its outcome was a matter of "life and death for France." Two concepts of France were supposedly at stake: Was France still able to play a major role in world affairs? Or did France's future lie in the "European Construction" in which some French leaders had placed so much store? Why should France be diminished to the status of "two defeated and three tiny countries," when nobody was asking Great Britain to do the same? In the end, the noes won by 319 votes to 264. Triumphant Communists, Gaullists, and other *anti-cèdistes* burst into a spirited rendition of "La Marseillaise."[60]

The EDC was blown up by the 30 August debate, and U.S. foreign policy toward Europe, hopes for a federal European state, and, seemingly, West Germany's chances of independence suffered collateral damage from the explosion. Fears surged that Washington would react by withdrawing to the European periphery, or that German public opinion would swing in favor of a deal with the Russians. Bonn had to be restored its national sovereignty— quickly. But how was this to be done without enraging French (and not only French) public opinion whose consent for German rearmament had rested upon the supranational element of the EDC?

The British became the honest broker in the diplomatic negotiations to solve the problems left by the EDC vote. According to Foreign Secretary Anthony Eden, he was in his bath in his cottage in western England on 5 September 1954 when the idea of extending membership of the Brussels Treaty came to him.[61] The Brussels Treaty was a European structure, after all, albeit an intergovernmental one. A nine-power (the six ECSC states, plus Britain, Canada, and the United States) intergovernmental conference was held in London between 28 September and 3 October 1954 to discuss German (and Italian) membership of the Brussels Pact. To win over the French, the British made an expensive commitment to maintain four divisions on the European mainland for as long as the other Brussels Pact member states wished. Adenauer reciprocated by promising that West Germany would not manufacture atomic, biological, or chemical weapons, guided missiles, warships of more than three thousand tons, or strategic bombers without the consent of a two-thirds majority on the Brussels Council. It would also limit its army to the twelve divisions foreseen by the EDC Treaty. Bonn also undertook not to use force to achieve border changes or to reunify Germany.

The revised Brussels Pact Treaty was signed in Paris on 23 October 1954, and the new organization, known as the Western European Union (WEU), became operational in May 1955. Concurrently, West Germany was restored full national sovereignty and admitted to NATO. Although the treaty's preamble stated that one of its goals was "to encourage the progressive integration of Europe," the WEU was never more than a talking shop. Security matters were handled by NATO; economic integration was the province of the European Economic Community (EEC) from 1958 onward. Nevertheless, the WEU was important. Had the security question posed by West Germany not been resolved, further advances in European integration would have been unthinkable. To this extent, the WEU negotiation arguably "marks the high point of the British contribution to European unity."[62]

IMPERIAL ECLIPSE

The hysteria surrounding the French rejection of the EDC has to be seen in the context of France's imperial decline. After World War II, France had been expelled from Syria by its British ally. It had vainly tried to cling on to its imperial presence in Indochina by waging war against the Viet Minh, which had established an independent republic in northern Vietnam after the end of the Japanese occupation. The conflict in Vietnam, which cost France more than twenty thousand lives, had only been possible because Washington, especially after China joined the communist camp in October 1949, had footed the bill. By the time of Dien Bien Phu, the United States was paying three-quarters of the costs of the war.[63]

Underlying this U.S. concern for the survival of French imperialism was the "domino" theory, which President Eisenhower articulated in January 1954 in justification of the scale of U.S. help to France. Vice President Nixon anticipated Eisenhower luridly in December 1953, warning that if Vietnam fell, "Thailand is put in an almost impossible situation. The same is true of Malaya with its rubber and its tin. The same is true of Indonesia. If Indochina goes under communist domination the whole of South East Asia will be threatened and that means that the economic and military security of Japan will be endangered also."[64]

France, a proud country, resented being turned into a foot soldier for American grand strategy. The early 1950s saw a wave of anti-American hostility in France. The Communist Party led the charge, naturally, but the Gaullist press rivaled it for the centrality of anti-Americanism in its ideological repertoire.[65] This hostility toward the United States found its symbol in the humble—or not so humble—bottle of Coke whose place on the bar shelves of France was portrayed by the communists as a sign that France was being *cocacolonisé*. The distribution of Coke in France was obstructed by officials in the health ministry until December 1953. As Richard Kuisel has put it, for those "who opposed the entry of Coca-Cola the affair was, in one form or another, a tiny effort at national self-assertion, a gesture that France might find a 'third way' in the Cold War."[66]

Britain greeted cultural Americanization with less resentment. But Britain's elites were no more pleased than France's at being eclipsed by the rise in American power. The Indian Ocean, which before 1942 and Japanese invasion had been a British lake, now became an area of strategic interest for Washington. Economic weakness and nationalist pressure compelled Britain to withdraw from India in 1947, and Washington swiftly began consolidating relations with the nations, especially Pakistan, born as a consequence of the end of the Raj. The United States supported Britain's efforts to ensure that Malaya—as it then was—did not fall into communist hands upon independence. Nevertheless, Britain's vast military effort in the Malayan peninsula, at a time when London urgently needed to rationalize its foreign and defense spending, was never quite enough for Washington, which caviled at every British plan to cut its commitments "East of Suez." The diplomatic construction of SEATO—the South East Asia Treaty Organization—prior to the signature of the Treaty of Manila in September 1954 was characterized by frequent differences of opinion, notably over Indian membership, between Dulles and Foreign Secretary Eden.

London worried that Washington's anti-communist obsession was a threat to world peace. One reason that Eisenhower did not intervene militarily on the side of the French in Vietnam during Dien Bien Phu was that Britain flatly refused to endorse such intervention, which might have broadened the war to include China. The Geneva conference, which would eventually divide Vietnam at the seventeenth parallel and bring the war to an end, began on 26 April 1954, with Chinese participation, and Eden wanted to do everything possible to find a diplomatic solution.

The United States had also supplanted Britain in the bastion of London's informal empire, the Middle East. President Truman's overt pressure for the creation of a Jewish state had precipitated the end of the British mandate in Palestine in 1948; in British judgment, the creation of Israel had destabilized the region and dangerously radicalized the Arabs. The British joined with Washington and Paris in May 1950 to sign a Tripartite Declaration that regulated arms sales to the states of the Middle East and provided a guarantee for the existing borders, but the likelihood of further war between Israel and its neighbors grew rather than declined in subsequent years.

The Americans also fumed at the geopolitical consequences of British colonialism in the region. In Iran, for instance, "informal empire" had allowed Britain to exploit the country's oil reserves cynically. Millions of Iranians lived in dire poverty and were turning to the Tudeh, the Iranian Communist Party, or to militant nationalism. In 1951, Mohammed Mossadeq became premier in Tehran. Mossadeq, seeking to make the Anglo-Iranian Oil Company pay a fair price for Tehran's oil, nationalized the oil fields. The Iranian premier's move angered the British government, which placed an ineffectual embargo on Iranian exports. In June 1953, the Eisenhower administration, alarmed by Britain's feeble response and by Tehran's increasingly radical rhetoric, mounted Operation AJAX, a covert intervention to bring Mossadeq down and to impose a leader, General Fazlollah Zahedi, who was more to Washington's taste. It was the first time "Washington had organized in detail the overthrow of a foreign government outside its own hemisphere."[67]

From June 1953 onward, Shah Reza Pahlavi and his country were part of the American sphere of interest, not the British. In the fall of 1955, Iran, along with Pakistan, joined the Baghdad Pact, a regional security system involving Turkey, Iraq, and Britain, but sponsored by the United States, which supplied arms and advice to the pact's members. Israel was drawn toward France for arms supplies and diplomatic support as a result of the pact; Egypt, meanwhile, looked to the Soviet Union.[68]

For all these reasons, by April 1955, when Eden replaced Churchill as premier, the Anglo-American "special relationship" was distinctly lukewarm. Eden and the Foreign Office found it difficult to play second fiddle to the United States, whose leaders, especially Dulles, they belittled as narrow-minded amateurs. But the British themselves were in denial. London's huge expenditures on overseas military commitments and on developing the technology necessary for superpower status, notably the atomic bomb and the means of delivering it, were an intolerable long-term burden for Britain's public finances and on the balance of payments. Britain could not do what its leaders thought it should do.

The British were also on the wrong side of the divide provoked by the rising national consciousness of Asian and African peoples. This consciousness found political expression in April 1955 at the Bandung Conference in Indonesia, where, led by President Sukarno, India's Jawarhalal Nehru, and Colonel Gamel Abdel Nasser of Egypt, the "Third World" formulated a position of non-alignment in the Cold War. The side that won their allegiance, the conference participants made clear, would be the one that did most to reduce racial and colonial injustice. Amateur or not, Dulles realized that this stance posed a major dilemma for Washington:

> For many years now the United States has been walking a tight-rope between the effort to maintain old and valued relations with our British and French allies on the one hand, and on the other hand trying to assure ourselves of the friendship and understanding of the newly-developed countries. . . . Unless we now assert and maintain our leadership, all of these newly independent countries will turn from us to the USSR.[69]

Washington would have been more credible with the protagonists of the anticolonial struggle had it refrained from carrying out coups d'état such as the one against Mossadeq in 1953, or the one that overthrew Jacobo Arbenz in Guatemala the following year. It also would have enjoyed far more credibility had black Americans been able to drink from the same water fountains as whites in Mississippi or Alabama. Such contradictions aside, however, Dulles was not mistaken: in the battle for the minds of the world's new nations, a legacy of colonialism was a huge handicap. In the mid-1950s, Britain was waging a brutal campaign against the Mau-Mau in Kenya, fighting Greek nationalists in Cyprus, supporting white rule in Southern Rhodesia, and propping up a client regime in Iraq. France was fighting a dirty war against revolutionary nationalism in Algeria, which was then part of French metropolitan territory. For the developing world, the colonial powers were public enemy number one and Washington sided with them, outside Europe, at its peril.

The Suez crisis from July to November 1956 was the culmination of the tensions brewing between the Eisenhower administration and its chief allies, between Eden and Dulles personally, and between the West and the nations of the developing world. Without alerting Washington, Britain and France conspired with Israel to attack Egypt on the eve of Eisenhower's re-election on 6 November 1956. Their action gave the USSR a pretext to crush the contemporaneous rebellion against communist rule in Hungary and to remind the West of its growing nuclear prowess.

The crisis had a proximate Cold War cause. Egyptian leader Nasser, who had been a key participant in the 1952 military coup against the pro-British King Farouk, and who had subsequently elbowed aside the coup's leader, General Mohammed Neguib, was playing off London, Moscow, and Washington for his own ends. After Britain relinquished its base rights in the Sinai peninsula in 1954, and followed a policy of rapprochement toward the Egyptian dictator, Nasser enjoyed a honeymoon with western statesmen in which his blandishments won Anglo-U.S. project financing for his plan to dam the Nile River at Aswan.

The Egyptian leader, however, soon changed tack. Intoxicated by success, he pursued a reckless game of tit-for-tat military provocation with Israel, undercut British influence in Jordan, and gave Algeria's rebels moral and material support. Such policies won applause from the Arab street but irritated Britain and France and infuriated conservative Arab leaders. Simultaneously, Nasser bought arms from Czechoslovakia. When Washington learned of Nasser's dallying with the Soviet bloc, it pulled its financial support from the Aswan dam on 19 July 1956. Two days later, Britain pulled the plug on its loans, along with the World Bank. It was "the first time that aid to underdeveloped countries had been openly used by the West as an instrument of policy."[70]

The construction of the dam was both a question of prestige and a vital national interest. Egypt's population was exploding, and the Cairo regime needed to expand the country's arable terrain. Nasser retaliated on 25 July 1956 by nationalizing the Suez Canal Company, the enterprise, headquartered in Paris, that administered the canal. He would pay for Aswan by raising the tolls paid by the world's shipping and by ensuring that the revenues mostly accrued to the Egyptian government, not Anglo-French shareholders. Of the nearly 14,700 ships that had passed through the canal in 1955, almost a third had been British. They carried the oil that kept British industry working.

The pro-British premier of Iraq, Nuri-es Said, who was in London when the crisis broke, reputedly told Eden that the British should "hit him. Hit him hard and hit him now."[71] In international law, this counsel was hard to justify. Egypt was within its rights to take ownership of the canal, provided compensation was paid and so long as the canal was kept open to shipping without discrimination of nationality. The Eisenhower administration favored a negotiated solution that would internationalize the management of the canal.

For these reasons, the British and French governments, though not ruling out the use of force to restore their position, allowed the summer of 1956 to be spent in lengthy talks between Nasser and the representatives of the Suez Canal Users' Association in Cairo, London, and the UNO, during which Nasser persistently rejected the notion of internationalization. Washington, failing to grasp the growing frustration of its allies, continued to advocate conciliation.

Top British officials were convinced that the British government could not let Nasser keep his grip on Britain's "wind-pipe," as the canal was called. Suez was a vital British interest. "If we sit back while Nasser . . . gradually acquires control of the oil-bearing countries, he can . . . wreck us," minuted the Permanent Under Secretary at the Foreign Office, Sir Ivone Kirkpatrick, at the height of the crisis.[72] Prime Minister Eden concurred and so did most of his government. French Foreign Minister Christian Pineau resorted to an overwrought domino theory to explain why France wanted military intervention. On 1 August 1956, he warned Dulles that failure to defeat Nasser might lead to collapse in Algeria and a subsequent dissolution of the French empire in black Africa. This would open huge new areas of the world to Soviet penetration.[73]

Public pressure for intervention was high in both countries: it was entirely normal to compare Nasser to Mussolini, and hence to regard the failure to take military action against Egypt as a return to Munich-style appeasement. Accordingly, in late October 1956, with the French taking the lead, the two European nations participated in a conspiracy. At top secret meetings at Sèvres near Paris, the British and French agreed with Prime Minister David Ben-Gurion that Israel, which had been the victim of repeated Egyptian raids on its territory, would attack Egypt in the Sinai and that Britain and France would intervene between the two sides, ostensibly to preserve the security of the canal zone and to separate the two warring parties. The deal was a "monument to French opportunism, the duplicity of Eden and Ben Gurion's paranoia."[74] On 30 October, Israeli paratroopers went into action. Britain and France issued an ultimatum to the two countries the following day. When

Egypt did not respond, on 31 October 1956, Anglo-French bombers knocked out Egyptian airfields, while Israel occupied the Sinai peninsula undisturbed.

International opinion went ballistic—almost literally, in the case of the USSR. The United States introduced a motion condemning Israel's attack to the Security Council of the UNO. It was vetoed by Britain and France. The matter was transferred to the General Assembly, which demanded Israel's withdrawal on 2 November. Washington was determined not to be blindsided by the USSR on this issue. As Eisenhower wrote: "Since the Africans and Asians almost unanimously hate one of the three nations, Britain, France and Israel, the Soviets need only propose severe and immediate punishment of these three to have the whole of two continents on their side."[75] Britain and France nevertheless ignored the General Assembly's plea for peace, which was especially strong from Commonwealth countries such as Canada and India.

On 4 November, after Egypt blocked the canal, British and French troops occupied the canal zone and shelled Port Said, causing heavy loss of life among civilians. The following day, Soviet Premier Nikolai Bulganin weighed in by sending stern letters to Ben-Gurion, Eden, and French Premier Guy Mollet. The letter to Eden asked the prime minister to reflect upon what Britain's situation would be if it were attacked "by a stronger power possessing all types of modern weapons of destruction" including "rocket equipment." In the meantime, however (see below, chapter 5), Russian troops exploited the world's preoccupation with the Middle East conflict to crush the Hungarian revolution against communist rule.

Bulganin's threat was disturbing, but not so decisive for British policy as the contemporaneous run on sterling on the international currency markets. At the height of the crisis, Chancellor Harold Macmillan, until that moment a Suez hawk, abruptly suffered a "sensational loss of nerve."[76] Britain's dollar reserves were leaching away and without a loan from U.S. banks or from the International Monetary Fund (IMF), the country faced the prospect of being unable to pay for its imports. A fraught British government belatedly realized that to get U.S. backing for such a loan, it needed to be in the Americans' good graces. On 6 November 1956, however, relations between Eisenhower and Eden were down to zero. Reluctantly, Eden agreed to a cease-fire and to the intervention of a force of UN blue helmets in the canal zone. In exchange, Britain got its IMF loan. Eden, whose bad health almost certainly affected his judgment during the crisis, resigned as premier and was replaced in January 1957 by Macmillan.[77] The new premier sensibly made restoring relations with Washington his overwhelming priority.

In Paris, the Americans' rejection of the Anglo-French action was regarded as betrayal. France's distrust of the Americans, and its determination to re-establish itself as a genuinely independent force in the world, grew as a consequence and would shortly find, in General Charles de Gaulle, a leader capable of translating desire into reality. But even at the height of the crisis, the wish to rebel against U.S. leadership was lurking beneath the surface. German Chancellor Adenauer, who was in Paris, told Mollet to "make Europe. It will be your revenge."[78] It is hard not to conclude that France subsequently followed his advice.

Suez was the most striking case during the early Cold War years of the West's divisions. But, in general, the notion that the United States was a benign hegemon artfully shaping the political arrangements of its European allies is a simplistic one. As Suez made abundantly clear, Washington exercised only partial authority over the proud nation-states in its sphere of interest. Eisenhower could no more tell the British and French what to do in the Middle East than he could promote economic reform in Greece, order Western Europeans to form a federal political union, compel the Italian Christian Democrats to ban the PCI, or even make the French drink Coca-Cola. This is not to suggest that the United States was powerless. Washington's influence was profound. But its imperial sway, like all liberal empires through history, was on sufferance and limited in scope.

NOTES

1. Stephen Ambrose and Douglas Brinkley, *Rise to Globalism* (New York: Penguin, 1997), 101.

2. Robert D. Schulzinger, *US Diplomacy since 1900* (New York: Oxford University Press, 2002), 12.

3. Geir Lundestad, "Empire by Invitation: The United States and Western Europe, 1945–1952," *Journal of Peace Research* 23 (1986): 263–77.

4. Raymond Aron, "The Imperial Republic," in Aron, *The Dawn of Universal History* (New York: Basic Books, 2002), 297 and 295.

5. The text of the speech can be found at: http://www.cvce.eu/content/publication/2002/9/9/7bc0ecbd-c50e-4035-8e36-ed70bfbd204c/publishable_en.pdf.

6. For the Brussels Pact, see Antonio Varsori, *Il Patto di Bruxelles: Tra integrazione europea e alleanza atlantica* (Rome: Bonacci, 1988).

7. Michael Hogan, *The Marshall Plan, America, Britain and the Reconstruction of Western Europe* (Cambridge: Cambridge University Press, 1987), 87.

8. "U.S. Objectives with Respect to the USSR to Counter Soviet Threats to U.S. Security," *Foreign Relations of the United States* (FRUS) (Washington, DC: Government Printing Office, 1948), 1: 663–69.

9. Lord Ismay, *NATO: The First Five Years* (Paris: NATO, 1954), chapter 1.

10. Matteo Lodevole, "Western Communists and the European Military Build-up, 1949–50," *Cold War History* 10 (2010): 203–28.

11. See Andrea Guiso, *La colomba e la spade: 'lotta per la pace' e antiamericanismo nella politica del Partito comunista italiano, 1949–1954* (Saveria Mannelli: Rubbettino, 2006), chapter 4, "La campagna antiatomica."

12. For the role of Koestler, see Michael Scammell, *Koestler: The Indispensable Intellectual* (London: Faber & Faber, 2009), chapters 32–33. The manifesto produced by the West Berlin meeting is reproduced in Peter Coleman, *The Liberal Conspiracy* (New York: The Free Press, 1989), 249–51.

13. For example, Frances Stonor Saunders, *Who Paid the Piper?: The CIA and the Cultural Cold War* (London: Granta, 1999).

14. In private, Stalin backed Togliatti rather than the Yugoslavs. See Elena Aga-Rossi and Victor Zaslavsky, *Togliatti e Stalin: Il PCI e la politica estera staliniana negli archivi di Mosca* (Bologna, Il Mulino, 2007), 233–34.

15. James E. Miller, "Taking Off the Gloves: The United States and the Italian Elections of 1948," *Diplomatic History* 7, no. 4 (1983): 43.

16. FRUS, 1948, vol. 3: 766.

17. FRUS, 1948, vol. 3: 769.

18. FRUS, 1948, vol. 3: 849.

19. Vittorio Ivella, "Favorable Omens in Italy," *Foreign Affairs* 27 (1948): 701.

20. "Italians at the Polls," *Economist*, 17 April 1948, 637.

21. *Economist*, 24 April 1948, 658.

22. Miller, "Taking Off the Gloves," 36.

23. Arturo Carlo Jemolo, *Italia Tormentata* (Bari: Laterza, 1951), 162.

24. Mario Del Pero, "Containing Containment: Rethinking Italy's Experience during the Cold War," *Journal of Modern Italian Studies* 8 (2003): 532–55.

25. Palmiro Togliatti, *Pace e Guerra* (Milano: Sera Editrice, 1949), 15.

26. For a detailed discussion of aid to Tito after the outbreak of the Korean War, see Beatrice Heuser, *Western Containment Policies in the Cold War: The Yugoslav Case* (London: Routledge, 1989), especially chapter 6, "Strengthening the Shield."

27. For the resolution of the Trieste crisis, see, in English, Roberto Giorgio Rabel, *Trieste, the United States and the Cold War, 1941–1954* (Durham, NC: Duke University Press, 1988).

28. Del Pero, "Containing Containment," 549.

29. See Del Pero, "American Pressures and their Containment," *Diplomatic History* 28, no. 3 (June 2004).

30. For Zahariadis's error, see John O. Iatrides, "Revolution or Self-Defense: Communist Goals, Strategy and Tactics in the Greek Civil War," *Journal of Cold War Studies* 7, no. 3 (2005), 31–33.

31. See Amikan Nachmani, "Civil War and Foreign Intervention in Greece," *Journal of Contemporary History* 25 (1990): 489–522.

32. Richard Clogg, *A Concise History of Greece* (Cambridge: Cambridge University Press, 1995), 146.

33. John Lamberton Harper, *The Cold War* (Oxford: Oxford University Press, 2012), 93.

34. See James Miller, *United States and the Making of Modern Greece: History and Power, 1950–1974* (Durham: North Carolina University Press, 2009), esp. chapter one, "The Greek Tar Baby."

35. Daniel Fernández de Miguel, "El antiamericanismo en la España del primer franquismo (1939–1953): el Ejército, la Iglesia y Falange frente a Estados Unidos," *Ayer* 62 (2006): 257–82.

36. Mark S. Byrnes, "Overruled and Worn Down: Truman Sends an Ambassador to Spain," *Presidential Studies Quarterly* 29 (1999): 268.

37. Byrnes, "Overruled," 276.

38. For France, see Anne Dolphy, "La France et la défense atlantique: le pacte hispano-américain de septembre 1953," *Revue d'histoire moderne et contemporaine* 49 (October–December, 2002).

39. NSC 5418/1, "U.S. Policy Toward Spain," FRUS, 1952–1954, vol. VI, part 2, Western Europe and Canada, Document 918.

40. Quoted in David Reynolds, ed., *The Origins of the Cold War in Europe: International Perspectives* (New Haven, CT: Yale University Press, 1994), 13.

41. Konrad Adenauer, speech to the Bundestag 20 September 1949, quoted in Gabriele D'Ottavio, *L'Europa dei tedeschi* (Bologna: Il Mulino, 2012), 31.

42. Dennis Bark and David Gress, *A History of West Germany*, vol. 1: *From Shadow to Substance 1945–1963* (Cambridge, MA: Blackwell, 1993), 259.

43. Konrad Adenauer, *World Indivisible* (New York: Harper's & Brothers, 1955), 39 and 42.

44. All quotations from the Schuman declaration, http://europa.eu/about-eu/basic-information/symbols/europe-day/schuman-declaration/.

45. See Marc Trachtenberg and Christopher Gehrz, "America, Europe and German Rearmament, August-September 1950," *Journal of European Integration History* 6, no. 2 (2000): 9–35, for U.S. pressure on the Europeans.

46. Pascaline Winand, *Eisenhower, Kennedy and the United States of Europe* (New York: St. Martin's, 1993), 27–28.

47. Foreign Secretary Anthony Eden speaking at Columbia University, 11 January 1952, quoted by D. R. Thorpe, *Eden: The Life and Times of Anthony Eden First Earl of Avon, 1897–1977* (London: Pimlico, 2004), 368.

48. Klaus Schwabe, "The Cold War and European Integration, 1947–1963," *Diplomacy and Statecraft* 12, no. 4 (2001): 26.

49. For Adenauer's frustration, see Hans Peter Schwarz, *Konrad Adenauer*, vol. 2: *The Statesman* (Oxford: Berghahn, 1997), 3–33.

50. An English translation of the note is to be found in FRUS 1952–1954, vol. VII, part 2, 169–72.

51. Caroline Kennedy-Pipe, *Russia and the World, 1917–1991* (London: Arnold, 1998), 101.

52. The quotation is from Janusz Kaźmiercazk, "The Community that Never Was: The European Defense Community and Its Image in Polish Visual Propaganda in the 1950s," *Journal of Cold War Studies* 11, no. 4 (2009): 123. Ironically, the Stalin note of 10 March had promised that the civil rights of former Nazis would be restored.

53. Quoted in Robert Osgood, *NATO: The Entangling Alliance* (Chicago: Chicago University Press, 1962), 93.

54. J. F. Dulles, *War or Peace* (New York: Macmillan, 1950), 213–15.

55. Craig Parsons, *A Certain Idea of Europe* (Ithaca, NY: Cornell University Press, 2006), discusses this "coalitional shift" in detail, 74.

56. The best analysis in English of the Soviets' plans is Geoffrey Roberts, *A Chance for Peace? The Soviet Campaign to End the Cold War, 1953–1955*, CWHP Working Paper no. 57 (2008).

57. For Molotov's proposal, see: http://www.wilsoncenter.org/publication/molotovs-proposal-the-ussr-join-nato-march-1954.

58. Kevin Ruane, *The Rise and Fall of the European Defence Community* (London: Macmillan, 2000), 92–93.

59. Anthony Eden, *Full Circle* (London: Cassell, 1960), 149.

60. Quotations from N. Laites and C. de la Malène, "Paris from EDC to WEU," *World Politics* 1 (1957): 193–219.

61. Eden, *Full Circle*, 151.

62. Anne Deighton, "The Last Piece of the Jigsaw: Britain and the Creation of the Western European Union, 1954," *Contemporary European History* 7 (1998): 196.

63. Bernard Droz, *Storia della decolonizzazione nel XX secolo* (Milan: Mondadori, 2007), 130–34.

64. Quoted in Odd Arne Westad, *Global Cold War* (Cambridge: Cambridge University Press, 2006), 119.

65. Lucia Bonfreschi, "Complotto contro la Francia: l'antiamericanismo nella stampa gollista della IV Repubblica," in *L'antiamericanismo in Italia e in Europa nel secondo dopoguerra*, ed. P. Craveri and G. Quagliariello (Soveria Mannelli: Rubbettino, 2004), 485–518.

66. Richard F. Kuisel, *Seducing the French: The Dilemma of Americanization* (Berkeley: University of California Press, 1996), 69.

67. Westad, *Global Cold War*, 122.

68. J. C. Hurewitz, "The Historical Context," in *Suez 1956: The Crisis and Its Consequences*, ed. Wm Roger Louis and Roger Owen (Oxford: Clarendon, 1991), 28.

69. FRUS 1955–1957, vol. XVI, 906.

70. Hugh Thomas, *The Suez Affair* (London: Pelican 1967), 35.

71. Originally cited in Thomas, *The Suez Affair*, 38. But see also Elie Podeh, "Regaining Lost Pride: The Impact of the Suez Affair on Egypt and the Arab World," in *The 1956 War: Collusion and Rivalry in the Middle East*, ed. D. Tal (London: Frank Cass, 2001), 211.

72. Quoted in Keith Kyle, "Britain and the Crisis, 1955–1956," in Louis and Owen, *Suez 1956*, 123.

73. Maurice Vaisse, "France and the Suez Crisis," in Louis and Owen, *Suez 1956*, 137.

74. Avi Schlaim, "The Protocol of Sèvres 1956: Anatomy of a War Plot," *International Affairs* 73 (1997): 530.

75. Quoted in Robert R. Bowie, "Eisenhower, Dulles, and the Suez Crisis," in Louis and Owen, *Suez 1956*, 210.

76. Keith Kyle, *Suez: Britain's End of Empire in the Middle East* (London: Weidenfeld & Nicholson, 1991), 465.

77. J. Pearson, *Sir Anthony Eden and the Suez Crisis: Reluctant Gamble* (London: Palgrave, 2003), sympathetically argues, 173, that by October 1956 Eden's illness had made him a "different man" and under pressure his judgment failed him.

78. Quoted in Keith Kyle, *Suez*, 467.

Chapter Five

1956: Communism in Turmoil

The year 1956 was a dramatic one for the communist parties and states of Europe. Soviet leader Nikita Khrushchev, who began the year by making the momentous "Secret Speech" to the Twentieth Congress of the Soviet Communist Party condemning the crimes of Stalin, wanted two incompatible things: to accelerate destalinization and retain political control of the satellite states of Eastern Europe. The Secret Speech critically undermined the ideological legitimacy upon which Soviet control rested. Leaders of the USSR had always claimed to possess the correct interpretation of history, to know infallibly where humankind was heading. The whole Soviet project was predicated on this arrogant assertion. When he made the Secret Speech, Khrushchev officially admitted that the high priest of history—Joseph Stalin—had been a psychopath and that the USSR had taken the wrong road under his erratic rule. An error of historical dimensions had been made.

Inevitably, Khrushchev's admissions brought about turmoil in the communist world. It was an open invitation to revolt and revolt punctually occurred. In Poland, Soviet leadership was contested by both party elites and by mass public opinion. In Hungary, the people—especially the young—spontaneously and courageously took to the streets to fight for greater freedom and political pluralism. By so doing, they presented their domestic leadership with an existential choice: side with the party and the USSR, or re-think your conviction in the historical inevitability of communism.

Imre Nagy, a reformist communist who regained power at the beginning of the Hungarian revolution (he had briefly been premier between July 1953 and January 1955), chose the latter course. It is for this reason that he is today remembered with great affection both in Hungary and elsewhere. János Kádár, a top Hungarian party functionary who had been a victim of the Rákosi regime, chose the former course of action. He colluded with the

USSR's oppression of his own people and, upon taking power, purged the country's intellectual, military, and political elites ruthlessly in order to reestablish the Communist Party's central role. Even though Kádár subsequently turned his country into "the best barracks in the Soviet camp," by allowing greater economic liberty and a greater openness to the outside world, his reputation was smeared indelibly by his betrayal in 1956.

Kádár was not the only figure to besmirch his historical reputation in 1956. One can make a good argument that until 1956, communism, despite the crimes of Stalin, had retained a patina of progressivism, at any rate in Europe. The events of Hungary wiped this spurious film away. Even on the left, communism became regarded as reactionary, as just another unscrupulous imperialism. This is why western communists who did not break with the USSR after 1956 were ethically hobbled thereafter. The French (and Italian) Communist parties, not to mention eminent intellectuals such as the British Marxist historian Eric Hobsbawm, unquestionably lost moral authority.[1] They continued to denounce the French Army's tortures in Algeria, or the crimes of "American capitalist imperialism" in Latin America, Greece, and Vietnam. But they were wide open to the charge that they weighed Soviet crimes on different, more forgiving scales.

THE THAW

Nikita Khrushchev had not been the favorite to succeed Stalin. He seized the top job in the Kremlin through a combination of low peasant cunning, ruthlessness, and complacency on the part of his rivals. In his memoirs, Soviet Foreign Minister Molotov loftily dismissed Khrushchev as "a man of meager culture . . . a fishmonger, a petty fishmonger, or man who sold cattle. . . . He was a shoemaker in matters of theory . . . a primitive man."[2]

Khrushchev was, however, Molotov's master in the low arts of political manipulation and sometimes his ally—nobody in the Politburo had friends—in the tortuous political infighting that ensued in the three years following Stalin's death. In the summer of 1953, Khrushchev, Molotov, and Georgy Malenkov, a cynical party bureaucrat who had risen through the ranks during the great purges in the 1930s and who had led the attack on the so-called Leningrad group within the party after 1945, ganged up to terminate the threatening supremacy of Lavrenti Beria. After Stalin's death, Beria, the dictator's most blood-stained henchman, had posed as a reformist, even a liberal. Beria had freed many political prisoners from the camps (a policy his successors continued), temporarily halted "Russification" of the Baltic states, and had even contemplated negotiating with the West to establish a neutral united Germany. This was a proposal that Molotov, for one, regarded as an ideological deviation and appalling act of appeasement.

Had Beria established his credibility as a reformer, he would likely have made scapegoats of his Politburo colleagues for the excesses of the Stalin era and purged them.[3] He was not given the chance. At a 26 June 1953 meeting of the Presidium (Politburo), Malenkov and Khrushchev attacked Beria for his "opportunism" and alleged links with western spies and Tito. Waiting gunmen, commanded by the war hero Marshal Georgy Zhukov, were called into the room and Beria was arrested. In the following days, Beria's top placemen within the security services were rounded up. In December 1953, Beria was "tried" by a kangaroo court in the Kremlin, charged with terrorism and espionage, condemned, dragged to the cellars, and shot in the head at point blank range.[4]

Khrushchev openly boasted of his role in the dramatic June 1953 meeting of the Presidium. He subsequently revealed that Malenkov had turned "white" at the climactic moment and that Beria had been green in the face and had "shat his pants."[5]

Khrushchev obtained the key position of party secretary after Beria's demise. In this post, Khrushchev led the drive to cultivate the fallow "Virgin Lands" of Kazakhstan and western Siberia. Hundreds of thousands of young enthusiasts were sent to the Soviet Union's badlands to grow wheat. By the mid-1960s, it had become apparent that the "Virgin Lands" policy was an ecological disaster of the first magnitude, but in 1954–1955 the campaign to raise wheat output gave Khrushchev an aura of leadership as grain yields initially increased.[6]

In February 1955, with the support of the Stalinist diehards Molotov, Kaganovich, and Mikoyan, Khrushchev forced Malenkov out of the premier's job (he became minister for electricity supply) after charging him with the heinous crime of "social democratism." Malenkov kept his place in the Politburo, however. The "petty fishmonger" then out-maneuvered Molotov himself, who was the only man who still rivaled him for prestige and authority. Molotov had no desire to change the Stalinist economic model and remained the "Mr. Nyet" of foreign policy. Khrushchev, however, had decided to break completely with the Stalinist era by restoring relations with Yugoslavia.[7] Molotov had shared with Stalin the decision to split the Cominform and sincerely regarded Yugoslavia to be a state that had betrayed socialism. In May 1955, Khrushchev led a Soviet delegation to Belgrade in Molotov's absence, and then led a ferocious attack on Molotov's supposedly retrograde attitudes in foreign policy in the July 1955 meeting of the Presidium. To keep his place in the chief organ of power, Molotov was forced to conduct self-criticism and admit his "political incorrectness."

The new openness toward Yugoslavia was part of a wider policy of conciliation toward the West pushed by Khrushchev and his Politburo allies. The spring and summer of 1955 was a period of Cold War détente. On 15 May 1955, after only brief negotiations, the Austrian State Treaty was signed.

Vienna regained its independence and was freed from military occupation by the former Allies. Austria became a neutral state in the heart of Europe. Bordering on Czechoslovakia and Hungary, its presence was a permanent reminder to the peoples of those states of an alternative to Soviet domination and communist rule. It was also perceived to be a possible model for a future united Germany.

The day before the signature of the Austrian Treaty, the USSR and its satellite states (Albania, Bulgaria, Czechoslovakia, the GDR, Hungary, Poland, and Romania) had signed the Warsaw Treaty, a NATO-like pact of mutual defense. The pact provided for a coordinated military command and established a "political consultative committee" of representatives of the member states to provide a forum for collective decision making. The USSR obviously called the shots within the new organization, but at least in principle the Warsaw Treaty did represent a dilution of centralized Soviet control: in future crises, indeed, there would be moments when the bosses of Moscow's so-called puppet regimes would urge hard-line policies upon a relatively cautious Soviet leadership.

The explicit motivation for the establishment of the new alliance was "the situation created in Europe by the ratification of the Paris agreements, which envisage the formation of a new military alignment in the shape of 'Western European Union,' with the participation of a remilitarized Western Germany and the integration of the latter in the North-Atlantic bloc." Despite this starting point, the pact's language was not bellicose—indeed, it explicitly evoked a spirit of détente. The pact's contracting parties vowed to "refrain in their international relations from the threat or use of force" and declared their "readiness to participate in a spirit of sincere cooperation in all international actions designed to safeguard international peace and security" and to eliminate nuclear weapons. The pact was open to all states, "irrespective of their social and political systems," that were willing to " assist in uniting the efforts of the peaceable states in safeguarding the peace and security of peoples"—whatever that meant precisely. Each contracting party further vowed to adhere to "the principle of respect for the independence and sovereignty" of the other member states and to "non-interference in their internal affairs."

Such language would look distinctly hypocritical less than eighteen months later when Soviet tanks crushed resistance in the streets of Budapest after Hungary suggested that it might leave the Warsaw Pact and become a neutral country like Austria. The unwritten clause of the organization created at Warsaw was that nobody could leave it without Moscow's consent.

In mid-1955, however, the West was willing to give the USSR an opportunity to expand upon its ideas for a lasting settlement for Europe. At the ceremony in Vienna, the Soviets accepted a joint invitation by Britain, France, and the United States to hold a heads of government meeting to discuss the future of Europe and of Germany. This idea had been first suggested by Churchill in May 1953, but had met little favor in Washington (or, indeed, within Churchill's own cabinet) until the question of the EDC, and West German integration into NATO, had been definitively decided. Now, the three NATO powers proposed that the two sides should meet in Geneva in mid-July.

The encounter between the heads of government in Geneva was freighted with significance. For the first time since Potsdam, the leaders of the wartime allies were going to sit round a table and try to build goodwill. As Eisenhower said in a TV message to the American people on the eve of the talks, the "purpose" of the meeting at Geneva was "to change the spirit that has characterized the intergovernmental relationships of the world during the past ten years."[8]

The Geneva conference was characterized by Moscow's proposal of a general "Treaty on Collective Security in Europe." Prime Minister Bulganin, who fifteen months later was menacingly to remind Great Britain of the Soviets' nuclear strike capability during the Suez crisis, put forward a plan for a pan-European Pact of Non-Aggression to which the United States would also be encouraged to adhere. Members of the new organization would improve trade and cultural links between themselves and would set up administrative machinery to make recommendations to the governments party to the agreement. The USSR argued, however, that the GDR, as well as West Germany, should adhere to the pact: in effect, an extension of diplomatic recognition to the East Berlin regime. Article 14 of the Soviets' proposals also stated that after a mutually agreed time limit had elapsed, the Warsaw Pact, the Western European Union, and the North Atlantic Treaty should be superseded by the new General Treaty. In the meantime, however, Moscow further suggested that the Warsaw Pact and NATO should sign an agreement to refrain from the use of force against one another and that withdrawals of foreign troops should begin from European territory.

The West's leaders thought that these proposals to establish European security were putting the cart before the German horse. As Secretary of State Dulles commented, the three "Western Powers" felt that "the prolonged division of Germany is in itself a threat to European security, whereas . . . the Soviet Delegation feels that the division of Germany can be almost indefinitely prolonged without endangering European security provided certain supplementary measures are taken."[9] Despite this fundamental difference of opinion, the conference concluded positively with warm professions by all four nations that they intended to pursue better relations and hold regular meetings of their foreign ministers. The "Spirit of Geneva" seemed to herald a real breakthrough in international relations. In Winston Churchill's archaic-sounding phrase, "Jaw-jaw [i.e., dialogue] was better than war-war." Especially when the war would be fought with nuclear weapons.

The emergence of Khrushchev had thus brought about a sea change in the direction of Moscow's policy. Beria had been "liquidated"; Molotov and Malenkov had been humbled (though not shot). Tito had become an interlocutor, if not a collaborator. In international affairs, the USSR was no longer hemmed in the Stalinist bunker, but taking bold new initiatives to end the stalemate in Europe and outflank the United States. Just as Khrushchev had played the high-stakes game of Kremlin corridor politics more ably than his chief rivals, the new leader in the Kremlin presumably thought that he could outsmart the Americans, too.

These events were accompanied by timid steps toward permitting freer discussion of Soviet life and recent history: the so-called Thaw. Named after a 1954 novel of this title by the literary critic and wartime propagandist Ilya Ehrenburg, the metaphor does capture the impact that Khrushchev's new course had on the Cold War. The ice seemed to be melting. Khrushchev's abandonment of the keystones of Stalinist policy improved the chances of reconciliation in Europe, but it also increased the odds of an explosion within the communist bloc and of a backlash by the hard-liners in the Kremlin and the satellite states.

THE SECRET SPEECH

Khrushchev was convinced that the legacy of Stalinism had to be rooted out if the party was to recapture what he regarded as the original idealism of Leninist theory and practice. Nevertheless, at the end of 1955, he was still surrounded by some very hard men who saw no need to make structural changes in the USSR's economy, foreign policy, and ideology. The Secret Speech was his attempt to set a new agenda.

William Taubman says that the Secret Speech was the "bravest and most reckless thing [Khrushchev] ever did."[10] The Twentieth Congress, when it convened on 14 February 1956, represented a new stage in destalinization. No portraits of Stalin hung on the walls, and few references were made to his name in the Congress's public sessions (though they were cheered). Khrushchev himself ignored Stalin in his set-piece opening speech. Yet behind the scenes, a tense argument was raging about the utility of there being a public denunciation of Stalin's record. A report, commissioned by Khrushchev and written by Pyotr Pospelov, "an extremely conservative party historian" who had himself "participated in many acts of mass repression in the 1930s," had confirmed in gruesome detail that Stalin's victims had run into the millions; that the dictator had himself signed the death warrants of more than forty-four thousand people in 1937–1938; that torture had been authorized and widely practiced throughout the USSR and its satellites.[11]

By now, moreover, hundreds of thousands of individuals—including the Soviet system's nemesis, Alexander Solzhenitsyn—had been released from the camps, or had been posthumously "rehabilitated." Khrushchev believed it was a moral and political necessity to underline Stalin's responsibility for the abuses that these citizens had suffered. The Politburo unenthusiastically agreed to let Khrushchev present Pospelov's report to a secret session of the Soviet delegates on 25 February 1956.

The decision was a historic one. Khrushchev spoke for four hours and larded the text provided by his speechwriters with numerous off-the-cuff anecdotes about Stalin's shortcomings, cowardice, and political errors. Although Khrushchev's revelations were several times interrupted with what the official text called "tempestuous applause," the Congress's delegates were stunned by what they heard. Taubman says: "The Soviet regime never fully recovered and nor did he."[12]

The Secret Speech was indeed a searing indictment of Stalin's methods of rule and leadership—of the so-called Cult of Personality that had transformed him into "a superman possessing supernatural characteristics akin to those of a god."[13] Party democracy, socialist legality, and Leninist principles had been neglected while Stalin and his sidekick, the "abject provocateur and vile enemy, Beria," carried out mass repressions of good communists. To the accompaniment of "indignation in the hall," Khrushchev gave facts and figures about the scale of the purges of delegates who had attended the Seventeenth Party Congress in 1934, more than half of whom had been arrested and shot for counter-revolutionary activity in the latter half of the decade.

The speech was, however, much more reticent on the millions of non-communists who had fallen victim to Stalin's paranoia. Indeed, it underlined that Stalin's pursuance of collectivization and forced industrialization had enabled the USSR to survive in a hostile international environment. Stalin's abuses began only in 1934, Khrushchev argued, after the key stages in the construction of socialism had largely been carried out. This distinction had the useful effect of exonerating Khrushchev himself from complicity in the dictator's crimes before that date: in fact, one reason the purges took place was to allow men like Khrushchev, Malenkov, and Beria to advance at the expense of the so-called Old Bolsheviks.

Even more dramatically, Khrushchev scornfully attacked Stalin's culpable willingness to trust Hitler; his incompetence, Khrushchev openly stated, had cost hundreds of thousands of lives. Indeed, Khrushchev came close to depicting Stalin as an "objective" collaborator of Hitler—one whose mistakes were so gross that they almost enabled the Nazis to win the war. "This is Stalin's military 'genius'; this is what it cost us!" Khrushchev ranted. To "thunderous and prolonged applause," he asserted that "the main credit for the victorious ending of the war belong to our Communist party, to the armed forces of the Soviet Union, and to the tens of millions of Soviet people uplifted by the party," not to Stalin.

To back up his words, Khrushchev distributed Lenin's "testament," a 1924 document that was subsequently published as a pamphlet in July 1956. In the "Testament," Lenin wrote that "Comrade Stalin . . . has concentrated enormous power in his hands; and I am not sure that he always knows how to use that power with sufficient caution." In a postscript, Lenin had added: "Comrade Stalin is too rude . . . and this fault . . . becomes insupportable in the office of general secretary. Therefore I propose to comrades to find a way to remove Stalin from that position."[14]

The speech did not stay secret for long. The leaders of the world's communist parties present were briefed on the speech's contents and a summary of Khrushchev's remarks was discussed in party meetings across the USSR. The Polish Workers' Party printed a large print run of several thousand copies for the use of militants. Before long, the speech had made its way to the West, where a translated version was published by the *New York Times* in June. Communists in Western Europe found themselves in the uncomfortable position of learning from the capitalist press that the worst accusations of oppression leveled against the USSR by its bourgeois critics had now been confirmed by the leader of the USSR in person. As the Italian intellectual Lucio Magri has written, Khrushchev's words "cut deep into the heart and brain of every militant."[15]

The communist world was thrown into confusion by Khrushchev's speech. Blaming Stalin's "errors" of judgment and condemning the "personality cult" for "distorting" Soviet reality was all very well, but such explanations could not hide the fact that there was darkness at what should have been noon. Even many communist loyalists doubted that terror on the scale described by Khrushchev could be attributed solely to the actions of Stalin and other renegades such as Beria. And if they could, what did that say about the nature of the political system that could produce such monsters?

Communist leaderships fought hard to prevent such heretical thoughts from gaining ground, but it was an uphill battle. The debate within the *direzione* (steering committee) of the PCI on 20 June 1956 gives a sharp insight into the kind of fierce arguments set off by the publication of the speech. Party leader Palmiro Togliatti came under open attack in plain Italian, not the usual bureaucratese, for having kept the party leadership in the dark since February 1956 and for having given a long interview on the topic of the speech to a party publication, *Nuovi Argomenti*, without the approval of the rest of the leadership. A party heavyweight, Pietro Secchia, who had been the leader of the PCI's revolutionary wing in the 1940s, remarked acidly that there had clearly been a "thaw" toward the outside world, but not in the internal management of the party.[16] In general, the debate within the *direzione* revolved around whether the party leadership should encourage open discussion of the speech's revelations or dampen the discussion down. The latter option was chosen. The party newspaper, *L'Unità*, did not reprint the speech. Togliatti's interview, which essentially put forth the bromide that the errors and crimes of the Stalin era, while real, had not "deformed the nature" of the Soviet project, became the party line. [17]

Togliatti's interview has been portrayed as daringly "Trotskyist" in its critique, insofar as the Italian leader admitted that "bureaucratic degeneration" existed in the USSR and acknowledged that Stalin's "mistakes" were not "merely personal" but had "blanketed" the reality of life in the Soviet Union. Togliatti's unorthodoxy should not be overinterpreted, however. Ultimately, it was a damage limitation exercise by an artful spin doctor. After reading the interview, one could continue to believe. No leader of any weight within the party resigned. The party chiefs merely "suppressed their consciences and intelligence, and pretended that nothing had happened." [18]

The PCI's reaction was nevertheless better than that of the French Communist Party (PCF). Its leader, Maurice Thorez, simply gagged all critical debate. According to Irwin Wall, Thorez told a senior party official who had obtained a copy of the speech that "we must act as if it did not exist." [19] *Humanité*, the PCF's daily newspaper, printed a photograph of Stalin on its front page on 5 March 1956 and throughout the spring of 1956 praised the Soviet leader's achievements and status in the pantheon of communism. When the Speech was published in June, the PCF warned that publication in the bourgeois press could only facilitate "speculations and maneuvers" by enemies of communism and stated adamantly that "the explanations given thus far" of Stalin's "mistakes" were inadequate. A proper "Marxist analysis" was needed. On 6 July 1956, such an analysis was attempted. A joint declaration by the PCF and the Soviet Party found that the "cult of personality" had originated in Stalin's own character, in Beria's nefarious activities, and in the need for discipline in the face of Trotskyism and the attacks of world capital. It was, in short, incidental, not intrinsic to the society achieved in the USSR, which had not succumbed to the degeneration identified by Togliatti. Thereafter, the Secret Speech became a taboo topic in the PCF and the text went unpublished in the party press. [20]

Within the Soviet bloc, the Secret Speech had the greatest political consequences in two countries: Poland and Hungary. The Hungarian revolution is discussed at length below, but the crisis provoked within the Polish Communist Party was almost equally dramatic. Communist rule in Poland was profoundly shaken by Khrushchev's speech. Party leader Bierut died of a heart attack while he was still in Moscow: the shock of Khrushchev's words, and what they portended, was seemingly too much for the Polish apparatchik. He was replaced by Edward Ochab. Had Bierut lived, he would have been submerged by a groundswell of indignation from ordinary party workers and citizens, who used the revelations of the Secret Speech to call communist rule into question. Throughout the spring, peasants demanded an end to collectivization, intellectuals denounced the privileges of the party hierarchy, students agitated for free speech, party members called for a purge of the Stalinists entrenched in the leadership. In April, *Po prostu*, a weekly magazine edited by young Marxist critics of the regime, published an article entitled "What Is To Be Done" that urged its readers to agitate in their workplaces and local party cells for immediate reforms, to bring about regeneration of the party from below.[21] In the face of this tumult, Jakob Berman, the party boss in charge of ideology and security matters, was forced to resign from his party and government positions in May 1956. Thousands of individuals jailed for no good reason between 1948 and 1953 were released and their sentences quashed. Some of the chief torturers of the Stalinist period were arrested, though the security police remained a baleful presence in political life.

In June 1956, the rejection of the political system spread to industrial workers at a major engineering plant in Poznań, Poland's fourth-largest city. Factory operatives—in theory, the chief beneficiaries of socialism—revolted against "acute economic distress."[22] Their protest soon took on a political aspect, however. Frustrated by the authorities' prevarication, the mass of the workforce struck on 28 June 1956 and marched on the town center, where they were joined by thousands of ordinary citizens. A labor dispute had become an uprising against the regime, against the USSR, and for political and religious freedom. "We want UN-supervised elections," "Down with the Red Bourgeoisie," and "We want God" were slogans that neither Warsaw nor Moscow could regard with equanimity, especially since there were a number of western reporters in the city, attending a trade fair.[23]

The protest quickly turned violent. The crowd sacked the local party headquarters and laid siege to the headquarters of the security police. A suspected secret policeman was lynched. The Polish Politburo authorized Marshal Konstantin Rokossovsky, a Russian citizen of Polish origin who commanded the armed forces, to quell the revolt. Under Rokossovsky's orders, troops and tanks fired on the crowds. More than seventy civilians were killed and hundreds wounded. The world's communist press blamed the uprising on the work of American-paid provocateurs, but in private, communist leaders well knew that the Poznań revolt was a sign that the revelations of the Secret Speech had made Polish citizens more inclined to question the brutal working and living conditions, unjust and undemocratic political system, and subservience to the USSR that were the hallmarks of the regime established in Poland since the end of the war.

The only way of restoring the party's authority was the return of a prodigal son. In October, after weeks of secret negotiations, Władysław Gomułka was readmitted to the Politburo and the Central Committee of the Workers' Party prepared—without consulting the USSR—to acquiesce in his demand that he should be made first secretary. Khrushchev, who was as suspicious of Gomułka's nationalism as Stalin himself, responded with an imposing show of "coercive diplomacy."[24] On 19 October 1956, as the Central Committee convened, Soviet troops in Poland were mobilized and columns of tanks converged upon Warsaw. Warships anchored menacingly off Gdansk. Russian troops were alerted in neighboring Ukraine and East Germany. Marshal Rokossovsky, whose primary loyalty was to the USSR, made preparations for a takeover. The risk loomed of clashes between troops loyal to Rokossovsky and troops loyal to Gomułka.

Most dramatically of all, the Soviet top brass invited itself to the Central Committee's meeting (or "plenum"). Two planes, the first carrying Molotov and other Kremlin heavyweights such as Anastas Mikoyan and Lazar Kaganovich, the second transporting Khrushchev himself, landed in Warsaw where they were greeted by Rokossovsky and other top Russian military officials. A day of intensive talks began during which Khrushchev accused the Poles of wanting to "turn their faces to the West and your backs on us." Gomułka responded with patience, but without the sycophancy hitherto typical in relations between the Soviet leadership and its subordinates. He bluntly told Khrushchev that he would preserve communist rule in his own way, without Moscow's interference. He added that the Soviet military presence in Poland had to be reduced and that Marshal Rokossovsky, whose presence was a humiliation, should be replaced.[25]

Remarkably, he got his way. After the impromptu Soviet delegation had gone home, the Central Committee duly elected Gomułka and voted to relieve Rokossovsky of his post. In his address to the Central Committee, Gomułka acknowledged that forcible collectivization had been an error (over 90 percent of the nation's collective farms were subsequently dissolved) and underlined that national sovereignty was a fundamental principle of international relations that had not always been respected by our "great and friendly neighbor" during the time of Stalin.[26]

Gomułka's uncompromising stance was genuinely popular. He managed to rally behind him "all patriotic Poles, including the spiritual leaders . . . of a nation that was still bitterly anti-communist and almost wholly Roman Catholic."[27] Huge crowds gathered in the country's main cities to show support for the beleaguered leader. Many of these demonstrations took "extremely radical forms" and led to clashes with the police and the destruction of monuments to the liberation of Poland by the Red Army.[28]

Either because the Soviet leadership shrank from using force on the scale necessary to quell the new course in Polish policy, or because they grasped that Gomułka was a tough customer able to preserve as much orthodoxy as possible, in the days following the Central Committee plenum the Kremlin decided to let Poland be. The tanks returned to the barracks. Rokossovsky was recalled to the USSR and Cardinal Stefan Wyszyński, the symbol of the Polish church's oppression by the communist state, was released from jail.

In the long run, Gomułka justified Khrushchev's trust. He was a conservative who preserved the essentials of the Stalinist system rather than a radical intent on a new departure. At the time, however, events in Poland appeared as a harbinger of a more pluralistic future for communism. As the French intellectual Marcel Péju wrote, it seemed as if a "second October revolution" was "sweeping away ten years of Stalinism across Europe."[29] The downfall of Polish neo-Stalinism, and the arrival in power of a leader able to make the Kremlin blink, was in particular an inspiration for reformers in neighboring Hungary, which rose in revolt just as Gomułka was confirmed in power.

THE CRUSHING OF BUDAPEST

The Hungarian revolution of October–November 1956, and its suppression by the Red Army, is one of the landmarks of the European Cold War. Thousands of Hungarians died during the fighting and tens of thousands more were persecuted once so-called socialist legality had been restored. More than two hundred thousand Hungarians fled the country, a diaspora that enriched the West's cultural and professional life as much as it impoverished Hungary's own.

Outside of Hungary, the crushing of the Hungarian revolt was the last straw for many intellectuals who had hitherto justified or supported the USSR. Just eight months after the Secret Speech, the USSR revealed itself to be as intolerant as ever of national divergences from the Soviet model. "Stalin's ghost," to borrow the French philosopher Jean-Paul Sartre's formulation, still haunted the communist movement. Even on the political left, communism now seemed to be no better than the imperialism that was oppressing Algeria, black Africa, and Central America. For many other European progressives, the bloody repression in Budapest was confirmation that communism was a form of society and government whose malaise was fundamentally incurable. Only diehard defenders of the Soviet state (a category that included the leaderships of the PCF and PCI) found it possible to regurgitate the official propaganda line that the Hungarian revolt had been an attempted coup carried out by former fascists and "reactionary elements."

The peculiar virulence of the Hungarians' revolt against their rulers was a consequence of the fact that alone among the Soviet bloc, Hungary's process of destalinization was interrupted by the return to power of the leadership who had ravaged the country in the 1940s and early 1950s. The process of destalinization had begun in June 1953 when Mátyás Rákosi and other top Hungarian leaders were called to the USSR and berated for the catastrophic state of the Hungarian economy and excessive use of terror. Lavrenti Beria, Stalin's chief executioner since 1939, even attacked Rákosi for having authorized torture against fellow communists: if ever there were a case of the pot calling the kettle black, this was it. Not long before, such failings would have led straight to a prison cell, if not a gallows. Now, however, Rákosi and his henchmen were merely ordered to take full public responsibility for their "mistakes." The Soviet leadership nominated Imre Nagy as its candidate for the premiership, but permitted Rákosi to keep the post of party first secretary. Ernő Gerő, a doctrinaire Stalinist, became deputy premier and minister of the interior.

Nagy was a Moscow-trained agricultural economist who had acted as an informant on his fellow Hungarians on behalf of the Soviet security services in the 1930s.[30] He had been minister of agriculture immediately after the war and had been the architect of a radical land reform that gave land to the peasants. Unlike Rákosi, Gerő, and other key Hungarian party officials, Nagy was not of "Jewish origin," a fact that the men in the Kremlin regarded as a definite plus. The least doctrinaire of the party's top functionaries (he had even attended his daughter's church wedding), and the only one with any popular following, the jovial "Uncle Imre" had been sidelined during the years of Rákosi's terror, though his connections with the Russian "organs" spared him the fate reserved for László Rajk.

Once in power, Nagy launched a "New Course" in economic policy, cutting the amount of investment in heavy industry and permitting the dissolution of collective farms if their members so chose. Wages were increased and prices reduced to give a boost to purchasing power and to stimulate consumption. Ideological orthodoxy was relaxed and political prisoners were released from the camps or allowed to return to Budapest from internal exile. By the autumn of 1953, the "Hungarian Gulag" had been "virtually eliminated."[31]

Such measures were anathema to Rákosi, who intrigued constantly, and to the Kremlin's ambassador to Budapest, Yuri Andropov (a future leader of the USSR), who, in Charles Gati's words, "played Iago to the Kremlin's Othello by implying that the alternative to Rákosi was chaos, not reform."[32] When the new course failed to bring about quick economic progress, and when Nagy began to rehabilitate communists, such as János Kádár, imprisoned during the terror, obstruction of the Hungarian premier became still more intense, especially after Nagy advocated greater democracy in party decision making to ensure that there was no repetition of past "sins."[33]

On 8 January 1955, the clash between Nagy and Rákosi, which was contemporaneous to the growing tensions between Malenkov and Khrushchev, was resolved during a summit between the Soviet Politburo and the chief Hungarian leaders. In a startling about-turn, Rákosi was now hailed by Molotov and the Kremlin diehards as the best available leader in Hungary:

Nagy was accused, among much else, of "antiparty" activity. Party functionaries had been shot for much less. Even Malenkov, Nagy's Kremlin sponsor, insisted that the Hungarian leader should subject himself to self-criticism. The meeting ended with a joint resolution that "the party's policies in the years before 1953 were fundamentally correct." Nagy's "New Course" was history.

Three weeks after this verbal battering, Nagy suffered a minor heart attack. While he was convalescing, his enemies moved against him. On 2 March 1955, the Central Committee of the Hungarian Workers' Party unanimously condemned his right-wing deviationism. Nagy had a second and worse heart attack. In April the Central Committee expelled him from both the Central Committee itself and from the Politburo. His place as premier was taken by András Hegedüs, a close supporter of Rákosi.

In the following months, Nagy was barred from returning to academia and, in November, stripped of his party membership. Yet he never sought to regain favor by making a ritual disavowal of his ideas and of the actions of his government. Nagy also developed his theoretical position after his exclusion from power. He circulated manuscripts among the intellectuals within the party who had come to the conclusion that only democratization could bring about political progress in Hungary. These manuscripts, which were published in the West after Nagy's death, advocated domestic and international policies similar to those of Tito's Yugoslavia, which in 1955 had taken the lead, at the Bandung conference in Indonesia, in forming the non-aligned movement. Nagy, by the time of the Secret Speech, wanted Hungary to be free to develop a model of socialism that conjugated greater pluralism in domestic politics with neutrality in the international sphere.[34]

The Secret Speech intensified dissent within Hungary. At the end of May, meetings of the Petőfi Circle began. This was a discussion club attended by the cream of the Hungarian intelligentsia, but also party officials. Its original purpose was to allow critics to let off steam and make suggestions for reform. Too much steam was simmering in the pot, however. On 19 June 1956, Julia Rajk, the widow of László Rajk, addressed the circle. Recently released from jail, she pointed the finger of blame at the party functionaries present: "You not only killed my husband, but you killed all decency in our country." Demanding justice, and the punishment of the murderers in power, she concluded her speech with the words "Comrades, stand by me in this fight!"[35] Mrs. Rajk received an ovation. The following meeting of the circle, on 27 June, was attended by thousands and turned into a rally in favor of freedom of speech and an attack on the official censorship that had banned the publication of the Secret Speech.

Alarmed by the growing mood of unrest, in mid-July the USSR sent Politburo member, and relative moderate, Anastas Mikoyan to Hungary on a fact-finding mission. Mikoyan immediately grasped that regime change was imperative: in a top secret report to the Politburo on 14 July 1956, he warned that "one can see how day after day the comrades are losing their grip on power."[36] Rákosi was instructed to retire from the party secretaryship, nominally on health grounds, and conduct self-criticism. On 19 July 1956, he obeyed orders. He was whisked off to the USSR, where he spent the evening of his life writing his memoirs. Months later, individuals far less steeped in guilt than he were hanged from Budapest's lampposts.

Rákosi's replacement was not Nagy, or some other leader of reformist instincts, but the worst possible choice: Ernő Gerő, who was incapable of interpreting the swelling mood of disenchantment among the Hungarian people. Hungary needed principled political leadership in the summer of 1956, but Gerő morally could not provide it.

The public mood boiled over in October 1956, after László Rajk had been ceremoniously rehabilitated and reburied and as Gomułka fought for his political life. On 23 October 1956, university students, who had already taken the illegal step of forming an autonomous association, showed solidarity for the Poles by marching to the statue of a Polish general who had been a hero of the Hungarians' struggle for national independence in 1848. The students had drawn up a sixteen-point list of demands, which included the withdrawal of Russian troops from Hungary, and they tried to get Radio Kossuth, an official broadcaster, to transmit it. It was refused. By nightfall, rebellious students and workers were milling about the squares of Budapest, a gigantic statue of Stalin had been pulled down, the first clashes had begun, Gerő had requested Soviet aid, and a crowd gathered in front of the Parliament building was chanting for Nagy.

A Gomułka (or a Khrushchev) would have turned the street against the party hierarchy. Nagy made the error of temporizing. He even began his speech by using the word "Comrades." This was a gaffe and he was loudly heckled. Later, he made a second error of agreeing to serve in the Politburo, and as premier, without insisting on a clean sweep of the Stalinists in the party leadership. As a result, when Soviet tanks arrived and the youth of Budapest were fighting them with a bravery that aroused the world's admiration, Nagy was tarred with Gerő's brush. Martial law was pronounced in his name. From then on, he struggled to regain credibility, both with the fighters in the streets and with the propagandists of Radio Free Europe (RFE), the Munich-based, U.S. government-financed broadcaster, which urged the Hungarians to rid themselves of the regime and recklessly implied that the Hungarians were not alone in their fight. RFE's rhetoric convinced many Hungarians that NATO intervention was in the offing. President Eisenhower understandably never contemplated an action that might have precipitated a world war.

Nagy began from 28 October to take the radical political steps demanded by the people and his own closest advisors. A cease-fire was negotiated. The

Politburo was purged of Stalinists; János Kádár, a "centrist," became the party's new leader. On 30 October, with the explicit approval of Mikoyan, the USSR's man on the spot, the government was opened to non-communist ministers, notably Zoltán Tildy, the postwar president and Peasant Party leader. Géza Losonczy, one of Nagy's inner circle, and a man whose experiences in Rákosi's jails had turned him into a passionate believer in democratic pluralism, also joined the government.

These changes were initially greeted positively by Moscow. The Politburo negotiated with Nagy's government about withdrawing its armed forces from Hungarian soil. When *Pravda* announced this decision on 31 October, "it created a sensation around the globe."[37] It briefly looked as if the USSR was willing to allow a "free, democratic and independent Hungary," to quote the words Nagy used in a radio address on 30 October. Yet just two days later, Kádár and other senior officials had packed their bags and left for Moscow. Five days later, Soviet tanks were back in Budapest and other urban centers around the country, and the revolution was being crushed by the redoubled use of force. What caused the almost instantaneous turn-about in Soviet policy?

The answer to this question is a combination of factors. Hungarian freedom fighters besieged the Budapest headquarters of the security police on 30 October and, after the police fired on the crowd, stormed the building and lynched officials. The episode was portrayed as "white terror" by the international communist press and was interpreted, certainly by the Soviet Politburo, as a sign that events were taking a reactionary turn. Anglo-French intervention in the Suez canal zone at the beginning of November 1956 (see above, chapter four) came at just the right moment. By creating worldwide uproar, it distracted attention from events in Hungary and enabled the USSR to act without incurring excessive international opprobrium.

Moreover, after learning that Soviet troops were returning to Hungary instead of leaving it, Nagy's government announced on 1 November that it was leaving the Warsaw Pact and declared neutrality in a "desperate last attempt at saving the revolution."[38] That Nagy should take such a step underlines the Kremlin's real reason for rethinking its original support for his government. Hungary was going beyond even Poland in its assertion of autonomy, and Nagy, unlike Gomułka, was spurring the mood of national assertiveness, not trying to rein it in. Objectively, Moscow faced the prospect of Hungary's becoming a second Austria. Its government would be led by the Peasant Party; the Church would reassert its role in Hungarian society; the Social Democrats would probably establish themselves as the principal party of the left. The USSR would be humiliated; its pretensions to represent the masses, already shaken by the Polish events, would be exposed as a sham.

Gomułka and Tito, let alone the Kremlin hard-liners or the Stalinists still in power in Prague and East Berlin, feared a domino effect. After obtaining

Kádár's agreement to head a Soviet-imposed government, Khrushchev conducted a whirlwind tour of Balkan states—Romania, Bulgaria, and Yugoslavia—to explain his changed intentions. Tito, the founder of the anti-imperialist non-aligned movement, raised no objections to the Soviet occupation of a neighboring sovereign state and pledged that he would strive to persuade Nagy to step down.[39]

On 4 November 1956, the Red Army threw its full weight into the battle against what *Pravda* called "the dark forces of reaction" who had seized power in Budapest.[40] More than 2,500 Hungarians, and 700 Soviet troops, were killed in the street fighting that followed. Nagy, after announcing to the world at 5.20 a.m. on the morning of 4 November that "Soviet troops [have] launched an attack against our capital city with the obvious intention of overthrowing the lawful, democratic Hungarian government," decamped for the Yugoslav embassy together with fourteen of his closest advisors and their families. In the following days, tens of thousands of other Hungarians fled toward Yugoslavia and especially Austria, which generously opened its borders and established refugee camps to host the flood of desperate human beings fleeing war and political persecution.

GUILTY MEN

Once the battle was over, Kádár consolidated his position with the aid of the security police. Hundreds of people who had fought in the insurrection were hanged. Tens of thousands were imprisoned or sanctioned in other ways. Nagy stayed in the Yugoslav embassy for nearly three weeks, which the USSR regarded as a breach of Tito's agreement with Khrushchev. Harboring such "bankrupt degenerates and accomplices of the counterrevolution" as "Nagy and Co" was treated by the Russians as a diplomatic slap in the face.[41] On the other hand, moving Nagy and his entourage to the Yugoslav capital, Belgrade, was also excluded: Kádár did not want a rival "government in exile" over the border. On 22 July Nagy left the safety of the embassy after Kádár gave Tito a guarantee of safe conduct. Kádár did not keep his word. Instead of being allowed to go home, Nagy and his group were seized and, when they refused to issue a statement supporting the new regime, were sent into exile to Snagov, in Romania.

Kádár, who knew that Khrushchev's rivals might restore Rákosi if he showed mercy, then pursued a vendetta against Nagy, urging upon the Soviet leader the need to eliminate Nagy physically.[42] In April 1957, Nagy and his chief supporters were arrested, taken to Budapest, and imprisoned for more than a year. They were finally "tried"—the quotation marks are obligatory—between 9 and 15 June 1958. Nagy; Pál Maléter, the revolution's defense minister; and Miklós Gimes, a journalist who was one of Kádár's most ferocious critics, were sentenced to death. They were hanged on 16 June 1958. József Szilagyi, Nagy's chief of staff, was hanged separately. Zoltán Tildy, who on 4 November 1956 had courageously waited in the Parliament building for the arrival of the Russian troops, was imprisoned for six years. Sándor Haraszti, an intellectual who was interned with Nagy in Romania, and Miklós Vásárhelyi, Nagy's press officer, were sentenced to six and five years, respectively. Other prominent figures in the revolution received sentences ranging from life imprisonment to five years' jail. Géza Losonzcy had already died of his treatment in prison.

Hungary's revolution had been betrayed by Khrushchev and Kádár, and left in the lurch by Tito. One should add to this list the Communist parties of France and Italy. The PCF gave unconditional support of the USSR's actions during the crisis—its headquarters in Paris was attacked by right-wing militants as a result. The PCI, by contrast, quarreled bitterly over the Hungarian revolt. The party leadership mostly adhered to the Moscow interpretation of events, although Giuseppe Di Vittorio, the head of Italy's largest trade union, the *Confederazione generale dei lavoratori* (CGIL), briefly rescinded from the party line. The party's intellectuals were more divided. One hundred and one intellectuals connected to the party, most of them university professors, signed a manifesto of support for the Hungarian revolution. Several prominent figures, notably the writers Italo Calvino and Vasco Pratolini, left the PCI in the months following the Soviet invasion. Some two hundred thousand party members did not renew their membership cards in 1957.

The PCI's eighth congress, which took place in December 1956, nevertheless made no public criticism of the USSR. The events in Hungary had occurred, party leader Palmiro Togliatti asserted, because Hungary had not corrected the errors of Stalinism in a timely manner and because "imperialist" agents had provoked disorder among "counterrevolutionary" elements of the population.[43]

Togliatti's line was ridiculed by the PCI's principal domestic opponents, Christian Democracy (DC). As an intriguing contemporary DC pamphlet argued, how—if communism was so successful—had a fascist revolutionary movement become powerful enough in Hungary to incite a whole people to "fight, suffer and die"? In Italy, like Hungary, the fascists had once been dominant. Now, they had become a derided minority. Why wasn't Hungary the same? For the DC, the "repugnant servility" of the PCI's reaction to the Hungarian events was proof that its leadership and party functionaries were "a fifth column" entrenched on Italian soil.[44]

One PCI leader, Antonio Giolitti, grandson of a liberal prime minister in pre-fascist Italy, dissented from Togliatti's line: for him, the refusal to interpret the facts of the Hungarian revolt for what they obviously were was an instance of *doppiezza*—a word usually translated as "duplicity." In this case, however, the best word in English is an Orwellian one: "doublethink," the ability always to know the politically correct thing to say, or act upon, irrespective of one's own most private thoughts. Giolitti, who subsequently joined the Socialist Party (PSI) and was an important influence on that party's shift away from a broadly pro-Moscow stance, courageously urged the PCI's congress to express its innermost doubts about the Soviet project frankly. The task of replying to Giolitti was left to a young parliamentary deputy called Giorgio Napolitano, who rallied the faithful by stating baldly that the Soviet "intervention" in Hungary had prevented Hungary from falling into "chaos" and had hence "contributed decisively . . . to saving peace in the world."[45]

Neither the intellectuals' protests, nor the derision of his opponents, nor the dissent of the party membership deflected Togliatti from his line. On 19 June 1958, he gelidly told the party newspaper that he had "no particular statement to make" about Nagy's execution. He mendaciously pointed out that the new Hungarian government had regained the confidence of the workers, that its courts functioned well, and that Nagy had been head of government at a time when people had "taken up arms to overthrow the people's government and bring the country into the camp of the imperialists, thus breaking with the socialist camp."[46] Just possibly, Togliatti thought that Nagy, Gimes, Losonczy, and Maléter had gotten their just desserts. Certainly, he knew he should imply that they had.

Thirty years later, in 1986, the PCI's supine support for the invasion of Hungary in 1956 was the object of a major polemic in Italy. The then leader of the PSI, Bettino Craxi, wrote an article entitled "Courage of the Truth," in the party newspaper *Avanti!* In this article, Craxi asked the PCI why, thirty years on, "nobody in the Communist camp has seen fit to begin the job of rehabilitating the figure of Imre Nagy."[47] The article provoked a torrent of personal memoirs, attempts at historical re-interpretation, and, behind the scenes, rethinking among the PCI's leadership. In private, the PCI knew that it had been on the wrong side of the barricades in 1956.

So, in their heart of hearts, did many other European progressives and communists. The Soviet clampdown in Budapest prolonged communism in Hungary and kept the lid on dissent within the Soviet bloc for another decade. But it dispelled any remaining aura of progressivism about the Soviet project.

NOTES

1. For a vigorous statement of this argument, see Tony Judt, "Eric Hobsbawm and the romance of Communism," in *Reappraisals: Reflections on the Forgotten Twentieth Century* (London: Vintage, 2008), 116–28.

2. William Taubman, *Khrushchev: The Man, His Era* (The Free Press: London, 2006), 231–32.

3. Taubman, *Khrushchev*, 245 in notes.

4. Dimitri Volkogonov, *The Rise and Fall of the Soviet Empire* (Harper Collins, 1998), 185–93. Vologokov records Khrushchev telling an aide on the day of Stalin's funeral that "as long as that bastard [Beria] is alive, none of us can feel safe."

5. Taubman, *Khrushchev*, 258.

6. Roy and Zhores Medvedev, *Khrushchev: The Years in Power* (New York: Norton, 1978), 34–37, 58–62.

7. Svetozar Rajak, "New Evidence from the Former Yugoslav Archives," *Cold War History Project Bulletin*, no. 12/13 (Fall/Winter 2001): 315–24, for the 1954 correspondence between Khrushchev and Tito that broke the ice between the two states.

8. President Eisenhower, text of Radio-Television Address, 15 July 1955, in *The Geneva Conference of Heads of Government, July 18–23 1955* (Washington, DC: Department of State, 1955), 13.

9. John Foster Dulles, quoted in *The Geneva Conference of Heads of Government*, 70.

10. Taubman, *Khrushchev*, 274.

11. Medvedevs, *Khrushchev: The Years*, 68.

12. Taubman, *Khrushchev*, 274.

13. This quotation, and the ones in the following paragraphs, is from the text of the speech at: http://www.theguardian.com/theguardian/2007/apr/26/greatspeeches1.

14. Bertrand D. Wolfe, *Khrushchev and Stalin's Ghost* (New York: Praeger, 1957), 262–63.

15. Lucio Magri, *Il Sarto di Ulm* (Milan: Il Saggiatore, 2009), 133.

16. Istituto Gramsci (Rome), Archive of the PCI, File MF 136.

17. Palmiro Togliatti, "Intervista a *Nuovi Argomenti*," in PCI, *Il Partito Comunista Italiano e il movimento operaio internazionale, 1956–1968* (Roma: Riuniti editori, 1969), 34–61.

18. Renato Mieli, *Deserto Rosso: Un decennio da comunista* (Bologna: Il Mulino, 1996), 99.

19. Irwin Wall, *French Communism in the Era of Stalin* (Westport, CT: Greenwood, 1983), 209.

20. Wall, *French Communism*, 211–12.

21. Pawel Machcewicz, "Intellectuals and Mass Movements: The Study of Political Dissent in Poland in 1956," *Contemporary European History* 6 (1997): 371.

22. Johanna Granville, "1956 Reconsidered: Why Hungary, not Poland?" *Slavonic and East European Review* 80 (2002): 660.

23. Machcewicz, "Intellectuals and Mass Movements," 363.

24. Mark Kramer, "The Soviet Union and the 1956 Crises in Hungary and Poland: Reassessments and New Findings," *Journal of Contemporary History* 33 (1998): 170.

25. For detailed accounts of Gomułka's position, see L. Gluchkowski, "Poland 1956: Khrushchev, Gomułka and the 'Polish October,'" *Cold War History Project Bulletin*, no. 5 (1995), and Krzysztof Persak, "The Polish-Soviet Confrontation in 1956 and the Attempted Soviet Military Intervention in Poland," *Europe-Asia Studies* 58 (2006): 1285–310.

26. Anthony Kemp-Welch, *Poland under Communism: A Cold War History* (Cambridge: Cambridge University Press, 2008), 101–2.

27. Edward Crankshaw, *Khrushchev: A Career* (New York: Viking Press, 1966), 241.

28. Machcewicz, "Intellectuals and Mass Movements," 365.

29. Marcel Péju, "Dal rapporto Kruscev alla tragedia Ungherese: Il comunismo nell'ora della verità," in *La Rivolta Ungherese*, ed. J-P. Sartre (Milan: Mondadori, 1957), 125. This is the Italian translation of the January 1957 edition of Sartre's journal, *Les Temps Modernes*.

30. János M. Rainer, *Imre Nagy: A Biography* (New York: I.B. Tauris, 2009), 29–30.

31. Rainer, *Imre Nagy*, 67.

32. Charles Gati, *Failed Illusions: Moscow, Washington, Budapest, and the 1956 Hungarian Revolt* (Palo Alto: Stanford University Press, 2006), 116.

33. Rainer, *Imre Nagy*, 78.

34. Imre Nagy, *On Communism; In Defense of the New Course* (New York: Praeger, 1957), see esp. chapter 5, "The 'Five Principles' of International Relations and Our Foreign Policy."

35. Quoted in *The Hungarian Revolution*, ed. Melvin Lasky (London: Congress for Cultural Freedom, 1957), 30.

36. For Mikoyan's report, see Csaba Békés, Malcolm Byrne, and János M. Rainer, eds., *The 1956 Hungarian Revolution: A History in Documents* (Budapest: CEU University Press, 2000), 143–47. It is also published on the website of the National Security Archive at http://www2.gwu.edu.

37. Gati, *Failed Illusions*, 180.

38. Csba Békés, "The 1956 Hungarian Revolution and the Declaration of Neutrality," *Cold War History* 6 (2006): 477.

39. A. S. Stykalin, "Soviet-Yugoslav Relations and the Case of Imre Nagy," *Cold War History* 5 (2005): 6.

40. Quoted in Lasky, *The Hungarian Revolution*, 227.

41. Stykalin, "Soviet-Yugoslav Relations," 7, quoting Foreign Minister Dimitri Shepilov.

42. Gati, *Failed Illusions*, 232–33.

43. "Elementi per una dichiarazione programmatica del PCI," December 1956, in *Il Partito comunista italiano e il movimento operaio internazionale*, 110. Communists who followed the party line on Hungary laid down by Togliatti were called "carristi," after the Italian word for tank.

44. Democrazia Cristiana, *La Rivoltà Ungherese e la crisi del comunismo* (Rome: Democrazia Cristiana, 1957), 13, 9, and 18.

45. Giorgio Napolitano became president of Italy in 2006 and remains in the office today. His political memoirs, *Dal PCI al socialismo europeo* (Rome: Laterza, 2005), contain a brief but unrevealing account of his role in 1956.

46. "Giudizio di Togliatti sulla sentenza Nagy," *L'Unità*, 19 June 1958, 1.

47. Bettino Craxi, "Il coraggio della verità," *Avanti!* 10 October 1956. Reprinted in *La Paura della verità: Ungheria 1956. Tutti i documenti del grande dibattito della sinistra italiana*, ed. Guido Gerosa (Milan: Edimac, 1987).

Chapter Six

The Berlin Crisis

The lull in the European Cold War represented by the Austrian State Treaty and the Geneva conference in July 1955 did not last long. The Suez affair and the repression of the Hungarian uprising against communist rule at once restored the crisis atmosphere. In the late 1950s, moreover, tensions worsened still further.

There were two root causes for the tension. The first was the still unresolved question of Germany. By the mid-1950s, when it joined NATO, West Germany was an economic miracle and a free society; its communist counterpart, the GDR, was by contrast the platonic ideal of a police state, where the Stasi, or security services, had permeated society with its spies. Brash and materialistic though the new West Germany appeared to some of its writers and artists, millions of East Germans could not look at their cousins' economic and political achievements without envy. Their own society would have reminded them powerfully of *1984*, had copies of Orwell's 1949 classic been smuggled through the iron curtain. Unable to vote freely for any party except the dominant SED of party leader Walter Ulbricht, East Germans increasingly began to vote with their feet, crossing into West Berlin and asking for asylum. From Berlin, such refugees were flown to West Germany to make a new life.

The second root cause of tension was the accelerating nuclear contest between the two blocs. In the mid-1950s, the United States possessed substantial superiority both in the number of strategic nuclear warheads and in the means of their delivery. A huge boost in military spending in the early 1950s had led to the construction of an intercontinental force of B-52 bombers capable of reaching the USSR and also to technological advances such as the miniaturization of atomic warheads. By the mid-1950s, huge, specially designed field guns enabled U.S. troops in Europe to fire shells with the same explosive yield as the bomb that destroyed Hiroshima. Had Soviet forces ever crossed the West German border, this artillery would have been used to obliterate their rearguard—along with millions of civilians. Moreover, rather than make an unaffordable investment in conventional forces, Britain and France also opted to concentrate on nuclear arms. In the absence of sufficient conventional forces to repel an invading Soviet army, the use of so-called tactical nuclear weapons was the principal arrow in NATO's quiver. First strike was first response.

The USSR, however, itself exploded a hydrogen bomb in 1954 and was catching up with the Americans in missile technology. The launching into orbit of Sputnik, a small communications satellite, on 4 October 1957, came as a bolt from the blue in Washington, since it seemingly showed that the USSR had developed the technical means to launch intercontinental missiles against American cities. The United States' fortunate geographic position, which hitherto had sheltered it from Soviet bombers, ceased to be a guarantee of homeland safety.

As it happened, this Soviet threat was more rhetorical than real (the USSR did not develop an advanced intercontinental ballistic missile capability until the late 1960s), but that did not stop Soviet leader Khrushchev from threatening to use his arsenal of destruction against the West. There were moments in Khrushchev's career when his interlocutors, including his Kremlin colleagues, must have feared that they were dealing with, if not exactly a madman, then certainly an overhasty bully who did not think issues through.

The centrality of nuclear weapons for strategic planning alarmed West Europeans, who began to fear for the survival of their civilization. The 1958–1962 Berlin Crisis, when Khrushchev's brinkmanship and Ulbricht's unremitting pressure for a harder Soviet line risked provoking catastrophe for Europe as a whole, was the spark that could have set off a conflagration. Had the Soviets and their East Germans ever lived up to their threats, and incorporated Berlin into the GDR, then the danger of a nuclear exchange would have become real.

For this reason, British Premier Harold Macmillan, despite having been a staunch critic of appeasement during the 1930s, tried assiduously to find a negotiated solution with the Russians. Macmillan had no intention of fighting a third world war for the sake of West Germany's amour-propre. This was important since the Kennedy administration listened closely to what he and the British government had to say. Adenauer was disenchanted by "Anglo-Saxon" insensitivity to West German principles during the Berlin crisis, and this led him to draw closer to French President Charles de Gaulle, who was stauncher in Germany's support.

THE TWO GERMANIES

West Germany was founded in May 1949. By 1955, as we have seen, it had become a sovereign state. It was a member of the WEU and NATO and was constructing an army to fulfill its role in those organizations. It was a founder member of the European Coal and Steel Community (ECSC) and was constructively involved between June 1955 and March 1957 in the negotiations that led to the signature of the two Treaties of Rome instituting the European Economic Community (EEC) and the European Atomic Community (Euratom).[1] Bonn's willingness to open its agricultural market to French competition and to pay for part of the costs of development of France and Belgium's colonies in Africa made the EEC Treaty possible. It is too reductive to say that the EEC amounted to "a Franco-German condominium, in which Bonn underwrote the Community's finances and Paris dictated its policies . . . the French 'Europeanized' their farm subsidies and transfers, without paying the price of a loss of sovereignty," but this formulation does capture the centrality of West Germany's role in the negotiations and highlights the significance of Bonn's relationship with Paris.[2] The first president of the European Commission, the body charged by the EEC Treaty with transforming the economies of Belgium, France, Italy, Luxembourg, the Netherlands, and West Germany into a single market, was Walter Hallstein, a senior official in the West German foreign ministry since 1951 and a close advisor to Adenauer. The "Hallstein doctrine," formulated in 1955, was a keystone of West German foreign policy. In substance, it stated that Bonn would extend no diplomatic recognition to any state that itself recognized the GDR as an independent nation. The appointment of such a high-profile individual was hence a striking confirmation of West Germany's integration into the West since 1949.

West Germany was willing to compromise with France over agriculture and over the political leadership of the EEC because its leaders knew that German industry would benefit from freer West European trade and the creation of a larger market—the raison d'être of the EEC Treaty. The German *Wirtschaftswunder* (economic miracle) was in full swing by the time the EEC came into operation. Under the leadership of Adenauer's economics minister, Ludwig Erhard, an ardent free trader, Bonn was constructing an innovative form of welfare state capitalism. Unlike Britain, where the Labour Party had nationalized the "commanding heights" of the economy, or France, where state planning of industry was the norm, the West German state limited its involvement in the marketplace. Business could freely set prices and wage levels and drive investment. Cartels were dismantled and taxes cut. The result of these pro-market principles was a surge in economic growth that outpaced even West Germany's booming neighbors. Overall output grew by over 8 percent per year in the first half of the 1950s and by 7 percent per year between 1955 and 1958. The EEC gave a further spur to growth in the early 1960s as German companies exported industrial manufactures to its community partners.

As in Japan and Korea in the 1960s and 1970s, and China today, such a rate of increase in economic activity meant that ordinary families could suddenly afford cars, telephones, refrigerators, and other appurtenances of the consumer society. Car production increased *twenty-sevenfold* between 1949 and 1966. The increase in growth also meant the elimination of joblessness. In the immediate postwar years, unemployment, boosted by the flood of refugees from the East, had been high. By the end of the 1950s, companies were employing "guest workers" from southern Europe since there were not enough local workers to staff the assembly lines. High growth also meant that Bonn could enact legislation that "soon made the Federal Republic into one of the world's most elaborate and encompassing welfare states."[3] German workers enjoyed pension rights and levels of worker protection that were the envy of the industrialized world. Workers were, moreover, given exceptional power in the management of larger firms. The 1952 Factory Constitution Law obliged all joint stock corporations to set aside one-third of the seats on their supervisory boards (i.e., the board of directors) for representatives of the workers and established "works' councils" to help manage industrial relations in smaller companies.

The visible improvements in the prosperity and social rights of ordinary German workers were a development of great significance in the Cold War. The essence of the communist claim against capitalism was that it *inevitably* led to slumps, unemployment, and impoverishment and that capitalist economies could not evolve democratically, but only through revolution. The postwar boom proved Marx to be wrong and hence eroded the chief theoretical justification for communist rule. In 1959, at Bad Godesberg, this ideological development was symbolized by the German Social Democrat Party's (SPD) explicit rejection of Marxist dogma. The SPD adopted a party program that stressed that the construction of a socially responsible market economy and a strong welfare state were the party's primary goals. The SPD completed its break from the intellectual legacy of Kurt Schumacher (who had died in 1952) by becoming a supporter of the process of European integration and of the western alliance.[4]

The SPD went down this path after it had been heavily defeated by Adenauer's CDU-CSU coalition in both the 1953 and 1957 elections. But its willingness to rethink its ideology was a sign of democratic vitality, of placing electoral competition ahead of doctrinal purity. Such signs were, in fact, everywhere. Almost 90 percent of the electorate voted in the 1957 poll; parliamentary institutions were esteemed; extremist parties of the left and right failed to get a foothold in the Bundestag (although in 1956, the Communist Party was banned), and the "Bonn state"—as GDR propaganda dubbed it—boasted a high caliber of free political debate in the media. A new generation of politicians was also emerging, notably the charismatic SPD mayor of West Berlin, Willy Brandt, and the young, dynamic, defense minister, Franz-Josef Strauss. Critics, especially two future Nobel Prize winners, Heinrich Böll and Günter Grass, could point to the crassness of the new Germany and complain that there was a selective amnesia about the country's Nazi past. But overall Bonn's democratic progress was undeniable.

The GDR, by contrast, was a Stalinist outpost. The economy of the socialist half of Germany also grew rapidly in the mid-1950s, despite not having the assistance of Marshall Plan aid. But the citizens of the GDR benefited little from economic reconstruction. Compulsory savings rates were high, as the state gathered resources for investment in heavy industrial production and in prestige projects: "Only by extracting a maximum of labor at the lowest cost in terms of consumer goods could the regime realize its goal of rapid, bootstrap industrialization."[5] Domestic consumption, especially housing, was neglected. The well-stocked supermarkets and neon signs of the new cities of West Germany were unknown. East Berlin boasted the imposing *Stalinallee*, but there were few cars to drive along it, and they mostly belonged to the party *nomenklatura*. Agriculture was partly collectivized, in the face of tenacious resistance from the peasants. Shortages were accordingly widespread, while imported foodstuffs were a rarity since foreign exchange was spent only on essentials, not frivolities like oranges and bananas.

All political competition had been abolished by the mid-1950s. In 1948 and 1949, in keeping with developments in the rest of the Soviet bloc, the SED was Stalinized. Former Social Democrats were compelled to bow to the Moscow line, and the party's functionaries were subjected to intensified ideological training. A witch hunt began against alleged bourgeois deviationists, Titoists, Zionists, and West German spies. While the GDR did not experience the bloodthirsty purges that characterized socialist development in Hungary, Romania, or Czechoslovakia, the atmosphere within the GDR was nevertheless distinctly Orwellian. As in *1984*, "nobody was kept under closer scrutiny than members of the SED itself." Party members were encouraged to spy on one another, report dubious remarks made by comrades or relatives, and show ideological "vigilance." Most denunciations were "petty and spiteful," and "individuals prone to exaggerated suspicions were . . . able to indulge their vendettas and wreak revenge on those who had crossed them."[6]

A giant state security apparatus, the so-called Stasi, was erected to investigate the ideologically suspect and to hunt for spies. Formally established in February 1950, the Stasi employed nine thousand people by 1955, not counting its tens of thousands of informers. Its official mission was "preventing or throttling at the earliest stages—by whatever means necessary—all attempts to delay or to hinder the victory of socialism." To this end it spread like a "cancer" through East German society, ensuring that its informers were present in every church congregation, block of flats, army unit, educational institute, and factory workshop in the country. Its activities were far more widespread, equally above the law, and of greater sophistication than Hitler's Gestapo.[7]

The SED, moreover, occupied the political system. Elections were a farce. Citizens could vote for a slate of candidates chosen in advance by the SED leadership upon which representatives of the SED, its controlled organizations, and four other carefully monitored political parties (the CDU, the Liberals, the Farmers Party, and the National Democrats) were listed. A negative vote had to be cast publicly, in effect transforming it into an open act of rebellion. Abstention was not easy either. Entire workplaces were marched to the voting booth to do their patriotic duty. Unsurprisingly, electoral turnout was usually over 95 percent and the official candidates tended to be elected by 99 percent margins. The Parliament was, in any case, a rubber stamp for decisions of the government, which was in its turn a conduit for decisions taken by the party's organs. Walter Ulbricht, the party secretary, not Otto Grotewohl, the premier, was the key figure in the GDR.

Unlike Hungarians or Czechs, however, East Germans had an escape route from the nightmare of everyday Stalinism. They could, at the cost of abandoning their homes and loved ones, literally take a bus to freedom by crossing into the western zones of Berlin. In 1952 through 1953, as the SED intensified collectivization and industrialization and as the witch hunt against deviant elements reached its peak, East Germans began to flee in large numbers. Nearly 200,000 GDR citizens left the country in 1952; 331,000 did so in 1953. Together, this was more than 3 percent of the population. The refugees, moreover, were mostly trained citizens whom the communist state could least afford to lose: communist dogma was no substitute for a university diploma when it came to the operating table or building a bridge.

The exodus persuaded the SED leadership to mitigate the rigor of its policies. After Stalin's demise, the party-state relaxed repression against the middle classes, farmers, and the Christian churches. It did not, however, rescind increased production norms for factory workers implemented in May 1953. On 17 June 1953, the workers of Berlin and other cities rose in revolt. Two days of street fighting followed until the revolt was crushed by Soviet troops with the loss (according to official figures) of twenty-one lives. A reign of terror followed in which hundreds were jailed, interned in labor camps, or hanged. The regime's propaganda blamed counter-revolutionary elements for the uprising and warned the citizens that they might forfeit the party's confidence. This was too gross even for the dramatist Bertolt Brecht, who was the most prominent intellectual associated with the Ulbricht regime. Brecht asked ironically, in a poem circulated to trusted friends, whether it would not be easier for the government "to dissolve the people and elect another."[8]

Brecht's remark illustrated the essence of the German problem. Politically divided Germany was a laboratory for "two experiments as to which model of society and government could best satisfy the material, spiritual and national needs of the German people."[9] As early as the mid-1950s, despite the many intellectuals and party members whose support for the regime was rooted in genuine idealism, and who believed that the GDR would, over time, evolve a superior form of society to its western counterpart, it was clear that the ordinary citizens of the GDR preferred the West to the socialist paradise being constructed on their behalf. The Ulbricht regime was detested by its own people. Ulbricht only survived 1956 as a result of a fortuitous—for him—combination of circumstances. Khrushchev's personal support, the lack of a Nagy or Gomułka figure within the SED's ranks, and a cowed East German population whose educated young had fled, or were thinking of fleeing, to the West, enabled him to hang on as leader. There was, in fact, a surge in East German asylum seekers in the second half of 1956, with some 280,000 people fleeing the country in the year as a whole: more refugees than left Hungary during the Soviet invasion. Nevertheless, unless the anomaly of Berlin was resolved, the fear that the regime might implode, with unpredictable consequences for peace in Europe, could not be allayed. But resolving the question of what to do with Berlin was a puzzle that admitted no easy solution.

THE BALANCE OF TERROR

Divided Germany was also a huge armed camp by the mid-1950s. On both sides of the border, armies pointed weaponry of unprecedented destructive power at one other. The USSR stationed five army corps in the GDR—as many as 380,000 men—and these troops were backed by the German *Nationale Volksarmee* (NVA), which was integrated into the Soviet command structure. The Soviet force in East Germany possessed powerful offensive capacities: its tank divisions were equipped with the T-34 battle tank and with the JS-3 (Joseph Stalin) heavy tank, a forty-six-ton monster "able to defeat any NATO tank."[10] In 1954, the T-54 medium tank, with its innovative design and 100mm gun, was added to the Warsaw Pact's armored forces. Soviet tank units were backed up by well-equipped artillery, motorized infantry, and airborne and engineering units that reinforced their ability to penetrate enemy defenses. Advancing Soviet troops could be protected from the air by MiG-17 fighter bombers capable of carrying a 500kg bomb load over a combat radius of 700km.

NATO generals assumed that Soviet forces would attack along several main fronts: along the Baltic coast and into Jutland; toward Hamburg; across the North German plain toward the Ruhr industrial zone and Mannheim; through Bavaria toward Stuttgart; and from Czechoslovakia in a pincer movement to surround Munich. Against such Soviet penetration NATO could field, by 1957, a five-division German conscript army, which would increase in size to twelve divisions by the early 1960s; three British armored divisions backed up by a Dutch army corps to defend northern Germany; the First French Army in southern Germany. Two U.S. army corps were stationed in the center of West Germany and Bavaria. British and American troops were equipped with the (excellent) Centurion and Pershing tanks, but not in numbers that could have rebuffed battle-hardened Soviet troops.

NATO forces were thus outnumbered and underequipped in conventional weapons. This point is crucial. There can be no doubt that had Soviet forces attacked, most of West Germany would have fallen under their control within days, absent a nuclear response by the West. Indeed, in the early 1950s, this had been the NATO planners' assumption. As early as 1954, however, American policy makers knew that in the event of a general war, "America would win, and the Soviet Union would be utterly destroyed."[11]

The reason for this confidence was the immense superiority achieved by NATO in miniaturizing nuclear weaponry. From 1952, U.S. artillery units in Germany were equipped with 280mm "atomic cannons" capable of firing the W19 shell just over 30 kilometers. The W19 exploded with a "yield" (i.e., explosive force) equivalent to the bomb dropped on Hiroshima in August 1945. Also in 1952, short-range Corporal missiles were deployed: these cumbersome weapons had a range of approximately 140 kilometers and a warhead with a yield of 60 kilotons: Hiroshima multiplied by four. The more mobile, truck-launched "Honest John" missile had a range of 6 to 38 kilometers and a 10-kiloton yield. Great Britain, which had exploded its first A-bomb in October 1952, also contributed to NATO's theater nuclear superiority. The bulky "Blue Danube" bomb, with a 20-kiloton yield, was developed by November 1953 and would have been used on bombing missions over Germany and Central Europe in the event of war. Cash-strapped Britain managed to maintain seven squadrons of jet bombers capable of carrying a nuclear payload.

Such tactical nuclear weapons would have been used to blast advancing Soviet tank forces and their supply links. They would unquestionably have wreaked massive damage. Germany's cities had been destroyed between 1942 and 1945 by the Anglo-American strategic bombing campaign. Yet a single W19 shell contained as much explosive power as a 1,000-bomber raid. A 1955 NATO planning exercise called "Carte Blanche" wargamed a Soviet attack on Western Europe in which 355 tactical nuclear weapons were employed, for the most part on German soil. The staff officers conducting

"Carte Blanche" concluded that 1.5 million to 1.7 million civilians would die and another 3.5 million would be wounded *in the first two days of battle.* Other deaths would follow from radiation sickness, burns, and exposure.[12]

But NATO strategy did not merely envisage using battlefield weapons. The United States had conducted a massive buildup of its strategic bombing force since the outbreak of the Korean War. The B-47 bomber, first deployed in 1950, was a qualitative leap in aviation technology: more than a thousand were built in the 1950s and many were based in the United Kingdom, within striking range of the USSR. The even more advanced B-52, which was capable of carrying eight nuclear bombs, was deployed from 1955 onward. These bombers had plenty of ordnance to carry: the stockpile of U.S. strategic weapons increased from 170, with a total yield of 4.19 megatons (i.e., 4.19 *million* tons), in 1949 to 2,123, with a yield of more than 9 *billion* tons by 1956.[13] The gigantic increase in yield reflected the increase in destructive potential generated by the detonation of the thermonuclear bomb (H-Bomb) on 31 October 1952.

President Eisenhower's strategic thinking was embodied in NATO planning document MC48, which was approved by the North Atlantic Council on 17 December 1954, and envisaged any attack on Western Europe being answered by systematic bombing, using thermonuclear devices, on the nuclear capacity, physical infrastructure, and industrial cities of the USSR. Once it was "clear" that the Soviets were to blame, "America and her allies had to open up with everything they had."[14] This did not necessarily mean waiting to be attacked. Indeed, MC48 entailed preemptive strikes to ensure that the ground war did not even begin. Once the NATO commanding officer (between 1953 and 1956, General Alfred Gruenther) was sure that a Soviet assault was imminent, he could, after consultations with the president, have authorized the B-52s to fly. In December 1956, NATO modified the strategic doctrine embodied in MC48 to give emphasis to its "shield," that is, its conventional forces, which, it was underlined, were to be the first instrument of resort in the event of Soviet incursions into Alliance territory, but outright invasion would still have been met with NATO's "sword," that is to say, recourse to so-called massive retaliation.

The principal West European powers colluded in this buildup of American power in Europe, since it freed them from having to choose between guns and butter. This was particularly the case for France, which was embroiled in an expensive colonial war in Algeria, and Britain, which possessed a far-flung empire full of trouble spots like Aden, Cyprus, and Malaya. British defense spending was second only to the United States' in the 1950s, as a percentage of national output. However, European leaders were acutely conscious of the cession of national sovereignty that they had made. In effect, they had handed over the sacred trust of national defense to the president of the United States and given him a blank check to reduce much of the continent to a smoking ruin.

Moreover, who could be sure that future U.S. presidents would even cash the check? As one leading European statesman argued, once the USSR had developed its own capacity to strike at the U.S. homeland, "it was unimaginable that the two rivals would ever come to blows except as a last resort."[15] Rather than risk nuclear destruction, a future U.S. president might leave Western Europe in the lurch. This is why the Soviet achievement of sending Sputnik into space signified more than an impressive feat of aeronautical engineering. Washington discovered, to the dismay of its allies, that the Soviet Union could build intercontinental ballistic missiles (ICBMs) and thus rob the United States of its territorial immunity. A panicky NATO drew the conclusion that yet more alliance firepower was necessary and authorized the installation of Jupiter intermediate-range missiles in Italy and Turkey in December 1957.

Even without ICBMs, the USSR possessed a nuclear strike force of imposing power. It could have supported its advancing troops with battlefield nuclear weapons in Germany (SS-1, or "Scud" missiles) and struck at other targets in Western Europe with its substantial bomber forces and array of intermediate range missiles. The USSR exploded an H-Bomb just months after the United States (in August 1953), and thermonuclear weapons were available to Soviet forces by 1956. The blast from a single Soviet one megaton bomb (i.e., a device with seventy to eighty times the explosive force of the bomb dropped on Hiroshima) would have literally obliterated the British industrial city of Birmingham, along with its 1.8 million inhabitants, and spread highly toxic fallout over an area of some four hundred to five hundred square kilometers.[16]

Accordingly, both Britain and France sought to construct their own independent nuclear deterrents. Britain spent lavishly to develop a ballistic missile called "Blue Streak" that would have been capable of hitting targets in the USSR. France, which was well behind in the nuclear race, wanted a *force de frappe* of its own (it exploded its first atomic bomb only in February 1960 on the eve of a visit to Paris from Khrushchev). Even Chancellor Adenauer harbored unrealistic hopes of possessing a West German deterrent. From 1958, the *Bundeswehr* (German armed forces) were equipped with tactical nuclear weapons (although the warheads remained under nominal American control), but Adenauer, despite West Germany's obligations under the WEU Treaty, chafed at not possessing the bomb.

President Eisenhower broadly sympathized with the Europeans' desire to control their own defense destiny. He considered that it was morally right that the Europeans should exercise sovereignty over their own defense, and in the late 1950s that meant possessing strategic nuclear arms. Had it not been for the 1946 Atomic Energy Act, which banned the United States from sharing nuclear secrets, Eisenhower might have armed the Europeans with U.S. weapons; as it was, his administration permitted de facto European control of tactical nuclear weapons and also encouraged the Europeans to take charge of their strategic destiny via NATO, by strengthening the European role in the alliance. In May 1958, Great Britain was given privileged access to U.S. nuclear secrets.

This was not good enough for Charles de Gaulle, the great war leader who returned to power in Paris in May–June 1958 amid the turmoil caused by the Algerian War. De Gaulle, whose mission was the restoration of France as a great power, was determined to renounce the "Atlantic docility" that had characterized French foreign policy during his absence from power. This meant acquiring "modern means of deterrence" and exercising national control over them.[17] De Gaulle immediately discarded an ongoing German-Italian-French plan to construct weapons together and intensified the French government's atomic research and development plans.

In September 1958, the General imperiously wrote to Eisenhower and Macmillan to question France's status in NATO. De Gaulle argued that the worldwide responsibilities of France, and its status as a soon-to-be-nuclear power, made it imperative that Paris should be admitted to the inner sanctum of NATO decision making, along with Britain. The alliance should be under "triple, not dual direction." When Eisenhower and Macmillan evaded his demand, de Gaulle quickly took steps to reduce France's commitment to the alliance. The French Mediterranean fleet was removed from NATO control in March 1959, and the Americans were prohibited from deploying tactical nuclear weapons on French soil.

The desire of West European governments to enter the nuclear arms club was controversial, especially in West Germany and Great Britain. The British Campaign for Nuclear Disarmament (CND) was launched by intellectuals associated with an influential political magazine, the *New Statesman and Nation*. In November 1957, the paper published an article called "Britain and the Nuclear Bombs," by J. B. Priestley, a best-selling novelist, who called for the abolition of nuclear weapons and for unilateral disarmament by Britain itself, irrespective of what other nations did. Rather than join an arms race, Priestley argued, Britain should take the moral lead in world politics, as it had so often done in the past. "Alone, we defied Hitler; and alone we can defy this nuclear madness into which the spirit of Hitler seems to have passed, to poison the world," Priestly exclaimed.[18]

On 17 February 1958, CND's inaugural meeting was held in London. The star speaker was a diplomatic historian, A. J. P. Taylor, whose scholarship had left him convinced that great wars could and usually did break out by accident. Taylor, after describing in gory detail what the effects of a thermonuclear explosion would be, asked rhetorically, "Is there anyone here who would like to do this to another human being?" Taylor broke the hushed silence that followed these words by saying, "Then why are we making the damned thing?" When the meeting ended, much of the overwhelmingly professional middle-class audience marched on the prime minister's residence in Downing Street and shouted "murderer" until the police arrived and used attack dogs to disperse them.[19]

Under the leadership of Kingsley Martin, the *New Statesman*'s editor; Taylor; and a committee of Britain's liberal establishment, CND subsequently organized mass demonstrations, notably the annual marches between London and Aldermaston, the research center where Britain's fissionable material was made. The movement split in 1960 over the question of civil disobedience. Against the wishes of the movement's founders, the "Committee of 100," whose figurehead was the philosopher Bertrand Russell, organized sit-ins and other illegal protests, most notably in September 1961 during the Berlin crisis when over a thousand people, including the eighty-nine-year-old Russell, were arrested in London's Trafalgar Square. Certainly, an inept remark by Foreign Secretary Lord Home, to the effect that "the British people are prepared to be blown to atomic dust if necessary," gave fresh impetus to the Committee's protests.[20] There was a limit to the stoicism even of the British.

The opposition Labour Party was deeply divided over the question of whether Britain should possess the H-Bomb. Priestley's *New Statesman* article was written in response to a statement made by Aneurin Bevan, Labour's spokesman on foreign affairs, at the party conference in October 1957. Bevan broke with his supporters on the left of the party by pleading with opponents of the British deterrent not to send him "naked into the conference chamber," without an H-Bomb as a bargaining chip. He added, brutally, that his unilateralist opponents' reasoning was a mere "emotional spasm."[21] Labour's leaders reluctantly shared the Macmillan government's view that terrible though nuclear weapons were, Britain would count for nothing in the world unless it had them. This is why, in Britain, resistance to nuclear weapons was predominately a question for civil society, not a party political affair.

In West Germany, by contrast, protests against nuclear weapons were actually led by the SPD, which launched its cheerily named "Campaign Against Atomic Death" (KdA) in early 1958, in conjunction with the founding of CND, though the two movements had only sporadic contacts. The two movements also used different rhetorical strategies. Whereas many CND supporters followed Priestley by suggesting that Britain would be living up to its liberal tradition by pressing for unilateral disarmament, German peace activists "had an entirely negative view of the past." "Everything which was wrong about the German past, everything which we can identify as the aberration of German history, blossoms again [in West German rearmament]," or so the protesters averred. The KdA added the potent thought that in the event of a nuclear war, "the German people on both sides of the border zones will be certain victims of nuclear death. There is no protection against it."[22]

The SPD-led campaign demanded that the West German government renounce any intention of possessing nuclear arms and support the institution of a nuclear weapons-free zone in central Europe, a stance that was confirmed in the 1959 Bad Godesberg program. SPD-controlled cities announced plans to hold referendums on the continuation of U.S. military bases in West Germany, but the Adenauer government successfully argued before the courts that such polls infringed its constitutional right to conduct foreign policy. Only in 1960 did the SPD evolve a less neutralist foreign policy, one that turned upon reinforcing the West's conventional military strength so that nuclear weapons need not be used and the risk of nuclear conflict would diminish.

By then, the antinuclear movement in Germany had lost momentum as a result of the renewal of the Berlin crisis after November 1958, which forcefully reminded German citizens that "there were real and immediate risks to a policy of disarmament."[23] It should be added, however, that the principal weakness of the case for nuclear deterrence was also on show during the crisis. The reliance on nuclear weapons for the defense of the West was based upon the premise that no communist leader would be so irrational as to risk certain destruction by engaging in military adventurism. Khrushchev's erratic behavior during the Berlin crisis cast doubt over this proposition. Despite being well aware that the Soviet Union's vaunted strength in missiles was nonsense, "he mounted a reckless foreign policy on a fragile fiction of superiority."[24]

THE BERLIN WALL

Khrushchev launched the second Berlin crisis on 10 November 1958. Speaking in Moscow, the Soviet leader claimed that the West, by establishing West Germany and rearming it, had violated the Potsdam Agreement. Since the fact of German division could not now be gainsaid, Khrushchev argued that the time had come to eliminate Berlin's anomalous status as an allied-occupied city, which was the source of "subversive" West German and American propaganda and a base for espionage by the western powers (this last charge, of course, was true enough; Berlin, along with Vienna, was spy central for both sides during the Cold War). So far as the USSR was concerned, Khrushchev warned, Berlin was the capital city of the sovereign GDR. Within six months, he added, the Soviet occupation forces would yield all authority over border crossings, land communications, and air space to the only rightful authority, the East German government. If the West refused to acknowledge the GDR's sovereign right to control its own territory, or contravened any restrictions that the GDR might enforce on freedom of movement in Berlin, the USSR would honor its obligations to its Warsaw Pact ally. If that meant general war, Khrushchev implied, so be it.

The Soviet Union followed up Khrushchev's speech with diplomatic notes to the three occupation powers in Berlin and to Bonn advocating a new regime for Germany. The two Germanies should be united in a confederation—a demand that the Soviet leader well knew would be rejected—and the wartime allies should sign a peace treaty with both nations. The western zones of Berlin would become a "demilitarized free city" "within the structure of the state in which it resides," that is, the GDR. The free city would be self-governing, but would not be allowed to conduct, or permit, hostile or subversive activity against the GDR or "any other state." The goal, obviously, was to neuter what was shortly destined to become "West Berlin" as a symbol for the peoples of East Germany, by making access to it more difficult and by curbing freedom of speech and political activity within the western zones.

In January 1959, the Soviet government further proposed that it would call a peace conference, to which the two Germanies would be invited, to settle the issue of the international standing of the German confederation, should it be formed. Germany should withdraw from the Atlantic Pact and the Warsaw Treaty; it should possess self-defense forces only; it should be prohibited from unification with Austria; all foreign troops should withdraw from German territory. Germany's borders should be the ones that had emerged at the end of the war, which implied accepting that the current Polish border was a permanent fact.

Khrushchev, of course, knew that he would not get everything he asked for. Rather, he was hoping to get a deal that would at least confer recognition on the GDR, fix the border with Poland, and terminate free Berlin's ability to act as a magnet for the people of East Germany. This last was certainly Walter Ulbricht's priority. East Germans were still streaming to the West, undermining the regime's ability to construct a functioning modern society. Indeed, it has even been argued that the Ulbricht tail was wagging the Soviet dog throughout the crisis, by reminding the Soviet leader of how much the communist cause stood to lose if the GDR collapsed.[25]

The West was faced with a set of demands that was wholly unacceptable to the Bonn government. Recognition of East German sovereignty and of the existing eastern border with Poland, disarmament and withdrawal of U.S. troops, and confederation with a communist regime were all anathema for Adenauer, who urged his allies to stand firm at all costs. On the other hand, Bonn was petrified at the thought of conflict. By the end of 1958, the West German government grasped that Germany—East and West—would cease to be a functioning civilization if war broke out. At bottom, Adenauer was prepared to make concessions over Berlin, so long as West Germany was not forced into unification with the GDR and so long as it could remain a member of NATO, and not be reduced to neutrality and military impotence. But he was strongly against concessions being given too quickly. De Gaulle was in fundamental agreement with the German chancellor. The General did not desire a united Germany (he reputedly said that he loved Germany so much he was glad there were two of them), but was adamant that West Germany's integration into the West had to be preserved. Above all, he thought Khrushchev was bluffing. The Soviet leader would back off if the West stood up to him, de Gaulle assured his allies.

De Gaulle certainly stood up to the Russians himself. When the Soviet ambassador to France took a leaf from his master's copybook and began threatening de Gaulle with the consequences of nuclear war for France, de Gaulle proved predictably immune to intimidation: "Well, my dear ambassador, we shall all have to die, but so will you."[26]

The British government was the weak link in the chain of the West's resolve. Premier Harold Macmillan had little love for the Germans, against whom he had fought in two world wars, and not much esteem for Adenauer (a disdain that was reciprocated), whose judgment he distrusted. The Americans, Macmillan thought, were allowing Bonn's tail to wag the American dog. As the sand trickled out on Khrushchev's six-month deadline, Macmillan decided in February 1959 to make a personal mission to Moscow to gauge what the Soviet leadership was thinking. Adenauer, for one, reacted with rage and contempt at what he saw as Macmillan's opportunistic behavior.[27] U.S. reaction was lukewarm at best—both Eisenhower and Dulles worried, unimaginatively, that Macmillan was imitating prewar premier Neville Chamberlain's peace missions to Hitler.

In Moscow, the British leader experienced Khrushchev at his most mercurial. The visit, which began on 21 February and lasted nearly two weeks, was marred throughout by Khrushchev's touchiness and bullying.[28] But, when Macmillan opened the door to negotiations on the German question, the Soviet leader became less belligerent. He waived his deadline for recognition of the GDR—to the disgust of Ulbricht. Macmillan's journey, for all the criticism that was leveled at it, did break the ice that had accumulated since November 1958.

A period of relative détente began. The foreign ministers of the four wartime allies (including Christian Herter in the place of Dulles, who had died in April 1959) met in Geneva between 11 May and the beginning of August 1959. In these marathon negotiations, the West made a bold response to the Russian January demands. The three western powers proposed that Berlin should become a self-governing city after free elections held under quadripartite or UNO supervision. Thereafter, a mixed committee composed of twenty-five West German and ten GDR delegates should be given the task of coordinating the integration of the two Germanies for a period of up to two and half years, at the end of which free all-German elections to a Constituent Assembly would be held. The new all-German government that emerged from the elections would have "full freedom of decision with regard to internal and external affairs"; would abide by the 1954 West German renunciation of chemical, biological, and nuclear weapons; and would take part in a peace conference at which, by mutual accord, a security pact for Europe, which would involve the withdrawal of "non-indigenous" troops from agreed areas of Central Europe, would be signed.[29]

The Soviet negotiator, Foreign Minister Gromyko, said *nyet* to these proposals, presumably because they reiterated the West's perennial demand that Germany should be reunited after free elections. They nevertheless represented a generous offer. Given the preponderance of socialists in East Germany, it was unlikely, for instance, that the Christian Democrat-Liberal coalition that had governed West Germany since 1949 would have won all-German elections. One critic destined for future greatness affirmed that the "Western 'package' plan" had "gone dangerously far" in the direction of a solution that "may lay the basis for the Soviet domination of all of Germany."[30]

The Soviet stalling did not derail détente. Khrushchev made his celebrated tour of the United States in September 1959, when he charmed ordinary citizens, marveled at American farms, and argued furiously with Americans who exercised free speech and condemned Soviet actions in Budapest and elsewhere. An encounter with Eisenhower, while characterized by the Soviet leader's eccentricities, led to an invitation to the American president to visit the USSR. A Paris summit of the four wartime allies was arranged for mid-May 1960 in Paris. The future of Germany was placed on the agenda.

It was a false dawn. At the beginning of May 1960, a U-2 spy plane flown by Captain Gary Powers was shot down over the USSR. When it transpired that the White House had authorized Powers's mission, Khrushchev felt betrayed by his new friend Eisenhower. Livid, the Soviet leader attended the Paris summit only to demand an apology from Eisenhower. The apology was not forthcoming. Eisenhower's tour of the USSR was canceled, and Europe was abruptly reminded, yet again, how much its future depended upon the whims, the egocentricities, the errors, and the strategic posturing of the two superpowers. De Gaulle was confirmed in his deep conviction that Western Europe had to start taking responsibility for its own affairs. If Western Europe could achieve unity of purpose, and possession of its own deterrence, it could begin a unilateral policy of détente with the Russians "from the Atlantic to the Urals" and achieve greater security through negotiation and the superseding of NATO. These heretical thoughts would make the French leader persona non grata in Washington before too long.

Khrushchev, who was under pressure from the Chinese for the ideological unorthodoxy of his détente with so-called U.S. imperialism, spent the fall of

1960 burnishing his Marxist credentials by attending the UNO in New York and attacking colonialism. He placed the Berlin question on the backburner until the U.S. presidential elections had concluded. The narrow election of J. F. Kennedy, who proceeded to blot his copy book almost immediately by the tragicomic failed invasion of the Bay of Pigs in Cuba in April 1961, was seen as a golden opportunity by the USSR to get its way over Berlin.

Khrushchev, like Adenauer, perceived the new president to be young and indecisive. When the two men first met, at Vienna on 4 June 1961, an inadequately briefed Kennedy received the same kind of verbal hazing as Khrushchev had meted out to Macmillan in February 1959. At Vienna, Khrushchev essentially insisted—and in this respect, his position was reasonable—that Kennedy should look at the German question from the Soviet point of view. Germany had killed tens of millions of Soviet citizens and ravaged the whole of Eastern Europe. It had to be curbed permanently. Yet, thanks to the United States:

> Now Germany, the country which unleashed World War II, has again acquired military power and has assumed a predominant position in NATO. Its generals hold high offices in that organization. This constitutes a threat of World War III which would be even more devastating than World War II.

Khrushchev thus asserted that it was not possible to have détente between the superpowers until a peace treaty ending World War II and extinguishing the hopes of West German "revanchists" had been signed. This meant recognition of the fact that two Germanies now existed: "A united Germany is not practical because the Germans themselves do not want it."

Actually, of course, Ulbricht and the SED leadership did not want it. The sheer numbers of people in the GDR voting with their feet amply proved that the desire for unity was strong among the ordinary citizens of the GDR. The Soviet position was unreasonable insofar as Khrushchev was openly asking the West, as the price of better relations between the two blocs, formally to divide Germany against the wishes of its inhabitants. It was a step that Kennedy could not take without losing all prestige with his allies. "No one would have any confidence in U.S. commitments and pledges," Kennedy pointed out.[31] Both men were constrained, in other words, by the preferences of their respective German constituencies.

There was a second unreasonable aspect to the Soviet position. As in 1958–1959, Khrushchev warned at Vienna that he would sign a separate agreement with the GDR that would leave the western zones of Berlin as an enclave dependent upon the GDR's goodwill for access to the West. In effect, the USSR was saying that if *it* voluntarily surrendered its occupation rights over Berlin to the East German state, then there was no reason why the other allies should not do the same. At bottom, this position was a legacy of the war. Khrushchev believed that since hundreds of thousands of Russians had died to capture Berlin, the USSR ought to have a greater say than the other allies in deciding its fate. Their rights existed only on Soviet sufferance.

When Kennedy duly warned Khrushchev not to risk a "miscalculation" that might lead to war, the Soviet chief took violent offence: a reaction that only confirmed Kennedy's fears that he was dealing with someone who might indeed push the envelope too hard if he were provoked. Since the U.S. president was being advised by Dean Acheson, the former secretary of state under Truman, who wanted to respond to any Soviet recognition of East Germany by sending a tank division along the highway to reinforce the garrison in Berlin, this was useful knowledge. In the months that followed, Kennedy followed a cautious strategy, similar to that being recommended by the British, of standing firm on what were called at the time the "three essentials:" an allied military presence in Berlin, freedom of movement throughout the city for accredited western diplomats, and the liberty of the citizens of Berlin *within the western zones*.

Khrushchev went public with his demands in the days following the Vienna summit, insisting that he would sign a peace treaty with the GDR by the end of the year. Ulbricht upped the ante at a press conference on 15 June 1961, by attacking the West for engaging in "trade in human beings" (i.e., helping asylum seekers) and warning that this practice would be terminated once East Germany had full control over its own borders—although he also lied that "no one has any intention of building a wall."

The result was predictable. Khrushchev and Ulbricht's post-Vienna blustering led to what the mayor of West Berlin, the SPD's chancellor candidate Willy Brandt, described as a "mass exodus" from East Germany.[32] Tens of thousands of desperate people realized that it was now, or perhaps never. More than thirty thousand people fled to the West in July. The socialist half of Germany was risking death by hemorrhage of its most qualified citizens. If it was to survive, it had to do something.

The something was the Wall. A summit meeting of the Warsaw Pact powers on 3–5 August 1961 gave Ulbricht approval to block off East Berlin from the western zones. On 13 August, East German paramilitary troops began constructing barbed wire barricades along the line separating the Soviet zone from the rest of the city. The day before, 12 August, some 2,500 people had sought asylum in the West. Communications links between the two halves of Berlin were interrupted, and East Berliners were henceforth allowed to cross over to the West only if they had been issued with a temporary passport. Non-Germans, including allied military personnel and diplomats, could only cross at one border crossing: the infamous Checkpoint Charlie. More than sixty thousand East German citizens who worked in the western zones suddenly found themselves without a livelihood. In a further provocation, the Ulbricht regime warned West Berliners to stay at least one hundred meters from the Wall for their own safety.

Deliberately impermanent until western reaction could be gauged, the Wall gradually became a three-meter-high monstrosity. Watchtowers were built and manned with snipers; buildings near the Wall were knocked down to ensure that there was a clear, floodlit zone across which any would-be escapee would have to run. Many still tried. On 17 August 1962, just over a year after the construction of the Wall, a young man called Peter Fechter was shot by East German border guards and left to bleed to death under the eyes of powerless West Berliners. Fechter's pitiless killing provoked demonstrations in West Berlin and attacks on buses carrying Soviet soldiers in the western half of the city.

The communist press in Western Europe did its best to put a good face on the construction of the Berlin Wall. The PCI's newspaper, *L'Unità*, for instance, headlined its 14 August 1961 edition "RDT [the Italian acronym for the GDR] takes security measures along the border with West Berlin." It added demurely that East Germany was merely introducing "the kind of controls that every state applies to its borders." The story was accompanied by a photograph of East German policemen unrolling barbed wire in front of a crowd of acquiescent citizens.

Horrible though the Wall was, it was also, as Kennedy quipped, "a hell of a lot better than a war." Willy Brandt subsequently wrote, "What came as a cruel blow to us in Berlin . . . appeared to others a relief or at least the lesser of two evils."[33] This was true even in Bonn. Adenauer, mindful perhaps of "Carte Blanche," accepted Ulbricht's action with only perfunctory protest; indeed, he waited a week even to visit Berlin and did not attend the huge protest rally organized by his rival, Brandt, on 16 August. It was a decision that cost him dear in West Germany's national elections in September 1961. Adenauer's Christian Democrat coalition lost five percentage points, while Brandt's SPD advanced by a similar margin. Adenauer was only able to form a coalition government after a messy period of bargaining.

From the West's point of view, the Wall was a propaganda triumph: communist East Germany had essentially admitted that its citizens could not be trusted to leave its borders. To boost morale in West Berlin, President Kennedy sent Vice President Lyndon B. Johnson and symbolically reinforced the American garrison with 1,500 troops. Despite such symbolic shows of strength, the Soviets kept up relentless pressure. On 23 August, claiming that "all kinds of revenge-seekers, extremists, saboteurs and spies are being sent from the Federal Republic of Germany to West Berlin," the Soviet government threatened to restrict access to Berlin by the three designated air corridors.[34]

It was to counteract such harassment that President Kennedy sent General Lucius E. Clay, a popular figure in Berlin because of his role in the

1948–1949 blockade, as special presidential envoy to the city. Clay, who arrived on 19 September, engaged in a series of high-profile confrontations with the Soviets and the GDR with the aim of ensuring that the East Germans did not nibble away at the rights of western diplomats and soldiers. The most notorious of these confrontations came in October 1961 when Soviet and American tanks faced off two hundred yards apart at Checkpoint Charlie, after East German border guards had denied access to allied diplomats. One of the iconic moments of the Cold War, the clash ended with an East German climbdown. Clay, who stayed in Berlin until the spring of 1962, did an energetic job of asserting the rights of the western powers within Berlin and of reassuring West Berliners that the West still cared about them.[35]

But it is important to realize that nobody, even Clay, was going to force a showdown over the rights of *Berliners* to visit their relatives and friends on the other side of the Wall, or to telephone them, or to send them gifts on their birthday, or simply to meet up for a beer. As Willy Brandt said, "the Wall has cut my city in half. . . . It separates father from son, mother from daughter, bride from bridegroom."[36] It constituted the grimmest physical representation to date of the fact that although the two superpowers were fighting the Cold War, Europeans, especially Germans, were *living* it.

AFTERMATH

In a famous essay, John Lewis Gaddis commented that thermonuclear weapons had had a "stabilizing effect on the postwar international system" by forcing national leaders "to confront the reality of what war is really like, indeed to confront the prospect of their own mortality."[37] Had the United States and the USSR merely been armed with cannons and muskets, or even tanks and flamethrowers, there would likely have been a war over Berlin. Great conflicts have been fought throughout European history with far less cause. Prestige concerns and the desire not to lose face, absent nuclear weapons, would have pushed one side or the other to resort to war at some point during the crisis. The huge nuclear arsenals of the two sides made any such self-indulgence by statesmen seem irrational (on 30 October 1961, the day after the conclusion of the standoff at Checkpoint Charlie, the USSR exploded a thermonuclear device with a yield of 50 megatons, i.e., nearly ten times more than all the explosives used in World War II). There could be no point in fighting a war whose human costs were bound greatly to exceed any possible gain. The same logic was to show itself during the Cuban crisis in October 1962, when Kennedy was willing to trade NATO's Jupiter missiles in Turkey for the removal of the Soviet weapons installed (disguised as palm trees) on Castro's Cuba, and when Khrushchev himself, faced by the

American quarantine around the island, turned his ships back and dismantled the bases constructed there.

Of course, it would have been better for everybody's nerves if Khrushchev had been less willing to posture on the brink of catastrophe. As Vladimir Zubok and Constantine Pleshakov have written, Khrushchev was "one of many Russian revolutionaries who acted according to Napoleon's motto '*on s'engage et puis on voit*,'"[38] It should be added, however, that Khrushchev was not the only one to blame. Under Eisenhower, the United States arguably rehabilitated West Germany far too quickly. Germans had only recently killed twenty million Soviet citizens without nuclear weapons. The Soviet leader's rant at Vienna was crude and his demands were impossible and unjust, but it was not unreasonable of him to be wary of the future political and military intentions of West Germany.

Indeed, in the fall of 1961 and the spring of 1962, the United States, encouraged by the British, and heartened by Khrushchev's decision to drop his end-of-year deadline for a peace treaty with the GDR at the Twenty-second Party Congress in October 1961, made a major effort to secure a German peace treaty on terms acceptable to both sides. Kennedy also made clear his absolute opposition to West Germany's ever possessing nuclear arms in a November 1961 interview with the Soviet journalist Alexei Adzhubei, who happened to be Khrushchev's son-in-law. The interview was "widely resented in Germany."[39] Over the next few months, U.S. diplomacy, led by Secretary of State Dean Rusk, offered the Soviets a generous deal: the United States would sign a non-aggression pact, recognize the Oder-Niesse line as the Polish border with East Germany, and ensure that West Germany stayed without nuclear arms. In exchange, however, Washington insisted that the USSR should guarantee a "free West Berlin, securely tied to the West, with western forces, and western forces alone, in the city as guarantors of its extraordinary status."[40] The USSR rejected the Americans' quid pro quo. The negotiation, which was carried on over the Germans' heads, irritated Bonn and drove Chancellor Adenauer toward de Gaulle, who in 1962 broke with the Americans and strove to build up the EEC as an independent third force in world affairs (see below, chapter 8).

President Kennedy's June 1963 visit to West Berlin, during which, to rapturous applause, he made his "Ich bin ein Berliner" speech, restored West German morale and symbolized Berlin's importance to the West. However, the signature, in Moscow on 5 August 1963, of the Partial Test Ban Treaty by the three main nuclear powers roiled relations with Bonn yet again. "Disgruntled German politicians and journalists compared the test ban treaty to the Treaty of Versailles, others saw it as a return to Yalta."[41] The treaty, which committed the three powers to "prohibit, prevent, and not to carry out any nuclear weapon test explosion," and to "refrain from causing, encouraging, or in any way participating in, the carrying out of any nuclear weapon test explosion," was "open to all states." The GDR signed within three days. West German leaders were infuriated both by this de facto extension of recognition of the East German regime and by the fact that the treaty signaled that the nuclear club wanted to limit its membership. Right-wing politicians such as Franz-Josef Strauss fumed that the Germans might turn to authoritarianism once again, if they were not treated as equals, but Washington was adamant. Bonn reluctantly signed the treaty on 19 August 1963. In hindsight, the rhetoric of some West German politicians, less than twenty years after the end of World War II, seems not a little presumptuous. The test ban treaty meant less radiation in the world's air and seas. It was hardly a Versailles-style diktat.

The West had an opportunity to show its support for Bonn within a year. The USSR signed a treaty of "Friendship, Mutual Assistance and Cooperation" with the GDR, on 12 June 1964. The treaty affirmed that a united Germany would only be achieved on the basis of agreement between the two sovereign German states and identified West Berlin as "an independent political unit." The three wartime allies, after consultations with Bonn, issued a tripartite declaration that underlined that West Berlin was not an "independent political unit" but part of Greater Berlin, over the government of which the four occupying powers retained rights and responsibilities. For good measure, they added that they did not recognize "the East German regime nor the existence of a state in Eastern Germany."[42] The stalemate seemed unassailable.

The man who would eventually find a way of upsetting the stalemate was Willy Brandt. At the height of the crisis, on 16 August 1961, Brandt wrote to President Kennedy urging the U.S. government to condemn the Soviet bloc's flagrant disregard of the UN's Declaration on Human Rights in the General Assembly of the UNO. Brandt further proposed holding a plebiscite in West Berlin on the desirability of the western allies' troops remaining until German reunification. Kennedy sent a reply by the hand of Vice President Johnson. It was distinctly cool in tone:

> Grave as this matter is . . . there are, as you say, no steps available to us which can force a significant material change in this present situation. Since it represents a resounding confession of failure and of political weakness, this brutal border closing evidently represents a basic Soviet decision which only war could reverse. Neither you nor we, nor any of our Allies, have ever supposed that we should go to war on this point.[43]

Kennedy's letter made a lasting impact upon Brandt. He realized that it meant that the GDR was a fact so long as the communist system survived. The primary question for German foreign policy thus became, or so Brandt concluded, the moral imperative of obtaining concrete human relief for the families and individuals whose lives had been shattered by geopolitics, even if this meant bowing to the reality of the existence of two Germanies. As he argued in October 1962, "It is precisely in Berlin, where the division of the world has been literally cemented in stone, and where the Soviet policy of coexistence is exposed in its naked reality, that one must insist that coexistence cannot be a synonym for the maintenance of the status quo."[44] When Brandt became chancellor in 1969, this conviction would guide his groundbreaking policy of détente with the Soviet bloc—Ostpolitik.

NOTES

1. For the negotiation of the EEC treaties, see Mark Gilbert, "The Treaties of Rome," in *The Oxford Handbook of the European Union*, ed. Erik Jones, Anand Menon, and Stephen Weatherill (Oxford: Oxford University Press, 2012), 95–106.

2. Tony Judt, *Postwar: A History of Europe since 1945* (New York: Penguin, 2005), 308.

3. Henry Ashby Turner, *Germany from Partition to Reunification* (New Haven, CT: Yale University Press, 1992), 108.

4. See Carl Cavanagh Hodge, "The Long Fifties: The Politics of Socialist Programmatic Revision in Britain, France and Germany," *Contemporary European History* 2 (1993): 17–34.

5. Turner, *Germany from Partition to Reunification*, 71.

6. Gareth Prichard, *The Making of the GDR, 1945–1953* (Manchester: Manchester University Press, 2000), 165.

7. Mary Fulbrook, *Anatomy of a Dictatorship: Inside the GDR 1949–1989* (Oxford: Oxford University Press, 1995), 47–52.

8. Bertolt Brecht, "The Solution," http://en.wikipedia.org/wiki/Die_L%C3%B6sung.

9. Brendan Simms, *Europe: The Struggle for Supremacy, 1453 to the Present* (London: Allen Lane, 2013), 407.

10. David Miller, *The Cold War: A Military History* (New York: St. Martin's Press, 1998), 263.

11. Marc Trachtenberg, *A Constructed Peace: The Making of the European Settlement* (Princeton, NJ: Princeton University Press, 1999), 158.

12. Robert McNamara, "The Military Role of Nuclear Weapons: Perceptions and Misperceptions," in *The Nuclear Controversy*, ed. William P. Bundy (New York: Council on Foreign Relations, 1981), 88.

13. Trachtenberg, *A Constructed Peace*, 181, quoting the *Bulletin of Atomic Scientists*.

14. Trachtenberg, *A Constructed Peace*, 159.

15. Charles de Gaulle, *Memoirs of Hope: Renewal and Endeavor* (New York: Simon and Schuster, 1971), 201.

16. Miller, *The Cold War: A Military History*, 372–373, quoting a NATO study from the early 1960s.

17. De Gaulle, *Memoirs of Hope*, 201–2.

18. J. B. Priestly, "Britain and the Nuclear Bombs," *New Statesman and Nation*, 2 November 1957, 554–56.

19. Kathleen Burk, *Troublemaker: A Life and History of A.J.P. Taylor* (New Haven, CT: Yale University Press, 2000), 214–15.

20. John Minnion and Philip Bolsover, *The CND Story* (London: Allison & Busby, 1983), 8.

21. The best account of this internal party dispute remains Michael Foot, *Aneurin Bevan: A Biography*, vol. 2: 1945–1960, 2nd ed. (London: Faber & Faber, 2008), 549–84.

22. Holger Nehring, "National Internationalists: British and West German Protests against Nuclear Weapons, the Politics of Transnational Communication and the Social History of the Cold War, 1957–1964," *Contemporary European History* 14 (2005): 568. A book-length study of the antinuclear movement is Mark Cioc, *Pax Atomica: The Nuclear Defense Debate in West Germany during the Adenauer Era* (New York: Columbia University Press, 1988).

23. Dennis L. Bark and David R. Gress, *A History of West Germany*, vol. 1 (Oxford: Blackwell's, 1993) 408.

24. Jonathan Haslam, *Russia's Cold War: From the October Revolution to the Fall of the Wall* (New Haven, CT: Yale University Press, 2012), 180.

25. This is the thesis of Hope Harrison, *Driving the Soviets up the Wall: Soviet-East German Relations, 1953–1961* (Princeton, NJ: Princeton University Press, 2003).

26. Jean Lacouture, *De Gaulle: The Ruler 1945–1970* (London: Harvill, 1991), 389.

27. Hans-Peter Schwarz, *Konrad Adenauer: The Statesman, 1952–1967* (Oxford: Berghahn, 1995), 396–98.

28. William Taubman, *Khrushchev: The Man, His Era* (London: The Free Press, 2006), 412; Alistair Horne, *Macmillan 1957–1986* (London: Macmillan 1989), 122–29, gives a colorful account of the British premier's "voyage of discovery."

29. Central Office of Information, *Berlin and the Problem of German Reunification* (London: HMSO, 1969), 66–67.

30. Henry Kissinger, "The Search for Stability," *Foreign Affairs* 37 (1959): 541–42.

31. The quotations in these paragraphs come from the American record of the conversation between Kennedy and Khrushchev at Vienna, 4 June 1961, FRUS 1961–1963, vol. XIV, document 32.

32. Willy Brandt, *My Life in Politics* (London: Penguin, 1993), 49.

33. Brandt, *My Life in Politics*, 49.

34. Central Office of Information, *Berlin and the Problem of German Reunification*, 42.

35. For an enthusiastic account of Clay's leadership, see W. R. Smyser, *Kennedy and the Berlin Wall* (Lanham, MD: Rowman & Littlefield, 2009).

36. Willy Brandt, *The Ordeal of Coexistence* (Cambridge, MA: Harvard University Press, 1963), 5.

37. John Lewis Gaddis, *The Long Peace: Inquiries into the History of the Cold War* (New York: Oxford University Press, 1987), 231.

38. V. Zubok and C. Pleshakov, *Inside the Kremlin's Cold War* (Cambridge, MA: Harvard University Press, 1996), 198. The phrase means "one goes into action and then one sees what happens."

39. Trachtenberg, *A Constructed Peace*, 341.

40. Trachtenberg, *A Constructed Peace*, 348.

41. Susanna Schrafstetter, "The Long Shadow of the Past: History, Memory and the Debate over West Germany's Nuclear Status, 1954–1969," *History and Memory* 16 (2004): 132.

42. The text of the Tripartite Declaration is to be found in Central Office of Information, *Berlin and the Problem of German Reunification*, 72.

43. The exchange of letters can be found in FRUS 1961–1963, vol. XIV, Berlin Crisis, documents 117 and 120.

44. Brandt, *The Ordeal of Coexistence*, 8.

Chapter Seven

Really Existing Socialism

One reason why Khrushchev encouraged the construction of the Berlin Wall was his long-term confidence in the superiority of the communist system over the various western variations of capitalism and social democracy. In his mind, the Wall was a temporary obstacle to prevent defectors from fleeing the rigors of life under Ulbricht and the Stasi, but sooner or later the GDR would achieve such gains in economic productivity, and such triumphs in the spheres of cultural and scientific achievement, that it would no longer need to fence itself off from the rest of the world. Again and again in the late 1950s and early 1960s, Khrushchev boasted that the Soviet bloc would supersede the West in economic production by the 1970s. In the fields of science and technology, moreover, the Soviet leader scarcely needed to advertise the USSR's triumphs. Communist parties across the world celebrated the achievements of the USSR in aerospace and rocket technology: Yuri Gagarin, the first cosmonaut, became the living symbol of the communist world's prowess in aeronautical engineering. [1]

Such claims were taken seriously by western leaders. The economic growth of the communist bloc looked impressive, and the USSR held an indisputable attraction for developing countries. It was to counteract this impression that the Kennedy administration mounted a major effort to improve relations with Yugoslavia and India, two of the principal actors in the non-aligned movement, and launched the "Alliance for Progress," a "kind of Marshall plan for the South," in Latin America. [2] Washington's foreign aid spending burgeoned.

But the United States' recent history and present policies weighed against it. An American-backed coup in Brazil in 1964; the bloody suppression, to American applause, of the Indonesian Communist Party by General Suharto in 1965–1966; and the CIA-supported coup d'état of Joseph Mobutu in the

133

Congo in November 1965 would have robbed the United States of progressive credentials in the developing world even had there been no Vietnam War. American involvement in Vietnam, of course, which began under Kennedy and was intensified by his successor, President Lyndon B. Johnson, was the final straw for its external reputation.

The Soviet bloc, however, failed to capitalize upon the worsening reputation of its ideological opponent, at any rate in Europe. In fact, the 1960s delivered a body blow to Soviet pretensions to be a model that the rest of the world could admire and imitate. The USSR, to the relief of its satrapies in Eastern Europe, turned its back on Khrushchev, via a palace coup in October 1964. Thereafter, the USSR and its satellites lapsed into a dull orthodoxy "ruled by increasingly pragmatic, cautious and self-interested élites."[3] Leonid Brezhnev, the man who replaced Khrushchev as party secretary, was the epitome of a "new class" of bureaucratic politicians who had been the principal beneficiaries of the construction of Soviet power since 1945.[4]

By the late 1960s, the reality of socialism in the USSR was so deeply unattractive that would-be revolutionaries in the West, no matter how contemptuous they were of western conformism, imperialism, and "repressive tolerance," nevertheless looked further east for a model.[5] Maoist China attracted the radicals who fought on the barricades of Paris, Rome, and Berlin in 1968, despite its Nazi-like hostility to the cultural achievements of the West and its criminal destruction of China's own civilization. In the 1960s, "the magical hysteria of the Mao cult" exercised a curious fascination for Europe's *bien-pensants*, especially in Paris.[6]

Within the Soviet bloc itself, all intellectual innovation was stifled. After Khrushchev's political demise, "dissidents"—scholars and writers who contested the system's norms—were punished zealously. When, moreover, the leadership of Czechoslovakia attempted to rethink communist ideology and economic practice, to liberalize the press, and to permit political and cultural pluralism, Brezhnev's USSR, prodded by its Warsaw Pact allies, sent in the tanks. The crushing of the "Prague Spring," as Czechoslovakia's heady experience of liberation in 1968 was known, was proof that "socialism with a human face" was regarded in Moscow, Warsaw, Budapest, East Berlin, and Sofia as a contradiction in terms. Nobody could challenge the central tenets of "really existing socialism" without paying a high price.

THE END OF THE MONOLITH[7]

Khrushchev's downfall had multiple causes. Indeed, it could be said to have been over-determined. The Soviet leader's blustering manner and habit of treating subordinates with petulant disdain had left him isolated in the party's top ranks. Men like Brezhnev toadied Khrushchev, but were ready to turn on him the moment his position slipped. For all Khrushchev's boasts that the USSR would overtake the West in living standards and cultural achievements, senior Soviet officials knew that agricultural policy, in particular, was a disaster. Despite possessing the supremely fertile Ukrainian plains, the USSR could not even feed itself adequately.

By the time of his downfall, Khrushchev's foreign policy had also split the world communist movement. His willingness to compromise with Tito's Yugoslavia won him the enmity of the die-hard Stalinist party of Albania, which feared Yugoslavia's hegemonic aspirations in the Balkans. The totalitarian regime of Enver Hoxha, whose omnipresence rivaled Ulbricht's GDR, insisted that Yugoslavia was "a Hell where the darkest terror reigns and where a clique of traitors, fed on American dollars soaked in the blood of the workers . . . [has installed] . . . a revisionist Trotskyist regime."[8] Albania's "ultra-leftism" won it the backing of China, whose leader, Mao Zedong, had never forgiven Khrushchev for attacking Stalinism so unambiguously in 1956. Mao's own cult of personality was as pharaoh-like as Stalin's, and his private life more sybaritic (indeed, it rivaled Tito's for excess). In the late 1950s and early 1960s, China was in the throes of the "Great Leap Forward," an imitation of Stalin's crash program of industrialization and agricultural collectivization. Mao, however, was outdoing even Stalin. Between eight and ten million citizens of the USSR had died of starvation or from the "liquidation" of the kulaks during the early 1930s. Mao's policy would bring about the deaths of an even higher number of hapless peasants.[9] Accordingly, Mao regarded Khrushchev as an opportunist and arch-revisionist. He resented, too, the USSR's leadership's assumption that it had the right to set the "line" of the entire world communist movement—a right evoked by Khrushchev at a fraternal conference of the world's communist parties in November 1957. If Khrushchev was in error, the "great helmsman," as Mao was sycophantically called, had the duty to set an alternative course. Albania's quarrel with Khrushchev offered the Chinese a way, in other words, of intensifying the ideological struggle for leadership of the world communist movement.

The struggle was fought out for the most part behind the scenes until 17 October 1961, when in his opening speech to the Twenty-second Congress of the Communist Party of the Soviet Union, Khrushchev accused Albania's leaders of Stalinist deviationism. Ominously, Khrushchev asserted that the USSR would do its "internationalist duty" to ensure that Albania marched "shoulder to shoulder" with its fellow socialist countries—exactly the kind of ponderous euphemism used during the Hungarian crisis to mean military intervention.[10] Instead of passively acknowledging the rebuke and admitting their "error," the Albanians asserted that the "anti-Marxist activities of N. Khrushchev and his followers" were endangering the "unity of the socialist camp." This brought the quick-tempered Khrushchev to the boil. On 27 October 1961, Khrushchev returned to the rostrum to tell the Soviet party, and its guests from communist parties all over the world, that "all that was reprehensible in our country in the period of the cult of the individual is manifested in its worst form in the Albanian Party of Labor." To illustrate his contempt for the "abnormal, evil situation" that existed in Albania, Khrushchev referred to the case of Liri Gega, a pregnant member of the Albanian Central Committee who had been shot some years before. Delegates shouted "for shame" as Khrushchev ranted that "even in the blackest days of rampant reaction, the Tsarist satraps, who tortured revolutionaries, scrupled to execute pregnant women."[11] Khrushchev compared the Albanians to Judas Iscariot, alleged that they would sell out world communism for thirty silver dollars, and suspended diplomatic relations with Tirana, the Albanian capital, in December 1961.

The polemics continued for the next three years, with Albania and China accusing Khrushchev of deviationism in ever-more hysterical terms and the USSR showing increasing impatience with the challenge of the Chinese Communist Party (CCP) to its leadership. On the other hand, Beijing portrayed Khrushchev's withdrawal from Cuba as a surrender to American imperialism. The Soviet leader's willingness to negotiate and sign the nuclear test ban treaty in August 1963 with Great Britain and the United States (a treaty that neither China nor France signed) only magnified Khrushchev's image in Beijing as a betrayer of the world revolution.

The communist world was, in fact, divided in three by 1963. On the far left, there were the Maoists, in other words China together with Albania and a number of developing world parties. On the right, were the Italians, who wanted more détente with the West and more democracy within the world communist movement. Back in November 1957, Togliatti, the PCI's leader, had argued in favor of "polycentrism," which meant that each country's party, and not Moscow, should judge how local circumstances might condition the building of socialism. The PCI had yielded to the Soviet assertion of leadership then, but in 1963–1964, it was ready to reassert its own position more forcefully. The PCI favored greater flexibility from the diktats and about-faces of Moscow since it would be freer to take advantage of democratic pluralism in Italy's parliamentary system, while redoubling its efforts to construct social hegemony for its ideas in schools, workplaces, and trade unions. Being seen as Moscow's stooge was an electoral handicap for the PCI. In Romania, polycentrism meant that the party leadership could press ahead with the construction of a heavy industrial base. Khrushchev had been opposing its plans, arguing that the various countries of the Soviet bloc should not duplicate one another's economic output but implement the principle of the "socialist division of labor."[12] In Hungary, by contrast, the party could experiment with economic reform and shift further away from the Stalinist industrial model. Khrushchev, vocally supported by the PCF and by loyalists behind the iron curtain such as Todor Zhivkov, the strongman of

Bulgaria, tried in vain to argue that the USSR should remain the sole ideological arbiter.

In August 1964, the Kremlin announced that delegates from twenty-six national communist parties would meet in Moscow on 15 December 1964 to resolve the problems facing world communism. Khrushchev's intention was clearly to reassert Moscow's domination and to isolate his critics, be they of the left or the right. His move failed, however. Togliatti, who died on 23 August 1964, responded with a (posthumously published) memorandum disassociating the PCI from any attempt to enforce obedience to Moscow. Given the strength of the forces of world imperialism, Togliatti argued, it was "unthinkable" to "exclude China and the Chinese communists" from the international communist movement. The best way to defeat the "unchecked and disgraceful" Chinese deviation was through dialogue, not mass expulsions or sterile polemic, and the articulation of constructive policies. Nor should communists pretend that there were no problems in the USSR and the other communist nations; the "worst thing," Togliatti contended (and it is likely that he had Hungary and the Berlin Wall on his mind), was "to give the impression that everything is going fine and then suddenly find ourselves obliged to discuss and explain difficult situations." Above all, Togliatti insisted in the concluding lines of his memorandum that it would be wise to abstain from "enforced uniformity toward the outside world" and better to strive to "establish and maintain unity" in consideration of "the diversity and full autonomy of each individual country."[13]

Togliatti's memorandum was like a cardinal publicly stating that the pope was interpreting scripture erroneously. The PCI was no longer treating the doctrine handed down by Moscow as if it were holy writ. Indeed, its leaders even "began to contemplate that 'the strongest communist party in the capitalist world' might become an international political actor on its own account; one, within the framework of the strategy of peaceful coexistence, able to influence both 'really existing socialism' and the western world in order to supersede the face-off between the two blocs and relax their internal tensions."[14]

Recent historiography has underlined the importance of Khrushchev's loss of prestige within the world communist movement as a cause of his downfall.[15] On 15 October 1964, Khrushchev was deposed as General Secretary of the CPSU by the other members of the Politburo and replaced by Leonid Brezhnev. In Orwellian fashion, Khrushchev became an unperson; amazingly, his "very name disappeared completely from the media and from the historical literature on the post-Stalin period."[16] He was not, however, subjected to the indignity of a show trial and execution; nor did a bloody purge of his followers and relations ensue. The watchword of the new leadership was caution.

DIVIDED HEAVEN

In addition to the polemics with Albania, Khrushchev's contributions to the Twenty-second Congress of the Communist Party of the Soviet Union in October 1961 stressed ambitious economic growth targets and returned to the theme of the need to root out Stalinism (subsequently, Stalin's corpse was expelled from its place of honor in the mausoleum to Lenin in the Red Square and buried). In Khrushchev's mind, the construction of socialism would have been achieved when the communist bloc eclipsed the material achievements of the West and when the legacy of Stalin's terror and totalitarian methods had been finally superseded. While Khrushchev himself employed repressive violence to quash challenges to the regime—striking coal miners in Russia paid a heavy toll in lives in 1962—it is clear that his aspiration was a society in which the Communist Party ruled with the masses' assent; acted, in short, as society's guardian, rather than its taskmaster. Khrushchev was no democrat, but he was motivated by a genuine idealism that marked him off from the bureaucrats who would push him out of power in October 1964.

It also marked him off from the rulers of the satellite states in central and Eastern Europe. Albania was an extreme Stalinist holdout, but most of the other regimes had liberalized little and were in the hands of unscrupulous boss politicians that had no inclination to renounce the party's role as a hard-driving overseer.

In the GDR, as we have seen, Ulbricht and the SED used the organs of state security, the Stasi, to monitor society on a vast and intrusive scale. Ulbricht was the arch-conservative of the Soviet bloc, the least willing to accept any flexibility in dogma. For him, the fall of Khrushchev came as a liberation. Flushed with East Germany's relative economic successes after the construction of the Wall, Ulbricht actually tightened the party's rule over "the developed socialist society" he boasted of having created. The GDR adopted a new constitution in 1968 that proclaimed it to be a "socialist state of the German nation" and that formalized the SED-dominated National Front list as the "sole organ through which the political parties and so-called mass organizations shaped the development of socialist society." Rights of free speech, assembly, and religion could only be exercised "in harmony with the principles of the new constitution," while the right to strike was abolished outright.[17] Why should workers want to strike against the state and party that represented their interests and acted in their name?

Bulgaria's destalinization was only partial, too. After the death of Stalin and the execution of Lavrenti Beria in December 1953, Vulko Chervenkov, who as Beria's protégé was tarred with the Stalinist brush, sought to preserve his position by sharing power with his principal rivals within the Bulgarian Communist Party. The party secretaryship was taken over by Todor Zhivkov in March 1954 and collective leadership became the order of the day. Chervenkov was replaced as prime minister of Bulgaria after the Secret Speech by Anton Yugov, a survivor of the 1949 purges, but a man chiefly remembered for conducting the persecution and judicial murder of the Agrarian Party leader Nikola Petkov (see above, chapter 3). Yet Chervenkov retained substantial power within the party apparatus and remained in the Politburo. The late 1950s and early 1960s were characterized by jockeying for power between the two men.

Both underestimated Zhivkov. Like Stalin and Khrushchev before him, Zhivkov used the mundane task of running the party machinery to build up a powerbase of supporters who owed him favors. After the Twenty-second Congress of the Soviet Party, sure he had a majority of the Bulgarian party's upper echelons behind him, he struck hard, condemning Chervenkov's Stalinist past and driving him out of political life. In November 1962, it was Yugov's turn. The premier was purged amid vicious personal attacks on his honesty, competence, and courage. Traicho Kostov, the party leader executed after a show trial in 1949, was rehabilitated—that is to say, it was admitted that the accusations against him had been false and had been obtained thanks to abuses of socialist legality—and the party acknowledged that the transition to socialism in the late 1940s had featured excesses (the accepted euphemism for mass murder and terror). Zhivkov became Bulgaria's absolute ruler, combining in his own person control over the state hierarchy, the party hierarchy, and the security services. Opponents in the party and the army were weeded out. Zhivkov cultivated a fatherly, "man of the people" image, but his regime remained hostile to any kind of radical political or economic change.[18]

According to Vladimir Tismăneanu, Romanian political culture after 1956 was based on "fear, suspicion, problematic legitimacy, spurious internationalism, populist manipulation of national symbols, unabashed personalization of power, and persecution mania."[19] Party leader Gheorghiu-Dej, an uneducated railwayman, was a ruthless intriguer. When, after the Secret Speech, two leading figures within the Romanian Party, Iosif Chişinevschi and Miron Constantinescu, challenged Gheorghiu-Dej's leadership, he successfully rallied the Politburo around him against the opposition group. He then used the political credit he had gained with the USSR during the Hungarian crisis (it will be remembered that Romania held Imre Nagy and other leading Hungarian officials in prison) to purge the party of their supporters: "In 1958-59, thousands of party members experienced again the frightful moments of terror from Stalin's years."[20] The numbers were boosted by thousands of others who had previously been officers in the royal army, landowners, members of opposition political parties, and "the children of all of the above."[21]

Many of those arrested were sent to penal colonies in the Danube delta where they worked, knee-deep in cold water, scything reeds for use in cellulose plants. In all, some sixty thousand prisoners performed forced labor; prisoners had to produce fifteen sheaves weighing about fifty kilograms each every day or else face punishment and reduced rations. Since food "consisted of several slices of bread and jam, and a cup of coffee substitute in the morning, and a piece of cold polenta and soup at lunchtime and in the evenings," it was certainly better to have full rations than otherwise. The camps, where the prisoners were housed in "unheated and uninsulated huts," were "sealed off with barbed wire and electrified fences" and patrolled by armed guards escorted by attack dogs. Medical care was poor, though many prisoners suffered from malaria, tuberculosis, and other diseases. Unknown thousands died in these Black Sea Belsens.

The Black Sea camps were not death factories like Auschwitz or Treblinka, or like the extreme punishment camps in the Soviet gulag. But they were still brutal places to be interned. They were "testimony" to a "mentality" that "saw the convicts as expendable slaves, worthy only of the barest of essentials to ensure work capacity but denied any care which might enhance it or indeed protect it."[22] It is worth reflecting upon the fact that they were operating, in Europe, just fifty years ago.

Gheorghiu-Dej was careful to take the Soviet side in the quarrel with Albania and China. He did not want to attract Khrushchev's wrath. Gheorghiu-Dej's favorite from 1961 onward was a man whose name would soon become notorious: Nicolae Ceauşescu. It was he who took charge of the party and this control of the party machine helped him grab the leadership after Gheorghiu-Dej's death. For Gheorghiu-Dej, Ceauşescu was the "perfect embodiment of the Stalinist apparatchik."[23] He was not an intellectual— indeed, was positively anti-intellectual—had not been trained in Moscow, and had served time in the jails of the pre-communist fascist dictatorship along with Gheorghiu-Dej himself.

By 1962, Gheorghiu-Dej was steering the Romanian party discreetly away from the USSR. Khrushchev's visceral anti-Stalinism was too much to stomach for the Romanian strongman. But it was, above all, the pressure upon Romania to specialize in the production of raw materials and agricultural produce that persuaded Gheorghiu-Dej to challenge the Soviet leader openly. Socialism, at any rate in the minds of its East European adherents, was so closely identified with the development of heavy industry that this plan seemed tantamount to saying to the Romanians that they were a backward people: a colony for more evolved nations.

In April 1964, after a year of verbal skirmishing over the issue, the Romanian Communist Party made a declaration of independence, arguing that it was a "sovereign right of each socialist state to elaborate, choose, or change the forms and methods of socialist construction." Romania thereafter took a position within the Soviet bloc akin to that of France in relation to NATO: half in, half out. The following year, Ceauşescu defeated the "the brutal and merciless head of the Securitate," Alexandru Drăghici, to become leader after Gheorghiu-Dej unexpectedly died of cancer in March 1965.[24] Like Caligula ascending to the imperial throne after the bloody reign of Tiberius, it seemed, at the time, like progress.

By comparison with the grim dictatorships in power in East Berlin, Sofia, Bucharest, and Tirana, Hungary and Poland were relatively liberal. In Budapest, the Soviets' hand-picked leader, János Kádár, purged supporters of the 1956 uprising and also re-imposed rural collectivization. But Kádár, unlike the other leaders discussed above, welcomed Khrushchev's renewed attacks on Stalinism at the Twenty-second Congress and moved to liberalize the regime by releasing political prisoners and experimenting with economic reform. Kádár did not demand the mass mobilization of the people in a national mission to build socialism; he merely asked for pragmatic acquiescence to communist management. The Hungarians, pulverized by Rákosi's terror and Khrushchev's tanks, were by the mid-1960s willing to go along.

It was Poland, however, that was the most ambiguous of all the countries within the Soviet bloc. After 1956, Gomułka was only able to preserve the party's rule by permitting considerable autonomy to the Catholic Church, by abandoning state ownership of agriculture, and by permitting a façade of pluralism and genuine political debate. In the 1960s, Poland was the only country in the Soviet bloc where the overwhelming majority of the population attended Catholic mass, where 80 percent of the land was in private hands, and where, within limits, the party line was open to questioning. The handful of non-communist parties in the Polish national assembly, the *Sejm*, occasionally voiced mild criticism of the party-state, even though they were closely monitored by the Polish United Workers' Party and were entirely composed of "fellow travelers" sympathetic to the party line. Poland was the weakest link in the Soviet chain. Precisely because Poland was freer than the other nations within the Soviet sphere, any disturbance within the Soviet bloc was bound to find an echo in Warsaw. For this reason, the party's rule became increasingly restrictive as the 1960s wore on. Gomułka, a shrewd politician, was well aware that he was walking on thin ice.[25]

This brief survey of the political struggles within the various states of the communist bloc will have underlined that they were anything but monochrome replicas of one another. Their institutions were broadly the same—a rubber stamp parliament and a single party whose principal decision-making bodies, the Presidium (Politburo) and Central Committee, were the de facto sovereign authorities of the state, too—but there were great differences in their approach to the building of socialism.

There were, however, important common features. Although Mark Mazower may be right to suggest that Eastern Europe in the early years of communism "was a lot less elitist than any previous kind of ruling system Eastern Europe had known,"[26] by the 1960s the *nomenklatura* system, which was all-pervasive in the Soviet bloc (and in Yugoslavia), meant that the communist states were no more fair in their distribution of social goods than capitalist states and were much *less* egalitarian than the welfare states of northern Europe. Rich material rewards were available to party bureaucrats. The system assigned privileges according to one's place in the hierarchy, and such perks were competed for and flaunted with a gusto that western bankers might have found excessive: genuinely austere officials like Gomułka were exceptions that illuminated the general rule. Senior party or state officials bought their food and drink in separate shops from the masses (and hence did not have to queue), vacationed in reserved party resorts, were housed more luxuriously, and had access to clinics reserved for party members and to both foreign travel and hard currency. [27] Of course, all such privileges were conditional upon the individual being in "good standing" with the party and could be taken away at whim by his or her superiors. It was a powerful inducement to political conformity.

Another common feature was repression of intellectual life. Blanket censorship prevailed in the media, propaganda filled the airwaves, school textbooks parroted party slogans, history was rewritten to reflect current political needs, and cultural policy depended upon the "tastes" of the party leaders. As a result of Khrushchev's personal intervention, Alexander Solzhenitsyn was allowed to publish his deeply moving account of life in the Gulag, *One Day in the Life of Ivan Denisovich*, in November 1962, but when the Politburo decided that such "slanders" on Soviet reality were counterproductive, unorthodox writers, including Solzhenitsyn, were subjected to mounting levels of persecution. [28] In 1966, in an internationally publicized case, two outspoken individuals, Yuli Daniel and Andrei Sinyavsky, were "tried" and condemned to long spells in prison for the "crime" of publishing abroad articles and stories critical of the Soviet system.

In East Germany, the writer Christa Wolf, an ambiguous figure, was allowed to publish the controversial novel *Divided Heaven* in 1963. Wolf subsequently became a candidate member of the SED's Central Committee, but was soon constrained to publish her work abroad. To put it mildly, Ulbricht's GDR did not enjoy a flourishing literary café society. In Poland, the philosopher Leszek Kołakowski, one of the true giants of twentieth-century political thought, was thrown out of his job for daring to call into question the sacred dogmas of Marxist-Leninism. [29] In Romania, in 1960, two of the country's leading intellectuals, the philosopher Constantin Noica and the literary critic Constantin Pillat, were tortured by the *Securitate* and sent to the camps, along with a group of their friends and colleagues, after they organized a private club to discuss the works of the great Romanian writers Emil Cioran and Mircea Eliade, both of whom had suspect right-wing views. [30]

In Prague, meanwhile, the desire of the Czechs for intellectual freedom was, in the mid-1960s, about to boil over, despite the authorities' best efforts to keep a lid on so-called dissent. The fourth "Writers' Congress" in 1967 featured a series of bold challenges to the regime, notably one by a young satirist called Václav Havel, the author of a withering lampoon of Marxist-Lenininst jargon called *The Memorandum*, who publicly lauded Solzhenitsyn's moral commitment.[31]

A third area of similarity across the communist bloc was impending economic obsolescence, although this was not necessarily apparent at the time of Khrushchev's downfall. The raw output of the Soviet bloc grew by 8 percent per year throughout the 1950s (Bulgaria, East Germany, and Romania all managed double-digit growth) and although growth slowed in the early 1960s, especially in Czechoslovakia and the GDR, it revived in the second half of the decade.[32] The communist countries of Europe produced no less than 30 percent of world industrial output by 1970. Such achievements were a godsend to the regimes' apologists, who ingenuously tended to equate growth in output with an increase in the quality of life and to imply that economic progress mitigated communism's glaring failures in the sphere of human and political rights.

But man cannot live by cement alone. The communist bloc's record in producing consumer goods or acceptable levels of housing or an adequate diet for its citizens was for the most part abysmal. In 1965 Russian workers had to wait for years to buy a washing machine, a television, or a car (which in any case cost the equivalent of three years' salary) and were constrained to live in ill-heated dormitories that provided each individual with a meager sixty-nine square feet of personal space and that often did not possess either running water or main drains. To get to work, unless they used the sumptuous Moscow subway, they had to rely on public transport that was so scarce that citizens spent several days a year just queuing for the bus. At dinner, if they did not want to pay black market prices, they were limited to the poor-quality meat and vegetables a grossly inefficient state distribution system had managed to haul along potholed roads from the countryside. Soviet families spent half their family incomes on food—more than double the amount in the West.[33]

East Germany, Hungary, and Czechoslovakia were better than the rest of the bloc at delivering consumer goods, though even they did not compare with their western counterparts. In East Germany, in particular, the percentage of people possessing a refrigerator, a television, or a "car" (it is doubtful that the East German Trabant, even by the standards of the 1960s, truly deserves this name) was comparable to that of Italy or Spain. Communist states also enjoyed a higher level of investment in social services than some western nations.

By the mid-1960s, however, the need to shift from extensive growth (i.e., growth driven by capital investment and greater workforce participation) to intensive growth (growth based upon technological innovation and rising consumption) was widely acknowledged everywhere in the Soviet bloc. The question was how to achieve this goal. The communist economies were run by administrative fiat, not by the market mechanism. The central planning agencies set production targets and allocated, usually incompetently, resources to the factories and farms that actually had to produce the goods. Such a system tended toward stagnation. Enterprises had no incentive to change their products to suit consumer demand and every incentive to meet or surpass the planned targets by churning out a limited number of drab standard products. Quality was less of a concern than quantity. The lack of competition for the state producers and the fact that unemployment was an ideological taboo guaranteed that firms could always sell whatever they produced. Nobody would shut the plant down.

In agriculture, the situation was even grimmer. The central problem with the collective farms common across the bloc was that the peasants who worked the farms did not regard themselves as owners. Peasants worked the bare minimum for the state and then cultivated their own private plots for sale in local markets. Private land was only a very small percentage of the arable land in the communist bloc, but it everywhere produced a disconcerting share (70 percent or more) of the national output of vegetables, fruit, eggs, and even meat.

In short, the communist economy was one where the individual consumer took what was doled out to her. And what was doled out did not begin to match what was on offer in the West. It was an acceptable situation only so long as the citizens of these states compared their lot with the grinding rural poverty of their peasant forebears, not with their peers on the other side of the iron curtain.

The communist leaderships experimented in the 1960s with a number of highly technical methods of introducing market mechanisms into their economic system: Professor E. Liberman of Kharkov University even made the front cover of *Time* magazine for advocating such changes.[34] Enterprises were given more latitude over how they met their plan targets and over the prices they charged; consumer products were allocated a greater share of overall resources (though heavy industry and the military continued to take far too much); some firms were allowed to make a profit and invest it, instead of having to negotiate investment with the planning ministry. Such measures were pushed farthest and fastest in Yugoslavia and in Kádár's Hungary, whose "New Economic Mechanism" was "the most lasting and important economic reform undertaken in communist eastern Europe."[35] Both countries soon began to seem much more "western" than anywhere else in the bloc to visitors.

Nevertheless, the speed of reform was hampered by the reflection that "greater latitude in the economy automatically raised the issue of whether there would be any redistribution of power and, if so, how this would be structured."[36] Economic change implied political change, and until 1968 no national communist party was willing to dilute its hold on power. This was in part for ideological reasons. Communist leaders believed that they were building a more evolved and less exploitative form of society than bourgeois capitalism or social democracy. In fact, they were year by year condemning their peoples to chronic economic backwardness.

THE PRAGUE SPRING

Czechoslovakia was the country where there was greatest desire to experiment with new forms of economic organization. The most innovative economist in the Soviet bloc, Otmar Šik, was a Czech, but his prescription for the malaise of the Czech economy—the creation of independent businesses able to operate freely in the market, even if this led to a loss of political control—was anathema for the party old guard. Šik was not alone. From the late 1950s onward, sophisticated Czech jurists, political scientists, novelists, and philosophers contested the core beliefs of communist dogma. Socialism, they argued, could—if it wanted—be pluralistic, and mindful of human rights. Its citizens could be political participants, not unquestioning subjects of an external authority.[37]

Czechoslovakia also had a leadership that was deeply compromised by the events of late Stalinism, and unlike Romania's Gheorghiu-Dej, it had never distanced itself from responsibility for those events. The direct beneficiaries of the Stalinist purges of the early 1950s remained in post until the early 1960s.[38] The party secretary, Antonìn Novotný, was a narrow-minded bureaucrat averse to any dilution of the party's grip on society. Although some of the surviving victims of the purges of the 1950s were released from jail in 1956 and 1957, the regime continued to present the trials of Slánský and his associates as an imperialist-Zionist plot. This falsehood undermined the regime's legitimacy, especially among intellectuals. After the Twenty-second Congress, the urge for renewal in the party leadership grew. At Khrushchev's insistence, a review of the 1949–1954 repressions was commissioned. This process, which was a potential bombshell for the regime, since a frank report was bound to lead to the removal of its chief figures, began in August 1962.

The Prague regime was especially threatened in Slovakia, where the domination of the Czechs was resented and where the desire for the rehabilitation of comrades persecuted for "nationalist" leanings was strong. In 1963, the Slovak intelligentsia, encouraged by the reformist first secretary of the Slo-

vak Communist Party, Alexander Dubček, forced the resignation of the
Czech prime minister, Viliam Široký, the party leader most deeply implicated in the postwar purges, and secured the rehabilitation, posthumous in some
cases, of the principal Slovak communists condemned during in the early
1950s. Dubček also permitted much greater freedom of intellectual life in
Bratislava, including the freest press in the Soviet bloc. In October 1967, at a
meeting of the national party's central committee, Dubček stood out as a
"vigorous proponent of reform" arguing for better treatment for Slovakia and
for a separation of party and state: he openly demanded that Novotný should
relinquish either the party leadership or his other position as national president.[39] Novotný, in his turn, denounced Dubček's "bourgeois nationalism."

As his autobiography makes clear, Dubček was convinced that communism could reacquire legitimacy only by driving economic and political reform. Rather than rely on Leninist dogma to justify its hegemonic role in
society, Dubček believed that the party had to inspire the masses to accept its
leadership by increasing democratic participation, strengthening fundamental
human rights, and achieving economic modernization and a higher standard
of living. Such beliefs were divisive. As he was ruefully forced to admit, for
the Soviet leadership, for the other leaders of the neighbouring communist
states, and for large sections of his own party hierarchy: "What we were
trying to do was . . . simply incomprehensible."[40]

Dubček became party secretary on 5 January 1968 after Novotný had
tried, and conspicuously failed, to get the USSR to back his rule. Dubček was
a fluent Russian speaker who had been trained in Moscow. There was no
reason for Moscow to think that he would be any more radical than János
Kádár, whose "goulash communism" was pacifying Hungary. Dubček was,
moreover, surrounded in Prague by men whose loyalty was not in question.
Within weeks, however, the Soviet leadership was regretting the nonchalance
with which it had regarded the question of Novotný's leadership as a purely
internal matter. Dubček was far more radical than Kádár, far more willing to
confront the past and present failures of the regime, and was leading a country that was intoxicated by its new freedom. Almost Dubček's first action
was to abolish press censorship. The result was a surge of press articles that
dissected the country's recent history with joyful precision.

On 14 March 1968, the Politburo instituted a process of rehabilitation for
the victims of the purges of the early 1950s. Holdovers from the Stalinist
period were forced out of key positions throughout February and March: on
30 March Novotný himself was ousted from the presidency and was replaced
by General Ludvík Svoboda, a noted reformer. Six leading figures from the
Novotný era were demoted from the Politburo at the Central Committee's
meeting on 6 April 1968, although that body still contained a number of
voting members, most notably Vasil Bil'ak, whose commitment to the reformist agenda was merely skin deep. Bil'ak would be, to use Dubček's own

uncompromising word, one of the principal "quislings" in August 1968, when Soviet forces invaded.[41]

The same meeting of the Central Committee also approved the party's "Action Plan," the intellectual centerpiece of the Prague Spring. This document's central theme was that Soviet-style communism had been superseded by history. Class antagonisms were no longer acute; the existing means of production, based as they were on heavy industry, were no longer in tune with society's needs; a technological revolution was occurring that required a superior level of scientific understanding and training among all sectors of society; the "democratization" of society was a precondition for the dynamism necessary to respond to the new forms of industrial society. In these circumstances, the Action Plan suggested, the unique role of the Communist Party was to "extend democracy and eliminate egalitarianism" by introducing a more meritocratic society, in which those who increased their skills levels or showed initiative could prosper.[42]

While the Action Plan's specific calls for market-based economic reforms and for the creation of federal institutions that would placate Slovakia's nationalist longings were vital parts of the document, and while its comment that Czechoslovakia would "pursue a more active European policy" by seeking better relations with the advanced capitalist economies aroused inevitable suspicion, the Action Plan's challenge to the rest of the Soviet bloc was conceptual, not political. In effect, it was implying that the notion of class struggle as the motor of history was as outmoded as the doctrine of the divine right of kings. But since the justification for one-party rule was precisely that the Communist Party was the instrument of the working class in the class struggle, the Action Plan undermined the ideological basis of the system.

The Action Plan suggested that the Communist Party's task was rather to act as an agent of renewal, *serving* society to the fullest in order to acquire an authority that would not be formal but "natural" since it would derive from the party's "capacity" and the "moral qualities" of its leaders. The despotic leaders of socialist states bordering on Czechoslovakia could be excused for thinking that this formula would lead to the dissolution of their personal rule. After all, they knew better than anyone what their own "moral qualities" were. In any event, the Action Plan was published only in an abridged version in the Soviet Union and was banned in Poland and East Germany.

Prague's most anxious neighbors were East Germany's Walter Ulbricht and Poland's Władysław Gomułka. Both feared "contagion" from Czechoslovakia. Indeed, in March 1968 Poland experienced widespread student uprisings, especially at the universities of Warsaw and Krakow, during which one of the protesters' most common chants was "Poland is awaiting its own Dubček."[43] The regime responded with characteristic brutality. Hundreds of professors were sacked and student demonstrators were beaten into submission. The sociologist Zygmunt Bauman and Leszek Kołakowski were forced to leave the country. Two thousand student activists were detained, some for long periods; more than 1,600 were denied the right to study or drafted into the army.[44]

Distastefully, associated with this wave of repression was an openly anti-Semitic propaganda campaign. The disturbances were blamed on Jewish agitators and Gomułka invited the country's (for obvious reasons, small) Jewish community to go to Israel if it did not like life in Poland. Thousands of Jews did indeed emigrate over the next months. Gomułka and Ulbricht could not understand why Dubček refused to use such tried and trusted methods on the party's critics in Prague.

On 23 March, during a summit meeting at Dresden, the Czechoslovak delegation, headed by Dubček, was berated for the growth of "counter-revolutionary tendencies" by the leaders of five other Warsaw Pact countries (East Germany, Poland, Bulgaria, Hungary, and the USSR); Ulbricht, indeed, argued that Prague had been too lax even under Novotný.[45] On 4–5 May 1968, the Czech leaders got another dose of the same medicine at a bilateral meeting in Moscow. Soviet leader Leonid Brezhnev compared the Czech press to "drunken peasants at a country fair," and insisted that "the counter-revolutionary forces, the successors of the bourgeoisie, are being given freedom to act as they please, and they are raging in full force."[46] He was especially infuriated by television pictures of demonstrators waving American flags during Prague's May Day celebrations. Military maneuvers were held by the Warsaw Pact on Czechoslovak soil in June, and Soviet troops remained for some days after the exercises had concluded.[47]

The last straw for Prague's neighbors came on 27 June 1968, when the literary journal *Literární listy* published "Two Thousand Words that Belong to Workers, Farmers, Officials, Scientists, Artists and Everybody," a manifesto written by the outspoken writer Ludvík Vaculík and signed by more than sixty prominent figures in Czechoslovak cultural life. This uncompromising document was an appeal to local associations of the party to nominate reformers as delegates to an extraordinary Congress of the Communist Party (KČE) scheduled for September to adopt the Action Plan and democratize the party's statutes. Aside from this political point, however, the "Two Thousand Words" manifesto was also a ringing condemnation of forty years of communist rule that had "transformed a political party and an alliance based on ideas into an organization for exerting power, one that proved highly attractive to power-hungry individuals eager to wield authority, to cowards who took the safe and easy route, and to people with bad consciences."[48]

The Czechoslovak Politburo criticized Vaculík's manifesto, but took no repressive action against either its writer or its signatories. This was not good enough for the Warsaw Pact hard-liners. On 14–15 July 1968, a summit meeting took place in Warsaw in the absence of the Czechoslovak leadership. In his speech to the summit, Ulbricht specifically referred to the "Two

Thousand Words" manifesto, citing it as proof that the goal of the "counter-revolutionary forces" was to "destroy the party's power." Ulbricht demanded "the elimination of hostile elements from the mass media" as the "absolute minimum of what must be done." Todor Zhivkov went still further: for him, "only by relying on the armed forces of the Warsaw Pact can we change the situation . . . in Czechoslovakia we must restore the dictatorship of the proletariat . . . we must prevent the social-democratization of the party." Brezhnev and Gomułka echoed these harsh strictures, with only Kádár making an embarrassed plea for tolerance. Brezhnev summed up the general mood best: "There has never been a case in which socialism triumphed and was firmly entrenched, only to have a capitalist order restored. This has never happened and we are certain it never will."[49]

The upshot of the summit was an aggressive letter to Prague containing an ultimatum to crack down on "counter-revolutionary" elements or face the consequences. The Czechoslovak leadership responded by denying there was any "objective reason to justify either the assertion that our current situation is counter-revolutionary or the allegation of an imminent threat to the foundations of the socialist system" and asked for bilateral meetings to enable them to press their case.[50]

A bilateral meeting with the Soviet leaders, Brezhnev and Premier Aleksei Kosygin, took place at the railway station of Čierna nad Tisou on the Slovak-Ukraine border on 29 July 1968. It was followed up five days later with another collective meeting of the Warsaw Pact in Bratislava. Dubček was badgered at both encounters to eliminate anti-Soviet comments in the press, suppress free inquiry into Czechoslovakia's recent history, crack down on non-communist political activity (since the spring, dozens of "clubs" with avowedly political objectives had emerged), and purge certain key individuals in the party and government hierarchies. Had Dubček gone along with these demands, he could perhaps have kept his hold on power. In a fascinating ninety-minute telephone call to Dubček on 13 August, Brezhnev dangled this course of action before the Czechoslovak leader in a way that irresistibly calls to mind Matthew 4, verses 1–11. You can "emerge triumphant," Brezhnev told Dubček, if you side with Bil'ak and give a "rebuff to the rightist forces."[51]

Dubček was not to be tempted, though his evasive reply that the Soviet leader should take "whatever measures" he believed necessary "may have been construed by Brezhnev as a tacit green light for military intervention."[52] Somewhat credulously, Dubček believed that the Soviet Union would not invade a fellow Soviet republic.[53] The communiqué of the Bratislava summit only two weeks before had reiterated that the states of the Soviet bloc would "improve all-round cooperation of their countries on the basis of the principles of equality, respect for sovereignty and national independence, territorial integrity, fraternal mutual assistance and solidarity," although it had also

contained ominous references to "the common international duty of all socialist countries to support, strengthen and defend the gains of socialism."[54]

Soviet elite units and troops from all the Warsaw Pact nations except
Romania began the invasion of Czechoslovakia on the night of 20–21 August
1968. The West was caught by surprise. President Johnson seemed not to
grasp the importance of the matter when he was told about it by Antonin
Dobrynin, the Soviet ambassador to Washington.[55] But the Johnson administration was not willing to jeopardize its efforts to negotiate a test ban treaty
and took no punitive action against the USSR, although Ambassador George
Crews McGhee in Bonn did underline that the invasion indicated that there
were "severe practical limits" on efforts to obtain détente and warned that
Washington should not accept the principle that the invasion was "a purely
internal Communist affair."[56]

Within a few weeks, four hundred thousand mostly Russian "liberators"
were on Czechoslovak soil. Dubček belatedly realized he was dealing with
"gangsters," not fellow socialists.[57] The Czechoslovak leadership issued a
dignified condemnation of the invasion but pleaded with its citizens not to
resist the invaders by force of arms.[58] Dubček, the premier Oldrich Černik,
and several other senior members of the KČE were taken forcibly to Moscow
where they were joined by other members of the Czech leadership, including
President Svoboda. Four days of intense negotiations followed. The Soviets
wanted to extort a confession of ideological error from the Czechoslovak
leadership, but they were already aware that they needed Dubček back in
power, which gave the hostages some bargaining power. Even with the backing of the Red Army, the Prague turncoats, led by Bil'ak and Alois Indra, a
candidate member of the Politburo, did not possess sufficient authority to
govern.

The outcome of the negotiations was the so-called Moscow Protocol, a
fifteen-point document that heralded the reintroduction of censorship, the
purging of the most noted liberals, the banning of political clubs, a return to
central economic planning, and the cancellation of the extraordinary party
congress (which was nevertheless held under clandestine conditions). No
promises were made for the withdrawal of the Red Army.[59] The KČE leadership reluctantly signed. They could see no other way of preserving any hope
for their nation, which had breached a hitherto unwritten law that communist
parties were not free either to abandon socialism or to destabilize socialism
elsewhere. *Pravda* made this point, which became known as the "Brezhnev
Doctrine," in two leading articles published while the Czechoslovak leadership was still in Moscow. On 27 August 1968, Dubček spoke emotionally
over the radio begging his people to accept the Moscow accord. On several
occasions, his composure broke. Tearfully, he asked his listeners to forgive
him for stopping: "I think you know why it is." As one of his countrymen
wrote, the Czechs and Slovaks knew that the "awful long pauses" in

Dubček's broadcast "contained all the horror that had befallen their country."[60]

Dubček remained in office until April 1969, but did not govern. His leading supporters were gradually squeezed out and "realists," most notably a Slovak former opponent of Novotný, Gustav Husák, came to the fore. Despair gripped the radicals in Prague and Bratislava. On 16 January 1969, a boy called Jan Palach doused himself with petrol in Prague's central Wenceslas Square and set himself alight. A letter was found in his coat pocket announcing that he had the honor of being "torch number one." Other torches would burst into flame if strikes did not break out in protest of the occupation and of censorship. In fact, no second torch did kill himself. But Palach's death prompted an outpouring of national grief. Some eight hundred thousand people attended his funeral. Dubček did nothing to restrain these demonstrations; indeed he plainly sympathized with them.[61]

Dubček's final disgrace came after a game of ice hockey. On 28 March 1969, Czechoslovakia beat the USSR 4–3 to win the world championship. Tens of thousands of Czechs took to the streets of Prague for a rowdy celebration that ended with the sacking of the office of the Russian airline, Aeroflot.[62] Military intervention was only avoided by a hair's breadth. On 17 April 1969, Dubček resigned as party leader. Husák took over and Dubček was forced to watch his successor steer "a reluctant Czechoslovakia back into the fold of political and economic orthodoxy."[63] A purge of so-called unreliable elements was started in the KČE. Hundreds of thousands of reformers lost their party cards and, in many cases, their jobs. Hundreds were imprisoned. The KČE went back to being a Stalinist "transmission belt" communicating the party elite's orders to the rest of society and enforcing them.[64] The universities and other cultural institutions were particularly hard hit.[65]

Dubček would subsequently become ambassador to Turkey for a brief period, be expelled from the party, and be forced to work, under constant surveillance from the secret police, as an obscure official in the Slovak forestry commission. For two decades he was what Orwell called an "unperson." But in the fall of 1989 he became a hero again.

The Prague Spring thus ended with "normalization"—which meant for most a return to drab conformity. In the communist bloc, 1968 exposed the huge lie at the heart of the Soviet system: namely, the lie that the party was representative of the people's will, or even the will of the most progressive section of society. The radicals of Western Europe, fighting on the barricades of Berlin, Paris, and Rome, were too preoccupied with conducting the struggle against American imperialism in Vietnam to analyze this development thoroughly, but they got the general point. Rudi Dutschke, the most prominent intellectual associated with the German students' movement, visited Prague in March 1968. The students and faculty of Charles University, desirous of achieving the freedoms that citizens of the West already took for granted rather than constructing the utopian socialism that Dutschke preached, gave the visiting radical a short course in the democratic socialist society that they hoped would emerge from the Prague Spring. But even before he went to Prague, Dutschke had admitted that what he called the "global authoritarian-socialist structure" dominating the Soviet bloc had exercised its role as "teachers and educators of the masses" in a "counter-revolutionary way."[66] Many western radicals believed something similar: the revolution had been betrayed by the bureaucrats of really existing socialism and only a new revolutionary consciousness, of the kind Mao was experimenting with in China (the so-called Cultural Revolution), could save really existing socialism from sclerosis. The masses had to terrorize the bureaucrats to rejuvenate the revolution. The reason that the Prague Spring truly represented "socialism with a human face" is that its proponents, both in the party and in civil society, did not want to terrorize anybody.

NOTES

1. The PCI newspaper *L'Unità* proclaimed Gagarin a "hero of the future" in a full-page article on 14 April 1961; its 16 April 1961 edition was headlined "The USSR is preparing a Space Craft for the Moon" and featured a lengthy front-page editorial on "The Cosmos and Society" that explained that the Soviet Union's leadership in space technology was a sign of its advanced cultural prowess, and not merely a one-off victory against the United States.

2. John Lamberton Harper, *The Cold War* (Oxford: Oxford University Press, 2012), 148.

3. V. Zubok and C. Pleshakov, *Inside the Kremlin's Cold War* (Cambridge, MA: Harvard University Press, 1996), 281.

4. See Milovan Djilas, *The New Class* (London: Thames & Hudson, 1957). Djilas, who was in prison when this book was published in the West, had his sentence extended as a punishment.

5. Herbert Marcuse, "Repressive Tolerance," in Robert Paul Wolff, Barrington Moore Jr., and Herbert Marcuse, *A Critique of Pure Tolerance* (Boston: Beacon Press, 1969), 95–137.

6. Simon Leys, *Chinese Shadows* (London: Penguin, 1974), 10.

7. I have borrowed the title of an excellent contemporary article by Walter Z. Laqueur, "The End of the Monolith," *Foreign Affairs* 40 (1962): 360–73.

8. William E. Griffith, *Albania and the Sino-Soviet Rift* (Boston: MIT Press, 1963), 46.

9. The latest estimates speak of forty-five million deaths in China during the "Great Leap Forward." See Frank Dikötter, *Mao's Great Famine: The History of China's Most Devastating Catastrophe, 1958–1962* (New York: Walker & Co, 2011).

10. Griffith, *Albania*, 228.

11. Quotes from Griffith, *Albania*, 233–35.

12. See R. V. Burks, "The Rumanian National Deviation: An Accounting," in *Eastern Europe in Transition*, ed. Kurt London, (Baltimore, MD: Johns Hopkins University Press, 1966), 93–113, for a contemporary discussion of the Romanian leadership's ambitions.

13. Palmiro Togliatti, "Promemoria sulle questioni del movimento operaio internazionale e della sua unità," in Roberto Bonchio et al., *Il partito comunista italiano e il movimento operaio internazionale 1956–1968* (Rome: Riuniti, 1968), 235–47, for quotations. The original Italian version appeared in *Rinascita*, September 1964; a translation was published in the *New York Times* on 5 September 1964.

14. Alexander Höbel, "Il Pci nella crisi del movimento comunista internazionale tra Pcus e Pcc (1960–1964)," *Studi Storici* 46 (2005): 516.

15. See, for instance, Paul Du Quenoy, "The Role of Foreign Affairs in the Fall of Nikita Khrushchev in October 1964," *The International History Review* 25 (2003): 2.

16. Jerry F. Hough and Merle Fainsod, *How the Soviet Union Is Governed* (Cambridge, MA: Harvard University Press, 1979), 252.

17. Henry Ashby Turner, *Germany from Partition to Reunification* (New Haven, CT: Yale University Press, 1992), 101–2.

18. Joseph Rothschild, *Return to Diversity: A Political History of East Central Europe since World War II* (Oxford: Oxford University Press, 2000), 213–15, was the main source for these paragraphs on Bulgaria.

19. Vladimir Tismăneanu, "Gheorghiu-Dej and the Romanian Workers' Party: From De-Sovietization to the Emergence of National Communism," CWHP, Working Paper no. 37, May 2002: 2. See also Tismăneanu's authoritative *Stalinism for All Seasons: A Political History of Romanian Communism* (Berkeley: University of California Press, 2003), chapters 5 and 6, for a longer discussion of the power struggles within the Romanian communist movement.

20. Tismăneanu, "Gheorghiu-Dej and the Romanian Workers' Party," 26.

21. Dennis Deletant, *Communist Terror in Romania* (London: Hurst & Co, 1999), 280.

22. Deletant, *Communist Terror in Romania*, 279, is the source for these details on the Romanian camps.

23. Tismăneanu, "Gheorghiu-Dej and the Romanian Workers' Party," 41.

24. Quotations from Tismăneanu, "Gheorghiu-Dej and the Romanian Workers' Party," 47 and 52.

25. This paragraph is based upon Norman Davies, *Heart of Europe: The Past in Poland's Present* (Oxford: Oxford University Press), 1–12.

26. Mark Mazower, *Dark Continent: Europe's Twentieth Century* (London: Penguin, 1998), 283.

27. The author had the life-changing experience of visiting Romania on an educational visit in the mid-1970s. One of the sights we were shown was the suburb of Bucharest reserved for high dignitaries of the party and other personalities such as the tennis player Ilie Nastase. The houses were extremely luxurious and well-appointed. When our guide asked us if we had any questions, a forest of hands went up. Visibly surprised, she asked a boy sitting at the front of the bus what his question was. He spoke for us all: "In a socialist country, isn't everybody supposed to be equal?"

28. For the publication of *One Day in the Life of Ivan Denisovich*, and the subsequent backlash, see Michael Scammell, *Solzhenitsyn* (London: Hutchinson, 1984), chapters 23–29.

29. Some of the work that got Kołakowski into trouble is collected in *Toward a Marxist Humanism: Essays on the Left Today* (New York: Grove, 1969).

30. Deletant, *Communist Terror in Romania*, 277.

31. Extracts of key speeches from the Czech Writers' Congress of 1967 are published in Jaramir Navratil, ed., *The Prague Spring 1968* (Budapest: Central European University Press, 1999), doc. no. 1; Havel's contribution is on page 9. *The Memorandum* can be found in Havel, *The Garden Party and Other Plays* (New York: Grove, 1993).

32. George Schöpflin, *Politics in Eastern Europe* (Oxford: Blackwell, 1996), 138.

33. This paragraph is based upon Timothy Sosnovy, "The New Soviet Plan: Guns Still Before Butter," *Foreign Affairs* 44 (1966): 620–32.

34. Quoted in Michael Kaser, "Kosygin, Liberman and the Pace of Soviet Industrial Reform," *World Today*, September 1965, 375–88.

35. Gale Stokes, *The Walls Came Tumbling Down: The Collapse of Communism in Eastern Europe* (Oxford: Oxford University Press, 1993), 79.

36. Schöpflin, *Politics in Eastern Europe*, 139.

37. I owe these brief comments on Czech intellectual ferment to Vladimir I. Kusin's fascinating *The Intellectual Origins of the Prague Spring: The Development of Reformist Ideas in Czechoslovakia* (Cambridge: Cambridge University Press, 1971 and 2002).

38. I use the word "beneficiaries" deliberately. According to Alexander Dubček, *Il socialismo dal volto umano: autobiografia di un rivoluzionario* (Roma: Riuniti editori, 1996), 107, the Communist Party leadership divided up the possessions of their murdered rivals after their

execution. English edition: *Hopes Dies Last: The Autobiography of Alexander Dubcek* (New York: Kodansha, 1993).

39. William Shawcross, *Dubček* (New York: Simon and Schuster, 1990), 108.

40. Dubček, *Il socialismo del volto umano*, 207.

41. Dubček, *Il socialismo del volto umano*, 227.

42. My translation from *La Via Cecoslovacca al socialismo* (Rome: Riuniti, 1968), 21–22 and 36–45. The fact that the Italian Communist Party should rush to translate the Czech text was significant. Jiři Hájek, Dubček's foreign minister, emphasizes the Action Plan's concern to go beyond the class struggle and its concept of the Communist Party as an innovator, earning the support of the masses through its behavior, not its ideologically defined role as an historical instrument, in his *Praga 1968* (Rome: Riuniti, 1978), 26 and 35.

43. Quoted in Mark Kramer, "The Czechoslovak Crisis and the Brezhnev Doctrine," in *1968: The World Transformed*, ed. Carole Fink, Philipp Gassert, and Detlef Junker (Washington, DC: The German Historical Institute and Cambridge University Press, 1998), 127.

44. Jerzy Eisler, "March 1968 in Poland," in Fink, Gassert and Junker, eds., *The World Transformed*, 248.

45. Jaramir Navratil et al., eds., *The Prague Spring 1968* (Budapest: Central European University Press, 1999), doc. no. 14: 64–72; henceforth, *The Prague Spring*. Ulbricht had good reason to be worried. The notion that there was only slight unrest in the GDR during 1968 has been disproved by scholars researching in the Stasi archives. Fulbrook writes: "Countless numbers of ordinary individuals were willing to risk disciplinary actions, arrest and possible imprisonment, by refusing to sign official documents, by demanding sympathy strikes or *Gedenkminuten*, by spreading leaflets or daubing graffiti, by making symbolic demonstrations of their opposition to the Ulbricht regime." See Mary Fulbrook, "Popular Discontent and Political Activism in the GDR," *Contemporary European History* 2 (1993): 276.

46. *The Prague Spring*, doc. no. 28, 124.

47. For Soviet strategic thinking during the crisis, see Vojtech Mastny, "Was 1968 a Strategic Watershed of the Cold War," *Diplomatic History* 29, no. 1 (2005): 149–77.

48. *The Prague Spring*, doc. no. 44, 177–81, quote 177–78.

49. *The Prague Spring*, doc. no. 52: 212–33. Brezhnev quote p. 228.

50. *The Prague Spring*, doc. no. 53: 234–37. The Czechoslovak reply is to be found in document 55: 243–49.

51. *The Prague Spring*, doc. no. 81: 345–56.

52. Kramer, "The Czechoslovak Crisis," 153.

53. Dubček, *Il socialismo del volto umano*, 208 and 223.

54. *The Prague Spring*, doc. no. 73, 327; Kramer, "The Czechoslovak Crisis," 149.

55. Anatoly Dobrynin, *In Confidence: Moscow's Ambassador to America's Six Cold War Presidents* (New York: Random House, 1995): 180–81. Mastny, "Was 1968 a Strategic Watershed?" says, 166, that "it was not [Johnson's] finest hour."

56. For McGhee's advice, see *The Prague Spring and the Warsaw Pact Invasion of Czechoslovakia in 1968*, ed. Günter Bischoff, Stefan Karner and Peter Ruggenthaler (Lanham, MD: Lexington Books, 2010), appendix 7, 457–59.

57. Dubček, *Il socialismo del volto umano*, 223.

58. *The Prague Spring*, doc. no. 100: 414–15.

59. *The Prague Spring*, doc. no. 119: 477–80.

60. Milan Kundera, *The Unbearable Lightness of Being*, trans. Michael Henry Haim (London: Faber & Faber, 1985), 69.

61. See Shawcross, *Dubček*, 171–76, for a vivid description of Palach's death and its aftermath.

62. The Cold War History Project has an excellent set of translated documents regarding these events at http://digitalarchive.wilsoncenter.org/collection/204/cold-war-on-ice.

63. Adam Roberts, "Socialist Conservatism in Czechoslovakia," *The World Today*, November 1970, 478.

64. The metaphor is Hájek's, *Praga 1968*, 197. He estimates that 475,000 people "left the party involuntarily" during normalization.

65. Stokes, *The Walls Came Tumbling Down*, 66, says the regime mounted "an all-out attack on cultural institutions."

66. I am quoting from an interview given by the German student leader to the German magazine *Konkret* (May 1968), translated into Italian in Rudi Dutschke, *Dutschke a Praga* (Bari: De Donato, 1968), 97.

Chapter Eight

The Reluctant Ally

When Charles de Gaulle came to power in May 1958, he was taking the reins of a rapidly modernizing, medium-sized West European nation with fractious politicians, an imperial legacy that weighed the country down psychologically and economically, and a Stalinist Communist Party with a substantial share of the vote. The savage war being fought to preserve French rule in Algeria had tarnished France's international reputation and put its democracy at risk; had de Gaulle been sick or otherwise incapable of fulfilling his destiny in the spring of 1958, a military coup and civil war would have been likely consequences: an instructive reminder of the importance of individual statesmen in history.

France, in short, shared many of the same problems as Italy, and then added a few of its own. Yet no political leader in Rome dared to think that Italy could be the pivot power in world politics: at most, politicians such as the Christian Democrat Amintore Fanfani enjoyed being a *tramite* (go-between or facilitator) during international negotiations. Even Great Britain had no illusions that it could do more than advise its cousins in Washington. Harold Macmillan, when he replaced Anthony Eden in January 1957, made restoring the "special relationship" between Great Britain and the United States his first priority. Britain would exert global influence by retaining its independent nuclear deterrent and by working closely with Washington. Macmillan cultivated his personal relationship with President Kennedy assiduously. Kennedy came to esteem the judgment of the bookish, occasionally histrionic British premier, despite the generation gap between them. De Gaulle, a genuinely great man, by contrast misjudged his ability to make France punch above its weight. He wanted to restore France's greatness, but did not possess the means to his end.

De Gaulle likely regarded the British compromise with Washington's greater power as an *unworthy* one. Nations did not adjust their foreign policy to suit the objectives set by others. The General's strategy was to boost France's standing in the world by building a nuclear deterrent, taking the lead in Western Europe, and following a foreign policy that befitted France's dignity. If that meant disagreements with Washington or London or Moscow . . . well, it was in the nature of things that great nations had their differences.

De Gaulle was a classic case of a political leader whose worldview and deepest political beliefs made him too shortsighted to see what was "under his nose"—namely, that France was too weak for the role that he wanted it to play. But the same worldview paradoxically made him a farsighted interpreter of the trends that were shaping international affairs in the 1960s. De Gaulle contested Washington's leadership, but not just for the sake of French *gloire*. Sooner than his peers, he realized that the Cold War division of Europe was potentially a parenthesis in its history.

CLEARING THE DECKS

Before he could mount his challenge, however, the French leader had to provide himself with the institutional machinery to govern France, and he had to liberate France from its debilitating colonial war in Algeria. When de Gaulle took power, he insisted that the French constitution should be drastically altered to provide for a president with sweeping powers over the conduct of foreign and defense policy, the maintenance of internal order, and the duration of any given parliament. Many at the time thought the new Constitution articulated an almost fascist concept of the role of the leader: The journalist and political thinker Raymond Aron more sedately suggested that de Gaulle was "the best possible monarch in the least bad of possible governments."[1] The Constitution was approved in a referendum at the end of September 1958 by an overwhelming margin. De Gaulle was nominated president by a college of some eighty thousand elected public officials in December 1958 (a subsequent constitutional reform provided for the direct election of the president), and he took office on 8 January 1959. Outgoing head of state René Coty summed up the national mood perfectly when he said that the "first of the French is now the first in France."[2] De Gaulle had an impregnable constitutional platform from which to guide France's policy toward the rest of the world.

The General, who had been brought to power by the failure of the governments of the IV Republic to deal with the Algerian insurrection, now flew to Algiers and told the recalcitrant white settlers of Algeria that he "understood" their opposition to Algerian independence. He proceeded to abandon them, offering Algeria the option of self-determination on 16 September 1959. This turnaround led to two coups against his rule in January 1960 and April 1961 by soldiers in Algeria, but de Gaulle quelled both by sheer strength of personality. Algeria became independent in July 1962. Throughout 1961 and 1962, near civil war raged in both Algeria and mainland France as the diehard colonialist OAS (Secret Organized Army) carried out bomb attacks and shootings. Thousands were killed or maimed.[3]

Termination of the Algerian conflict was the price de Gaulle had to pay to be able to take the lead in European and transatlantic politics. It also won him kudos in Washington, which had been critical of human rights abuses by the French army throughout the Algerian war and which had exercised pressure on France to get out of its colonial imbroglio.[4] Yet rather than rest on his laurels, and concentrate on domestic policy, de Gaulle picked a fight with the "Anglo-Saxons" by blocking, in January 1963, the American-backed application of Great Britain to join the EEC, which Prime Minister Macmillan had initiated at the end of July 1961. De Gaulle did not pick this fight by chance. It was an ideal way of asserting France's independence from Washington.

The Eisenhower administration had been a strong backer of the EEC, believing that it was a process that would lead to a West European federal state and thus strengthen the West as a whole. When the EEC Treaty was signed, moreover, the United States had enjoyed a trade surplus with Western Europe and could thus afford to be generous about the protectionism intrinsic to the EEC concept. By the early 1960s, circumstances had changed. Europeans, now thoroughly recovered from the war, were reducing their trade deficits with Washington by exporting manufactures, while American companies were investing in Europe on a large scale.

Since Western Europe now stood firmly on its own two feet, Secretary of State Dean Rusk spoke in December 1961 of the administration's "Grand Design" to unify the non-communist world in a free trading community. In February 1962, President Kennedy signed the Trade Expansion Act and called for the fullest possible liberalization of trade between democratic industrialized nations. As a contemporary observer wrote: "By the spring of 1962 . . . the United States' objective in economic policy was to bring the whole of the non-Soviet world under the same regime of generally freer trade and payments, but within this world it saw an emergent grouping of two major centers of power—the United States and an integrated Western Europe including Britain."[5] Excited policy intellectuals in Washington even spoke of the emergence, in the long term, of an "Atlantic Community" replete with political institutions.

De Gaulle had plans of his own for the EEC's development that made Washington's sudden enthusiasm for a transatlantic trade community and British membership of the EEC unwelcome. As we saw in the previous chapter, he had proposed, in September 1958, that the West should be led by a triumvirate of Britain, France, and the United States. The two "Anglo-Saxon" powers intimated in return that they regarded such pretensions as excessive. As Macmillan wrote in his diary, France was first of all aspiring to join a club that did not exist—for the British and the Americans, while they enjoyed close relations, did not actively collude to set policy—and second, was making an "absurd" claim to parity in the absence of any nuclear capacity. De Gaulle's missive, when it was publicized, aroused resentment among the other EEC nations. Yet as Macmillan shrewdly remarked, "I think it would never enter into de G's head to doubt the general acceptance of the thesis that France is to be treated on a different level to any other power—equal certainly to UK and also to the U.S."[6]

Rebuffed by London and Washington, de Gaulle accordingly decided to build up the EEC into a rival power center that the "Anglo-Saxons" would have to heed. From September 1960 onward, the French leader urged the rest of the Six to extend European integration into the key fields of foreign policy, defense, and culture. In the fall of 1961, this vision crystallized into a proposal (the Fouchet Plan, so called because it emerged from a committee chaired by de Gaulle's close collaborator, Christian Fouchet) for an "indissoluble" "Union of States." The union's key institution was to be a council composed of the heads of government of the Six's member states as well as bimonthly meetings of the foreign ministers. The council was to be served by a "Political Commission," which was to consist of senior officials of the foreign affairs ministries of each member state. The new organization was to be based in Paris.

Such ideas were audacious, especially when one remembers that they were put forward just weeks after the construction of the Berlin Wall and at the height of the confrontation at Checkpoint Charlie. By putting defense and foreign policy on the table, the Fouchet Plan represented a leap forward for European integration, and hence was instinctively popular among West European leaders, most of whom were committed to the ideal of European unity. The Plan's "intergovernmentalism" was less attractive to them. De Gaulle believed that in matters of high policy, only the most authoritative representatives of the member states could make decisions. The Fouchet Plan reflected his views to the letter.

The EEC's member states pointed out other flaws. First, would the "Union of States" supersede NATO and the EEC, or be compatible with them? Fouchet was ambiguous. Second, would Great Britain be admitted to membership? Third, the Dutch disliked the politicization of the European project. Dutch leaders saw European integration as desirable so long as it served "the ultimate goal" of "making European politics and Atlantic trade liberalization identical phenomena." They were not bothered about posturing on the world stage. [7]

The Netherlands redrafted Fouchet's proposals to insert language favorable to NATO and to the autonomy of the EEC. Angered by their presumption, in January 1962 de Gaulle exposed the other five member states to shock therapy by imposing a second draft (Fouchet II) that removed all references to NATO and included economic policy as a core competence of the Union (and hence implied that the EEC would be subsumed within the new organization). It was a graphic reminder of who would call the shots if the Union of States was ever formed.

The Dutch persevered. De Gaulle's second draft was also amended to provide guarantees for NATO and the EEC. The crucial question became British membership. In April 1962, Britain, instigated by The Hague, asked to participate in the political union talks. Belgian foreign minister Paul-Henri Spaak, a former secretary general of NATO and a passionate Atlanticist, and his equally pro-American Dutch counterpart Joseph Luns bluntly stated that they would reject any treaty that did not include Britain as a member. The talks collapsed as a result.

President de Gaulle was furious. Why? *Lèse majesté* is certainly one reason. More to the point, however, his hopes of dominating a West European bloc that would speak with one voice within NATO had been sabotaged by two small Atlanticist countries and the British, Washington's key ally. Like many great men, de Gaulle did not know how to put himself in the shoes of lesser beings and look at circumstances from their point of view. As a distinguished French diplomatic historian has pointed out, de Gaulle's plan assumed that the EEC's member states "would place independence from the American superpower ahead of security." In fact, they preferred to "prosper" beneath the "American umbrella" rather than "shelter under the notional influence offered by a France which could not yet boast a nuclear strike force." De Gaulle's high-handed attitude had not helped his cause, either. It had "awoken memories of Louis XIV and Napoleon" and made the United States' "distant tutelage" seem like a better bet.[8]

Washington wisely kept a low profile during the Fouchet negotiations, but the General's reverse gave quiet satisfaction. De Gaulle was seen by the Kennedy administration as a loose cannon who needed to be tied down. His determination to make France an independent nuclear power was also the source of no little alarm. Whereas Eisenhower had tolerated the spread of nuclear weapons, and actively facilitated the British acquisition of nuclear technology, the Kennedy administration quickly concluded that nuclear proliferation needed to be checked.

Indeed, just a week after the Dutch rejection of the Fouchet Plan, Secretary of Defense Robert McNamara told a NATO Council meeting that it was necessary to "centralize the decision to use nuclear weapons" and that it would be "intolerable" if "part of the strategic force" was launched "in isolation from our main striking power." For good measure, he added that small-scale deterrents were useless anyway and could only serve to induce nuclear strikes on the countries that possessed them.[9] The Kennedy administration began to talk up the idea that NATO countries should have access to nuclear weapons only as part of a "multilateral force" (MLF) whose atomic weapons would be under strict American supervision. The whole trend of the Kennedy administration's policy was toward harmonization of the West under Washington's guidance and leadership.[10]

De Gaulle's rejection of British membership of the EEC in January 1963 was hence an act of rebellion against Washington's tightening grip. First, the General ensured he had the backing of Konrad Adenauer. Between November 1958 and mid-1962, the two leaders met on fifteen occasions, had more than one hundred hours of talks, and wrote to each other more than forty times.[11] Adenauer made an official visit to France in July 1962 and de Gaulle hailed him as a "great German, a great European, a great man who is a great friend of France."[12] In September 1962, de Gaulle visited Bonn, where he aroused massive popular approval by declaring his admiration for the "great German people." Nobody had talked to the Germans in this way since 1945 (or even 1870). Dazzled by de Gaulle; contemptuous of Macmillan, the appeaser of Khrushchev; and resentful of Kennedy's negotiating over his head on Berlin and the future of Germany, Adenauer made France, which had been staunch during the Berlin crisis, the point of reference for his foreign policy. It would soon become clear that his judgment was not shared by either his foreign minister, Gerhard Schröder, or his heir apparent, Ludwig Erhard.

Matters came to a head in mid-December 1962 when de Gaulle met Macmillan at Rambouillet castle in France. De Gaulle broke the bad news that he was leaning against British membership of the EEC to the prime minister, who became deeply emotional: the General reputedly assured his ministers that he had nearly told the British premier "*ne pleurez pas, milord.*"

Macmillan had good grounds for distress. The previous month, immediately after the Cuban crisis, Washington had told London that the Skybolt air-launched missile, with which the British were intending to deliver their atomic warheads, was unreliable and that the program would have to be terminated. Since Britain had already canceled its own "Blue Streak" ballistic missile in April 1960, the Macmillan government was stuck with costly hardware that it could not get off the ground. De Gaulle's intimation that entry to Europe was also in doubt thus came as a second slap in the face in the space of a few weeks. Macmillan's foreign and defense policy was in tatters.

The British premier rallied quickly. At the Nassau Conference on 18–21 December 1962, Macmillan persuaded Kennedy to let Britain buy American sea-launched Polaris missiles. This meant building a fleet of oceangoing submarines, but the British were determined to stay in the nuclear game.

Washington wanted any British fleet to integrate into NATO's forces (hitherto Britain's nuclear forces had not been), but at Nassau the president, to the frustration of many of his advisors, who saw a golden opportunity to end Britain's nuclear independence, acknowledged that when supreme national interests were at stake, a British premier could order Polaris to be fired without waiting for the say-so of the NATO commander. This generous gesture toward a personal friend and longtime ally overturned the logic of the MLF.

Kennedy was prepared, with British support, to offer the same missiles to de Gaulle on the same conditions. Without unconditional control over the weapons, however, France was not interested. France, moreover, possessed neither the submarines nor the warheads necessary to utilize Polaris. De Gaulle was also indisposed at being presented with a deal that the French government had played no part in negotiating. Last but not least, Under Secretary of State George Ball, a keen supporter of the MLF, visited Paris and Bonn in the second week of January to press the idea on America's partners. De Gaulle was not amused. [13]

The General accordingly, in Vaisse's words, "broke lances" with Washington across the board. [14] First, he publicly dismissed British prospects for entry into the EEC at a 14 January 1963 press conference. After loftily explaining that Britain's agricultural arrangements and ties to its former empire had proved stumbling blocks throughout the negotiations, de Gaulle made abundantly clear that his principal objection was that British membership might lead to American domination of the EEC. If Britain was admitted to membership, he argued, other countries would follow. The "eleven member, then thirteen-member, then perhaps eighteen-member Common Market that would be built would . . . hardly resemble the one the Six have built." He went on:

> Moreover, this Community, growing in this way, would be confronted with all the problems of its economic relations with a host [*une foule*] of other states, and above all with the United States. It is likely that the cohesion of all its members . . . would not survive for long and that in the end there would appear a colossal Atlantic Community dependent on America and under American control that would swiftly absorb the European Community. [15]

France, de Gaulle insisted, wanted a "purely European construction." De Gaulle's veto was followed up, on 22 January, by a second action offensive to Washington, namely the signature of a Franco-German Treaty of Friendship during a visit by Adenauer to Paris. The treaty established that the heads of government would meet each other twice a year; the foreign ministers would meet every three months. Regular meetings between officials were to take place to ensure the coordination of the two countries' policies in the areas covered by the treaty, namely foreign, defense, and education policy and policy toward cultural exchanges for young people (a particular interest of Adenauer's). In foreign policy, the two countries pledged to "consult each other, prior to any decision, on all important questions . . . with a view to arriving, so far as possible, at a common position." EEC, NATO, and East-West matters were singled out as areas where Franco-German coordination was essential. These decisions went much further than the diplomats attending the summit had expected. By signing the treaty, Adenauer was overtly siding with de Gaulle in his quarrel with London and Washington. Indeed, French foreign minister Maurice Couve de Murville officially terminated negotiations with Britain on 29 January 1963.

In the long run, the Élysée Treaty (as it is usually called) laid to rest decades of Franco-German hatred and provided a vehicle for progress in European integration. Historians have retrospectively characterized it as a farsighted act of statesmanship. At the time, it was construed, especially in Washington but also by many in West Germany, as a cynical French bid to detach Germany from NATO and drag Bonn toward Cold War neutralism.

Washington, aware that bullying de Gaulle was not an option, pressured West Germany's political elite mercilessly to go back on Adenauer's decision: The episode in fact is an authentic instance of the United States acting imperiously toward a European ally during the Cold War. Like the Eden cabinet during the Suez crisis, the West German government abruptly discovered that if the Americans compelled them to make a choice between Washington and Paris, it really had no choice at all. When the Bundestag ratified the treaty, a preamble was added to the text to say that West Germany's commitments to NATO were unaffected by it. Adenauer, who was nearing ninety, was unsentimentally deposed from the leadership of the CDU in April 1963 and replaced by Ludwig Erhard, the most Atlanticist, unGaullist, free-trade enthusiast the party could muster. Erhard became chancellor in the fall of 1963. Some of the emotion that surrounded Kennedy's visit to Berlin in June 1963 among top German politicians was due to relief that the Americans, despite Adenauer's unwise deviation from orthodoxy, were apparently still on Bonn's side.

FROM THE ATLANTIC TO HANOI

De Gaulle was not quelled by Washington's show of strength over the Élysée Treaty. He accepted the U.S. intervention philosophically, but soon returned to the attack on four separate fronts: monetary policy and the hegemony of the dollar; defense policy and NATO, from which France took a semidetached position in 1966; relations with the communist bloc; Vietnam, which de Gaulle presciently foresaw would end in catastrophe. It was a message that Washington did not want to hear.

In short, de Gaulle took upon a gadfly role toward Washington in the latter half of the 1960s. It is not clear that his activities amounted to a coherent alternative foreign policy or to an "all-out crusade against U.S. preponderance and the established global order."[16] Rather, it might be more accurate to regard them as a series of provocative gestures that could (and did) do little to change the nature of Western Europe's relationship with the United States. But the gestures undeniably caused a stir on both sides of the Atlantic. The General was willing to express heartfelt doubts about the general trend of U.S. policy that other European leaders often shared, even though most were reluctant to state their views openly.

The General's stand was widely dismissed as "anti-American" at the time, but this diagnosis was somewhat glib. Not every case of plain speaking about the shortcomings of U.S. grand strategy should be regarded as being motivated by envy of the American way of life or by distaste for democracy, though too often this assumption has conditioned Washington's reaction to European criticism. Sometimes, plain speaking can be the action of a candid friend.[17]

De Gaulle's challenge over monetary policy was the result of his dissatisfaction with Washington's privileged position (as he saw it) in the world economy. The postwar economic order established at the Bretton Woods conference of August 1944 had planted the dollar at its heart. Under Bretton Woods, an ounce of gold was given the fixed price of $35.20 and other currencies were pegged to the U.S. currency in relation to this value. Revaluations within the system, such as the substantial devaluation of sterling in 1949 and 1967, were political crises with major knock-on effects that the industrialized democracies did their best to avoid. Countries with a surplus of dollars could, if they wanted, exchange dollars for bullion from the Federal Reserve. In theory, this meant that U.S. politicians in government and Congress should be prudent stewards of the domestic economy, managing demand carefully in order to ensure that the U.S. economy did not overheat and lead to too great an outflow of dollars (and hence present foreigners with the opportunity to drain the United States of its gold reserves).

In practice, from the late 1950s onward, the United States tried to have both guns and butter. The federal government increased spending on welfare while failing to cut the growing costs of the American military presence around the world (indeed, after the Vietnam commitment began to intensify in 1964, it increased them). High spending by the government pumped money into the economy, boosting growth and sucking in imports. Concurrent high growth in Western Europe led to conspicuous U.S. direct investment. Already when J. F. Kennedy took office in January 1961, Washington was beginning to get nervous about the United States' shrinking surplus on its balance of payments—a surplus that would become a serious deficit by the end of the decade.[18]

The Kennedy administration solved the problem by urging its allies to foot more of the bill for the common defense. West Germany indeed committed itself to buy more arms as a way of offsetting military costs for the U.S. balance of payments. But this, of course, was grist to de Gaulle's mill. As we have seen, he thought the Europeans should be conducting a foreign and defense policy that coincided with their own interests, not one that tamely followed the Americans' strategic goals. But now the United States was asking Europe to *pay* for a policy whose goals and costs had been decided in Washington.

Starting in 1964, France began building up its gold reserves and selling dollars. On 4 February 1965, de Gaulle gave this policy a public rationale by calling for the abolition of Bretton Woods. There was no reason, the French president argued, to treat the dollar as a surrogate for gold. By allowing the United States to pay its debts in dollars instead of gold, "which has real value, and which one possesses only if one earns it," Washington could indebt itself for free.[19] As one scholar has expressed de Gaulle's gripe: "The power to print the world's currency conveyed the ability to finance a global strategic role without commensurately taxing U.S. citizens."[20]

The new policy was accompanied by various dramatic gestures—instead of keeping his gold in the Federal Reserve, de Gaulle theatrically flew it home to France—and it sparked off an equally dramatic transatlantic controversy. An American columnist, Russell Baker, satirized de Gaulle's action by comparing "Gaullefinger" to the James Bond villain "Goldfinger," who of course tried to *steal* the gold in Fort Knox before he was foiled by special agent 007. Other contributions were less tongue-in-cheek and spoke openly of a "gold war."[21]

Despite the vaudeville, the crisis had serious implications. By unloading dollars, de Gaulle was hinting that European possessors of U.S. promises to pay (which is what paper money is) could not rely upon the United States to preserve the dollar's value. If it suited U.S. policy makers, Washington might devalue its currency and leave its allies to pick up the tab. Europeans, de Gaulle was suggesting, should not *trust* the United States so much, hence the row. No nation, especially an ally, likes being accused of untrustworthiness.

A similar logic was behind the French president's decision partially to withdraw from NATO in March 1966. Under Kennedy and Johnson, Washington had moved away from the strategic doctrines of the Eisenhower era. Instead of "massive retaliation" to any Soviet attack, the Kennedy administration pressed the doctrine of "flexible response" upon its European allies. Once the USSR possessed enough submarine- and land-launched ballistic missiles capable of escaping a first strike by U.S. forces and of mounting a counterattack on U.S. soil—which by the mid-1960s it did—U.S. strategists unsurprisingly no longer wanted to resort automatically to the use of nuclear arms. Instead, Washington urged its allies to ramp up their conventional forces in order to be able to repel, or at least slow, a Soviet advance into Germany. Tactical nuclear weapons would only be used at a second stage, and ballistic missiles would not be employed except in retaliation for Soviet escalation of the conflict. Use would be "late and limited."[22]

"Flexible response" was greeted askance by the Europeans, not least because it theoretically required an enormous increase in their defense spending (which was never forthcoming). It nevertheless became official NATO policy in 1967, with the adoption of policy document MC 14/3. By then, however, France had left the alliance's command structure. In de Gaulle's view— and this is why he was so determined to acquire a French *force de frappe* capable of destroying Soviet cities—Europeans could not and should not rely on Washington taking a conflict to the ballistic stage. Why should *les américains* commit suicide? More generally, de Gaulle believed that the issue was one of fundamental principle. How could any state worthy of its name not take primary responsibility for its own national defense?

At a press conference on 9 September 1965, de Gaulle gave a masterly overview of his thinking. The present epoch, he argued, with its large numbers of new states; the "preponderant power" acquired by two countries, "America and Russia," which naturally tended them to exercise "their hegemony over the peoples under their sway"; the rising power of China, which was bound to become a power of the first rank; not to mention the terrifying power of nuclear weapons and the speed of industrial change, was one of "almost infinite hopes, but also gigantic dangers."

What was France's role in such a situation? There were "some" in France who wished to "subordinate her to Moscow," de Gaulle darkly warned—this was a ritual hit at the PCF. There were also others who on the strength of "arbitrary theories" believed that France should "submerge its personality" in international organizations dominated "from within or without" by the United States—this was a sniping reference to NATO and the EEC. De Gaulle countered that either policy amounted to an unjustifiable "national abdication." France had "to have a policy that is her own." For this reason, by 1969 at the latest, when the NATO Treaty was to be renewed, France would bring to an end the "qualified subordination" foreseen by membership of NATO, although it would remain an ally of the NATO countries for so long as the "solidarity of the western peoples" appeared necessary for the defense of Europe.[23]

For similar reasons, between June 1965 and January 1966 France was involved in the so-called empty chair crisis of the European Economic Community (EEC), where France fought (and won) a lengthy battle to maintain a veto over decisions taken by a qualified majority of the EEC's governing body, the Council of Ministers.[24]

On 21 February 1966, with Washington ever more deeply involved in the Vietnam conflict, de Gaulle returned to the question of France's status in

NATO, but in more polemical terms. The world had changed since April 1949, he contended. As a result of "interior and external evolution" within the communist bloc, the "western world is no longer threatened today as it was when the American protectorate was organized in Europe under the cover of NATO." For good measure, de Gaulle added that though the odds of a general war were receding in Europe, one could not tell whether the conflicts in which America was embroiled elsewhere in the world—such as Vietnam—might not lead to a "general conflagration" in which Europe would be involved against its will.[25] Two weeks later, de Gaulle warned President Johnson of France's intention to "regain on her whole territory the full exercise of her sovereignty, at present diminished by the permanent presence of allied military elements or by the use which is made of her airspace; to cease her participation in the integrated commands; and no longer to place her forces at the disposal of NATO."[26]

Washington reluctantly went along with de Gaulle's démarche. President Johnson laconically remarked that "when a man asks you to leave his house, you don't argue; you get your hat and go."[27] When one considers that the United States had provided France with $4.2 billion in military aid since 1945 (nearly half of the amount granted to all NATO states), Johnson's reaction showed commendable restraint.[28] France's decision meant, moreover, shifting SHAPE (NATO high command) from the outskirts of Paris to Belgium and the movement of the organization's headquarters to Brussels. The alliance's operational ability was impaired, especially by the denial of French airspace to NATO aircraft, and its logistical chains were disrupted. U.S. troops were nevertheless out of France by April 1967. They left behind facilities, which were taken over by the French army, worth nearly $1 billion.[29] The General's policy, in short, was not cost-free for France's allies. Nor, incidentally, was it popular with French elite opinion. "Almost all the principal political figures and organs of the press were more or less hostile to the General's decision," says French historian Maurice Vaisse.[30]

Once France was semidetached from NATO, the General was free to take his independent foreign policy in a new direction: launching unilateral détente with Brezhnev's USSR. De Gaulle had famously talked in the past of his wish for a peaceful Europe "stretching from the Atlantic to the Urals." He now made this vision a basis for policy.

De Gaulle, who had already aroused American ire by recognizing China in 1964—as Nixon would do to international acclaim in 1972—embarked upon a lengthy twelve-day visit to the USSR on 20 June 1966. The French president crisscrossed the USSR, visiting Moscow, Novosibirsk in Siberia, Leningrad, Kiev, Volgograd (as Stalingrad had been renamed), and Baikonur, the "aerospace city" that was the Soviet equivalent of Cape Canaveral, before returning to Moscow. No foreign leader had ever before been received with "such solemnity" by Soviet Russia.[31]

De Gaulle's regal progress around Russia achieved few concrete results, but was perhaps not meant to. The message it sent to the world was contained in a speech made in the Kremlin, the day after his arrival, in which he hoped that new relationships of détente, understanding, and cooperation might be forged between Western Europe and the East in such a way that there would be a "restoration" of Europe into a "fertile whole" rather than one "paralyzed by sterile division."[32] It was Europe's task to overcome its divisions and find solutions to its problems. The implication, of course, was that *La Russie* was a European nation, unlike the United States. In conversation with Brezhnev on 29 June 1966, at the end of his visit, de Gaulle made this point explicit. He told the Soviet leader that "the renaissance of Europe was impossible" without the USSR. Brezhnev confirmed, unsurprisingly, that he, too, would like to see an "independent Europe, one freed from all external interference." Responding to a bitter attack by Brezhnev on U.S. policy in Vietnam, de Gaulle even told his host that he regarded the USSR by contrast as "a great peaceful power"—a compliment that bordered on sycophancy toward his host.[33]

Yet the visit amounted to much more than mere appeasement of the Soviet *hyperpuissance*. As Vaisse says, the General's "initiative" served to "make détente respectable."[34] Thereafter, talking to the Soviets was no longer taboo for European leaders. One wonders whether, without de Gaulle's voyage of reconciliation, West European nations would have found the courage to begin the process of détente that would lead to the signing of the Helsinki Accords on human rights in August 1975, or whether West Germany's leaders would have launched the policy of *Ostpolitik* after 1969 (see below, chapter 9). De Gaulle's central point was that Europe's destiny could only be decided by Europeans themselves, not by the superpowers negotiating over their heads.

De Gaulle's fourth divergence from Washington came over the Vietnam War. De Gaulle explained to both Eisenhower and Kennedy that the only solution to conflict between the two Vietnams was "a neutral, unified Vietnam, with no foreign troops on its soil."[35] Such a nation might well be under the control of Hanoi, and hence communist, but de Gaulle thought that this was a secondary consideration. With his firm conviction in the centrality of national identity for deciding foreign policy, he guessed that the Vietnamese communists would not be in the pocket of the Soviets or the Chinese, and that their influence would not set off a cascade of dominoes.

U.S. policy was the exact opposite. Eisenhower and Kennedy propped up the autocratic regime of Ngo Dinh Diem in Saigon until its failure was evident (and then backed a murderous coup d'état to get rid of the Vietnamese leader). Under President Johnson, U.S. direct military intervention against North Vietnam escalated and, after the dubious August 1964 Gulf of Tonkin incident and subsequent resolution by Congress authorizing Johnson to assist any South East Asian country menaced by communist aggression, led to the insertion of combat units in March 1965 and the onset of air strikes on North Vietnam. The United States soon had more than five hundred thousand troops embedded in South East Asia.

The General watched these developments with growing dismay, but remained publicly silent until 1 September 1966 when he attacked U.S. policy in the course of an official visit to Cambodia. With a perceptible tone of defiance, de Gaulle urged Washington to follow the French example in Algeria by putting an end to "sterile conflicts." This meant beginning negotiations with Hanoi and committing to gradual U.S. withdrawal—in effect, the strategy that would subsequently be followed by President Nixon, when he "Vietnamized" the conflict in 1972. [36]

De Gaulle's speech in Phnom Penh provoked consternation among some U.S. policy makers, who did not accept that there was any parallel, moral or strategic, between Algeria and Vietnam. "De Gaulle appears to heap all the blame for the situation, its origin and development in Indochina, on the U.S. explicitly," Ambassador Chip Bohlen minuted plaintively from Paris. [37] Washington's mood worsened when the French president used his end-of-year address to the nation to denounce a war that was all the more "detestable" because a "great power" was "ravaging" a small one. [38] His remarks struck a chord with public opinion. There is little doubt that Washington's policy of trying to bomb North Vietnam into submission made de Gaulle's controversial prior withdrawal from the NATO command structure more presentable to the French people and to peoples elsewhere in Western Europe. In July 1967, France and North Vietnam resumed diplomatic relations. When, toward the end of his presidency, and after years of aerial bombardment that had cost hundreds of thousands of lives, Johnson decided to open negotiations with Hanoi, France naturally became the intermediary between the two sides. The talks that ended direct U.S. military involvement during President Nixon's second term in office were held in Paris.

De Gaulle's willingness to take a strong stance against the Vietnam War contrasted sharply with the line taken by Ludwig Erhard in Bonn and Prime Minister Harold Wilson in London (Wilson's Labour Party had narrowly defeated the Conservatives in the October 1964 general election). Both men supported the U.S. campaign against Hanoi in principle while resisting, for domestic political reasons, U.S. pressure for greater commitment to the war in practice. Like Macmillan, Wilson attempted during his premiership to act as an honest broker between Washington and Moscow but, unlike Macmillan, did not possess the international standing to be taken seriously in that role, certainly by Washington. [39]

Erhard's loyalty toward Washington alienated de Gaulle, especially after Bonn criticized de Gaulle's initiation of diplomatic ties with China, ignited public opinion within Germany, and failed even to placate the United States' incessant demands for more German spending on American weaponry to "offset" Washington's expenditure on the defense of West Germany. During a December 1965 summit in Washington, Erhard came under intense U.S. pressure to commit German support troops to the conflict—which would have breached the West German Basic Law—and when the chancellor politely demurred President Johnson "towered over the chancellor and raised his voice to a thundering volume" and "reminded Erhard in no uncertain terms of all the United States had done for West Germany during the past decades." Erhard "left the meeting shaken and near despair."[40]

In the following months, the West German government managed to convince Washington that troop commitments to South East Asia were a political and constitutional impossibility, but top U.S. officials accordingly switched their attention to the question of the German financial contribution for European defense, which Erhard was vainly aspiring to reduce. The Americans were all but contemptuous of the Germans' failure to do their trivial bit for the struggle against world communism. A September 1966 summit between Johnson and Erhard was very nearly as humiliating for the German chancellor as the previous encounter in December. When Erhard returned to Germany, he had lost all credibility as a leader with German public opinion. He resigned as head of government on 1 December 1966. Kurt-Georg Kiesinger replaced him as leader of the CDU, and a "great coalition" government was formed in Bonn between the CDU and the SPD.

Erhard's experience underlines the underlying rationale for de Gaulle's policy in the second half of his reign as president of France. For the General, it was simply undignified for the leaders of great European nations to go cap in hand to Washington. De Gaulle may have overestimated France's role in the world and pushed his opposition to Washington's policies to extremes. Buttering up Brezhnev in the Kremlin was hardly his finest hour. But nobody in Washington would ever have dreamed of treating him like an inept servant, or an unwanted guest, which is what happened to Erhard and Wilson respectively. De Gaulle showed by his actions that Western European leaders could be treated as equals by U.S. policy makers, if only they did not beg.

CONTESTING THE AMERICAN EMPIRE

The only other European country where leading politicians critiqued U.S. policy in Vietnam in the same way as de Gaulle was social democratic Sweden, which was a Cold War neutral. Sweden's long-standing premier, Tage Erlander, who had been in post since October 1946, emphatically took the view that neutrality should not be equated with passivity or imply a refusal to pass judgment. Sweden, despite its tradition of good relations with the United States, should not hesitate to express its condemnation wherever abuses of human rights took place. The Vietnam War was a case calling for a stand on fundamental principles. As the Swedish government officially stated in a debate in the *Riksdag* (Parliament) on 21 March 1968, few events since World War II had "affected" the Swedes so "deeply" as the Vietnam conflict. It was a "great disappointment" for the Swedes that "a country that has meant so much for the liberty and prosperity of our own continent" should "pursue" a policy in Vietnam that was irreconcilable with "democratic evaluations."[41]

Swedish government spokesmen, notably Erlander's heir-apparent, Olof Palme, gave vent to outspoken criticism of U.S. policy in South East Asia. At a demonstration in Stockholm against the Vietnam War in February 1968, for instance, Palme gave a succinct account of the causes of the Vietnamese conflict, which was, he asserted, "a long history in which events have evolved with a terrifying logic." Instead of building democracy in South Vietnam, and raising the living standards of the peasants, Washington had backed French colonialism and a corrupt, authoritarian regime. It had sided with privilege against social justice. It had dropped more bombs on Vietnam than had been dropped on Nazi Germany. It was now paying the inevitable price for its stupidity. Palme stated bluntly: "The United States maintains that it wants to defend the democratic rights of the Vietnamese people against foreign invaders. But if one is to speak of democracy in Vietnam it is obviously represented to a much higher degree by the National Liberation Front than by the United States and its allied juntas. . . . A regime which needs the help of 500,000 American soldiers to survive for a day can only have the people against it." Palme concluded that it was untrue to say that one small group motivated by a "fanatical hate of America" were opposed to the war in Vietnam. The "overwhelming majority of the people of Europe," he claimed, wanted the bombing to stop. Their sentiment was not anti-Americanism, but simply humanitarianism.[42]

"Strident" Swedish rhetoric against the war in Vietnam may have been a way of masking a broader shift toward a more balanced neutrality in the Cold War.[43] Certainly, the Swedes' condemnation of the Soviet invasion of Czechoslovakia, while unambiguous, lacked the edge of outrage that characterized their statements on Vietnam, or on events in Greece, where a military junta supported by the United States was rooting out and crushing opposition forces (see below, chapter 10). Nevertheless, the outrage Palme was expressing so fervently was widely shared.

This was especially true among the young. The Vietnam conflict was one of the principal issues evoked in the student protests that swept across Western Europe in 1967 and 1968. In Spain, protesters fought street battles against the creaking anachronism of the Franco regime. In Italy, tens of thousands of young people regarded postwar democracy as a gigantic fraud in which the two dominant parties, the DC and the PCI, colluded to prevent social progress. In West Germany, students rebelled against their fathers' generation: the creation of the "great coalition," under the leadership of a man who had held office under the Nazi regime, opened a Pandora's box of suppressed anxiety. German youth was almost hysterically concerned not to fall into the same error as their parents' generation; accordingly it went to the opposite extreme and saw signs of incipient Nazism everywhere it looked. Student upheaval broke out in West Germany in 1966 on the occasion of an official visit by the "fascist" shah of Iran. The scale of the ensuing violence (by both protesters and police) aroused uncomfortable memories of the Weimar Republic. Youth everywhere considered universities to be antiquated, overcrowded institutions out of touch with contemporary mores. Young people disrupted lectures and rioted in the streets for the right to read less Aristotle and Dante, more Marx and Gramsci, and, naturally, for greater sexual liberty.

Such concerns would have provoked widespread social tensions even had there been no Vietnam War, even had there been no "Amerika" to mobilize political animosity. The young were *enragé*. But the Vietnam War unquestionably rubbed salt on the wounds. A generation in rebellion against the society its parents had created regarded the war as emblematic of the West's fundamental *hypocrisy*. So much of what was happening in Vietnam was so obviously an atrocity, the rhetoric of the war's defenders was so obviously ludicrous, and the reaction of European leaders, de Gaulle apart, was so obviously servile that it was impossible to do other than rebel. A tour made by Vice President Hubert Humphrey around West European capitals in March–April 1967 aroused a paroxysm of mass anger. In Rome, Florence, Paris, Bonn, Berlin, and Brussels, Humphrey was greeted by violent crowds throwing paint and eggs and denouncing him as a murderer. [44]

In the year after Humphrey's visit, the sense of disillusionment with the U.S. elite and disquiet at its Vietnam policy only grew. The editor of a distinguished Italian political review, for instance, worried in February 1968 that "nothing is more disheartening than to contemplate how the Americans behaved around Florence [in 1944] to save the city and the way in which they have behaved at Hue and in all Vietnam." South Vietnamese forces, with U.S. support, were guilty of "violations of international law." Prisoners were being mistreated; heinous weapons were being used; "exclusively civilian targets" were being destroyed. Such practices, moreover, were the norm, not an exception. One could not even exclude—since U.S. policy makers openly discussed the question—that nuclear weapons might be employed: "So far as we are concerned, one question stands out: Can we continue to be the allies of a country that, in all seriousness, discusses whether or not to use atomic bombs? Does this alliance really improve our security? If they use atomic weapons, what will happen in Italy?" [45]

The Vietnam War, in short, coming as it did at the end of a long series of blatant interventions in the domestic politics of other developing countries, essentially caused the United States to lose its aura of progressivism in Europe, in much the same way that the invasion of Hungary was, for all but die-hard communists, a belated death knell for the USSR's reputation as a force for progress in world affairs.

It was in France, however, where the generational revolt came closest to destabilizing the national government and provoking a political crisis with Cold War implications. Paris, along with Prague and Berkeley, was the epicenter of the revolt of the world's youth in 1968. Opposition to the Vietnam War, which took off in France in February 1965 and was initially fronted by the great names that had opposed the war in Algeria, Jean-Paul Sartre above all, was the crucible in which the May 1968 upheaval in Paris was forged. The students who fought street battles with the police, occupied the buildings of the Sorbonne (the historic heart of Paris university), and were swept up in an ardent, nonstop debate about the essence of the new humane socialism the "revolution" (as it was briefly called) was going to bring to the world, cut their teeth in the campaigns of the innumerable left-wing student groups against the Vietnam War. May 1968 surprised the French authorities, but it perhaps should not have done. The anti–Vietnam War organizations were able to rally thirty-five thousand young people in Paris on 21 October 1967; *la lutte* against the U.S. intervention was one of the few things that ideologically sectarian young communists, socialists, Maoists, Trotskyists, and libertarians could actually agree on. Anti-imperialism, specifically anti-American imperialism, supplanted the struggle against French colonialism as the core theme of the radical left's worldview and propaganda. When anti-imperialism merged with opposition to the consumer society, the belief system that animated the radicals of 1968 emerged. [46]

The upheaval in France in 1968 was disconcerting for its scale and intensity. Starting with the radicalized workers of the huge Renault car plant at Billancourt near Paris, a generalized "revolt against authority" began: lawyers, journalists, doctors, film directors, shop workers, even professional soccer players formed spontaneous "action committees" and seized their workplaces in imitation of the vanguard intellectuals of the Sorbonne. The "middle and professional classes appeared to be rising up against the bureaucratic structures through which their lives were governed." [47]

By the last week of May, the national "psychodrama," as professor-journalist Raymond Aron notoriously defined it, was beginning to threaten the stability of the state. De Gaulle's rhetoric, so effective with paratroops in Algiers, was simply derided by the radical young. Both de Gaulle *and* the opposition PCF seemed unmanned by the challenge facing them. On 28 May, the leader of the parliamentary left, François Mitterrand, opportunistically announced that he was ready to run for president and stated that he had already chosen Pierre Mendès France, whose role during the EDC affair has already been documented, as his future prime minister. Mendès was the most acceptable figure in the political establishment to the radical left occupying the universities.

The PCF (and presumably its Soviet controllers) feared that Mitterrand would be less able than de Gaulle to retain France's independence from the United States. *L'Humanité*, the PCF paper, warned frankly on 27 May 1968 that the party would not go along with any "plot" that would "open the way for a regime dominated by anti-communism and subservient to American policy." The PCF announced a giant demonstration in Paris for 29 May, intimating that it would not tolerate competition on the left. Hitherto, the PCF had acted as a safety valve during the crisis. Like the PCI, its leaders had consistently criticized the student rebels and had emphasized their belief that France was not in a revolutionary situation. Would the PCF rally be the cover for a change of line and for an overt attempt to seize power?[48]

De Gaulle, who had been shaken by his inability to control events, chose this tense moment to disappear. On 29 May, he made a secret visit to the commander of the French army on the Rhine, General Jacques Massu, to get his support for military action if it was necessary. His will stiffened by Massu's bluff encouragement, de Gaulle returned to Paris and reasserted his authority. On 30 May he spoke by radio to the nation. He announced that elections would take place unless a "party that is a totalitarian enterprise" blocked them. He warned unambiguously that if the current "situation of coercion" continued, he would "seek ways other than the ballot box" to maintain order. France was threatened with the "dictatorship" of "totalitarian communism exploiting the ambition and hatred of rejected politicians." Nevertheless, the "Republic will not abdicate." Later the same day, five hundred thousand uplifted Gaullists marched through Paris shouting "Mitterrand, charlatan," and "de Gaulle, you are not alone."

This denouement gave the General a final opportunity to appear in his time-honored role as national savior. The frenzy of May was abruptly replaced by the victory of the so-called silent majority who had concluded that the alternative to de Gaulle was, in Raymond Aron's words, "an absolute void."[49] The Gaullists won a smashing victory in parliamentary elections held at the end of June. Nevertheless, the 30 May broadcast and subsequent triumph at the polls was the old hero's last show-stopping performance: Although he lingered in office for another year, the crisis had shown France that new actors were needed on the national stage.

Anybody who reads the documents produced by the "events of May" expecting to find brilliant, analytically rigorous analyses of the nature of American imperial hegemony will be severely disappointed. The historian Michel Winock has acidly commented that the "ardor" of the debates in the "superheated" atmosphere of the Sorbonne will "never suffice to erase their absurdity."[50] This does not mean, however, that there was no serious French commentary on the role of the United States in the world in the late 1960s. The editor of *Le Monde Diplomatique*, Claude Julien, contended, in his *L'Empire américain* (1968), that the American ideology of "manifest destiny" had driven its global expansion. To maintain control, however, the United States now was engaging in actions, and not only in Vietnam, that were antithetical to western values and were bound to lead to a long-term rejection by victim peoples of the American model. Europeans, Julien believed, should keep this fact in mind when they were making their strategic economic and geopolitical choices.[51]

Even those—and they were many—who continued to preach support for the Atlantic alliance and to defend Washington's role as a necessary bulwark against communism began to perceive the United States as an "imperial republic" whose postwar altruism in Europe had emphatically served its own interests, while unquestionably fostering economic progress and human liberty.[52]

Even outright admirers of the U.S. economic model, such as the French publisher and public intellectual Jean-Jacques Servan-Schreiber, were nevertheless alarmed by the scale of the "American challenge" to Europe, and to France in particular. U.S. business, with its greater efficiency and deeper pockets, was skillfully exploiting the single market created by the EEC and was much better placed to exploit the shift to a postindustrial model, in which more wealth was produced by leisure activities, than was European industry. Americans were more productive, technologically advanced, and innovative. Unless Europe united in a federal state with a coherent industrial strategy, Western Europe risked being "overtaken and dominated, for the first time in our history, by a more advanced civilization." Servan-Schreiber's essential message—that the United States and Europe were at root competitors, not, as Atlanticist rhetoric would have it, partners—unquestionably struck a chord with well-educated Europeans.[53]

De Gaulle's foreign policy was ultimately rooted, albeit for different reasons than Servan-Schreiber's, in a similar fundamental vision of the need to compete with the United States and challenge the rationale for its leadership. Neither France, nor democratic Europe, should remain passive in the face of American cultural, economic, and political hegemony. De Gaulle's actual foreign policy, if one pierces the aura that glimmers retrospectively around the General's every action, was flimsy in substance. France's use of the bully pulpit did not alter the superpowers' behavior. Washington carried on bombing Vietnam; the USSR invaded Czechoslovakia; the United States kept running up deficits and expecting its allies to soak them up. But de Gaulle's strictures were ahead of their time. In the 1970s West European leaders began to follow his lead and become much more assertive in their relations with both Moscow and Washington. The European Cold War entered a new phase after 1968, one in which the protagonists were mostly homegrown.

NOTES

1. Raymond Aron, *Memoirs: Fifty Years of Political Reflection* (New York: Holmes & Meier, 1997), 258.

2. Jean Lacouture, *De Gaulle: The Ruler 1945–1970* (London: Collins Harvill, 1991), 228.

3. De Gaulle himself was a target in September 1961, when a roadside bomb almost blew up his car, and in August 1962, when gunmen peppered his car with bullets. The unruffled general told Prime Minister Georges Pompidou that the would-be assassins had "shot like pigs." Madame de Gaulle, who was traveling with her husband on both occasions, was equally imperturbable. Lacouture, *De Gaulle: The Ruler*, 328.

4. For the role of U.S. foreign policy during the Algerian conflict, see Irwin M. Wall, *France, the United States, and the Algerian War* (Berkeley: University of California Press, 2001).

5. Max Beloff, *The United States and the Unity of Europe* (London: Faber & Faber, 1963), 113–14.

6. Peter Catterick, ed., *The Macmillan Diaries*, vol. II: *Prime Minister and After 1957–1966* (London: Pan Books, 2011), 163–64.

7. Mathieu Segers, "De Gaulle's Race to the Bottom: The Netherlands, France and the Interwoven Problems of British EEC Membership and European Political Union, 1958–1963," *Contemporary European History* 19 (2010): 117.

8. Maurice Vaisse, *La grandeur: Politique étrangère du general de Gaulle 1958–1969* (Paris: Fayard, 1998), 190.

9. Marc Trachtenberg, *A Constructed Peace: The Making of the European Settlement* (Princeton, NJ: Princeton University Press, 1999), 316.

10. This is the view of Frank Costigliola, "The Failed Design: Kennedy, de Gaulle, and the Struggle for Europe," *Diplomatic History* 8 (1984): 227–51; see also Denise Artaud, "Le Grand Dessein de J. F. Kennedy: Proposition mythique où occasion manqué?" *Revue d'histoire Moderne et Contemporaine* 29 (1982): 235–66. Pascaline Winand, *Eisenhower, Kennedy, and the United States of Europe* (New York: St. Martins, 1993), and Jeffrey Giauque, *Grand Designs and Visions of Unity: The Atlantic Powers and the Reorganization of Europe, 1955–1963*, (Chapel Hill: University of North Carolina Press, 2002), give a more positive spin to U.S. policy, but Giauque admits (p. 124) that the Kennedy administration was afraid that "without strong American leadership a uniting Europe might forsake America's interests."

11. Charles de Gaulle, *Memoirs of Hope: Renewal* (New York: Simon and Schuster, 1971), 180.

12. Hans-Peter Schwarz, *Konrad Adenauer: The Statesman, 1952–1967* (Oxford: Berghahn, 1995), 621.

13. Vaisse, *La grandeur,* 155–57; Trachtenberg, *A Constructed Peace*, 369.

14. Vaisse, *La grandeur* , 157. In English, we would say "crossed swords."

15. Charles de Gaulle, *Discours et Messages,* vol. IV: *1962–1965* (Paris: Plon, 1970), 69.

16. Frédéric Bozo, "France, 'Gaullism,' and the Cold War," in *The Cambridge History of The Cold War*, vol. II: *Crises and Détente*, ed. Melvyn P. Leffler and Odd Arne Westad (Cambridge: Cambridge University Press, 2010), 173.

17. This is the thesis of Max Paul Friedman, *Rethinking Anti-Americanism: The History of an Exceptional Concept in American Foreign Relations* (New York: Cambridge University Press, 2012).

18. See Diane Kunz, *Butter and Guns: America's Cold War Economic Diplomacy* (New York: The Free Press, 1997), 94–107, for Kennedy's deficit worries.

19. De Gaulle, *Discours et Messages,* 4: 332.

20. Dana H. Allin, "De Gaulle and American Power," in *Charles de Gaulle's Legacy of Ideas*, ed. Benjamin M. Rowland (Lanham, MD: Lexington Books, 2011), 105.

21. Quoted in Friedman, *Rethinking Anti-Americanism*, 169.

22. Robert C. McNamara, "The Military Role of Nuclear Weapons: Perceptions and Misperceptions," in *The Nuclear Controversy*, ed. William P. Bundy (New York: Council on Foreign Relations, 1985), 82. In fact, "flexible response" was a myth perpetuated for political reasons. See Francis J. Gavin, "The Myth of Flexible Response: United States Strategy in Europe during the 1960s," *International History Review* 23 (2001): 847–75.

23. De Gaulle, *Discours et Messages*, 4: 383.

24. The best account of de Gaulle's relationship with the EEC is N. Piers Ludlow, *The European Community and the Crises of the 1960s: Negotiating the Gaullist Challenge* (London: Routledge, 2007). This book contains an outstanding chapter on the "empty chair" crisis.

25. De Gaulle, *Discours et Messages*, 5: 18.

26. De Gaulle, letter 7 March 1966 to Lyndon B. Johnson. Available at http://www.cvce.eu.

27. Quoted in Thomas Allen Schwarz, *Lyndon Johnson and Europe: In the Shadow of Vietnam* (Cambridge, MA: Harvard University Press, 2003), 145.

28. Michael Harrison, *The Reluctant Ally: France and Atlantic Security* (Baltimore, MD: Johns Hopkins University Press, 1981), 33. I also owe the title of the chapter to this book.

29. Harrison, *The Reluctant Ally,* 149.

30. Vaisse, *La grandeur* , 388.

31. Vaisse, *La grandeur* , 426.

32. De Gaulle, *Discours et messages*, 5: 43.

33. Vaisse, *La grandeur* , 426.

34. Vaisse, *La grandeur* , 429.

35. John L. Harper, "The Road to Phnom Penh: De Gaulle, the Americans and Vietnam, 1944–1966," in *Charles de Gaulle's Legacy of Ideas*, ed. Rowland, 60.

36. De Gaulle, *Discours et Messages*, 5: 74–78.

37. FRUS 1964–1966, vol. XII (Western Europe), doc. 66.

38. De Gaulle, *Discours et Messages*, 5: 130.

39. See Jonathan Colman, *A "Special Relationship"? Harold Wilson, Lyndon B. Johnson and Anglo-American Relations "at the Summit," 1964–68* (Manchester: Manchester University Press, 2004) for Wilson's overactive diplomacy.

40. Eugenie M. Blang, "A Reappraisal of Germany's Vietnam Policy, 1963–1966: Ludwig Erhard's Response to America's War in Vietnam," *German Studies Review* 27 (2004): 348.

41. *Documents on Swedish Foreign Policy 1968* (Stockholm: Royal Ministry for Foreign Affairs, 1969), 14.

42. *Documents on Swedish Foreign Policy 1968*, 122–29.

43. This is the thesis of Carl-Gustaf Scott, "Swedish Vietnam Criticism Reconsidered: Social Democratic Vietnam Policy a Manifestation of Swedish Ostpolitik," *Cold War History* 9 (2009): 243–66.

44. Friedman, *Rethinking Anti-Americanism,* 191.

45. Enzo Enriques Agnoletti, "Osservatorio," *Il Ponte*, no. 2 (1968): 155–56.

46. Laurent Jalabert, "Aux origines de la generation 1968: Les étudiants français et la guerre du Vietnam," *Vingtième Siècle*, no. 55 (1997): 69–81.

47. Bernard E. Brown, *Protest in Paris: Anatomy of a Revolt* (Morristown, NJ: General Learning Press, 1974), 16.

48. Lacouture, *De Gaulle: The Ruler*, 542. See also Mattei Dogan, "How Civil War Was Avoided in France," *International Political Science Review* 5 (1984): 245–77.

49. Raymond Aron, *Elusive Revolution: Anatomy of a Student Revolt* (New York: Praeger, 1969), 85.

50. Michel Winock, *La febbre francese: dalla Comune al maggio 68* (Rome: Laterza, 1986), 274.

51. Claude Julien, *L'Empire Américain* (Paris: Grasset, 1968). This book in many ways anticipates the thesis of Odd Arne Westad's *Global Cold War*.

52. Raymond Aron, "The Imperial Republic," in Aron, *The Dawn of Universal History* (New York: Basic Books, 2002), 403.

53. Jean-Jacques Servan-Schreiber, *The American Challenge* (London: Pelican, 1969), 45.

Chapter Nine

Détente and Solidarity

The Soviet Union's oppression of the Prague Spring came at a delicate moment. Western governments had been nurturing "détente" with the Soviet bloc and were anxious to consolidate the gains achieved by their diplomacy. The Soviet crushing of the Prague Spring, and the chill season of "normalization" that followed, might have put all such diplomatic overtures on the backburner.

In fact, the opposite happened. Led by West Germany, the countries of the European Community (EC) intensified relations with the Soviet bloc. They were backed by Europe's neutral states: Austria and Finland were especially active in the process of building better East-West relations. The culmination of détente was the signature in August 1975 of the "Final Act" of the Conference on European Security and Co-operation (CSCE) by thirty-three European states from both sides of the iron curtain, plus the United States and Canada. Though conservative commentators in the United States argued that the Helsinki Accords would not improve the lives of the peoples under communist rule and that the policy of the Nixon and Ford administrations might lose Europe to communism, both administrations yielded to their European allies' determination to press ahead with their chosen course.

In part, détente's American critics were right. The Soviet Union and its satellites ignored the Final Act's clear injunctions to respect human rights. But by failing to do so, they exposed their moral bankruptcy. The season of détente also encouraged greater economic exchange between the two halves of the continent. Trade and investment in the East increased. But here, too, the failings of the communist system were exposed in stark detail. Most of the Soviet bloc countries, anxious to raise the technological level of their economies, rushed to borrow from the West from the mid-1970s onward. Western bankers, with their unerring eye for credit risk, were quick to advance loans. By the end of the decade, the communist bloc was crippled with debt and its economy was lagging even further behind its western neighbors than it had been in 1970. Moreover, since investment in agriculture had been neglected, some parts of the bloc were increasingly reliant on imports to feed themselves—an absurdity for a region that ought to have been the farm belt of Europe.

The country that epitomized this moral and economic bankruptcy was Poland. The 1970s was a grim decade for Poles. Faced with persistent social unrest, the Polish leadership maintained power by alternating repression with bribery in the form of artificial surges in consumer spending. By 1980, austerity was the only way the regime could balance the books. But Polish industrial workers would not swallow cuts in their already low standard of living. Between July 1980 and December 1981 in Poland, "the first genuine workers' revolution in history developed under the sign of the cross against a 'Workers' State.'"[1] Workers joined with the intellectuals to form a mass social movement—the independent trade union, Solidarity—that mounted an exhilarating challenge to the party bureaucracy. It was a tragedy, and a final indictment of the bankruptcy of European communism, that this inspiring revolution was brought to a temporary end by the imposition of martial law and the seizure of power by a man, General Wojciech Jaruzelski, who behaved (and even looked) like a Latin American colonel.

OSTPOLITIK

The reaction of the Italian Communist Party to the Soviet invasion of Czechoslovakia is a useful starting point for understanding the acceleration of détente in Europe in the late 1960s. On 23 August 1968, the PCI expressed its "serious disagreement" with the invasion since it was unable to justify "violations of the independence of any state." The PCI called for the withdrawal of the Warsaw Pact's forces, suggesting that an occupation of Czechoslovakia would make any "policy leading to the superseding of the military blocs" and a "new framework of international relations that guarantees peace and the emancipation of peoples" more difficult to attain. The PCI reiterated the point in one of the official "theses" presented to its party conference in October 1968. There it was argued that the "fundamental strategic choice" of the "revolutionary workers' movement" was the achievement of peace, and it was stated, quite explicitly, that the USSR's "violation" of the fundamental rule of noninterference in the internal affairs of another nation had put peace in jeopardy.[2]

The PCI was reminding Moscow that its actions had undermined a common position taken by European Communist parties at the July 1966 meeting of the Warsaw Pact powers in Bucharest. At that meeting, and even more vigorously at Karlovy Vary (Carlsbad) on 26 April 1967, European Communist parties had called for "a conference of all European states on the question of security and peaceful co-operation in Europe" and had appealed for the "withdrawal of foreign troops" and the "abolition of foreign military bases" throughout Europe. It had demanded acceptance by the "Bonn state" (West Germany) of the outcome of World War II, and specifically had urged the West German government to guarantee the existing borders of Poland and Czechoslovakia and to admit the existence of "two sovereign and equal German states." The Karlovy Vary meeting's communiqué concluded: "The peoples of Europe are capable of deciding questions of peace and security on their own continent. May they take the destinies of Europe into their own hands!"[3]

This gambit had not been rejected out of hand by the West, although its strategic implications were considerable. The North Atlantic Council, the governing assembly of NATO, had responded cautiously but positively. Through the initiative of the Belgian foreign minister, Pierre Harmel, NATO had begun in 1966 a review of the future tasks facing the alliance. This review reported in December 1967 and recommended a policy of engagement with the Soviet bloc. NATO member states were encouraged to play "their full part in promoting an improvement of relations with the Soviet Union and eastern Europe, bearing in mind that the pursuit of détente must not be allowed to split the alliance."[4]

This commitment to détente survived the invasion of Czechoslovakia. In March 1969, meeting at Budapest, the Warsaw Pact countries reiterated their demand for a "pan-European" peace conference. Crucially, they dropped the requirement that "foreign troops" should be withdrawn. In May 1969, pressed behind the scenes by the USSR but also for good reasons of its own, neutral Finland responded to this proposal by offering to host the conference.[5] NATO gave a constructive response to the Soviet bloc's proposal in its ministerial meetings in Washington in April 1969 and in Brussels in December of that year, but underlined that such a conference could only take place if the question of Germany had been resolved first.

In October 1969, Willy Brandt became chancellor of West Germany. As he recounts in his biography, "I had to ask myself: what can your state do, what can the Federal Republic of Germany do, to make peace more secure?"[6] Brandt's answer to this question was to make peaceful coexistence in Europe possible by unilaterally recognizing the territorial status quo in Europe and acknowledging the existence of the GDR. In his first speech to parliament as chancellor on 28 October 1969, Brandt proclaimed that his foreign policy would "preserve the unity of the nation by easing the tenseness of relations between the two parts of Germany" and breached a taboo by saying "even if two states exist in Germany, they are not foreign countries to each other; their relations with each other can only be of a special nature."

Brandt's defense minister, the future chancellor Helmut Schmidt, summed up so-called *Ostpolitik* in one brief paragraph in a lucid 1970 essay:

> The impelling motive of our eastern operation was the recognition that security through deterrence is only one essential element of stabilizing the framework of international relations and that security through lessening tension is a supplementary one, no less essential. . . . Since the partition of our continent and our country cannot be overcome, at least we must want to overcome the separation of the peoples; since borders cannot be shifted about any longer, we must bend all our efforts to render their presence more tolerable. This, basically, is what *Ostpolitik* is all about.[7]

There is no space here to describe the burst of active diplomacy carried out by Brandt; by Brandt's chief of staff and diplomatic envoy, Egon Bahr; and by Walter Scheel, the leader of the Free Democrat Party (FDP), who was Bonn's foreign minister after October 1969. By the end of 1970, after just fourteen months in office, Brandt had negotiated de facto peace treaties with the Soviet Union (12 August 1970) and Poland (7 December 1970). The Moscow Treaty—which had been preceded by an explicit West German renunciation of nuclear weapons, support for the plan for a pan-European peace conference, and a trade deal—underlined that peace in Europe could only be safeguarded if the existing frontiers, including Poland's western frontier along the Oder-Niesse line, and the existing boundary with the GDR were considered "inviolable."

The word "inviolable" was carefully chosen. It was a compromise between Moscow's demand that the frontiers should be considered *immutable* and the German desire to keep open the possibility of a return of the large areas lost by Germany at Soviet behest in 1945 *if the peoples of those areas so wished*. The Warsaw Treaty embodied the same language. But in the collective memory, the precise wording of the Warsaw Treaty is less remembered than Brandt's repentance for Nazi war crimes while visiting the Polish capital to sign the treaty. Taken to the Warsaw ghetto memorial, Brandt, in his own moving phrase, "did what human beings do when speech fails them." He knelt in contrition to the "millions of victims of murder."[8] Brandt's gesture communicated the idea that German policy was a genuine attempt to rebuild bridges between the two halves of the continent and to achieve lasting security.

The Moscow and Warsaw deals were criticized in Bonn for having abandoned the prospect of German unity. Brandt's answer was that he had not surrendered anything that "had not long since been gambled away" by the "criminal regime" of Adolf Hitler.[9] Brandt added that the practical goal of Ostpolitik was ending the separation of the German *people*. "Wandel durch Annäherung" ("change through rapprochement") was the slogan of Ostpolitik. The phrase implied that German unity might be achieved by the erosion of the East German regime from below: through human contacts, trade, and the gradual intertwining of the two states' daily lives.

The problem with this strategy was that East Berlin's leadership was less willing than Moscow or Warsaw to make concessions. In March 1970, Brandt met East German Premier Willi Stoph in the town of Erfurt, a meeting that was followed up by a second encounter in the West German town of Kassel. The Erfurt meeting was a public relations disaster for the communist regime. Placards decorated with the single letter "y" to show support for the West German chancellor decorated houses along the route to Erfurt taken by the federal chancellor's train. "Unscripted crowds" took to the streets of Erfurt to cheer "Willy." The massive Stasi presence in the town was unable to avoid a crowd gathering to applaud outside Brandt's hotel—though Stasi chief Erich Mielke reported subsequently to the GDR Politburo that "those people who chanted or in other ways made themselves evident by their negative actions were documented and will be worked on." Brandt sensibly avoided any gesture that might have inflamed the crowd's feelings further, but he and his aides were deeply moved by the bravery and warmth of Erfurt's citizens.[10]

The Kassel meeting turned into a near-riot as West Germans protested Stoph's presence. Brandt anyway found negotiations with Stoph "hardly worth the effort." The East German statesman read out dogma from cue cards and even called the Berlin Wall "an act of humanity."[11] The West Germans realized that they had to use their new leverage with the Russians to make the East German regime more flexible.

The USSR was willing to listen. In May 1971, Walter Ulbricht was replaced on Soviet orders as secretary of the SED by Erich Honecker. Ulbricht's removal facilitated the "protracted and difficult negotiations" between the four powers (France, Great Britain, the United States, and the Soviet Union) occupying the former German capital for a lasting solution to the Berlin question.[12] On 3 September 1971, the "Quadripartite Agreement" was signed. In substance, the four powers agreed that sovereignty over West Berlin lay in the hands of the three western powers, though its citizens could carry West German passports; that West Berlin was likewise *not* part of the GDR; that citizens of West Berlin should be granted greater opportunity to visit their relatives in the eastern part of the city; and that trade and communications between the two halves of the city should be eased. The treaty was silent about East Berlin.

Ostpolitik's defusing of the German question had a series of consequences. For Brandt, it led to his being awarded the Nobel Peace Prize in November 1971. It also led to a period of angst in West German domestic politics as the Christian Democrats resisted ratification of the Warsaw and Moscow treaties. The charismatic leader of Bavarian Christian Democracy, Franz Josef Strauss, was an especially vocal opponent of Brandt's policy. In the end, the two treaties were passed only after the symbolic abstention of the CDU and Strauss's *Christlich-Soziale Union* (CSU).

The Christian Democrats' hostility to Ostpolitik, however, turned out to be an electoral liability. Negotiations with East Germany intensified after the ratification of the Moscow and Warsaw treaties. Brandt asked for a new electoral mandate in order to bring the negotiations to a close. The general elections of November 1972 were, in effect, a referendum over the wisdom of Brandt's foreign policy. Over 90 percent of the electorate voted and the SPD gained six seats, becoming, with 230, the largest party in the *Bundestag* for the first time since 1949. The CDU/CSU lost seventeen seats, falling to 225 representatives. The FDP, however, gained eleven seats, arriving at a total of 41. After November 1972, the FDP became the kingmaker in German politics, able to make governments or break them (as they would do in 1982 when they switched their support from the SPD to the CDU).

On 21 December 1972, West and East Germany signed a treaty that committed the two equal "states" to developing "normal relations" between themselves and that recognized their mutual border as "inviolable." The two states agreed to exchange permanent missions to their respective capitals, though they stopped short of full diplomatic recognition. Bonn was ready to treat the GDR as a sovereign state *within* Germany, not as an independent nation like Poland or Czechoslovakia (Bonn signed a treaty with Czechoslovakia in December 1973). Nevertheless, article four of the treaty stated that neither state would claim to represent the other internationally: to claim to be, in other words, the sole legitimate Germany. In return for these concessions, West Germany obtained promises that the two states would conclude further agreements on cross-border traffic, economic questions, judicial relations, post and telecommunications, science and technology, health, culture, sport, and the environment.

By signing the treaty with the GDR, the Bonn government recognized that only a policy of gradual improvement of human and social contacts "held out the prospect of improving conditions for the millions of Germans who had to live behind the barbed wire, mined landstrips and masonry walls that the SED regime had constructed around the GDR to keep them from fleeing."[13] Both Germanies promised to respect the Charter of the United Nations, and they were, in fact, formally admitted to the General Assembly in 1973.

By 1973, Ostpolitik had transformed the European political scene. Such independence of action in foreign policy would not have been possible had West Germany not emerged as a major industrial power in the 1950s and 1960s. Nevertheless, West Germany's achievement was not just the result of its economic prowess. It was testimony to the power of inspiring leadership to change the course of events: Willy Brandt, though he was not without faults, was one of the most imaginative leaders of Europe's Cold War.

HELSINKI AND HUMAN RIGHTS

This unmistakable rise in West Germany's relative position might have provoked more alarm, given Germany's history, than it actually did. Henry Kissinger patronizingly worried that Brandt would not be able to manage the forces that he had unleashed.[14] Was West Germany hoping to play off one half of the continent against the other, risking "Finlandicization" by the Soviets in the process? Such geopolitical fantasies were soon dispelled by Brandt and Scheel's actual policy, which united Ostpolitik with a due concern for a common European foreign policy. Walter Scheel proclaimed that the EC was "On the Move" in a revealing fall 1971 article for an American audience.[15] The EC member states were adamant that their intention was to "transform," as the October 1972 summit of the community in Paris proclaimed, "the present complex" of its member states' relations into a "European Union" by 1980. Ostpolitik and German foreign policy activism were thus tethered to (though not controlled by) the lumbering ox of emerging independent European strength.

The ox is not an animal capable of multitasking, and the EC's foreign policy ambitions soon stumbled (see below, chapter 10). But over the issue of relations with the Soviet bloc, the ox showed the virtue of constancy. Between 19 November 1970, when the foreign ministers of the EC "Six" met to choose their priorities for foreign policy, and November 1972, when formal talks to decide the agenda of the CSCE began in Finland, the notion that human rights were of central importance to the peace and security conference became the distinctive element of the EC's attitude toward the negotiation.[16] As a result, the USSR discovered during substantive negotiations in Geneva from mid-September 1973 to July 1975 that it had either to accept that the conference would lead to specific pledges on human rights or else renounce the confirmation of the postwar status quo that the CSCE would guarantee.[17]

Daniel C. Thomas has argued that the EC was motivated to take this principled line by the logic of its own self-perception. Since the early 1960s, the EC had argued that community membership was conditional upon acceptance of the principles of human rights and democracy. The EC, therefore, when it made foreign policy a priority, simultaneously made extending respect for these principles one of its goals (even though EC policy makers did not necessarily expect the policy to be a success).[18] The argument is plausible, but it is worth remembering that human rights were placed high on the agenda by events during the Helsinki process. "Normalization" in Czechoslovakia; the bloody repression of students, intellectuals and industrial workers in Poland (see below); the difficulties experienced by the tens of thousands of Jews in the USSR who wished to go to Israel; the persecution of writers, scholars, and human rights activists, all made human rights in the Soviet bloc a high-profile issue.

The case of Alexander Solzhenitsyn is illustrative. Solzhenitsyn was expelled from the writers' union (and hence deprived of the right to publish) in 1969, denied the opportunity to travel to Stockholm to collect the Nobel prize for literature awarded to him in October 1970, and subjected to persistent harassment and public denigration. After the publication in December 1973 of chapters from the *Gulag Archipelago*, his memoir-based study of the Soviet concentration camp system, Solzhenitsyn was expelled from Russia in February 1974.[19] After the publication of the *Gulag Archipelago*, comparisons of Stalinism with Nazism, hitherto restricted to right-wing conservatives, became more usual, especially in France, where the Soviet myth had lingered longer than elsewhere.

Despite his woes, Solzhenitsyn was a relatively fortunate Soviet "dissident." His fame had shielded him from the worst kinds of persecution. In the early 1970s, an average of more than a hundred writers, scholars, and human rights activists per year were sentenced to long spells in prison, sent to labor camps, or condemned to psychiatric "treatment" for the "crime" of speaking their minds, even as Soviet diplomats glibly debated the human rights' clauses of the CSCE.[20] To individuals who had lived under the pervasive surveillance of the secret police, the EC's efforts during the Helsinki process to commit the USSR to the principles of human rights thus appeared as a bizarre distraction from the real issue. The whole process seemed uncomfortably like persuading cannibals to make a declaration in favor of vegetarianism. In a speech given to an American audience shortly before the final convocation of the CSCE to sign the "Final Act," Solzhenitsyn, now a free man in the West, ranted against the whole process of European détente:

> The European negotiations of the 35 countries have been for two years now painfully continuing. . . . During these two years of negotiations, in all East European countries the pressure has been increasing, the oppression intensified . . . and it is precisely now that the Austrian Chancellor says, 'We've got to sign this agreement as rapidly as possible.' What sort of agreement would this be? The proposed agreement is *the funeral of Eastern Europe*. It means that Western Europe would finally, once and for all, sign away Eastern Europe.[21]

The point Solzhenitsyn missed was that once the cannibals had publicly acknowledged that eating people was wrong, others could hold them to their word. The Helsinki agreements were to have "strong repercussions" in the USSR and other communist bloc countries precisely because they were "the first international agreements on human rights to be published in the Soviet press."[22]

The "Final Act" of the CSCE, signed in Helsinki on 1 August 1975, consisted of three principal chapters, or "baskets." The first basket was "Questions Relating to Security in Europe," which mostly consisted of a ten-point declaration of the "principles guiding relations between participating states." The second basket dealt with "Co-operation in the field of economics, of science and technology and of the environment"; basket three with "Co-operation in humanitarian and other fields."

The first basket gave the USSR and its allies the security guarantees they wanted in a language they found acceptable. All thirty-five states signing the "Final Act" committed themselves to refraining from "the threat or use of force against the territorial integrity or political independence of any state," a promise that rang hollow in Czechoslovakia. The participating states further agreed to "regard as inviolable all one another's frontiers as well as the frontiers of all States in Europe and therefore they will refrain now and in future from assaulting these frontiers," although they accepted that "their frontiers can be changed, in accordance with international law, by peaceful means and by agreement." The participating nations would further refrain "from any intervention, direct or indirect, individual or collective, in the internal or external affairs falling within the domestic jurisdiction of another participating state, regardless of their mutual relations."

These pledges safeguarded the Soviet bloc from an improbable invasion by a revanchist EC or from a U.S. strike via Alaska. More seriously—and it was this that aroused the disdain of individuals like Solzhenitsyn—they seemingly condemned the Baltic states to permanent subjugation inside the USSR. In return, the communist states expressed their determination to "respect human rights and fundamental freedoms, including freedom of thought, conscience, religion or belief"; to "promote and encourage the effective exercise of civil, political, economic, social, cultural and other rights and freedoms"; and to "act in conformity with the purposes and principles of the Charter of the United Nations and with the Universal Declaration of Human Rights."

The communist states could not keep such pledges without altering their entire system of rule. Their negotiators must have believed that these pledges were ephemeral. After all, as members of the UN General Assembly, the communist states had paid mere lip service to the Universal Declaration of Human Rights since 1945. The Final Act also stated that all participating states should respect one another's "right freely to choose and develop [their] political, social, economic and cultural systems" as well as each state's "right to determine its laws and regulations," which Soviet bloc lawyers regarded as a clear get-out clause. "Final Acts" are, in any case, not regarded as legally binding; the Finnish government was bidden by the conference to send the document to the United Nations together with a letter making plain that the Final Act was not a treaty or agreement as defined by article 102 of the UN treaty.[23]

The second basket exhorted the signatories to improve economic, trade, technological, tourist, and academic links: it might have been called the "basket for exchanges," for increasing exchanges of people, goods, visits, and technology was its central theme. Here, too, however, there was an underlying human rights dimension. Even a seemingly innocuous clause like the second basket's pledge that the participating states would "promote the publication and dissemination of economic and commercial information at regular intervals and as quickly as possible" had profound implications for a society in which even telephone directories were not freely available and in which statistics were official propaganda rather than performance indicators. The spirit of the second basket's approval of the "holding of national and international conferences, symposia, seminars, courses and other meetings of a scientific and technological character" could only be fulfilled by permitting the communist bloc's leading writers, scientists, and scholars to visit the West. The risk was that such individuals would "defect," to use the euphemism for "choose freedom" that was widely employed in the 1970s.

The third basket, on "Cooperation in humanitarian and other fields," committed the thirty-five states to "facilitate freer movement and contacts, individually and collectively, among persons, institutions and organizations of the participating States." Specifically, they promised to ensure that "contacts and regular meetings" between members of the same family (i.e., West Germans wanting to visit relatives in the East) would be favorably considered; that they would "deal in a positive and humanitarian spirit" with people who wished to be reunited with their family (i.e., East German grandmothers wanting to join their grandchildren in the West); that requests to marry a citizen from another of the participating states would not be unduly obstructed.

The participating states further expressed their intention to "facilitate" wider travel by making visa requirements easier and to "facilitate . . . the dissemination" of foreign newspapers and publications and the "promotion" of "books and artistic works." A greater variety of "recorded and filmed" broadcasts from other participating states would be shown, and working conditions for journalists would be improved. All these pledges held out the possibility of real improvements in the quality of everyday life for Soviet bloc citizens, especially intellectual workers such as teachers.

Predictably, the communist states did not keep their promises. True, it became possible to buy *Le Monde* or *Corriere della Sera* at a handful of news kiosks in Moscow, Leningrad, Prague, and Bucharest, but purchasers were monitored closely. Jamming of western radio broadcasts ceased until 1980. International artistic and scholarly exchanges were held in greater numbers, although visas were never issued contemporaneously for the families of the scholars, artists, or scientists allowed to leave the country. More foreign books were translated and distributed, but the works of George Orwell, Arthur Koestler, or Solzhenitsyn, not to mention a regiment of less perilous writers, still had to be published in *samizdat* (underground literature). Independent publishing was rigorously controlled (it was, for instance, impossible to buy stencils or printers' ink without a permit), and unauthorized publishers were admonished by stiff prison sentences when caught.

Visits from the West were permitted in greater numbers, but with the partial exception of Hungary, such official tours were kept under tight surveillance and followed a predictable route (the three-hour, statistic-filled trudge around an agricultural cooperative was de rigueur), and opportunities to encounter ordinary citizens were limited. Obviously, no effort was made to permit greater political liberty; indeed, several Soviet bloc nations, the USSR included, made constitutional changes to strengthen the central position of the Communist Party. After lengthy negotiations, post-Helsinki East Germany allowed freer travel and telephone communication from the West, but it made West Germans pay a high price in hard currency for the privilege of visiting their grannies on the wrong side of the Wall. Only old and sick citizens of the GDR were allowed to make the opposite journey, despite the fact that three hundred thousand East Germans applied to emigrate to the West in the three years that followed the signature of the Helsinki Accords. Most applications made explicit reference to the human rights provisions of the Final Act.[24]

The USSR initially showed tolerance for the groups of activists that publicized the rights acquired under the Helsinki Accord. The Moscow Helsinki Group, founded on 12 May 1976 by Yuri Orlov, a veteran oppositionist whose "dissent" dated back to the aftermath of Khrushchev's Secret Speech in February 1956—whose members included Ludmilla Alexeyeva, Elena Bonner, Aleksandr Ginzburg, Vitaly Rubin, and Anatoly Scharansky—was quickly followed by the creation of a Christian Committee for the Rights of Religious Believers and, in January 1977, by the Working Committee for the Abuse of Psychiatry. Committees for the emigration of Soviet Jews were also formed since would-be emigrant Jews were being persecuted ruthlessly in the early 1970s and, in some cases, were subjected to 1950s-style show trials.[25] The Moscow groups regularly relayed to the signatory governments of the Helsinki Accords the cases of human rights abuses that were brought to their attention. Tolerance for the groups' activities evaporated as a consequence. Bonner, Orlov, and their comrades soon faced intense persecution by the authorities.[26] In East Germany, Bulgaria, and Romania, human rights groups were not even given the chance to emerge.

In Czechoslovakia, by contrast, outspoken intellectuals held the regime to the promises it had made at Helsinki. The Charter 77 group was instituted in Prague on 1 January 1977, with three prominent critics of the regime, playwright Václav Havel, former foreign minister Jiří Hájek, and the renowned philosopher Jan Patočka, serving as its original spokesmen. Charter 77 was born to publicize the Kafkaesque case of the Plastic People of the Universe, a rock band arrested in September 1976 and charged with being an illegal organization. Charter 77's manifesto was published on 6 January 1977, and republished in various European languages on the following day. It emphasized that "basic human rights in our country exist, regrettably, on paper alone." The document insisted that Charter 77 would not carry out "any oppositional political activity" or "set out its own platform of political or social reform or change," but would rather "conduct a constructive dialogue with the political and state authorities" over issues of human and civil rights with the goal of enabling "all citizens of Czechoslovakia to work and live as free human beings."[27] The Charter was signed by more than two hundred of Czechoslovakia's leading intellectuals and dozens of other citizens added their names in the following year. Despite its cautious tone, the Charter represented a major challenge to the regime. The Chartists were saying, "We are not going to pretend any longer. We are going to call things by their proper names."[28]

The official press was soon filled with slanders on the patriotism of the Charter's signatories; dozens of Chartists were arrested; almost all lost their jobs and were forced to do menial work in factories, breweries, or the fields. Many were imprisoned. Professor Patočka died of a heart attack after interrogation by the police in March 1977. The ferocity of the regime's repression, which intensified in 1978–1979, induced ordinary citizens to be prudent: Ludvík Vaculík, the author of "Two Thousand Words," even worried that the Chartists would become a small band of heroes, cut off from normal society.[29]

The most famous essay produced by the Charter 77 movement, Havel's "The Power of the Powerless," starts from precisely this dilemma.[30] Havel begins his analysis of "post-totalitarian society" by interpreting the motives of a greengrocer who places the slogan "Workers of the World Unite" among the onions and carrots in his shop window. What are his motives? Havel contends that what the greengrocer is doing is signaling his conformity in a way that is consistent with his dignity. If the poster had said, "I am afraid and therefore unquestioningly obedient," the greengrocer would have been far less willing to bend his knee, since nobody likes to admit being scared. As it is, he can shrug his shoulders and say to himself, "What's wrong with the workers uniting?" By making this concession, Havel argues, he *lives within the lie* and, for the sake of a quiet life, becomes part of the system itself. Were he to take the sign down, retribution would be quick to follow. His pay would be reduced, or he would lose his post as shop manager or be denied a chance to take a family holiday at a seaside resort in Bulgaria, or he would see his daughter deprived of her place at university. These petty sanctions would themselves be implemented by persons faced with the same dilemma: for if they did not persecute the greengrocer, they themselves would become suspect. And so the system perpetuated itself endlessly. How could people be locked up for copying banned books if there were not policemen willing to catch them, lawyers to prosecute them, judges to try them, secretaries to type the charge sheet, jailers to lock the doors? Every trial of a "dissident" was an act of injustice committed by people who knew they were doing injustice, but who nevertheless eased their consciences by saying they were *observing the law*.

Havel's argument was that the only exit strategy was for people to live within the truth, that is, according to their conscience, and simply accept the personal consequences of their choices. His *hope* was that it might be possible to construct a "counter-polis," a parallel society of nonconformists that would become a "social phenomenon of growing importance" able to change official society. Hope came from within: if people rejected orthodoxy, the system would crumble, since *nobody* believed any longer that it would ever achieve its ends. Ultimately, Havel's essay, which has rightly been called "one of those arresting works that seem to embody the thought of an era," rested on the conviction that communism as practiced in Czechoslovakia was a fraud in which everybody was complicit.[31] Pointing the fraud out was *not* a misplaced sense of heroism, but a moral (and patriotic) necessity.[32]

Havel was jailed for five years in 1979. But the courage of Charter 77 and the Moscow Helsinki Group by then had had a huge impact on world politics. The follow-up conference to Helsinki, held in the capital of Yugoslavia, Belgrade, in the summer of 1977, saw the new U.S. administration of Jimmy Carter take the lead in condemning the Soviet bloc states for failing to implement the Helsinki Accords. Carter had started his presidency by corresponding with the Soviet human rights activist Andrei Sakharov: the distinguished Russian scientist's appeals to the West to expose breaches of the Helsinki Final Acts unquestionably influenced the United States' stance.[33]

In general, the Soviet bloc's mean-spirited persecution of its bravest and most gifted citizens was yet another nail in the coffin of its reputation. What historian François Furet called the "passing of an illusion" had definitively taken place in the West by the end of the 1970s.[34] It would be another dreary decade before the greengrocers of Prague took their placards from their shop windows and showed how strong the powerless can be when they are roused. But outside the Soviet bloc, only a few communist diehards maintained that really existing socialism represented the future of humanity.

In Italian writer Leonardo Sciascia's brilliant 1977 reworking of Voltaire's *Candide*, the protagonist, Candido Munafò, a naïf who always tells the truth, however inconvenient it may be, says to his comrades in 1970s Turin: "How is it that none of us wants to go to the Soviet Union? . . . We should all be wanting to go there. We're socialists." Candido's comrades sat in "chill silence" and then, even though it was unusually early, "everyone got up and left."[35]

REVOLT AND REPRESSION IN POLAND,
DECEMBER 1970–DECEMBER 1981

As Havel himself recognized, a "counter-polis" already existed in Czechoslovakia's neighbor, Poland, by the end of the 1970s. This was attributable to two peculiarities of Polish society under communism: the position of the peasants and the strength of the Catholic Church. The Polish peasants had resisted collectivization in the 1950s; as a result, rural communities and traditional values were thriving. The Church had achieved considerable independence since the period of postwar Stalinism and was respected for its refusal to compromise on human rights issues. During the 1968 upheaval, for instance, the dynamic archbishop of Krakow, Karol Wojtyła, had sermonized against the authorities' rejection of dialogue with young Poles and had sheltered students on church premises during police crackdowns.

More than anywhere else in the Soviet bloc, moreover, Polish industrial workers had been alienated from the party that theoretically ruled in their name. The first breach between the workers and the party came in December 1970, just days after the signature of the agreement with West Germany, when steep price rises were imposed on basic foodstuffs without any compensation in the form of wage increases. Workers took to the streets in the northern shipbuilding ports of Gdansk, neighboring Gydnia, and Szczecin (Stettin) on the border with East Germany. In all three towns, social conditions were extremely poor with workers being constrained to work long shifts, live in squalid hostels, and wait for years to obtain a small apartment (and hence to be able to marry). The price rises set this tinderbox alight. Between 12 and 14 December 1970, the three cities' shipyards were closed by strikes and Communist Party headquarters were stormed by crowds and burned to the ground.

The authorities' reaction was ruthless: under orders from the minister of the defense, General Jaruzelski, more than twenty-seven thousand troops were mobilized. On 16–17 December, security forces fired on the crowds in all three cities: dozens of protesters were killed (the official death toll was forty-four, but the true figure was far higher) and hundreds were wounded. Arrests took place on a major scale.[36] Subsequently, strike leaders were subjected to reprisals, with many being sacked, beaten, or even murdered. As a shipyard activist from Gdansk reflected in his memoirs: "December 1970 was a disaster for us . . . it convinced us that we would have to find other solutions."[37] The activist was, of course, Lech Wałęsa, who took a prominent role in the disturbances.

The scale of the disturbances was a defeat for the party, too. Party leader Gomułka, having jeopardized détente, became the scapegoat for the crisis: he was replaced by the party boss in Silesia, Edward Gierek.[38] The new leader rescinded the price increases in March 1971. For the next four years, Gierek "strove for a rapid improvement in living standards at the same time as he dramatically raised the level of investment."[39] Another scholar puts it more bluntly: "Puritan frugality was replaced by cavalier extravagance."[40] The Polish state, in brief, pumped money into the economy by building new factories and social amenities and raised living standards by increasing wages and keeping foodstuffs, notably meat, at artificially low prices via huge subsidies. The state financed this ambitious program by obtaining credit from western banks, which were keen after the oil price spike of 1973–1974 to recycle petrodollars deposited with them by the oil-producing nations.

Gierek's gamble was that Poland could pay off its debt in the short term by exports of natural resources (coal, copper, sulphur), while steadily enhancing the country's manufacturing capacity in order to be able to export high-value goods in the future. For five years, his plan gave the economy a shot in the arm: output increased by 9 percent per year between 1971 and 1976 and real wages grew by over 40 percent from 1971 to 1976. Meat consumption soared. By 1975, the average Pole was chomping 70kg of meat per year, more than most West Europeans.[41]

The dice soon started to roll the wrong numbers, however. Gierek's plans neglected agriculture, which was unable to meet demand, and stimulated so many imports of food, luxury goods, and machine parts that Poland ran a trade deficit of $3 billion per year in 1975 through 1976. Polish management was not skilled enough to direct the new manufacturing ventures, and the local engineering industry could not make advanced components. Most new industrial investments as a result turned out to be white elephants. A plant to make Massey-Ferguson tractors and diesel engines, for instance, was started in 1974, was completed only in 1980, and turned out a mere two thousand tractors per year instead of the twenty-five thousand foreseen by the plan. Each tractor required $4,000 of imported parts.[42]

By the summer of 1976, the need to reduce demand in the economy had become obvious, but the only solution the Politburo could advance was the old ploy of raising food prices without consultation. Cushioned from the concerns of the hoi polloi by their access to party shops and high salaries, the party leaders discovered: (a) that a policy of "let the workers eat sausage" did not work if the sausage doubled in price overnight; (b) that since higher wages among even the better-off categories of worker had been accompanied by killing increases in workloads (by as many as seven hundred extra hours per worker per year in the Gdansk shipyard, according to Wałęsa), they were now compelling the Polish proletariat to endure ten-hour working days, including weekends, while slashing their purchasing power.[43] Unsurprisingly, "public rejection of the new prices was instantaneous and nationwide."[44] In the town of Radom, street clashes at the end of June left two thousand demonstrators injured and several dead. *Nomenklatura*-only shops were sacked, and the party headquarters was set ablaze.

The scale of popular reaction was such that the party leadership was forced to rescind the price rises. The authorities nevertheless began reprisals against the ringleaders of strikes and revolts. The rise in food prices was brought in by stealth, with better-quality foods being reserved for special access shops, while the working class was left to chew on much inferior products. It was this mean-spirited policy of repression and immiseration—to use the appropriate Marxist terminology—that caused links between the intellectuals and the working class to flourish and that made the "counterpolis" theorized by Havel a reality in Poland by the late 1970s.

Poland's intellectuals had not been tardy in exploiting the Helsinki Accords to protest against human rights abuses. On 5 December 1975, Polish scholars, led by Professor Edward Lipiński, presented the Polish *Sejm* with the "Manifesto of the 59," which protested against the party's desire to consecrate the "leading role of the party" in the constitution and to give Poland's "eternal alliance" with the USSR constitutional status. The fifty-nine intellectuals further appealed for freedom of conscience, religion, information, and expression. Tens of thousands of ordinary (but there was nothing ordinary about such people) citizens openly backed the Manifesto and other human rights initiatives taken at this time. On 23 September 1976, KOR, the Committee for the Defense of the Workers, met for the first time in Lipiński's Warsaw flat. KOR was an impressive gathering of intellectuals of different ages (Lipiński, the oldest, was eighty-seven), beliefs, and professions. Several founder members, including Jacek Kuroń, who became KOR's public face, had served prison sentences for opposition to the regime; several of the older members were wartime resistance heroes. This group of intellectuals, which was soon joined by other opponents of the regime, notably the young political thinker Adam Michnik, became the nucleus of a network of sympathizers throughout the country, who voluntarily distributed publications, reported on cases of police violence or victimization, and provided legal assistance for workers on trial for political offenses. "KOR was but the governing body of a huge popular movement."[45]

KOR's politics were democratic socialist, though open to other currents of opinion in Polish society. Another opposition group, ROPCiO (Defense of Human and Civil Rights), was formed in March 1977 with the explicit goal of taking "joint action" to "adhere to, and monitor adherence to, all human and civil rights, and human dignity;" and to publicize breaches by the regime of human rights and liberties. The so-called Flying University organized lectures on taboo topics and exposed the mendacious interpretation of recent Polish history propagated in official textbooks. Underground publishing houses such as NOWA thrived as they by-passed the censorship process and published translations of anti-totalitarian classics.[46]

In April 1978, the Free Trade Unions movement (FTU) began to "organize the defense of the economic, legal and humanitarian interests" of the working class in the Baltic sea ports. The FTU's founders (who included Wałęsa) asserted that the official unions had become "an extension of the Polish United Workers Party and an obedient tool to operate a system of organized exploitation of all social strata in Poland" and appealed to all "for solidarity in the struggle for a brighter future." The FTU's *samizdat* newspaper, *Robotnik*, written and edited by KOR members, reached as many as two hundred thousand readers and was decisive in raising the political consciousness of Polish workers. Kemp-Welch says that such a publication had "no precedent" in Eastern Europe.[47] One index of raised consciousness was the number of workers who attended a commemoration service for their comrades killed in December 1970. Year by year after 1976 the number of workers attending the illegal ceremony grew: in 1979 several thousand people mourned.

Above all, there was the Catholic Church. In 1977, the Church "was actually bigger under the Communists than it had been before the war."[48] The Church could call upon two cardinals, seventy-five bishops, nineteen thousand priests, thirty-six thousand monks and nuns, and *twenty million* communicants. There were more than fourteen thousand churches and forty-five seminaries. Catholic publications were widely read and mostly uncensored by the state. In general, the Church trod a fine line between rejecting the regime's values and working with it, though simply by existing it provided a haven for activities outside official control. Its influence in rural Poland was profound. When, in October 1978, Karol Wojtyła became pope, the immense *presence* of the Catholic faith in Poland became evident. Charismatic, deeply principled, acutely intelligent, Pope John Paul II was to prove one of the most striking personalities of the twentieth century. His elevation to the Holy See aroused an outpouring of national pride in Poland. His first papal visit in June 1979 attracted more than twelve million people to gigantic outdoor masses. The Communist Party and the organs of the state wisely kept a low profile as Wojtyła ministered to his flock.[49]

In *A Path of Hope*, Lech Wałęsa compares the situation in 1980 to a river: "Thus the trickles of water meet to form streams, and the streams join to produce a river. Sometimes it's a majestic and irresistible force, at other times it's blocked, compelled to go underground. Our movement was like that river."[50] The river burst from underground in August 1980. It flooded the whole of Poland. But as its waters engulfed the nation, its force dissipated, allowing the crumbling institutions of the party state to make one last desperate stand.

The first sign of inundation came on 9 August 1980 when one of the leading activists in the FTU movement, a welder and crane driver called Anna Walentynowicz, was sacked for misconduct just five months before retirement, a punishment that deprived her of a pension. The sacking was a piece of political spite. It came, moreover, at a moment in which the Gierek regime was once again raising prices. Poland's economic problems had worsened, détente was on the wane following the 1979 Soviet invasion of Afghanistan, and western bankers had turned off the credit tap. Poland had to pay back $5.2 billion in principal in 1980 as well as make nearly $2 billion in interest payments on over $20 billion of foreign debt, yet was running a current account deficit of nearly $3 billion. Poland's entire export earnings to the West came only to about $7 billion. Had western governments not lent Poland money in the late 1970s, these problems would have surfaced earlier, but from 1980 onward they became inescapable.[51] The Gierek binge was over, but the regime did not possess the moral authority to impose austerity. Strikes were already sweeping the country when Walentynowicz was fired.

On the morning of 14 August 1980, leaflets signed by the FTU's organizers were distributed to shipyard workers in Gdansk as they went to work urging them to defend Walentynowicz's rights. Wałęsa, who was banned from the shipyard, hopped over a fence and took over leadership of the protest, which swelled in the following days across the Gdansk region, with dozens of other workplaces showing their solidarity through strike action. The authorities quickly backed down and offered the shipyard a pay raise, a monument to the men killed in December 1970, and the reinstatement of Walentynowicz, Wałęsa, and a third worker. The strike committee, headed by Wałęsa, recommended acceptance. Workers from nearby repairs yards and enterprises, who had risked their livelihoods by joining the strike and who feared reprisals, regarded the quick deal as a surrender. Wałęsa, judging the mood, reneged on the deal he had struck and a "strike in solidarity" began. An inter-enterprise strike committee was formed on 18 August and put forward a twenty-one-point set of demands on 22 August.

The demands were of unprecedented boldness for a communist society. They included recognition of the right to form trade unions independent of the employers or the party; a guaranteed right to strike; freedom of expression, with concrete steps being taken to end the suppression of nonparty publications; the liberation of political prisoners; withdrawal of privileges from members of the party hierarchy, military, and police; lowering of the retirement age to prerevolutionary levels; an immediate pay raise and index-linked pay; adequate child-care facilities and maternity leave for female workers; better housing; and the right to free Saturdays, with Saturday work being given extra compensation.[52]

In *Path of Hope*, Wałęsa says he knew the workers had won a "major victory" when deputy premier Mieczysław Jagielski was sent by Warsaw to negotiate on the basis of the twenty-one points.[53] Talks lasted nine days, but the best cards were now in the hands of the workers and the advisors from KOR that they insisted on having present at the negotiations. The party could only have restored its authority by worse bloodshed than in 1970. But had that course been followed, western governments would have pulled the economic plug. On 31 August the Gdansk agreements were signed by Jagielski on behalf of the party and, with a giant pen portraying the pope, by Wałęsa on behalf of *Solidarność* (Solidarity), as the workers' movement had now been baptized. Solidarity acknowledged the leading role of the party in the state, but its other chief demands, above all the right to organize free trade unions, to free expression, and to strike, were agreed to in principle by Jagielski.[54]

The political fallout from the Gdansk accord was immense. On 3 September 1980, the Soviet leadership, showing scant respect for the principle of noninterference in the internal affairs of other countries that it had demanded at Helsinki, cabled Warsaw to express its view that "the agreement, in essence, signifies the legalization of the anti-socialist opposition." It urged the Polish communists to "prepare a counterattack and reclaim the positions that have been lost among the working class and the people" by using propaganda, infiltration of Solidarity, and selective implementation of the Gdansk accords. Above all, "overriding significance to the consolidation of the leading role of the party in society" should be given.[55] Its cable also demanded that the Polish party be renewed with healthy elements: taking the hint, Gierek checked into hospital with sudden heart trouble and was replaced by Stanisław Kania, a close ally who had been in charge of the security services since 1976.

The Gdansk accord liberated workplaces across the country. Branches of Solidarity sprang up in every factory and the union soon had millions of members—9.5 million workers would eventually be represented at Solidarity's first congress, held in Gdansk in September 1981. While the Polish courts insisted that Solidarity should recognize the leading role of the party in the nation's political life, the union had become by the end of 1980 the dominant social interlocutor of the party in the nation's economy—which naturally made it a political actor. This political role was strengthened by Rural Solidarity, an independent union of private farmers, whose creation evoked the specter of the Peasants' Party, postwar Poland's most popular political party until it was smashed by the Communists in 1947.[56]

Solidarity's emergence as a political force infuriated East Germany and Czechoslovakia, whose leaders, Honecker and Husák, gave powerful support for Soviet intervention. Plans were laid for a 8 December 1980 intervention by Warsaw Pact troops. At a Moscow summit on 5 December 1980, Poland was saved from calamity by Kania, who pleaded for a stay of execution: "Even if angels entered Poland . . . they would be treated as bloodthirsty vampires and the socialist ideas would be swimming in blood."[57] Whatever this meant exactly, it swayed Brezhnev against invasion, much to Honecker's disgust. Bogged down in Afghanistan, conscious of the costs of occupying Poland, and also aware that crushing a manual workers' movement like Solidarity would be an ideological debacle, Moscow decided to rely on Poland's leaders. The Soviet leadership was nevertheless unanimous, in the words of foreign minister Andrei Gromyko, that "we simply cannot and must not lose Poland."[58]

In Soviet esteem, Kania was eclipsed by General Jaruzelski, the defense minister, who became premier on 10 February 1981. Kania must have seemed to Brezhnev like a second Dubček, evasive and unwilling to crack down, while Jaruzelski at least talked like a hard-liner. Yet both were humiliated on 27 March 1981, when Solidarity brought the country to a standstill to protest the beating up of three of its activists by undercover police in Bydgoszcz, a town northwest of Warsaw. Rather than risk a general strike, Kania and Jaruzelski made concessions to Wałęsa, including the legalization of Rural Solidarity and restrictions on the use of the paramilitary police. In return, Wałęsa called the strike off, and by so doing split Solidarity itself. Many activists thought the time had come to take power; many others thought that Wałęsa was too autocratic in his decision making. Wałęsa, on his side, was convinced that the politicization of Solidarity would mean Soviet invasion.[59]

The argument would rumble on within Solidarity until the national congress, which began on 5 September 1981. The conference passed a radical program that, while stopping short of demanding free elections, called for political pluralism and industrial self-management (a euphemism for private enterprise). On the congress's fourth day, a Solidarity veteran, *Robotnik* editor Andrzej Gwiazda, read out an "appeal to the working people of Eastern Europe," whose unions had not, of course, sent fraternal delegations (more than twenty western unions had), urging them to follow Solidarity's example. The appeal was passed by acclamation. For the Soviet press, the congress was an "anti-socialist and anti-Soviet orgy." At the end of the month, Wałęsa was elected leader only by a narrow majority (55 percent) of the 896 delegates' votes.[60]

The anti-Soviet tone of Solidarity's congress ended Kania's career. Kania had been elected party leader at the party congress in July. A brief wind of change had blown through the party's ranks and numerous party conservatives were voted out of the central committee and the Politburo. By the fall, this reformist mood had disappeared. Hundreds of thousands of disillusioned reformers had left the party to join Solidarity; the ones who remained were against reform. Economic conditions had worsened: production had plummeted (output fell by 12 percent in 1981, a collapse of Great Depression proportions) and queues snaked outside every butcher. After Politburo criticism in October, Kania was replaced by Jaruzelski.

Behind the scenes, Jaruzelski was steeling his nerve to launch a coup d'état. Contrary to later assertions that he acted because the Soviet Union was on the point of intervention, Jaruzelski actually pleaded for military assistance from the USSR: a well-known scholar has said that "Jaruzelski's donning the mantle of the nation's saviour was a travesty."[61] On 13 December, Poles awoke to the sound of the national anthem and a general in full military uniform telling them that he had decided to act for their own good and had enacted a Military Council of National Salvation to help him.[62] The coup went like clockwork: suppressing democracy was one thing at which the regime excelled. Bloodshed, by Pinochet standards, was limited; the 1967 coup in Athens is a fairer comparison. Solidarity was caught off guard. Its offices were shut down, workplaces that resisted were crushed by armed police, and the union's leaders, including Wałęsa, were interned (as was Edward Gierek). Although the pope wrote to Jaruzelski insisting that "every effort" should be made "so that our compatriots will not be forced to spend this Christmas under the shadow of repression and death," martial law lasted until July 1983.[63] Many leading Solidarity supporters remained in prison long after that date.

International criticism reversed the pattern set by the Greek colonels. The United States, this time, was vocal in its condemnation: President Ronald Reagan proclaimed 20 January 1982 to be "Solidarity Day," a day on which "we the people of the Free World stand as one with our Polish brothers and sisters. Their cause is ours."[64] In Europe, reactions were more muted. Although fifty thousand Parisians took to the streets to protest, West German public opinion was notably ambiguous. The large peace movement in Germany (see below, chapter 10) relativized the suppression of Solidarity, pointing out that the United States was supporting dictators all over the world: the prominent Green Party activist Petra Kelly was one of the few German radicals who considered that "a clear statement on Afghanistan and Solidarity was a yardstick of the peace campaign's credibility and legitimacy."[65] The West German chancellor, Helmut Schmidt, all but welcomed Jaruzelski's action and quickly invited the new Polish government to Bonn for talks on economic aid.

There was, in fact, a general West European disinclination to allow the Polish crisis to derail détente. Throughout the 1970s, East-West trade had been improving: West Germany and Italy were by 1980 sourcing 5 percent of their imports from the Comecon countries and exporting similar percentages.[66] Above all, in 1981, France, Italy, the United Kingdom, and West Germany signed an important energy deal with the USSR to source natural gas via the SNGP (Siberian Natural Gas Pipeline). The project required substantial investment from the European partners and significant technology transfers, but promised a flow of cheap energy to Western European economies. The Reagan administration, which had disapproved of the pipeline from the outset, mounted a concerted effort to block the project throughout 1981, arguing that it would make Europe dependent upon Soviet energy and provide the USSR with a new influx of hard currency that would prop the communist system up. More generally, the deal would "forge an economic link with Europe that will inevitably increase Moscow's influence among our allies."[67]

In the wake of the suppression of Solidarity, the Reagan administration slapped heavy economic sanctions on Poland itself and placed an embargo on the export of U.S. gas and oil equipment technology to the USSR. This mattered since U.S. firms such as Caterpillar and General Electric manufactured components necessary for the pipeline's construction. The administration's move was regarded as inept in European capitals. A summit, held in Versailles, France, in June 1982 temporarily cooled tempers, but a subsequent unilateral decision by Washington to extend its embargo on gas and oil technology to non-American firms that possessed U.S. subsidiaries or used U.S. technology on license turned up the heat beneath the dispute. Executives of offending firms were even made liable to criminal sanctions.

The U.S. claim to extraterritorial rights over European citizens was rejected indignantly by all Washington's principal partners, many of whose firms stood to lose substantial contracts. Britain's minister of trade—an ardent free-market conservative—pointed out in an acerbic parliamentary speech that it was "inequitable" that the United States should continue to export "large quantities of grain" to both Poland and the USSR while leaving the burden of the sanctions to fall on America's European allies.[68] This was unfair—U.S. companies such as Caterpillar were hard hit too—but there was truth to the charge that the Reagan administration's anti-communist zeal lost momentum when it impinged upon the pecuniary interests of Republican-voting farm belt states. The West European allies openly advocated noncompliance with the embargo and eventually forced Washington to rethink its policy.

The transatlantic squabble over the Siberian pipeline was symptomatic of relations between the United States and its allies in the 1970s. It was hardly the first row to have strained the Atlantic alliance since Richard M. Nixon had been elected president in November 1968. Washington's weak dollar policy, its unease over the EEC's attempts to establish a "common foreign policy," President Jimmy Carter's uncertainty over the deployment of intermediate-range nuclear missiles, the political consequences of democratization in the Mediterranean, and the Soviet invasion of Afghanistan had all previously generated transatlantic tensions. These tensions are the topic of the next chapter.

It should be said, however, by way of conclusion to *this* chapter, that western nations could fall out among themselves because their historical opponent was no longer the moral and economic rival it had once appeared to be (though in firepower terms it was a much greater military threat). In retrospect, we can see that the communist states were offered a golden opportunity to civilize their regimes in the 1970s. Both the West and the regimes' internal critics did everything consonant with human dignity to avoid provocation and to invite reform. The response had been philosophers made to clean windows in Prague, writers injected with mind-altering drugs in Soviet psychiatric clinics, industrial workers beaten into submission in Gdansk. Such actions preserved the communist regimes' grip on power, but only at the cost of exposing their ideological bankruptcy.[69] By December 1981, the Soviet emperor's lack of new clothes was obvious. It was still not clear whether anybody would have the courage to point out the grossness of his nudity.

NOTES

1. Timothy Garton Ash, "The Significance of Solidarity," in *Poland under Jaruzelski: A Comprehensive Sourcebook on Poland during and after Martial Law*, ed. Leopold Labedz (New York: Charles Scribner's Sons, 1984), 49.

2. The two documents are reprinted in *Il Partito Comunista italiano e il movimento operaio internazionale, 1956–1968*, ed. Roberto Bonchio et al. (Rome: Riuniti Editore, 1968), 312–13 and 371–83.

3. "Statement by the European Communist and Workers' Parties on European Security" (Karlovy Vary, 26 April 1967), *Centre Virtuel de la Connaissance sur l'Europe* (CVCE), http://www.ena.lu.

4. Final Communiqué of the Ministerial Session of the North Atlantic Council (Brussels, 13–14 December 1967), http://www.nato.intl.

5. For background, see Thomas Fischer, "A mustard seed grew into a bushy tree': The Finnish CSCE Initiative of 5 May 1969," *Cold War History* 9 (2009): 177–201.

6. Willy Brandt, *My Life in Politics* (London: Penguin, 1993), 172.

7. Helmut Schmidt, "Germany in the Era of Negotiations," *Foreign Affairs* 49 (1970): 46.

8. Brandt, *My Life*, 200.

9. Timothy Garton Ash, *In Europe's Name: Germany and the Divided Continent* (London: Vintage, 1993), 73.

10. M. E. Sarotte, "A Small Town in (East) Germany: The Erfurt Meeting of 1970 and the Dynamics of Cold War Détente," *Diplomatic History* 25, no. 1 (2001): 93-96. Sarotte's book, *Dealing with the Devil: East Germany, Détente and Ostpolitik 1969–1973* (Chapel Hill: University of North Carolina Press, 2001), is in my opinion the best work in English on Ostpolitik.

11. Brandt, *My Life*, 211.

12. Henry Ashby Turner Jr., *Germany from Partition to Reunification* (New Haven, CT: Yale University Press, 1992), 155.

13. Turner, *Germany from Partition to Reunification*, 162.

14. See Henry Kissinger, *Years of Upheaval* (London: Phoenix Press, 2000), 143–46.

15. Walter Scheel, "Europe on the Move," *Foreign Policy*, no. 4 (Autumn 1971): 62–76. Brandt had made the same points in April 1968: Willy Brandt, "German Policy to the East," *Foreign Affairs* 46 (1968): 476–86.

16. For EC policy, see Daniel C. Thomas, *The Helsinki Effect: International Norms, Human Rights, and the Demise of Communism* (Princeton, NJ: Princeton University Press, 2001), 40–59, and Angela Romano, *From Détente in Europe to European Détente* (Brussels: Peter Lang, 2009).

17. Svetlana Savranskaya, "Unintended Consequences: Soviet Interests, Expectations and Reactions to the Helsinki Final Act," in *Helsinki 1975 and the Transformation of Europe*, ed. Oliver Bange and Gottfried Niederhart (Oxford: Berghahn, 2008), 187.

18. Thomas, *The Helsinki Effect*, 39–43 and 259–61. Thomas argues for this "constructivist" argument as against various "realist" or "neo-realist" explanations.

19. For the events leading up to Solzhenitsyn's expulsion from the USSR, see Michael Scammell, *Solzhenitsyn* (London: Hutchinson, 1984), 829–46.

20. Ludmilla Alexeyeva, "The Human Rights Movement in the USSR," *Survey* 23, no. 4 (1977–1978): 82, gives the following figures: 125 imprisoned in 1969; 146 in 1970; 92 in 1971; 91 in 1972; 81 in 1973; 106 in 1974. The figures then fall away to fewer than 50 per year until 1979. Figures were based on reports in the *samizdat* newspaper *Chronicle of Current Events*. See also the seminal work by Sidney Bloch and Peter Reddaway, *Russia's Political Hospitals: The Abuse of Psychiatry in the Soviet Union* (London: Victor Gollancz, 1977).

21. Alexander Solzhenitsyn, speech to the AFL-CIO union, 30 June, 1975, *Survey* 21, no. 3 (1975): 128. Bruno Kreisky was president of Austria. Italics are in the original.

22. Alexeyeva, "The Human Rights Movement in the USSR," 74.

23. I owe these insights into the legal subtleties of the Final Act to Harold S. Russell, "The Helsinki Declaration: Brobdingnag or Liliput?" *The American Journal of International Law* 70 (1976): 242–72.

24. For implementation of Bonn-East Berlin détente, see Lawrence S. Whetton, "Scope, Nature and Change in Inner-German Relations," *International Affairs* 57 (Winter 1980–1981): 60–78.

25. See Bernard Levin, "The Blood Trial Revived," and "The Bloody Trial Concluded," in *Taking Sides* (London: Cape, 1979), 48–56. In these two articles, originally published in *The Times* on 28 November 1974 and 7 January 1975, the British journalist campaigned on behalf of a doctor, Mikhail Stern, who had been put on trial for swindling and corruption (but was threatened with charges of child murder). His real crime was his desire to emigrate to Israel. During the trial, a number of Dr. Stern's patients refused to recite the scripted evidence that the authorities had provided them. Dr. Stern received an eight-year sentence in a labor camp, but was released after international pressure.

26. Official persecution closed down the Helsinki group's operations in 1982. By that time, only a handful of activists remained free; many had had to leave Russia. Yuri Orlov was sent to a labor camp in 1977, released in 1986, and then expelled to the United States.

27. See http://libpro.cts.cuni.cz/charta/docs/declaration_of_charter_77.pdf for the original typescript in English.

28. Miroslav Kusy, "Chartism and 'Real Socialism,'" in Václav Havel et al., *The Power of the Powerless: Citizens Against the State in Central-Eastern Europe* (New York: Sharpe, 1985), 170.

29. Quoted in Abbott Gleason, *Totalitarianism: The Inner History of the Cold War* (New York: Oxford University Press, 1995), 187.

30. Václav Havel, "The Power of the Powerless," in Havel, *Open Letters* (London: Faber & Faber, 1991), 125–214.

31. Gleason, *Totalitarianism*, 184.

32. Havel makes similar points, but with a strong patriotic emphasis on the Czech national culture, in another famous essay: "Letter to Dr. Gustav Husak," *Survey* 21, no. 4 (1975): 167-90.

33. Jimmy Carter, *Keeping Faith: Memoirs of a President* (New York: Bantam Books, 1982), 146.

34. François Furet, *The Passing of an Illusion: The Idea of Communism in the Twentieth Century* (Chicago: Chicago University Press, 1999), especially chapter 13, "Epilogue."

35. Leonardo Sciascia, *Candido* (London: Harvill Press, 1995), 115.

36. For the December 1970 uprising, see Anthony Kemp-Welch, *Poland under Communism: A Cold War History* (Cambridge: Cambridge University Press, 2008), 180–88.

37. Lech Wałęsa, *A Path of Hope* (London: Collins Harvill, 1987), 75.

38. For the fall of Gomułka, see Adam Bromke, "Beyond the Gomulka Era," *Foreign Affairs* 49 (1971): 480–92.

39. Jerry F. Hough, *The Polish Crisis: American Policy Options* (Washington, DC: Brookings Institution, 1982), 12.

40. Joseph Rothschild and Nancy M. Wingfield, *Return to Diversity: A Political History of East Central Europe since World War Two* (New York: Oxford University Press, 2000), 196.

41. For the Polish economy, see Kazimierz Poznanski, "Economic Adjustment and Political Forces: Poland since 1970," *International Organization* 40 (1986): 455–88.

42. Derek H. Aldcroft and Steven Morewood, *Economic Change in Eastern Europe since 1918* (Aldershot, UK: Elgar, 1995), 164.

43. Wałęsa, *Path of Hope*, 82.

44. Kemp-Welch, *Poland under Communism*, 208.

45. Jan Josef Lipski, "The Founding of KOR," in Labedz, ed., *Poland under Jaruzelski*, 78.

46. See Adam Bromke, "Opposition in Poland," *Problems of Communism* 26, no. 3 (1978): 37–51, for a very useful overview.

47. Kemp-Welch, *Poland under Communism*, 219.

48. Carl Tighe, "Cultural Pathology: Roots of Polish Literary Opposition to Communism," *Journal of European Studies* 29 (1999): 182.

49. Marcin Zaremba, "Karol Wojtyła the Pope: Complications for the Comrades of the Polish United Workers' Party," *Cold War History* 5 (2003): 317–36.

50. Wałęsa, *Path of Hope*, 107.

51. Statistics in Hough, *The Polish Crisis*, 17. For a lucid explanation of the communist states' economic problems, see the interview with Lawrence Brainard, in Michael Charlton, *The Eagle and the Small Birds: Crisis in the Soviet Empire from Yalta to Solidarity* (Chicago: Chicago University Press, 1984), 164–67.

52. An English translation of the Gdansk agreement is to be found in *Survival* 23, no. 5 (1981): 228–31.

53. Wałęsa, *Path of Hope*, 133.

54. These stirring events are depicted in Andrzej Wadja's film *Man of Iron* (1981), one of the greatest realist postwar films, and one that includes a cameo role by Lech Wałęsa.

55. Mark Kramer, "Poland 1980–81: Soviet Policy during the Polish Crisis," *Cold War History Project Bulletin* no. 5 (Spring 1995): 118–19.

56. The best account of the spread of Solidarity is Timothy Garton Ash, *The Polish Revolution: Solidarity*, 3rd ed. (New Haven, CT: Yale University Press, 2002).

57. Vojtech Mastny, "The Soviet Non-Invasion of Poland in 1980/81 and the End of the Cold War," CWHP Working Paper no. 23 (1998): 6.

58. Kramer, "Soviet Policy during the Polish Crisis," 118.

59. Wałęsa, *Path of Hope*, 185–91, for his side of this crisis.

60. Kemp-Welch, *Poland under Communism*, 322.

61. Mastny, "The Soviet Non-Invasion," 14.

62. The text of the statement is reprinted in Labedz, ed., *Poland under Jaruzelski*, 7.

63. Letter quoted in Wałęsa, *Path of Hope*, 224.

64. Ronald Reagan, presidential proclamation 4891, 20 January 1982.

65. Quoted in Robert Brier, "Poland's Solidarity as a Contested Symbol of the Cold War: Transatlantic Debates after the Polish Crisis," in *European Integration and the Atlantic Community in the 1980s*, ed. Kiran Klaus Patel and Ken Weisrode (New York: Cambridge University Press, 2013), 93.

66. For precise figures, see N. Piers Ludlow, "The Unnoticed Apogee of Atlanticism: U.S.-Western European Relations during the Early Reagan Era," in Patel and Weisbrode, eds., *European Integration and the Atlantic Community*, 25.

67. Assistant Secretary of Defense Richard Perle, quoted in Ksenia Demidova, "The Deal of the Century: The Reagan Administration and the Soviet Pipeline," in Patel and Weisbrode, eds., *European Integration and the Atlantic Community*, 65.

68. Lord Arthur Cockfield, quoted in Demidova, "The Deal of the Century," 78.

69. For this point, see the interview with Lezek Kołakowski in Charlton, *The Eagle and the Small Birds*, 131–34.

Chapter Ten

Resentful Allies

The 1970s and early 1980s were characterized by moments of genuine tension between the United States and its principal European partners. The Atlantic relationship, though it did not finish in divorce, did not lack public bickering. It is hard to apportion blame. The United States was undoubtedly high-handed in its treatment of its European allies at various times between the late 1960s and the mid-1980s. In different ways, both President Nixon and President Carter neglected their allies' concerns, yet were irritated when their allies showed resentment. President Reagan's crusading rhetoric after he took office in 1981 alarmed policy makers in democratic Europe. As an American commentator wrote, Reagan's policy seemed like "bravura" of a kind that could easily "stumble into disaster." Certainly, it generated an "upsurge in neutralist and pacifist sentiment" among a section of West European public opinion, which was more inclined to march against the U.S. military bases on its doorstep than protest the Soviet missiles pointed at its head.[1]

On the other hand, Europeans made the relationship fraught as well. By the late 1960s, U.S. living standards were matched by several economically advanced European countries. Rising prosperity produced greater assertiveness on the part of West European elites, who no longer saw the need to defer to American wishes. Leaders like Willy Brandt, British Premier Edward Heath, and de Gaulle's successor as president of France, Georges Pompidou, desired to give the European Community a foreign policy dimension that it had hitherto lacked. As we saw in chapter 9, they actually succeeded in the field of human rights. European "political cooperation" turned out to be harder to achieve in other fields, however, and over the 1973 Arab-Israeli conflict, and subsequent OPEC boycott of the United States, the EC's bid to distinguish itself from Washington led only to humiliation.

Western Europe's distancing of itself from Washington was not merely a function of its growing economic power. While the United States continued to speak as if it were a beacon for humanity, the European allies were less in thrall to American moral leadership than before. The Watergate allegations were crucial in this respect. It was difficult for the United States to retain the leadership of the democratic world when its president was being investigated for subverting the democratic process. The Vietnam War only compounded America's image problems. Every Vietnamese child burned by the "Free World's" napalm was a brutal argument on behalf of the many Europeans who regarded the two superpowers as moral equivalents. U.S. relations with Sweden were particularly tense. Premier Olof Palme's long-standing criticism of the Vietnam conflict kept pace with President Richard M. Nixon's intensification of the war. By the early 1970s, Palme was accusing the United States of assuming "the mantle of the old colonial imperialism" and of colluding with the USSR to divide the world into "spheres of interest." Palme promoted an alternative foreign policy for European nations based upon advocacy of peace and disarmament, substantial aid transfers to the developing world (Sweden made and kept a pledge to invest 0.7 percent of GDP on development), environmentalism, and the establishment of "a more democratic international community" in which multinational corporations were made accountable to the communities that they exploited.[2]

The progressive neutralism advocated by Olof Palme (but also in Great Britain after 1979 by the Labour Party, and in Italy by the PCI), nevertheless persuaded few. The United States' European allies were not ready to cut the transatlantic apron strings and go it alone. In the early 1980s, the West European allies risked unpopularity to strengthen the transatlantic link by siting American cruise missiles on their soil. The marriage between Washington and Western Europe remained solid, though in the long decade 1968 to 1984, it was anything but placid.

MONEY MAKES THE WORLD GO ROUND

The trouble in the transatlantic relationship began with the dollar. The view of many leading European statesmen was that the dollar was the anchor of the postwar economic edifice constructed by the United States: Washington could not neglect it without putting at risk its overall leadership. In the 1970s, however, the fears de Gaulle had raised in the mid-1960s about the long-term reliability of the American currency became fact. Washington's promises to pay were less than golden, as the General had predicted. The United States' backsliding on its commitments was unquestionably one of the principal underlying causes of instability in the Atlantic alliance.

The 1944 Bretton Woods agreements established that the U.S. dollar should possess a fixed value redeemable in gold (one ounce of gold was worth $35) and other international currencies should possess a fixed value in relation to the dollar, though these values could be adjusted by mutual agreement to assist economies that were suffering balance-of-payments problems. Britain, for instance, was obliged in November 1967, after a debilitating struggle, to reduce the pound's value from $2.80 to $2.40. Together with fixed currencies went a powerful American commitment to free trade. By and large, the European nations reciprocated. Agriculture apart, the EC opened up its restrictions on imports from the rest of the world, as did large non-EC economies such as Britain (Britain joined the EC in 1973).

The United States thus shored up its role as the West's principal military power by promoting commerce in dollars between the countries within its sphere of influence. The problem with this strategy was that it worked almost too well. European (and Japanese) products poured into the United States in the 1960s, eroding the trade surplus it had enjoyed with the rest of the world since the end of the nineteenth century. In the second quarter of 1971, America actually ran a trade deficit of $800 million dollars.

This weakening trade performance was important for two reasons. First, it meant that foreigners accumulated large "overhangs" of dollars that they could exchange for Washington's limited reserves of gold bullion (by the summer of 1971, foreign banks and companies held more than $70 billion; the United States' gold reserves were only $12 billion); second, the United States began to run deficits in its balance of payments since its trade surpluses no longer compensated for its outlays in overseas military expenditure or for the outflow of dollars in direct investments by U.S. multinationals.

By the summer of 1971, the Nixon administration had concluded that this situation could not go on. Pressure was growing on Capitol Hill to impose tariffs on Japan and to reduce troop numbers in Europe. Both of these solutions would have diplomatic consequences that Nixon did not want to risk. He had, moreover, an election to win in November 1972. Nixon planned to engineer a consumer boom in time for the election, but this strategy would fail if the money pumped into the economy was spent on foreign goods and turned the trade deficit into a campaign issue. There was, moreover, the issue of equity. As Nixon saw it, other countries were now nearly as rich as the United States; they should therefore make greater sacrifices for the common cause against communism, not abuse American generosity. As Nixon's treasury secretary, the Texan John Connally, averred: "My philosophy is that all foreigners are out to screw us and it's our job to screw them first." This was not the language of postwar liberal internationalists like George C. Marshall, George F. Kennan, or Dean Acheson, but of a new class of American leaders who feared the emergence of economic rivals that might aspire to political leadership. As Nixon himself remarked: "It's terribly important that we be number one economically because otherwise we can't be number one diplomatically or politically."[3]

The crunch came in August 1971. Speculators began shifting money into safer havens abroad. The British, anxious for the value of their dollar hoard, asked the United States on 13 August 1971 to exchange $3 billion dollars for gold. Within forty-eight hours, Nixon, after consultations at Camp David with his economic policy advisors, announced a "New Economic Policy." In brief, the United States "suspended" convertibility of the dollar for gold, imposed a 10 percent "surcharge" on imports, reduced income and consumer taxes, and made token cuts to federal spending and overseas aid. It was a reflationary package, designed to stimulate the economy in time for the election while minimizing the effects on the trade deficit. U.S. public opinion cheered the president's boldness, and Wall Street registered a huge gain on the day following Nixon's speech.

In Europe, nobody applauded, although Secretary Connally sneered, "So the other countries don't like it. So what?" Two things worried the Europeans. First, the attitude exemplified by Connally's remarks. If the United States was going to act as a bully, how should Europe respond? For Nixon to have transformed global economic policy without even a charade of consultation sent a powerful message to every European leader. Second, Europeans were worried about the long-term effects on the dollar. If the dollar, shorn of its gold guarantee, were to decline sharply, European exports would become much dearer in the United States. Even worse, the dollar would likely decline more sharply against the mark than against the lira, the pound, and the franc. This would lead to "asymmetry" between European exchange rates and give a commercial advantage to those countries whose currencies had strengthened by less. The EC had only completed the customs union foreseen by the 1957 Treaty of Rome in 1968. The Europeans had no way of knowing whether their newly created trading regime could survive the political tensions engendered by fluctuating exchange rates. Truly, Nixon had "decided to put the domestic economy first and let the international chips fall where they might."[4]

Nixon's August 1971 démarche initiated a bout of international monetary diplomacy during which the major industrial nations tried to patch up the Bretton Woods system. In December 1971, they agreed in Washington to establish new fixed rates for the major currencies: the yen and the mark in particular were revalued substantially against the dollar. It was also agreed that currencies would fluctuate within "bands" of +/- 2.25 percent of their par value against the dollar. This device was known as the "tunnel." On 7 March 1972, anxious to restrict currency fluctuations still further, the EC Six, joined subsequently by Britain, instituted the so-called snake within the tunnel by which they agreed that fluctuations between their own currencies would be limited to just 1.125 percent above or below par values. The "Snake," in other words, was an attempt to "lash the EEC's currencies together like boats in a harbor that would rise and fall together as the dollar tide advanced and ebbed."[5]

None of these devices restored order to the money markets. In February 1973, the dollar was sold off and lost value against the franc, the mark, and the Swiss franc. The free-market price of gold surged. The United States did nothing to support the price of the dollar, even though Arthur Burns, the president of the Federal Reserve, warned that "our failure to offer to intervene would be taken in Europe as an abdication of leadership and responsibility."[6]

Burns was right. It was. On 9 March 1973, in Paris, the G-10 group of largest industrial nations, together with the other member states of the EC, acknowledged that Bretton Woods had drawn its last breath. The member states of the EC had been presented with a fait accompli. Their reserves of dollars were now a diminishing asset, and the common market had been robbed of part of its rationale by the introduction of exchange rate uncertainty. While this state of affairs was not entirely Nixon's fault, there is no doubt that the Nixon administration's willingness to jettison the economic regime the United States itself had imposed upon the rest of the industrialized world shook U.S. standing and left a strong impression in Europe's capitals that Washington was a declining hegemon.

THE "YEAR OF EUROPE"

On 23 April 1973, less than two months after the burial of Bretton Woods, NSC chief Henry Kissinger launched the so-called Year of Europe with a New York speech that argued that the United States and her allies needed to rethink the Atlantic alliance to take into account changing global political realities. Kissinger contended that the emergence of the EC and Japan as major industrial powerhouses, and the USSR's emerging strategic "near equality," had changed the logic of the international situation with which the Atlantic alliance had to deal. In an unfortunate turn of phrase, Kissinger suggested that the new generation of European leaders were underestimating "the unity that made peace possible and to the effort required to maintain it." In particular, they were not contributing "a fair share of the common effort for the common defense." Kissinger urged that by the end of the year, President Nixon should be able to visit Europe to sign a new "Atlantic Charter" that would embody a new and less one-sided transatlantic relationship.[7]

Kissinger's speech was greeted gelidly by the EC states. First, his initiative was mistimed. Europe was still simmering over the dollar debacle. Second, European leaders assumed that Kissinger's initiative was designed to check the EC's expanding role in international affairs. In October 1972, the

Paris summit of the six EC member states and the three nations on the point of joining (Great Britain, Denmark, and Ireland) had proclaimed that by 1980 they would establish a European Union, with its own currency and a common foreign policy that would "establish its position in world affairs as a distinct entity determined to promote a better international equilibrium." In his speech, Kissinger had spoken of the EC as a bloc with purely "regional interests," which sounded as if he thought that the EC should leave the big stuff to Washington. Certainly, this was the interpretation of the French government, whose foreign minister, Michel Jobert, argued that Kissinger's scheme would "consecrate American hegemony over the western world" and intrigued from day one against it.[8] West Germany's Willy Brandt and French President Georges Pompidou both gave lukewarm receptions to Kissinger's speech in meetings with President Nixon in May 1973.[9] A third reason Kissinger's initiative was mistimed was the fact that Edward Heath, the only postwar British prime minister who was an unambiguous supporter of the broad ideals of the European movement, backed the objective of greater European foreign policy independence from the United States and was willing to let the French take the lead on this issue.

The EEC's doubts were compounded in June 1973 when Nixon and Brezhnev, meeting in Washington and California, signed the Soviet-American "declaration of common resolve" on the prevention of nuclear war (PNW). Article 4 of the PNW declaration, which committed the United States and the USSR to "enter into urgent consultations with each other" "if at any time relations between the Parties or between either Party and other countries appear to involve the risk of a nuclear conflict," was particularly controversial, though from the form of words chosen, it is hard to understand why. The Europeans were, in fact, abnormally sensitive to any idea that the United States and the USSR would form a "condominium" to decide nuclear matters over their heads. A tacit nuclear nonaggression pact between the two superpowers would leave Europe vulnerable.[10] Foreign Minister Jobert was especially irate about Washington's high-handedness, although as Marc Trachtenberg has pointed out, the idea that there was no consultation is a myth.[11]

Overall, William Bundy's disparaging critique of the Nixon administration's foreign policy, namely that it weaved a "tangled web" that created troubles for itself, is demonstrated in its relations with the EC in mid-1973.[12] Probably unwittingly, as a by-product of hyper-activity, by the summer of 1973 U.S. initiatives had created the perception that Washington was trying to keep the EC from being anything other than a satellite.

The EC responded to Kissinger's speech with a period of consultation dictated by the fact that the European Political Community (EPC)—its foreign policy mechanism—was still in its procedural infancy. The Nine agreed in Copenhagen in July 1973 to draw up a common response to the draft of the Charter proposed by the United States by September and that in the meantime they would not engage in bilateral discussions with the Americans: They should be what French minister Jobert called "a Europe of the Nine, not the Ten."[13] Kissinger therefore was shut out. As he said in his memoir *Years of Upheaval*, this was "totally at variance with the practice of intimate consultations of more than two decades."[14] Over the summer of 1973, the idea that there should be a declaration of common transatlantic principles took hold. The EC dispatched Danish foreign minister Knud B. Anderson to Washington at the end of September 1973 with a draft document that took care to eliminate any reference to Atlantic "partnership" or "interdependence," but which underlined that Europe was now a "distinct entity" in world affairs. Washington reacted with dismay, not least because Anderson could only act as a "messenger boy" and had no freedom to draw up a compromise text.[15]

In Kissinger's view, the "single most corrosive factor" explaining this setback was the Watergate scandal. The problem in fact went deeper. Europe was trying to assert its independence. By the fall of 1973, transatlantic relations were a powder keg waiting for a match, or, to use Kissinger's own simile, U.S. relations with her allies were like a quarrelsome family whose suppressed "frustrations" were ready to "explode with disproportionate fury."[16]

The explosion came as a result of the attack by Egypt and Syria on Israel on 6 October 1973. The United States took Israel's side in the crisis, provoking the oil-producing nations of the Middle East to use energy supplies as a geopolitical weapon. Oil prices, which had been diminishing in value along with the dollar, were raised by 70 percent on 16 October, and on 20 October an embargo on countries that supplied Israel was announced. The conflict also produced a risky surge of tension between the United States and the USSR. The Soviets proposed a joint U.S.-Soviet peacekeeping force to impose and police a cease-fire in the Middle East and hinted that they might unilaterally send "peacekeepers" to the region. The U.S. response was to put its armed forces on full nuclear alert on 25 October, a move that understandably created panic in European capitals. European leaders were not consulted for the good reason that Washington "could not have accepted a judgment different from our own."[17]

The Europeans, who depended upon the Arab nations for their oil supplies, now set out deliberately to challenge the United States' strategy in the Middle East.[18] Only Portugal and the Netherlands allowed U.S. transport planes flying to Israel to use their territory as a base; the others banned such aid. On 6 November 1973, ten days after the fighting ended, EC foreign ministers called for Israeli withdrawal to the 1967 borders as a necessary condition for achieving a lasting peace. In December, as OPEC states more than doubled the price of oil, the EC Nine announced that they would start a dialogue with the oil producers to achieve a "global regime" that would balance the economic development of the industrial nations with "reasonable prices" for the oil producers. On 14 December, the EC's foreign ministers produced a "Declaration on European Identity," a document that stressed the community's values and its need to unite if it was to count in world affairs, but which gave no ground on the key issue of drawing the United States into their decision-making process. [19]

Washington gave a bare-knuckled response to this European posture, by proposing the creation of a consumers' cartel of the largest industrial nations who would negotiate as a group with OPEC. In Washington in February 1974, the United States bullied the Europeans into accepting it scheme. U.S. speakers, from President Nixon down, linked the energy question to the issue of European security and openly threatened troop withdrawals from Europe if the EC did not back down. Only France stood out against this pressure; the rest joined the U.S.-sponsored International Energy Agency in November 1974. [20]

Britain, France, and Germany all changed their leaders in the spring of 1974, which facilitated Washington's broader push to rein in EC foreign policy independence. [21] By the so-called Gymnich Castle agreement in April 1974, the EC agreed that its member states could consult with Washington whenever they took foreign policy initiatives. At the end of June 1974, just before Nixon's resignation, NATO member states finally signed the "Declaration on Atlantic Relations," as it was now officially known. [22] The language of the declaration was anodyne, for the most part. In hindsight, it is hard to understand why the EC did not acquiesce in some such formulation a year earlier. By opposing Kissinger's initiative so bitterly, the EC states had conferred excessive significance upon it. [23] The "Year of Europe" had come to an end, but as its principal architect bitterly reflected: "An affirmation of unity requiring no concrete action that nevertheless takes fourteen months to negotiate is hardly a sign of moral rededication." [24]

Nixon's political demise in the summer of 1974 and the arrival of the affable Gerald Ford in the White House soothed tensions. Ford was an extremely popular president in European capitals, and on his watch "quadripartite consultation" between Washington, London, Bonn, and Paris became the norm. [25] Unlike Nixon, who had dragged his feet on the Helsinki process, saying for instance in a 5 June 1974 speech that the United States "would not welcome the interference of other countries in our domestic affairs and we cannot expect [the Soviet bloc] to be cooperative when we seek to intervene directly in theirs," Ford agreed that the human rights clauses of the Helsinki Final Act would work an improvement in conditions within the communist world, and thus contribute to peace, and stuck to his position despite the intense domestic heat that this stance engendered. [26]

WAGES OF SIN

By August 1975, when Gerald Ford signed the Helsinki Accords on behalf of the United States, Greece and Portugal—authoritarian right-wing regimes long supported by the United States—were in a state of transition toward democracy. Spain was about to join them. Italy was democratic, with a free press, vibrant civil society, and competitive elections, but the corrupt, socially conservative government of Christian Democracy was widely despised and political violence was rife. Young people in all four countries were unwilling to tolerate regimes whose policies were guided by priests, bespectacled, reactionary politicians, and the local American embassy.

The upsurge of democracy across the Mediterranean was a heartening development, but it soon became another source of disagreement between Washington and Western Europe. Washington naturally feared a growth in communist influence. Secretary of State Henry Kissinger, in particular, was inclined to take the Manichean view that the Mediterranean might be lost for the West. Nor was Kissinger alone. *The Economist* warned hysterically on 10 August 1974 that "the fluid situation in southern Europe has provided the greatest opportunity for the westward expansion of communist governments in Europe since the immediate aftermath of Hitler's war."[27] In fact, if the United States did lose influence in the Mediterranean in the 1970s, it was because the process of democratization overthrew static, old-fashioned, corrupt regimes that had enjoyed U.S. backing. To use a slightly melodramatic phrase, Washington paid the wages of sin.

The first country to complete its transition to democracy was Greece. Democracy in Greece had been subverted in April 1967 by a military coup led by Colonel Georgios Papadopoulos. "A cunning political operator," Papadopoulos amassed power after the coup.[28] He also enjoyed the overt support of Washington, which had watched the turmoil in Greece since the early 1960s with alarm. The United States' favorite in Greek politics, Konstantinos Karamanlis, had retired to exile in France in 1963. Elections led to the victory of the "Center Union," a party headed by a veteran (and pro-American) politician called Georgios Papandreou. His government was disrupted, however, by the ambitions of his economist son, Andreas, who wanted to introduce radical social reforms—a fact that made him persona non grata at the U.S. embassy in Athens. Ambassador William Phillips Talbot intrigued with King Constantine II to neuter Papandreou's government, and though the U.S. embassy did not collude with Papadopoulos's putsch, the United States backed the military's seizure of power despite the thousands of human rights violations that were recorded as the new regime consolidated its grip on the country.

There were strategic arguments for this policy of engagement with a dubious regime: the USSR was stepping up its naval presence in the Mediterranean and the Pentagon wanted to construct a home port in Greece for the U.S. fleet.[29] The Nixon administration also mysteriously regarded the Greek junta as a force for stability in the East Mediterranean region. The opposite was true, but such sentiments no doubt seemed suitably realist to Kissinger and the president. Nixon reportedly said of the junta, indeed, that "I am the best friend they've got."[30] The junta never enjoyed popular support, however, and many of its actions, such as the quixotic attempt to ban miniskirts and impose short haircuts on men, simply rendered it ridiculous: it "attracted widespread derision from the Greek intellectual elite."[31]

Papadopoulos, encouraged by the United States, eventually placed a fig leaf of respectability over his regime. In May 1973, the junta formally deposed the monarchy and made Greece a presidential republic. Papadopoulos was duly "elected" in July 1973 for an eight-year term, but his self-elevation over the regime's other key members, and his relative openness to what the junta called "guided democracy," made him suspect to hard-liners and paradoxically weakened his position.

The predictable result of propping up the Athens regime was a major political crisis that rapidly took on Cold War overtones. In mid-November 1973, after army units cleared the campus of Athens Polytechnic University of protesters in a bloody operation in which dozens of students lost their lives, Papadopoulos was replaced as president by General Phaidon Gizikis. Real power passed to the regime's hatchet-man, police chief Dimitrios Ioannidis. The regime's international credibility and domestic popularity sank to new lows. To distract public opinion, the junta remembered the old adage that patriotism is the last refuge of a scoundrel.

The patriotic issue Ioannidis chose to exploit was Cyprus, which had been a British colony until 1960 and which was populated by both Greeks and a substantial Turkish minority. The island's political arrangements—a "witches' brew" according to one observer—had been created by the 1961 Zurich agreements that had established an independent, unitary state presided over by a Greek—the wily Archbishop Makarios—but with a Turkish vice president with wide powers of veto. Greece, Turkey, and Britain all retained the right to intervene on the island should either community seek to undermine the Zurich arrangements.[32] In 1964 attacks by Greek nationalists on the Turkish community in Cyprus had already provoked a dangerous crisis between Greece and Turkey. Only the personal intervention of President Lyndon B. Johnson had prevented a Turkish invasion. Then, former U.S. Secretary of State Dean Acheson had suggested that Cyprus should be partitioned, with most of the island being unified with Greece, but with a Turkish zone left free to join Turkey. This plan had been rejected out of hand by the Greek community on the island.

To compound the problem, Archishop Makarios was despised by the junta in Athens, who regarded him as a communist and as a traitor to the cause of *enosis* (union) with Greece.[33] On 15 July 1974, the Cypriot military, instigated by Athens, launched a coup on the island. Makarios escaped from the presidential palace in Nicosia by the back door and fled to London. To the dismay of the Athens junta, on 20 July, Turkish troops established a bridgehead on Cyprus's north coast. War was averted only by the collapse of the Greek regime. Ioannidis's colleagues, well aware of Greece's inability to fight the Turks, rebelled against their leader. On 23 July 1974, the colonels surrendered power to a committee of notables headed by a pre-coup premier, the distinguished intellectual Panayiotis Kannellopoulos. The committee took the decision to recall Karamanlis, who returned to "a welcome verging on delirium" in Athens.[34]

Even the arrival of Karamanlis could do nothing to save the Greek position in Cyprus. On 8 August 1974, talks began in Geneva between Greece and Turkey, with British Foreign Secretary James Callaghan as honest broker.[35] Turkey, backed behind the scenes by the USSR, made no effort to negotiate seriously. Starting on 14 August 1974, Turkish troops occupied a third of the island and expelled Greeks from the Turkish enclave at gunpoint. Nearly two hundred thousand Greeks were forced across the demarcation line imposed by the Turkish army. Turks living in Greek areas fled to the zone controlled by the Turkish army. To Greek fury, the U.S. government remained silent in the face of these abuses of international law. Karamanlis withdrew from NATO in protest. As a contemporary analyst argued, "Kissinger had made a cold-blooded strategic decision that Turkey was more important to U.S. national security interests and to the NATO community than the new and unpredictable Greek government and its volatile electorate."[36]

The silver lining of the Cyprus debacle was that the Greeks at least rid themselves of non-communist Europe's most embarrassing government. In subsequent months, Karamanlis renewed democracy with commendable speed: in November 1974, his New Democracy party won elections with 54.4 percent of the vote. A month and a half later, the country voted decisively (69 to 31 percent) to abolish the monarchy. It was the sixth plebiscite on the monarchy in the twentieth century, but the size of the abolitionist vote was such that it finally removed the issue from Greek political debate. Karamanlis promptly introduced a constitution (9 June 1975) that provided for a strong, though not directly elected, presidency. Greece subsequently negotiated entry into the EC in 1978–1979 and joined on 1 January 1981. Athens reentered NATO in October 1980. Thanks largely to Karamanlis, one of the shrewdest European leaders since 1945, the United States regained an ally that its Machiavellianism had nearly lost.

What the United States did lose was the confidence of the Greek people. Not by chance, Karamanlis's successor as premier in 1981 was Andreas Papandreou's Pan-Hellenic Socialist Party (PASOK), which took 48 percent of the vote in the 1981 elections. Papandreou followed an erratic course in foreign policy, moving Greece into a flirtation with the Soviet bloc and confrontation with Turkey, and vented a marked anti-Americanism in his public pronouncements. There was an audience for such rhetoric. Washington's support for the colonels, and its de facto pro-Turkish policy in the summer of 1974, had alienated those sections of Greek society that were not already disgruntled by Washington's postwar paternalism.[37]

In hindsight, the remarkable thing about the collapse of authoritarianism in Portugal is that it took contemporaries by surprise: the CIA, for example, by its own admission had "gone out to lunch" when the crisis broke.[38] It was not as if Portugal's problems were unknown. The country had been ruled by the dictatorship of Antonio Salazar since 1926 and was embroiled in unaffordable wars against independence movements in the vast African empire to which Portugal clung for reasons of national pride.[39] It was nevertheless a founder member of NATO whose strategic position in the Atlantic—notably its naval base in the Azores—gave it leverage over Washington, which winked at the regime's shortcomings.

When Salazar died in 1969, he was replaced by Marcelo Caetano, an intelligent man who was not ruthless and hence was overtaken by events. Caetano inherited a social catastrophe. Portugal had the "lowest level of housebuilding . . . the smallest number of doctors, the highest levels of infant mortality . . . the lowest public expenditure on education and the highest levels of illiteracy" in Europe.[40] The dwellers of the shanty towns scattered around Lisbon were ideal tinder for a social revolution. So long as the lion's share of government spending was spent on the conflicts in Mozambique and Angola,[41] conditions could not be improved. By the early 1970s, many senior officers regarded the war in Africa as pointless. Many junior officers, radicalized by their experience in the field, regarded Portugal itself as a colony, or as a mercenary for American capitalist-imperialism. After Nixon took office, the United States sold Caetano large quantities of arms and equipment—including napalm—to carry on the African war. Many Portuguese soldiers were opposed to doing Washington's dirty work in a conflict against African independence movements whose worldview they increasingly shared.

In February 1974, a senior officer, General Antonio di Spínola, published a book called *Portugal and the Future*, which called for a democratic "Lusitanian Federation" in the place of the imperial regime. "The future of Portugal depends on an appropriate solution to the problems raised by the war which, by consuming lives, resources and talent, increasingly compromises the rhythm of development which we must have to catch up with other countries," Spínola sensibly wrote.[42] *Portugal and the Future* identified Spínola as a useful ally for the Armed Forces Movement (MFA), a clandestine movement of mostly Marxist officers who decided he would be a valuable figurehead for their own plans.

On 25–26 April 1974, troops led by MFA commander Major Otelo Sareiva de Carvalho overthrew the regime. Caetano was exiled to Brazil and Spínola became head of a "Junta of National Salvation" pledged to hold free elections within a year, establish political freedoms, abolish the secret police, and lay "the foundations for an overseas policy leading to peace."[43] Vast crowds celebrated the "carnation revolution," which attracted modish radicals, including the inevitable Jean-Paul Sartre, from all over Europe. For a while, sexually repressed Lisbon enjoyed a carnival of personal liberation—a fact that scandalized the country's conservative north.

So far so good, but the Portuguese revolution soon became a Cold War crisis as the Portuguese Communist Party (PCP) and the radical wing of the MFA compelled Spínola to accept Vasco Gonçalves, a communist fellow traveler, as premier and then squeezed Spínola himself from power at the end of September 1974. According to the *Economist*, Portugal was "set fair to become a second Cuba or a second Peru, depending on how much power the majors want."[44]

The PCP and its leader, Alvaro Cunhal, took an increasingly prominent role in the government from January 1975 onward. Against the opposition of the Socialists (PSP), the government unified the trade unions into a single body under communist control. On 12 March 1975, the MFA instituted a "Council of the Revolution" as the supreme organ of the state and nationalized the banks. Important newspapers became mouthpieces for official propaganda, and the nongovernment press was subjected to perpetual harassment.

Elections in April 1975 to choose a constituent assembly gave Portuguese citizens an opportunity to state their verdict on the revolution's direction. The clear winners, with almost 40 percent of the vote, were the PSP, whose leader Mario Soares was a hero of the struggle against Salazar and had served as foreign minister between May 1974 and March 1975. The next largest party, with over a quarter of the votes, was the right-wing Popular Democrats (PPD). The PCP came third, with a mere 12.5 percent, with the far-left Portuguese Democratic Movement (MDP) taking 4.1 percent. As in Hungary or Poland after World War II, the PCP had no mandate to press for the transformation of society along communist lines.

The PCP nevertheless acted as if it represented the real will of the Portuguese electorate. Cunhal notoriously told the Italian journalist Oriana Fallaci: "If you think the Socialist Party with its 40 percent and the Popular Democrats with its 27 percent is a majority . . . you are the victim of a misunderstanding. I'm telling you the elections have nothing or very little to do with the dynamics of the revolution. . . . I promise you there will be no parliament in Portugal."[45] In mid-July 1975, the PSP and PPD withdrew in protest from the government, as the PCP and its controlled organizations strengthened their grip.

The PCP was viewing Portugal through a Marxist-Leninist lens. Back in the real world, foreign investment had ceased, tourists were staying away, hundreds of thousands of *retornados* were flooding into the mother country from the now-liberated colonies, and the north of the country was in open revolt. Turning Portugal into a European Cuba was impossible without Soviet economic aid or a majority within the "Council of the Revolution" willing to use totalitarian methods. Fortunately for the Portuguese, neither condition prevailed. The USSR had no wish to derail détente (the Helsinki Accords, it will be remembered, were signed in August 1975) and could anyway not afford to become the revolution's banker. Neither the PCP nor ideologues like Carvalho possessed the strength within the MFA to impose dictatorship on the country as a whole.

In the *verão quente* (hot summer) of 1975, key moderates in the MFA, orchestrated by the foreign minister, Ernesto de Melo Antunes, led a fight-back against the PCP. In August, leading soldiers ousted Gonçalves from the premiership and from the inner circle of the MFA. Gonçalves's downfall was greeted with relief in both Washington and Brussels, which gave large sums of emergency aid to the Portuguese government. Nevertheless, October and November 1975 were characterized by political violence. The Constituent Assembly itself was seized by striking workers on 12 November 1975 and held hostage until the government caved in to the workers' demands. Rumors that the PCP or the militant left would seize control of Lisbon were rife. On 25 November 1975, a coup attempt by a regiment of ultra-Marxist paratroopers was crushed by troops loyal to the government. The MFA had signaled that it would use force to defend the supremacy of the constitutional process.

The Constituent Assembly subsequently produced a fascinating constitution that committed Portugal to a democratic "transition to socialism." Actually, its future, as its more level-headed politicians well knew, was in the EC. On 25 April 1976, Portugal voted and made Soares's PSP, which received a solid 35 percent of the vote and 107 seats, the largest party in parliament. Colonel António Ramalho Eanes, the soldier who had suppressed the coup on 25 November 1975, was elected on 27 June 1976 to the powerful presidency, with nearly 62 percent of the vote. The country has remained democratic ever since.

It had been a close-run thing. PCP leader Cunhal was a graduate of the Ulbricht school of democracy and would have imposed a one-party state without a qualm had he been strong enough. The PSP and its leader Mario Soares, together with the MFA's realists, managed to fend the PCP off. It was a stand that was made possible in the PSP's case by generous financial support from the West German Social Democrats.[46] The PSP was kept afloat, and this enabled Portugal's voters to go to the polls and vote, with impressive maturity, for the political parties that had opposed Salazar's authoritarianism but did not want a leftist dictatorship in its stead.

As in the case of Greece, the United States had been spared the consequences of its own foolishness by the good sense of the Portuguese people and the ability of Portugal's leaders: Soares, Antunes, and Eanes were able men who figured out what they had to do to stop Portugal becoming a communist regime and did it. Washington, by contrast, had sided with Salazar's *Estado Novo* while it dug its own grave and then spent the two-year crisis in a stew about the likelihood of a PCP takeover. Throughout the crisis, Kissinger believed the communists were "slowly but relentlessly gaining control of the country," but was dismissive of the efforts of the men, above all Soares, who were trying to prevent this from happening. In the fall of 1974, Kissinger told Soares to his face that he was "a Kerensky," a reference to the liberal Russian premier who was deposed by the Bolsheviks in 1917. The United States, against West European advice, insisted on Portuguese exclusion from NATO's nuclear planning group so long as there were communist ministers in its government, and in November 1974 sent Frank Carlucci III to the Lisbon embassy at the head of a team of diplomats who had been in post in Brazil in 1964 at the time of the U.S.-backed coup against President João Goulart. The hint was unsubtle, though Carlucci disappointed Kissinger by giving him essentially the same advice as the Europeans—back Soares and don't panic.[47]

By the April 1975 elections, an overwrought Kissinger was espousing an "inoculation theory." Convinced that Southern Europe as a whole was becoming an anti-American hotbed, the secretary of state came to the conclusion that a PCP-led coup in Portugal would actually be "a better outcome for the United States" since it would scare the European allies into facing up to the growing communist peril. Such apocalyptic prescriptions found few takers on the other side of the Atlantic.[48]

Kissinger's feverish thinking was attributable to developments in Italy, the most important of all the Mediterranean countries. There the PCI was on the march. The DC's hold over the political system had been supported by the PSI since the early 1960s, when DC leaders Aldo Moro and Amintore Fanfani had, with U.S. acquiescence, carried out the so-called opening to the left to strengthen its parliamentary majority.[49] The DC and the PSI governed together until 1972, but with limited success. Social reforms were not implemented, and protests by students and radicalized workers swept the country at the end of the 1960s. The DC nevertheless won the 1972 election with 38 percent of the vote, but the PCI, led by Enrico Berlinguer, a Sardinian and a man of exceptional personal integrity, inched forward to 27 percent. The neofascist Italian Social Movement, meanwhile, polled 2.8 million votes. Over the next three years, weak DC governments failed to solve economic problems caused by rising oil prices and were tainted by corruption scandals that reached the highest offices of the state. The "great white whale," as the DC was nicknamed, was floundering.

Moderate Italian voters increasingly regarded the PCI as a genuine alternative. Government by the disciplined, cautious PCI seemed to offer the prospect of greater order in society. By 1975, after a series of communist advances in local elections, there was open talk of a PCI *sorpasso* in the 1976 general elections. The PCI might become the largest party and have the right to form a government. This possibility propelled domestic Italian politics into a Cold War issue. The people most conscious of this fact were the leaders of the DC and the PCI. On 28 September 1973, in the wake of the tragic events in Chile, where troops commanded by General Augusto Pinochet had overthrown the elected government of Salvador Allende and were establishing a military dictatorship with lethal efficiency, Berlinguer published an essay entitled "Imperialism and Coexistence in the light of the events in Chile," in which he affirmed that "no serious person can dispute that the presence and intervention of North American imperialism played a decisive role in the events in Chile."[50]

In articles in the following weeks, Berlinguer asked what that fact meant for the PCI, since it was the most likely communist electoral winner in the West. Would a PCI victory be followed by a coup orchestrated in the U.S. embassy?[51] Berlinguer concluded that to allay fears the PCI should construct a "democratic alternative" with "popular forces of catholic inspiration, as well as other forces of democratic orientation"—in short, with the DC and its centrist allies. Berlinguer called this policy a "historic compromise" between the political forces that "bring together and represent the overwhelming majority of the Italian people."[52] Only in this way, Berlinguer thought, could the country's huge socio-economic problems be addressed.

Berlinguer's "historic compromise" for Italy was linked to a new vision for Europe. Speaking in Brussels in January 1974, and many times subsequently, he imagined the construction of a Western Europe that was "antifascist, democratic, and peaceful, free from economic subordination to the United States and multinational corporations, and bent on eliminating any kind of neo-colonial relationship with the developing world."[53] Together with the leader of the still-banned Spanish Communist Party (PCE), Santiago Carrillo, Berlinguer made the achievement of a free Spain a crucial first step in this process at a July 1975 meeting of the two parties in Livorno (Leghorn), Italy.[54] The new trend in West European communism toward political pluralism inspired by Berlinguer and Carillo's ideas became known as "Eurocommunism," a word that inspired a massive but today largely forgotten academic and policy debate both within the Communist Parties of Europe and in transatlantic academic institutions and think tanks.[55]

Some of the DC's leaders, notably Aldo Moro, were willing to contemplate the PCI's presence in a government in Rome; others were strenuously opposed. So, emphatically, was Washington. In his memoirs, Henry Kissinger described the Italian situation in 1975 as being "analogous to that of the Weimar Republic of the early 1930s which had led to the collapse of democracy in Germany."[56] This diagnosis was off the mark precisely because the PCI, unlike the German Communist Party during Weimar, still less the Nazis, was genuinely committed to preserving democracy.

Berlinguer did everything within his power to soothe the Americans' fears. On 15 June 1976, just five days before national elections, the PCI leader gave a startling interview to the Milanese newspaper, *Corriere della Sera*, in which he claimed that the PCI's "autonomy" from the USSR was "total." Berlinguer argued that unlike the USSR the PCI did not treat Marxism as "a closed body of principles whose literal formulation should provide answers for everything," but took a pragmatic approach that respected political pluralism and contrary ideas. There was too little popular participation in decision making in the USSR, Berlinguer affirmed, somewhat euphemistically. The PCI had no intention of "calling into question" the Atlantic alliance, he added. He "felt safer over here." There were "fewer restrictions" on building the kind of socialism he wanted to see in the West than in the East: Dubček's fate, which he clearly regarded as a tipping point in the PCI's relations with Moscow, "had unquestionably been unjust."[57]

Berlinguer did not fail to criticize what he regarded as the global injustice of American imperialism, but his interview was an unambiguous disavowal of the other side in the Cold War and, as such, it was a message that moderate Italian voters wanted to hear. In the elections on 20 June 1976, the PCI obtained 12.6 million votes, 34.4 percent of those cast. It was arguably the best electoral performance by any communist party in a free election anywhere, ever—a fact often overlooked. The DC, boosted by a Cold War press campaign, nevertheless took 14.2 million votes (38.7 percent) and avoided the dreaded *sorpasso*.

Neither party could govern without the other. A government of "national solidarity" was formed, presided over by a DC conservative acceptable to Washington, Giulio Andreotti, and composed of DC ministers only. The PCI gave external parliamentary support to the new government's attempts to rein in public spending (indeed, Berlinguer made a personal philosophy out of the need for greater austerity—moral as well as economic—in public life). The PCI supported the DC in the struggle against domestic terrorism, which culminated in April–May 1978 with the kidnapping and murder of Aldo Moro by "Red Brigade" terrorists.

The PCI's sacrifices for the common good were rewarded with merely token recognition, however, despite an intense debate in Italy and in the U.S. foreign policy circles over the wisdom of doing so.[58] Many veteran anti-communists both in Italy and the United States believed that the time had come to put the PCI to the test; the new Carter administration's ambassador to Rome, Richard Gardiner, and Carter's National Security Advisor Zbigniew Brzezinski were resolutely against. Under Carter, accordingly, the United States followed a compromise policy of not intervening in Italian domestic politics—but of not being indifferent to the PCI's prospects, either.[59]

U.S. preoccupations were comprehensible. Although many commentators were inclined to make a progressive symbol out of the PCI in the 1970s, not all its leaders were cut of the same cloth as Berlinguer. In a book published in January 1978, Berlinguer's deputy, Giorgio Amendola—theoretically a PCI reformist—made the surely mendacious assertion that he learned of Stalin's oppressions from the Secret Speech and suggested that the PCI's support for the Soviet intervention in Hungary in 1956 was justified because reactionary forces headed by Cardinal Mindszenty had "aimed at a violent restoration of capitalism."[60] The book was ostensibly about "renewing the PCI." It was reasonable for foreign analysts to believe that the PCI's transformation was only skin deep. Keeping the PCI out of the government was also in U.S. interests. Had the PCI been in power in Rome at the end of the 1970s, the task of siting intermediate-range nuclear missiles in Europe (see below) would undoubtedly have become much more difficult.

It was nevertheless probably a mistake not to engage more intently with Berlinguer. The Carter administration took the PCI partly out of quarantine, but it also propped up the DC's hold on power until the PCI's momentum had ebbed away. With the aid of the PSI, which shifted to a pro-NATO, pro-capitalist orientation in the late 1970s under the leadership of Bettino Craxi, an ambitious young politician who projected an image of modernity, the DC was, in effect, kept in power by Washington. The wages of sin, in this case, were paid by the Italians, for few democracies have ever been so badly governed as Italy was in the 1980s. In one scholar's eloquent phrase: "Berlinguerian austerity gave way to the irresponsibility of steadily rising deficits. Systematic clientelism gave way to its most exuberant phase."[61]

The transition to democracy in Spain, which began in November 1975 when Franco died after a long decline, aroused less alarm in Washington. Power passed into the hands of King Juan Carlos, who initially retained the last premier of the Franchist era, Carlos Arias Navarro, a former mayor of Madrid whose nickname was "the butcher." The Spanish Socialist Party (PSOE), headed by a young lawyer called Felipe Gonzalez, and the Communist Party of Spain (PCE), under the leadership of Santiago Carrillo, behaved with conspicuous moderation in the months after Franco's death. The two parties swiftly concluded that a *ruptura democratica* (democratic break: i.e., a Portuguese-style election of a constituent assembly) was not in the cards. Only a *ruptura pactada* (negotiated break via the institutions of the former regime) was practical politics, if Spain was to avoid a coup by unrepentant Franchists in the army.

In July 1976, Juan Carlos told the U.S. Congress—it was significant that the king felt obliged to go to Washington to announce his intentions—that his policy was to ensure, "under the principles of democracy," "the orderly access to power of distinct political alternatives in accordance with the freely expressed will of the people." The speech had an "electrifying impact in Spain."[62] Juan Carlos chose Adolfo Suarez Gonzalez, a young man with an impeccable past as a Franco supporter, as Arias Navarro's successor.

Suarez was an inspired choice. "Intelligent, pragmatic and loyal, Suarez was ready to serve the king and democracy as steadfastly as he once served Franco and fascism."[63] With the assistance of the king's former tutor, Torcuato Fernandez-Miranda, the president of the Cortes (the Spanish parliament), Suarez and Juan Carlos managed in less than a year to introduce democratic freedoms, legalize the PCE, and convince the Cortes to pass a Political Reform Act that provided for the democratic election of the Cortes itself. It was a feat of artful tightrope walking: had they ever gone too far, too fast, the army would have stepped in—as it did on 23 February 1981 when die-hard officers held the Cortes and government hostage and took over several cities. Only the intervention of King Juan Carlos, who made a de Gaulle-style televised appeal to the soldiers, avoided catastrophe.

The "23F" coup was one good reason for Spain's politicians wanting to join NATO. Placating the generals mattered. U.S. pressure was another powerful force. The centrist government of Leopoldo Calvo Sotelo accordingly steered Spain into the organization in 1982. NATO membership became a major issue in the general elections of October 1982. The PSOE, which won the elections with 48 percent of the votes, campaigned hard against membership of the alliance. It was a popular stance. Opinion polls in the early 1980s recorded over 70 percent opposition to U.S. bases and to Washington's foreign policy. Once in power, however, PSOE leader Gonzalez changed tack and kept Spain in the organization pending a referendum on membership. This was held only in March 1986, when passions had cooled. A narrow majority of 52.5 percent of the Spanish voted to stay in NATO, so long as the American military presence—seen as a legacy of U.S. support for Franco—was reduced.[64] Spain was the Mediterranean country that caused fewest problems for the transatlantic relationship in the 1970s and 1980s, but only because it enjoyed political leadership of the highest order. The transition to democracy might easily have gone horribly wrong. It is interesting to speculate how Washington would have reacted had the generals taken power in 1977 or 1981.

GEORGIA ON THEIR MINDS

The democratization of the Mediterranean was a crucial development for Europe. In an important sense, the construction of the "West" had been completed only when Athens, Lisbon, and Madrid became capitals of democratic societies. For West European public opinion, membership of the western club of nations meant being opposed to fascism, not just communism. Totalitarianism came in two forms.

The threat posed by the USSR was nevertheless the principal challenge facing the West. Here, too, however, there was a split in the late 1970s and early 1980s in transatlantic relations. Gerald Ford's short presidency proved to be a lull before a fresh storm between Washington and its European allies. President Jimmy Carter antagonized the Germans as much as Richard Nixon and Henry Kissinger had infuriated the French. Schmidt defined Carter as "idealistic and fickle" in his political memoir, *Men and Powers*.[65] Presumably only politeness stopped him from writing "moralizing and undependable," for that is what he meant. By 1980, Schmidt's contempt was reciprocated by the White House.

On close examination, we can see that Carter's rows with his European partners derived from three authentic shortcomings in his administration's political strategy. First, and most comprehensibly, Carter fell out with his European allies over defense. Carter, despite the fact that he attributed great importance to success in reducing the number and destructive power of the superpowers' nuclear arsenals and pushed a new round of the Strategic Arms Limitations Talks (SALT II) with vigor, was slow to respond to the Soviet Union's deployment from 1976 onward of "intermediate" (or "gray area") weapons like the Backfire bomber and SS-20 missiles, which were technologically on a par with the best NATO equipment and which enabled the USSR to strike anywhere in the European "theater" without employing its strategic nuclear forces.

It was Chancellor Schmidt who best articulated the Europeans' position on the strategic imbalance, most notably in an October 1977 speech at the International Institute for Strategic Studies (IISS) in London. Schmidt's position was that the West, despite its commitment to détente, should not permit the USSR to achieve such a position of military supremacy that it could exercise political leverage over Western Europe. He argued that since the USSR "has given no clear indication that she is willing to accept the principle of parity for Europe, as she did for SALT . . . we shall have to rely on the effectiveness of deterrence."[66]

Carter initially offered to deploy a battlefield weapon, the so-called neutron bomb, which was quickly denounced by the communist press as a "capitalist" weapon because it killed advancing troops while leaving property intact. When public revulsion mounted both in the United States and Europe to this horrible weapon, Carter announced in April 1978 that the weapon would not be made after all. His decision was harshly criticized by the European politicians, especially Schmidt, who had expended considerable political capital in winning domestic support for developing the weapon. As Carter legitimately pointed out in his memoirs, however, none of the allies was willing to commit itself to actually *deploying* the weapon.[67] Since the weapon was designed for use against invading conventional forces in Europe, especially tanks, the Europeans' reluctance made investing billions of dollars in development and testing pointless. Nevertheless, "Carter's about-face generated growing concerns about the leadership qualities of the U.S. president."[68]

The growing Soviet threat might have been confronted by the Europeans' increasing conventional defense spending significantly or by taking the plunge and developing an autonomous "European" nuclear force. But the former would have cost a fortune and the second was never a real option. As a 1979 official German statement on defense policy admitted, "Europeans need the protection afforded by the nuclear deterrent of the United States . . . even if Western Europe were to achieve political unity, the nuclear protective function of the United States would still be indispensable."[69] But so long as Europe depended on U.S. strategic power to defend it from the Soviets, there rested "the paradox that NATO's doctrine rests on an American response even when American soil is not attacked."[70] At bottom, transatlantic tensions in the late 1970s were due to a problem that had existed since the USSR developed the means to deliver strategic nuclear weapons against American cities in the late 1950s: would the Americans risk a nuclear holocaust to defend their allies?

Carter agreed, at a Guadeloupe summit with France, Britain, and West Germany in January 1979, to furnish the Europeans with cruise and Pershing missiles to redress the "gray area" imbalance. In December 1979, NATO announced it would deploy 572 warheads, mostly in the form of land-based cruise missiles, by the fall of 1983. Concurrently, Britain upgraded its nuclear submarine fleet by buying Trident missiles. Having got what he wanted, Schmidt, under pressure from his increasingly pacifist parliamentary majority, started backtracking. On German insistence, the alliance advocated a "dual track" procedure, whereby deployment would be linked to arms reductions talks—this despite the fact that Soviet leader Brezhnev had pooh-poohed any such idea publicly and had threatened to meet any NATO deployment of cruise missiles with additional SS-20s.[71]

Subsequently, in June 1980, after the Soviet invasion of Afghanistan, Schmidt proposed in Moscow that a moratorium be called on intermediate nuclear weapon deployment, a dilution of the common NATO position that provoked a showdown between Carter and Schmidt at the Venice summit of the G7 during which the chancellor ranted that West Germany was not the

United States' "fifty-first state." President Carter described this encounter as the "most unpleasant personal exchange I ever had with a foreign leader."[72]

The second problem that roiled Helmut Schmidt's relations with the Carter administration was its neglect of the dollar. As an astute contemporary observer pointed out: "Had President Carter succeeded in evolving a coherent economic policy earlier and managed to maintain a stable dollar in the markets, many of his other so-called eccentricities and fumblings in the political and security fields would have been forgiven him."[73] During Carter's tenure in the White House, the dollar plummeted from 2.90DM to just 1.70DM in 1980, a decline whose effects cascaded over West European economies. Yet the U.S. balance-of-payments deficit, along with domestic inflation, continued to rise throughout Carter's presidency. Instead of putting their own house in order, by giving the U.S. economy a dose of deflation, U.S. policy makers urged the Germans to act as a "locomotive" for world growth by reflating their economy. They argued that rapid growth in Europe and Japan would suck in U.S. exports and solve the United States' balance-of-payments problems at a higher mutual level of prosperity. In May 1977, at a London summit of the industrialized nations, the U.S. government bullied the Germans and the Japanese until they agreed to aim for growth rates of over 5 percent of GDP.

Helmut Schmidt's contempt for Carter's economic policy is palpable in *Men and Powers*, where he derides the "locomotive" theory as a "monster of the Loch Ness type" that kept "coming up for air." More seriously, however, he stated that both the Carter and the Reagan administrations "acted according to the comfortable rule that whenever the American public began to feel the unpleasant results of national economic policy, Japan and Germany (sometimes the entire European Community) were to be made scapegoats."[74] From Schmidt's perspective the United States wanted to have its cake and eat it. As a brilliant German political scientist wrote at the end of the 1980s, Nixon and Carter's economic policies in the 1970s had "signaled the abrogation of the post-war economic compact." The "essence" of this compact was that the United States "would be willing to make economic sacrifices in return for political privileges."[75] In Schmidt's view, Washington was no longer making the economic sacrifices its hegemonic role demanded of it, but nevertheless still claimed the right to call the political tune.

In the spring of 1978, Schmidt and French President Valèry Giscard D'Estaing lost patience and took a bold initiative to regain European monetary sovereignty. The European Monetary System (EMS), which was adopted at a June 1978 summit in Bremen, West Germany, was a conscious attempt to isolate the EC from the side effects of fluctuations of the dollar by creating a rival European means of exchange, the European Currency Unit (ECU), for denominating payments within the EC and by linking all EC currencies except sterling (Britain refused to participate) to the German mark in a renewed "Snake." The EMS procedure was forbiddingly technical, but it was accompanied by rhetoric that was plainly designed to send a transatlantic message of enhanced European independence.

The dollar did not even rate an entry in the index of Carter's memoir, *Keeping Faith*. This points to the third problem posed by the Carter administration for democratic Europe's leaders: its apparent neglect of their concerns. Europeans wanted the United States to continue as the West's *primus inter pares*; as a team leader, not as a distant benefactor. In addition to relations with the USSR, which were obviously central, Carter palpably regarded East Asia and the Middle East as more important for U.S. foreign policy than Western Europe.[76] He may have been farsighted in making this geopolitical judgment call, but he underestimated the consequences of downplaying Europe's role.

Western Europe's growing disenchantment with U.S. leadership became visible in the months that followed the Soviet invasion of Afghanistan in December 1979. Carter sounded the bugle for a return to the Cold War, but his European allies responded with derision. By then, they had a stake in détente. Trade was growing rapidly with the Soviet bloc and Russian gas was coming on stream, reducing Western Europe's dependence on Middle East oil. West European leaders saw no point in risking a new freeze in the Cold War on behalf of a landlocked mountain state in Central Asia. Helmut Schmidt responded to Carter's hyperbolic claim that Afghanistan was the "greatest threat to peace since the Second World War" by tartly remarking that Warsaw Pact troops were stationed thirty miles from his home in Hamburg. Both Schmidt and Giscard D'Estaing visited Soviet leader Leonid Brezhnev within months of the invasion. Only three NATO members (West Germany, Norway, and Turkey) joined the United States' boycott of the 1980 Moscow Olympics.[77]

As the Carter presidency ended, the German commentator Josef Joffe ironized, "the main conflict in Europe was no longer between East and West but between the United States and its own allies."[78] Western Europe's leaders, with Schmidt to the fore, openly saluted "the new self-confidence and determination" represented by the election in November 1980 of President Reagan and reminded the United States that only "by mobilizing each partner's potential for the common cause, will Americans and Europeans be able to make their contributions to the world's political and economic balance."[79] But though Western Europe's leaders were broadly happy with the new president, a large swath of European public opinion was not. The first Reagan presidency would see a degree of public mobilization against NATO policy that in sheer numbers and geographical spread "dwarfed all previous protest movements in western Europe in the post-war period."[80]

EVIL EMPIRES

A British historian with a taste for irony has described President Reagan as being "quite unwittingly, one of the peace movement's most active recruiting agents."[81] Reagan, many Europeans concluded, was not a safe pair of hands. His anti-communist rhetoric and commitment to increased defense spending led the U.S. president to be caricatured as a trigger-happy cowboy whose objective was to get even with the bad guys in the Kremlin even if he had to waste Europe in the process.

At the same time, Moscow looked even more dangerous. Leonid Brezhnev was a dying man by the time of Reagan's election: he had ceased to function properly long before his death in 1982. His successors, the former KGB chief Yuri Andropov and, after Andropov's death, Kostantin Chernenko, were both plagued with health problems—Chernenko was effectively senile. President Reagan's chief defect, in democratic Europe's eyes, was that he was throwing down the gauntlet to these grim dinosaurs. What would happen if they picked it up? The old joke about the only alternative to peaceful coexistence with the USSR being warlike nonexistence made few smile in Western Europe in 1981. Many Europeans agreed with the eminent British historian E. P. Thompson, one of the founders of END (European Nuclear Disarmament), that Europe was "pig-in-the-middle while an interminable and threatening argument between born-again Christians and stillborn Marxists goes on over our heads."[82]

The hubbub surrounding the installation of cruise missiles has to be seen in this context. During Reagan's first term, Western Europe essentially experienced a war scare that only ended after Mikhail S. Gorbachev became Soviet leader in 1985. The height of the scare was between the summer of 1981 and December 1983, when the missiles were deployed. There were three surges of protest during this period. In the autumn of 1981, hundreds of thousands of protesters took to the streets of European capitals in concurrent protests: four hundred thousand marched through Amsterdam alone on 21 November 1981. In June 1982, similar crowds greeted a presidential visit by President Reagan. In October–November 1983, on the eve of deployment, protest reached another peak. A seventy-two-mile "human chain" involving two hundred thousand people was formed between the German city of Stuttgart and an American airbase in Ulm; more than five hundred thousand people (4 percent of the population) marched through The Hague, the Dutch administrative capital; 300,000 gathered in London's Hyde Park for a rally coordinated by the revived Campaign for Nuclear Disarmament (CND) (see above, chapter 4). CND's membership quintupled after 1979, reaching nearly one hundred thousand in 1984.[83]

Such great rallies were "only the tip of the peace movement iceberg."[84] More typical were local activities: candle-lit vigils, poetry readings, "die-ins" where protesters faked death, prayer meetings, showings of the anti-nuclear film *The Day After*. Petitions against cruise missile deployment garnered four million signatures in West Germany and an amazing three and a half million (a quarter of the population) in the Netherlands. Peace groups of every imaginable kind sprang up: medical and physical scientists were especially active in highlighting the devastating likely consequences of a nuclear exchange for Europe's populations.

Feminist groups and women in general took a prominent organizational role in the antiwar movement: it was often asserted that militarism was a "male" trait symbolized by the overtly phallic cruise missiles and could be overcome only by the caring, life-enhancing values allegedly inherent to women. One of the most emblematic protests against the deployment of cruise missiles was the "Women's Peace Camp" at the U.S. airbase at Greenham Common in Berkshire, England. From 1982 onward men were not allowed to frequent the camp, which was the site for several mass protests at which tens of thousands of women from all over Europe chained themselves to the perimeter fence, attempted to break through the base's security cordon in order to dance on the missile silos, or, on 1 April 1983, dressed as teddy bears and held a picnic inside the base.

More pragmatically, there was even an organization—"Generals for Peace and Disarmament"—of retired senior military men critical of the strategic thinking behind NATO's missile deployment. Their main argument was that once one factored in the French and British independent nuclear deterrents, the supposed Soviet strategic advantage in Europe was a mirage.

Unlike the events of 1968, the protests were for the most part peaceful. This was despite the fact that in the late 1970s protests in West Germany and other European countries against the building of nuclear power stations, or the transfer of nuclear waste, had led to battles between the police and environmentalists. The Green Movement became an authentic political force in Germany in the early 1980s, winning over 5 percent of the vote in the 1983 Bundestag elections. Ecologists were in the forefront of the protests against the nuclear missiles, as were other far left radicals. The French Communist Party spearheaded opposition to NATO in France. Nevertheless—and this is why the protests remained overwhelmingly peaceful—radicals were a vocal but ultimately small minority of the peace campaigners, who were typically under forty, well-educated, politically progressive, but not extreme and very often actuated by religious conviction. In the Netherlands, for instance, the peace movement's efforts were largely coordinated by the *Interkerkelijk Vredesberaad* (Interdenominational Peace Council: IKV); Quakers were very active in Britain; in Italy, progressive Catholics organized protests alongside the PCI. For all such people, "thou shalt not kill," rather than any political nostrum, was the motivating force behind their actions.

It is fair to say, however, that the peace movement broadly subscribed to one political position: opposition to what E. P. Thompson called, in a famous essay, "Exterminism." What Thompson argued was that the two superpowers had become mirror images of each other: both were political systems dominated by a blind search for military and technological supremacy. "Superpowers which have been locked, for thirty years, in the postures of military confrontation increasingly adopt militaristic characteristics in their economies, their polity and their culture." On the one hand, the American "military-industrial complex" had conditioned politics to the point that American representative democracy was a sham; on the other hand, the Soviet Union was like an "ill-run, security conscious university" in which "a huge and over-mighty engineering department" (its technical-military establishment) called the shots. In this situation, where there were two parallel empires whose raison d'être was producing the technology of mass destruction on an ever greater scale, an accident, miscalculation, or a "hot flush of ideological passion" might detonate a conflict that would eliminate European civilization and perhaps all human life. Thompson argued that it was vital for a broad alliance "which takes in churches, Eurocommunists, Labourists, East European dissidents (and not only dissidents), Soviet citizens unmediated by Party structures, trade unionists, ecologists" to summon up the "internationalist élan" necessary to "throw the cruise missiles and the SS-20s back."[85] How exactly Soviet citizens and East European dissidents were going to stop the deployment of SS-20s was wisely left unexplained.

The right-wing journalist and scholar Walter Laqueur dubbed this way of thinking "Hollanditis" in a well-known 1981 article.[86] It was nevertheless a very widely held set of beliefs—the 1983 election manifesto of the British Labour Party, which stated that its "most pressing objective" in international policy was "to prevent the deployment here or elsewhere in Western Europe of Cruise or Pershing missiles," was permeated by such thinking, for instance.[87] Whereas the United States had once been a symbol of freedom for the peoples of Western Europe, it was now seen by European public opinion as—at best—a hulking security guard keeping Europe safe, or even as a militaristic and materialistic empire indifferent to Europe's imminent demise under an atomic mushroom.

In a different way, the years 1968–1984 also compelled Western European leaders to adopt a more realistic assessment of the United States' attitude toward shouldering the burdens of the whole non-communist world. The United States would put its own economic and security interests first and leave its allies to cope with the consequences as best they could. The Reagan administration in this respect was no better from the European point of view than previous administrations. Reagan's military spending program was financed by giant budget deficits, which the administration paid for by issuing high yielding bonds that global investors naturally snapped up. "Reaganomics" caused the dollar to soar back almost to 1971 levels and seriously disrupted other industrial economies in the process.[88] The United States was an "elephant in the boat" of the world economy and one, moreover, that wouldn't even sit still.[89]

This does not mean that Europe's leaders reneged on the December 1979 decision to deploy the cruise missiles. An able foursome of conservative leaders—Italy's Francesco Cossiga, Germany's Helmut Kohl, Britain's Margaret Thatcher, and the Netherlands' Ruud Lubbers—met the peace movement's challenge with decision, although the scale of the protests in the Netherlands compelled Lubbers to postpone deployment until 1985. Two socialists, Italy's Bettino Craxi and France's François Mitterrand, who in February 1983 pressed a disconcerted German Bundestag to accept the missiles on the occasion of the twentieth anniversary of Adenauer and de Gaulle's Franco-German Treaty, were also staunch. Nevertheless, by 1984 European leaders were as ready as their publics for new thinking about the Cold War. This is why they were so receptive to new Soviet leader Mikhail S. Gorbachev.

NOTES

1. Flora Lewis, "Alarm Bells in the West," *America and the World 1981* (New York: Council on Foreign Relations, 1981), 555.

2. Olof Palme, Speech to the *Riksdag*, 31 January, 1973, in *Documents on Swedish Foreign Policy 1973* (Stockholm: Royal Ministry of Foreign Affairs, 1976), 16–18.

3. Richard Reeves, *President Nixon: Alone in the White House* (New York: Simon and Schuster, 2002), 343.

4. Diane Kunz, *Butter and Guns: America's Cold War Economic Diplomacy* (New York: Free Press, 1997), 218.

5. Mark Gilbert, *Surpassing Realism: The Politics of European Integration since 1945* (Lanham, MD: Rowman & Littlefield, 2003), 130.

6. Burns quoted in Kunz, *Butter and Guns*, 215.

7. Quotes from Henry Kissinger, "The Year of Europe," *Department of State Bulletin*, 14 May 1973, 593–98.

8. Quoted in Marc Trachtenberg, "The French Factor in U.S. Foreign Policy during the Nixon-Pompidou Period, 1969–1974," *Journal of Cold War Studies* 13, no. 1 (2011): 26. In addition to providing a magisterial picture of U.S. strategy, this article helpfully synthesizes a vast literature in French.

9. Claudia Hiepel, "Kissinger's Year of Europe: A Challenge for the EC and the Franco-German Relationship," in Jan van der Harst, ed., *Beyond the Customs Union: The European Community's Quest for Deepening, Widening and Completion, 1969–1975* (Brussels: Bruylant, 2007), 283–84.

10. On this point, see Maurice Vaisse, "Les relations spéciales franco-américaines au temps de Richard Nixon et Georges Pompidou," *Relations Internationales* 119 (Fall 2004): 358.

11. Trachtenberg, "The French Factor," 35, has a lengthy footnote documenting the consultation.

12. William P. Bundy, *A Tangled Web: The Making of Foreign Policy in the Nixon Presidency* (New York : Hill and Wang, 1998).

13. Pascaline Winand, "Loaded Words and Disputed Meanings: The 'Year of Europe' Speech and Its Genesis from an American Perspective," in van der Harst, ed., *Beyond the Customs Union*, 313.

14. Henry Kissinger, *Years of Upheaval* (Boston: Little, Brown, 1982), 188.

15. Hiepel, "Kissinger's Year of Europe," 289–90.

16. Kissinger, *Years of Upheaval*, 707.

17. Kissinger, *Years of Upheaval*, 713.

18. In 1973, Britain imported about 59 percent of its oil from the Arab world, France 72 percent, and Germany 75 percent. The United States, by contrast, only imported 16 percent of its energy needs and Middle East oil accounted for just 2 percent of America's total requirements. See Richard J. Barnet, *The Alliance: America, Europe, Japan Makers of the Postwar World* (New York: Simon and Schuster, 1983), 327.

19. For the full text, see "Declaration on European Identity," *Bulletin of the European Communities* (12/1973): 118–22.

20. For the Washington conference, see Fiona Venn, "International Cooperation versus National Self-Interest," in *The United States and the European Alliance since 1945*, ed. Kathleen Burk and Melvyn Stokes (Oxford: Berg, 1999), 71–98.

21. Heath narrowly lost the February 1974 general elections; Pompidou died in April 1974; Brandt was forced to resign in May 1974 after it was discovered that a close aide was a spy. He was replaced by Helmut Schmidt.

22. The text can be found at: http://www.nato.int/cps/en/natolive/official_texts_26901.htm?.

23. A point made by Trachtenberg, "The French Factor," 31.

24. Kissinger, *Years of Upheaval*, 1161.

25. For the positive European reaction to President Ford, see N. Piers Ludlow, "The Real Years of Europe? U.S.-West European Relations during the Ford Administration," *Journal of Cold War Studies* 15, no. 3 (2013): 136–61.

26. Nixon quoted in Daniel C. Thomas, *The Helsinki Effect: International Norms, Human Rights, and the Demise of Communism* (Princeton, NJ: Princeton University Press, 2001), 78.

27. "The Battle for Southern Europe," *Economist*, 10 August 1974.

28. Richard Clogg, *A Concise History of Greece* (Cambridge: Cambridge University Press, 1995), 164.

29. For a very useful discussion of the strategic considerations that weighed in the decision to work with the junta, see Konstantina Maragkou, "Favouritism in NATO's Southeastern Flank: The Case of the Greek Colonels, 1967–74," *Cold War History* 9 (2009): 347–66.

30. Quoted in E. G. H. Pedalieu, "'A Discordant Note': NATO and the Greek Junta, 1967–1974," *Diplomacy and Statecraft* 22 (2011): 107.

31. Nancy Bermeo, "Classification and Consolidation: Some Lessons from the Greek Dictatorship," *Political Science Quarterly* 110 (1995): 443.

32. Henry Kissinger, *Years of Renewal* (London: Weidenfeld & Nicholson, 1999), 197.

33. Among other things. The day after the coup, a drunken Ioannidis told an informant of the U.S. embassy that Makarios was a "rotten priest homosexual; he was perverted, a torturer, a sexual deviate and the owner of half the hotels on the island." Quoted in Ivar-André Slengesol, "A Bad Show? The United States and the 1974 Cyprus Crisis," *Mediterranean Quarterly* (Spring 2000): 112.

34. Richard Clogg, "Karamanlis's Cautious Success: The Background," *Government and Opposition* 10 (1975): 332.

35. James Callaghan, *Time and Chance* (London: HarperCollins, 1987), 339–55, for the British role in the crisis.

36. Laurence Stern, "Bitter Lessons: How We Failed in Cyprus," *Foreign Policy* 19 (Summer 1975): 74.

37. On this point, see Antonio Varsori, 'L'Occidente e la Grecia: dal colpo di Stato militare alla transizione alla democrazia (1967–1976)," in Mario Del Pero, Victor Gavin, Fernando Guirao, and Antonio Varsori, *Democrazie: L'Europa meridionale la fine delle dittature* (Milan: Mondadori, 2010), 5–94. Pedalieu, "A Discordant Note," 117–18, adds that U.S. policy toward Greece also soured its relations with NATO countries like Denmark, the Netherlands, and Norway, which had wanted the alliance to sanction Greece.

38. CIA official Cord Meyer, quoted in Kenneth Maxwell, *The Making of Portuguese Democracy* (Cambridge: Cambridge University Press, 1997), 45.

39. The Salazar regime diffused a map showing Portugal's colonies superimposed on a map of Europe under the slogan "Portugal não é um país pequeno." See Heriberto Cairo, "Portugal Is Not a Small Country: Maps and Propaganda in the Salazar Regime," *Geopolitics* 11 (2006): 367–95.

40. Ben Pimlott, "Socialism in Portugal: Was It a Revolution?" *Government and Opposition* 12 (1977): 341.

41. The two principal Portuguese colonies. Portugal was also facing revolts in Guinea-Bissau and Cape Verde. It had lost its enclave in India (Goa) in 1961, and East Timor declared independence in 1975.

42. Quoted in Douglas Porch, *The Portuguese Armed Forces and the Revolution* (London: Croom Helm, 1977), 85.

43. MFA program, in Porch, *The Portuguese Armed Forces*, appendix III, 247.

44. "Kerensky with a Monocle," *Economist*, 5 October 1974.

45. Maxwell, *The Making of Portuguese Democracy*, 148.

46. For the role of the SPD, see Ana Maria Fonseca, "The Federal Republic of Germany and the Portuguese Transition to Democracy, 1974–1976," *Journal of European Integration History* (2009): 35–56.

47. This paragraph is greatly indebted to Mario Del Pero, "Which Chile, Allende? Henry Kissinger and the Portuguese Revolution," *Cold War History* 11 (2011): 629–32.

48. Del Pero, "Which Chile, Allende?" 638–39.

49. For a succinct account of the diplomatic origins of "opening to the left," see Leopoldo Nuti, "The United States, Italy, and the Opening to the Left 1953–1963," *Journal of Cold War Studies* 4, no. 1 (2002): 36–55. The literature in Italian is *sterminata*.

50. Enrico Berlinguer, "Imperialismo e coesistenza alla luce dei fatti Cileni," in *Enrico Berlinguer: La passione non è finita*, ed. Miguel Gotor, (Turin: Einaudi, 2013), 27. This is an anthology of Berlinguer's writings and interviews from 1972 to 1983.

51. The U.S. ambassador's name was John Volpe. Left-wing Italians called him, only half-joking, "John Golpe"—"John the Coup."

52. Berlinguer, "La crisi italiana e il compromesso storico," in *Enrico Berlinguer: La passione non è finita*, 49 and 54.

53. Berlinguer, "Costruire un'Europa nuova," in *Enrico Berlinguer: La passione non è finita*, 75.

54. See Enrico Berlinguer and Santiago Carrillo, *Una Spagna libera in un'Europa democratica* (Rome: Editori Riuniti, 1975).

55. For a broad overview, see Silvio Pons, "The Rise and Fall of Eurocommunism," in the *Cambridge History of the Cold War*, vol. III: *Endings* (Cambridge: Cambridge University Press, 2010), 45–65. The intensity of suspicion engendered in Washington by "Eurocommunism" can be tasted by reading some of the "analysis" produced by right-wing Washington think tanks and academic institutions. For an egregious example, see *The Political Stability of Italy* (Washington, DC: Center for Strategic and International Studies, 1976), a report of an April 1976 conference attended by Washington policy-making grandees at which the keynote speakers were Clare Boothe Luce and former Secretary of Treasury John B. Connally.

56. Kissinger, *Years of Renewal*, 627.

57. Berlinguer, "La PCI e la NATO," interview with Giampaolo Pansa, in *Enrico Berlinguer: La passione non è finita*, 83–93.

58. PCI officials were granted visa rights to the United States and were invited to the U.S. embassy in Rome—minor novelties that nevertheless were interpreted as a sign of relaxation in Washington's attitude.

59. See Richard Gardner, *Mission Italy: On the Front Lines of the Cold War* (Lanham, MD: Rowman & Littlefield, 2005), and Olav Njølstad, "The Carter Administration and Italy: Keeping the Communists Out of Power without Interfering," *Journal of Cold War Studies* 4, no. 3 (2002): 56–94.

60. Giorgio Amendola, *Il rinnovamento del PCI* (Roma: Editori Riuniti, 1978), 124 and 134.

61. Patrick McCarthy, *The Crisis of the Italian State: From the Cold War to the Fall of Berlusconi* (New York: St. Martin's Press, 1995), 116. "Clientelism" is an Anglicization of *clientelismo*: pork barrel politics.

62. Paul Preston, *Juan Carlos: Steering Spain from Dictatorship to Democracy* (London: Harper Perennial, 2005), 349.

63. Stanley Meisler, "Spain's New Democracy," *Foreign Affairs* 56 (1977): 193.

64. For Spanish membership of NATO, see Kenneth Maxwell and Steven Spiegel, *The New Spain: From Isolation to Influence* (New York: Council on Foreign Relations, 1994), 32–38.

65. Helmut Schmidt, *Men and Powers* (New York: Random House, 1989), 181.

66. Helmut Schmidt, "The 1977 Alastair Buchan Memorial Lecture," 28 October 1977, in *Survival* (January/February 1978): 4.

67. Jimmy Carter, *Keeping Faith: Memoirs of a President* (New York: Bantam Books, 1982), 225–29.

68. Helga Haftendorn, *Coming of Age: German Foreign Policy since 1945* (Lanham, MD: Rowman & Littlefield, 2006), 247.

69. "White Paper on Defence, Federal Republic of Germany" (1979), reprinted in *Survival* (November/December 1979): 274.

70. Gregory F. Treverton, "Nuclear Weapons and the 'Grey Area,'" *Foreign Affairs* 57 (1979): 1083.

71. The background to the "dual track" decision has been explored in a monograph-length article by Kristina Spohr Readman, "Conflict and Cooperation in Intra-alliance Nuclear Politics: Western Europe, the United States and the Genesis of NATO's Dual-track Decision, 1977–79," *Journal of Cold War Studies* 13, no. 2 (2011): 39–89.

72. Carter, *Keeping Faith*, 537–38.

73. David Watt, "The European Initiative," in *America and the World 1978* (New York: Council on Foreign Relations, 1979), 587.

74. For quotations, see Schmidt, *Men and Powers*, 266.

75. Wolfram F. Hanreider, *Germany, America, Europe: Forty Years of German Foreign Policy* (New Haven, CT: Yale University Press, 1989), 306.

76. This comment is borne out by the index of Carter's *Keeping Faith*. Thus Schmidt, the most cited West European leader, gets eleven index lines. The European Community gets two lines. By contrast, the Camp David accords between Israel and Egypt in 1978 get fifty-nine lines; the protagonists of that accord, Egyptian leader Anwar Sadat and Israeli premier Menachem Begin, both get thirty-two lines each, far more than, say, Leonid Brezhnev (twenty-three). The Palestine Liberation Organization (PLO), together with the general entry on "the Palestinians," merits thirty-five index lines. Iran, even before the 1980 hostage crisis, is accorded more index lines than any West European country, as are China, Egypt, Israel, Jordan, Saudi Arabia, and Panama.

77. The debate was especially intense in Great Britain, where Premier Margaret Thatcher was a convinced supporter of the boycott and put great pressure on the British Olympic Committee. See Paul Corthorn, "The Cold War and British Debates over the Boycott of the 1980 Moscow Olympics," *Cold War History* 13 (2013): 43–66.

78. Josef Joffe, *The Limited Partnership: Europe, the United States and the Burdens of Alliance* (Cambridge, MA: Ballinger, 1987), 1.

79. Helmut Schmidt, "A Policy of Reliable Partnership," *Foreign Affairs* 59 (1981): 745.

80. Thomas R. Rochon, *Mobilizing for Peace: The Antinuclear Movements in Western Europe* (Princeton, NJ: Princeton University Press, 1988), xvi.

81. Donald Sassoon, *One Hundred Years of Socialism: The West European Left in the Twentieth Century* (London: I.B. Tauris, 1996), 717.

82. E. P. Thompson, *Beyond the Cold War: A New Approach to the Cold War and Nuclear Annihilation* (New York: Pantheon, 1982), 37.

83. Figures for CND from Rochon, *Mobilizing for Peace*, 12.

84. Rochon, *Mobilizing for Peace*, 6.

85. Quotations are from Thompson, "Notes on Exterminism," in *Beyond the Cold War*, 41–79.

86. Walter Laqueur, "Hollanditis" in *America, Europe and the Soviet Union* (New Brunswick, NJ: Transaction Publishers, 1983), 33–48.

87. The Labour Party, "The New Hope for Britain," http://www.politicsresources.net/area/uk/man/lab83.htm.

88. Kunz, *Butter and Guns*, 286, points out that "Reagan accumulated more national debt in six years than all presidents combined in the preceding 190 years." In all, the national debt rose by more than $1,000,000 million between 1981 and 1987.

89. Robert Solomon, "The Elephant in the Boat? The United States and the World Economy," *America and the World 1981* (New York: Council on Foreign Relations, 1981), 573–92.

Chapter Eleven

1989: The Year of Revolutions

When 1989 opened, Europe was still divided into communist and democratic halves, but there was a mood of impending change. Since March 1985, the general secretary of the Soviet Communist Party, Mikhail S. Gorbachev, had been striving to restructure the Soviet economy and political system: a policy that had become known throughout the world by the Russian word of *perestroika*. When these efforts had run into opposition from the party bureaucracy, Gorbachev had liberalized political life in the USSR through the parallel process of *glasnost* (openness) and by democratizing the Communist Party's internal selection of its leaders.

In international affairs, Gorbachev and President Ronald Reagan had put aside the enmities of the past to engage in genuine dialogue over nuclear disarmament. West European leaders, notably Spanish premier Felipe Gonzalez (with whom Gorbachev struck up a warm friendship), Premier Margaret Thatcher, and Chancellor Helmut Kohl, encouraged the new détente once they became certain that Gorbachev's new course was not mere propaganda. Gorbachev, in Thatcher's famous phrase, was a man they "could do business with."[1]

Twenty years after the Prague Spring, in short, another Dubček had taken power, but in the heart of the Soviet empire, not in Prague. "Gorbymania" swept Europe in the late 1980s. The Soviet leader's charm, intelligence, and good faith were palpable and represented a striking contrast to the sclerotic bureaucrats who had been the public face of the USSR since the late 1970s. Indeed, Gorbachev's public persona was more attractive than the Olympian cynicism of French president François Mitterrand, the stridency of Thatcher, the moral bankruptcy of Italy's political bosses, and the Hollywood optimism of Reagan. The West responded on a human level to Gorbachev's innovations: even conservatives wanted him to succeed.

Within the Soviet empire, Gorbachev's actions caused consternation among the elites running the USSR's satellite states. Some imitated the Soviet leader's initiatives and, indeed, were driven toward political pluralism faster than Gorbachev himself. The leaders of East Germany, Czechoslovakia, and Bulgaria, and the tyrant of Romania, Nicolae Ceauşescu, by contrast regarded Gorbachev as a sorcerer's apprentice, or even as an outright counter-revolutionary.

They were right to be fearful. In 1989, the regimes of those countries, which had long lost the respect of the peoples that they ruled, found they could no longer even intimidate them. The bluff of last resort, that Russian tanks would restore "Soviet legality," was trumped: nobody believed Gorbachev would send the tanks in. Emboldened, Václav Havel's greengrocer straightened his back, took the sign saying "workers of the world unite" out of his shop window, and took to the streets. Almost immediately, more immediately than Havel himself had imagined possible, the communist system collapsed.

The Italian intellectual Renzo Foa, writing in a communist newspaper, memorably called 9 November 1989 "Europe's most beautiful day."[2] The day before Foa published his essay, the Berlin Wall had been breached by incredulous citizens of the GDR. Such an event *was* a thing of fascinating beauty. A great many scholars have since explained the social and economic causes for communism's demise in Europe. But unless one grasps that the revolutions of 1989 were ultimately about millions of people regaining their dignity and asserting their most fundamental rights, one misses their defining feature. To quote Gale Stokes:

> Yes, [the people of central Europe] wanted sausages and bananas and fresh air in the literal sense, but more than that they wanted to step into what they dreamed would be the fresh air of freedom. Chanting words like "Freedom," "Democracy," and "Solidarity" . . . hundreds of thousands of ordinary citizens, rarely mobilized before or since, toppled the rotted Communist regimes of East Germany, Czechoslovakia and Romania, and to a certain extent Bulgaria, too.[3]

The collapse of communism in Central and Eastern Europe ended the illusion that it was an alternative way of organizing society to democratic pluralism and the market economy. It was a belief that had been strangely slow to die out in Western Europe; not even the crushing of the Prague Spring, or the repression of Solidarity, or the dismal spectacle of Soviet citizens, seventy years after the revolution, queuing for toilet paper and toothpaste had entirely extinguished it. "Gorbymania" was the last flaring up of this illusion: underlying the adulation was a sincere hope that the Soviet leader would find the tonic that the communist system needed to revive itself.

But by 1989, communism's malaise went too deep for any single politician to restore it to vitality.

PERESTROIKA

Aged only forty-seven when he became central committee secretary with responsibility for agriculture in 1978, Mikhail S. Gorbachev had entered the Politburo as a full member in 1980. By comparison with the drooling dinosaurs seated beside him, he was young, dynamic, and hence potentially threatening. Gorbachev became Kostantin Chernenko's deputy after the death of Brezhnev's successor, Yuri Andropov, in February 1984. His performance as deputy convinced even such hardy perennials as Andrei Gromyko, the foreign minister since 1957, that he deserved promotion to the top job when Chernenko himself died in March 1985. It was Gromyko who proposed Gorbachev's name to the Politburo, and his support ensured that the other conservatives within the leadership fell into line. Gorbachev was nominated for the general secretaryship with celerity, and his Politburo colleagues competed with each other to praise his outstanding qualities for the post.[4]

Had the party barons guessed what the new leader thought about the inadequacy of the communist system, Gorbachev would never have been nominated to run a tractor plant in the Urals. Gorbachev had arrived at the top by a combination of hard work (he was a provincial from Stavropol in southern Russia and came from peasant stock, not the *nomenklatura*); brains (his academic prowess enabled him to attend Moscow University, the most prestigious in the country); and, above all, learning how to disguise his opinions. Gorbachev arrived in the Politburo on the recommendation of Andropov, who despite his posthumous reputation as a would-be reformer was hardly a closet liberal, and Mikhail Suslov, a full member of the Politburo from 1955 to 1982 and a granitic defender of ideological orthodoxy. Indeed, even after he joined the Politburo, Gorbachev had either to accept the decisions taken by the innermost circle of leaders or "begin a descent from power which would have been strikingly faster than his rise through the party ranks."[5]

By the eve of his promotion to general secretary, Gorbachev had concluded that radical change was necessary if Soviet communism was to survive. In December 1984, he made an untimely speech urging restructuring for the economy and democratization of the political system (within, of course, the confines of the one-party state). The speech's contents were heavily censored by the party newspaper, *Pravda*. Gorbachev, however, knew that "we can't go on living in this way." He concurred with another young Politburo reformer, Eduard Shevardnadze of the Soviet Republic of Georgia, who had confided his belief that "everything's rotten. It has to be changed."[6]

Shevardnadze would subsequently become Gorbachev's foreign minister and one of his key allies.

Gorbachev moved swiftly to consolidate his position in 1985 through 1986: "Gorbachev regrouped ministries and replaced cadres on a scale not seen since Stalin."[7] The new men promoted (there were few women) favored experimenting with economic reforms, but few outside of Gorbachev's inner circle wanted political liberalization. Gorbachev accordingly had to walk a fine line between pressing ahead with his agenda and reconciling the die-hards to the changes being proposed.

Drastic action was certainly required. By the mid-1980s, the Soviet bloc was grinding to a halt. Economic growth was almost zero even according to the unreliable official figures. The only sector of the economy that continued to thrive was the military-industrial complex, which drained skilled workers, research resources, and a large part of output into the construction of the contemporary equivalent of pyramids. The rest of the economy, meanwhile, was stuck in the mechanical age, with the use of microprocessors, robots, and computers lagging a decade behind the advanced capitalist economies.

There was, moreover, an impelling need to rebuild the country's capital stock. The infrastructure constructed during the USSR's postwar moderniza-tion was falling to pieces, as the April 1986 meltdown at the Chernobyl nuclear power plant in Ukraine, which spread poisonous fallout over Ukraine and Belarus, so tragically underlined.[8] In addition, the energy-rich USSR was burdened with the costs of preserving socialism in the countries of Central Europe. In effect, the USSR exported gas and oil to its satellite states at artificially low prices and received as payment shoddy consumer goods that nobody else would buy.[9] Without this imperial subsidy, Poland would not have been the only communist country to collapse in the early 1980s. To get higher growth, and to get growth that made people's lives less drab, it was necessary to move toward an economy where more activity was driven by market mechanisms.

But this meant unmaking the omelet for which so many millions of eggs had been broken: admitting, in other words, that building communism had been a mistake with catastrophic human costs. Gorbachev himself, let alone the regime's diehards, was reluctant to face this stark fact. His book *Peres-troika: New Thinking for Our Country and the World* (1987) repeatedly emphasized the need to get back to the true Leninist path, which Gorbachev interpreted as being the one followed during the period of the New Economic Policy (NEP) from 1921 to 1928, in which small-scale private enterprise had been encouraged and during which, at any rate while Lenin was still alive, some measure of intra-party democracy had been allowed.[10] It has been argued that Gorbachev's "new thinking" proved that communism was a be-lief system unexpectedly capable of inspiring a last period of innovation and even idealism.[11]

The economic reforms undertaken in the first two years of Gorbachev's period in office fitted into this framework. Perestroika began in May 1985 with a campaign against one of the principal causes of low productivity: rampant alcohol abuse. Semi-prohibition was imposed, with tight limits being placed on the sale of vodka. This measure stimulated the free market, since bootleggers filled the gap left by the state with brews even more noxious than the official brands, but it also led to a rise in organized crime and a fall in tax revenues for the government, which actually compounded the USSR's economic problems. The anti-vodka campaign was relaxed at the end of the decade.

Gorbachev also introduced several measures inspired by the Hungarian "new economic mechanism," which since the late 1960s had encouraged private enterprise to function side by side with state-owned enterprises. The Law on Individual Labor Activity (November 1986) legalized black-market activity in such areas as taxis, domestic repairs, and the giving of private lessons. The Law on State Enterprises (June 1987) allowed state enterprises greater latitude to set prices and wages, although this reform's chief legacy was higher prices for the consumer. The Law on Cooperatives (May 1988) allowed three or more producers to form a private firm and to hire contract workers. In the crucial agricultural sector, Gorbachev encouraged state farms to lease land to independent groups of peasants, but the farm management bureaucracies were reluctant to cede control over production and access to farm machinery. By 1990, there *was* a burgeoning private sector in the USSR, but its share of the economy remained small by comparison with the gigantic state-owned firms and farms that employed most people, commanded most resources, and generated most economic activity. [12]

It is interesting to contrast the scale of the challenge facing Gorbachev with, say, the difficulties faced by Spain's democratic forces a decade before perestroika was launched. Prime Minister Adolfo Suarez had to deal with a military-aristocratic caste of reactionaries who wished to preserve their sinecures. It was an unenviable task. Gorbachev, however, also had to overcome a caste of reactionaries, but in his case, the Communist Party was almost twenty million strong, dominated the army, controlled the secret police, and believed its role in running the economy and society to be ordained by history. Spain, while its state enterprises were shielded from international and internal competition, at least had not had to build a private sector from scratch. Gorbachev's challenge was, in short, of a different order: Seweryn Bialer has insightfully compared it to the task faced by President Franklin D. Roosevelt during the Great Depression, namely "to save the system from its own follies by a process of evolutionary reformation." [13]

By 1987 Gorbachev had acknowledged that the chief obstacle to systemic change was the Communist Party. Undaunted, he introduced greater pluralism of opinion—glasnost—into the political process. Gorbachev loosened controls on dissidents, most notably by allowing Andrei Sakharov and Elena Bonner to return from internal exile; encouraged social scientists and academics to publish unorthodox analyses of the Soviet economy and society; and reduced censorship. The Chernobyl catastrophe, where the Soviet regime's initial failure to admit that an accident had taken place at all angered its neighbors, was a particular spur to greater openness.

By 1988, Soviet citizens could openly buy the *Gulag Archipelago*, or Orwell's *1984*, or read magazines full of articles critical of the "period of stagnation" under Brezhnev. *Argomenti i Fakty* (Arguments and Facts), a weekly specializing in investigative journalism, had a readership of more than thirty million![14] For a people used to bookstores stacked high with unread (and unreadable) copies of Brezhnev's collected works, the new climate of free thinking was a liberation.

Such intellectual ferment alarmed the diehards. In March 1988, Gorbachev had to fight off a major challenge to his authority following the publication, in the newspaper *Sovetskaya Rossiya*, of an anti-perestroika letter: in effect, a manifesto for a return to ideological orthodoxy. Written by a Leningrad scientist, Nina Andreeva, the letter was praised by an opponent of glasnost within the Politburo, Yegor Ligachev, and republished across the USSR and in East Germany. Ligachev's action was backed by several Politburo heavyweights and had the chief reformers not stood by Gorbachev, the affair might have led to a Kremlin coup similar to the one that ousted Khrushchev in 1964.

Gorbachev's narrow escape spurred his determination. In June 1988, at its Nineteenth All-Union Conference, the Soviet Communist Party opted to experiment with limited democratization. Specifically, the conference agreed to replace the Supreme Soviet (the USSR's nominated "parliament" that met annually) with a "Congress of People's Deputies," one-third of which would represent a broad range of political and social organizations (such as the Academy of Sciences or Komosol, the party youth organization) and two-thirds of which would be territorial representatives. The Central Committee was reserved one hundred seats. Elections to the new body could be contested, though only candidates with support among party-dominated organizations stood a chance of making the ballot paper. In all, the new body would have 2,250 members. Its main task would be to act as an electoral college to choose a new Supreme Soviet, which would, in its turn, become a real legislature, in session eight months a year, rather than a rubber stamp for decisions taken by the party hierarchy. As Gorbachev told the Supreme Soviet on 29 November 1988, before it voted for its own transformation: "Political reform is a kind of oxygen needed for the vital activity of the public organism."[15]

Elections to the Congress of People's Deputies were held on 26 March 1989. They generated genuine enthusiasm. Ninety percent of eligible voters went to the polls and many critics of the regime did well. Boris Yeltsin, a former leader of the Moscow Communist Party who had been forced out of the Politburo in November 1987 and had subsequently become an advocate of accelerating perestroika, got on the ballot paper and won by a landslide. Andrei Sakharov was elected despite the efforts of the Academy of Sciences' bureaucrats to keep him out, as were numerous other intellectuals with unorthodox ideas.

The Supreme Soviet selected by the Congress was still dominated by party hacks. Yeltsin, for instance, was excluded until another deputy stood down to make way for him. Nevertheless, the impact of the elections should not be underestimated. By the spring of 1989, at the peak of Gorbachev's political strength, the USSR had unmistakably shifted toward a more open political system, albeit one that differed enormously from the multiparty democracy Europeans and Americans took for granted. For the dinosaurs in East Berlin, Bucharest, and Prague, it was an alarming sight. Borrowing from Richard E. Neustadt's classic work on the U.S. presidency, we can say that in 1988 through 1989 Gorbachev was able to push through democratic reforms because his *personal* "power to persuade" was considerable. Combined with his institutional power as general secretary, his high personal standing enabled Gorbachev to push the bureaucracy in a direction that it abhorred.

Gorbachev had acquired this standing chiefly through his diplomatic triumphs. By establishing better relations with the United States and by becoming Europe's most admired political figure, he had built up political capital that he was able to spend on his domestic agenda. Gorbachev had to be careful not to provoke the diehards into mounting a coup, but Ligachev and his cronies equally had to remember that displacing Gorbachev would arouse international opprobrium and take the world back to a Cold War that the USSR was no longer strong enough to fight.

Gorbachev had hit the ground running in foreign policy. From day one in 1985, he showed no sign of an inferiority complex. There is no question that Gorbachev was decisive to bringing the Cold War to an end, although his achievement would have been impossible without the flexibility shown by western leaders, perhaps especially the two Cold War hawks, President Reagan and Prime Minister Margaret Thatcher.

Gorbachev's chief foreign policy innovation was that he said yes to reasonable proposals. He was not cast in the Molotov or Gromyko mold. His chief advisers on foreign policy—Foreign Minister Shevardnazhe; Alexander Yakovlev, a former ambassador to Canada; and his close aide Anatoly Chernyaev—were even more daring than Gorbachev himself. In effect, Gorbachev and his advisers echoed the arguments of Andrei Sakharov, who had contended since the 1960s that the USSR's relations with the rest of the world should rest on the "universal values" that transcended individual political regimes rather than on the "empirical-competitive" methods of traditional diplomacy whereby nations compete to maximize their prestige and power, even at the cost of war. Sakharov, the father of the Soviet hydrogen bomb, warned that "thermonuclear war cannot be regarded as a continuation of politics by other means (according to the formula of Clausewitz). It would be a means of universal suicide." He drew the conclusion that it was the moral duty of world statesmen to overcome divisions and abolish the risk of war. [16] In practice, this meant that the superpowers should work together to solve the great issues facing humankind such as pollution, overpopulation, and hunger, and should abstain from imposing their belief systems on unwilling peoples, be it in Guatemala or Czechoslovakia.

Under Brezhnev, such views, particularly when combined with human rights activism and condemnation of the USSR's Stalinist past, had meant a one-way ticket to jail or a psychiatric ward. They now became the basis of official Soviet policy. Gorbachev's speech to the Twenty-seventh Party Congress in March 1986, which called for "new thinking" in foreign policy, launched precisely these themes; his book, *Perestroika*, dedicated a long chapter to the need for the superpowers to abandon the nuclear option and to recognize that "security is indivisible." By the time *Perestroika* was published, the Soviet leader had already met U.S. President Ronald Reagan in Geneva, Switzerland, in November 1985 and again in Reykjavik, Iceland, in October 1986.

The Reykjavik summit, in particular, sent shock waves around the world. The two leaders proposed drastic cuts in medium-range missiles in Europe and even mooted the destruction of all thermonuclear weapons—a proposal that staggered West European leaders, who feared they would be left semi-defenseless before the Red Army. [17] The summit ended without agreement, however, since Reagan refused to abandon the Strategic Defense Initiative (SDI, popularly known as "Star Wars"), a projected anti-missile defense system in space. Gorbachev, meanwhile, flatly refused to cut warhead numbers unless the Americans amended the 1972 Anti-Ballistic Missile Treaty to suspend SDI research and testing for ten years.

Despite this setback, the Reykjavik meeting did enable both leaders to see each other without ideological blinkers. Both men realized that they could have peace if only they were bold enough. In June 1987, speaking before the Brandenburg Gate in divided Berlin, Reagan upped the ante with one of the most memorable speeches of modern times: "General Secretary Gorbachev, if you seek peace, if you seek prosperity for the Soviet Union and Eastern Europe, if you seek liberalization: Come here to this gate! Mr. Gorbachev, open this gate! Mr. Gorbachev, tear down this wall!"

Gorbachev was not yet ready to go so far. But in December 1987, in Washington, D.C., the two leaders signed a treaty dismantling intermediate nuclear forces in Europe—the "zero option" advocated by the peace movement in the early 1980s—and pledged to reduce their nuclear stockpiles to

4,900 each. In order to get these deals, Gorbachev voluntarily gave way on SDI and accepted asymmetrical cuts in the Soviet nuclear arsenal. Reagan and Gorbachev thereafter trusted each other in a way that had no precedent between a Soviet leader and an American president. The June 1988 Moscow summit was a triumph for their personal friendship, with Reagan being cheered by students when he gave a lecture at Moscow University on the merits of democracy. In December 1988, speaking at the United Nations, Gorbachev unilaterally cut Soviet combat forces by five hundred thousand troops. Six tank divisions were to be withdrawn from the GDR, Czechoslovakia, and Hungary as part of these cuts. In 1989, Soviet troops finally pulled out of Afghanistan, the Soviet Union's "Vietnam." Although top officials in the incoming Bush administration still worried in 1989 that Gorbachev might be "Brezhnevism with a paint job," the Soviet leader had won over the rest of the planet. [18]

The Bush administration's doubts were attributable to the sheer daring of Gorbachev's ideas and their possible consequences for the U.S. position in Europe. U.S. accounts of the end of the Cold War naturally stress the summit meetings held between the Soviet leader and his American counterparts. But Gorbachev's diplomacy with the principal European capitals was actually even more intense. Between March 1985 and December 1989, Gorbachev met Prime Minister Thatcher six times and made two high-profile visits to the United Kingdom. He met President François Mitterrand no fewer than eight times, including three visits to Paris. In the same four-year span, Gorbachev met Italian leaders and the pope in Rome in November 1989; hosted Spain's Felipe Gonzalez twice in Moscow; and held summits with the leaders of Austria (four times), Denmark, Finland, the Netherlands, Portugal, and Sweden. [19] Relations with West Germany were frostier, not least because in October 1986 Chancellor Helmut Kohl committed the huge gaffe of comparing Gorbachev's gifts as a propagandist to those of Joseph Goebbels'. Kohl nevertheless met Gorbachev three times in the late 1980s and President Richard von Weizsacker visited Moscow once. [20]

The chief outcome of this interaction with democratic Europe's leaders was Gorbachev's vision of the need to construct a "common European home." By this, Gorbachev meant a nuclear-free Europe; one which revived the Helsinki process to obtain security by creating a continent-wide community of nations that would respect human rights and stimulate cooperation on economic, cultural, and ecological issues. Washington worried that this idea was a plot to dilute U.S. influence in Europe, and, indeed, there probably was an element of calculation in Gorbachev's thinking. [21] By 6 July 1989, however, when the Soviet leader spoke to the Assembly of the Council of Europe in Strasbourg, the sincerity of his commitment to overcoming the Cold War division of Europe was evident. Quite explicitly, the Soviet leader insisted that the USSR was in favor of "eliminating all nuclear weapons by the turn of the century"; in favor of "a radical reduction in conventional arms and armed forces to a level of reasonable defense sufficiency that would rule out the use of military force against other countries for the purposes of attack"; in favor of "complete withdrawal of all foreign troops from the territories of other countries"; in favor of "dismantling military blocs and launching immediately a political dialogue between them to that end." The message could not have been clearer. Gorbachev was saying, "The Cold War is over." This suggestion naturally had enormous appeal for Europeans.

In his Strasbourg speech, Gorbachev signaled the end of the Cold War in a second way. The concept of a common European home obviously implied respect for the neighbors and for their ways of life. By the time Gorbachev spoke at Strasbourg, the Hungarians were dismantling the communist system as fast as they could and Poland had just held free elections in which the Communists had been routed. He nevertheless chose this delicate moment to say unambiguously:

> The fact that the states of Europe belong to different social systems is a reality. The recognition of this historical fact and respect for the sovereign right of each people to choose their own social system at their own discretion are the most important prerequisite for a normal European process.
>
> The social and political order in some particular countries did change in the past, and it can change in the future as well. But this is exclusively a matter for the peoples themselves and of their choice. Any interference in internal affairs, any attempts to limit the sovereignty of states—whether of friends and allies or anybody else—are inadmissible.[22]

It was a green light, whether Gorbachev intended it to be or not.

THE ICE CRACKS

Perestroika showed that change was possible within the Soviet empire. Nevertheless, even as late as July 1989 few observers predicted the imminent wave of protest that would sweep away the regimes of Central Europe. While recognizing, in Tocqueville's much-quoted words, that "it is not always when things are going from bad to worse that revolutions occur. It more often happens that when people who have long endured an oppressive regime without complaint suddenly find it relaxing its pressure, they rise up violently against it," most commentators assumed that the communist bloc regimes would somehow stagger on.[23]

Nevertheless, conditions for revolt objectively were ripe. Thanks to television, and family visits from the other side of the iron curtain, the peoples of the Communist bloc, especially East Germans and Hungarians, were well aware of the disparity in living standards between their own countries and neighboring countries in democratic Europe such as Austria or West Germany. They were equally aware that living standards were doomed to fall. Economic growth, already low in the second half of the 1970s, slumped in the first half of the 1980s, to barely more than 1 percent per year. Income per head, taking 1975 as 100, had risen by 1987 to 110.7 in Bulgaria, 116 in Czechoslovakia, 128.9 in East Germany, 117 in Hungary, and 131.9 in Romania. It had fallen to 97.3 in Poland.[24] These modest gains were wiped out in 1988 as economies across the bloc experienced falls in real purchasing power caused by the regimes' need to pay back debt. East Germany's fall in living standards was particularly dramatic: In effect, the country's citizens lost over a decade's income growth in a single year. The bloc's overall debt burden was huge. Gross hard currency debt reached nearly $100 billion by 1988, with Poland and Hungary being particularly exposed.

Paying off these loans was bound to be arduous, as the example of Romania showed. Romania was turned into a siege economy in the 1980s in order to pare down its foreign debt, which peaked in 1982 at nearly 20 percent of GNP. Dennis Deletant has written that these measures were "unparalleled even in the bleak history of East European communist regimes."[25] Foodstuffs were rationed to ensure that as much as possible of agricultural production went for export. In 1988, adults received 750 grams of sugar, 0.5 liters of cooking oil, 0.5 kilograms of flour, and 1 kilogram of pasta *per month*. Bread was limited to 300 grams per day.[26] Meat and dairy products were luxury goods. In apartment blocks, hot water was permitted just one day per week while electricity and gas were cut off as a matter of routine even in winter. Poverty, plus strict controls on contraception and abortion as the regime tried, for propaganda reasons, to push the population over thirty million, meant the abandonment of tens of thousands of children into state orphanages. The plight of these infants, as starved and brutalized as concentration camp inmates, was one of the most dreadful legacies of the end of communism.

President Nicolae Ceauşescu, party leader since 1965, and his sinister wife, Elena, lived meanwhile in the bubble of their own personality cult.[27] There was no money for gas and eggs, or starving orphans, but copious funds were found for the policy of so-called systemization. Vast areas of Bucharest were demolished and were replaced by grandiose boulevards (few people could afford a car) and the colossal "House of the Republic," the largest public building in the world after the Pentagon. In the countryside, hundreds of villages were marked for replacement by "agroindustrial complexes," though the regime happily collapsed before most fell to the bulldozer. Resistance to the Ceauşescu regime briefly broke out in the town of Braşov in 1987, but the *Securitate* made sure that such outbreaks were rare. Typewriters were as tightly restricted as machine guns. Unsurprisingly, Romania produced only a handful of dissidents—the most famous of whom was Doina

Cornea, a heroic university teacher of French literature. But a whole people was pushed to the limit of human endurance by Ceauşescu and his family in the 1980s.

Citizens of the other communist states did not necessarily know of the appalling hardships being inflicted upon the Romanians, but they could guess that their own future was grim. But by the end of the 1980s, all the communist regimes, not just Romania, had long lost any power they might once have had to ask their peoples to make such sacrifices.

East Germany was a police state in the purest sense of the word. The Stasi's vast network of informers snuffed out dissidence with baleful efficiency. Only the churches, both protestant and catholic, provided a limited haven from the watchful eye of the state, though even in the privacy of a church hall, one never truly knew whether one's neighbor was an informant or not. The border between the two Germanies, and with Austria, was protected from its own people by watchtowers, armed guards enforcing a "shoot to kill" policy, and attack dogs, although, in a liberal gesture, landmines and automatically triggered machine guns were mostly dismantled in the mid-1980s.[28]

Each year, hundreds nevertheless attempted escape, although a relatively easier way of getting to the West was simply applying to emigrate. Would-be emigrants were often arrested on trumped-up charges and then ransomed to West Germany in exchange for hard currency (prices reached 100,000 marks per head in the regime's dying days). Hundreds of thousands of people filed for permission to emigrate from the mid-1980s onward. The leadership of the GDR, like the Politburo during Brezhnev's last years, was aging and narrow-minded. In particular, Erich Honecker, party leader since 1971, and Erich Mielke, the head of the Stasi, were a byword for close-mindedness. In private, Honecker was a virulent critic of Gorbachev and his reforms.

Czechoslovakia was ruled over by Gustav Husák, the agent of post-1968 "normalization," until 1987, when, after a visit to Prague by Gorbachev, he was shifted to the country's presidency and was replaced by Miloš Jakeš, a dour party hack. Jakeš's promotion illustrated, to quote Joseph Rothstein, that the regime "had degenerated into an oligarchy, incapable of reassessing, let alone repudiating, its reinstallation by the Soviet invasion two decades earlier."[29] The cream of the country's intelligentsia was either in prison or the victim of endless petty discrimination in their everyday lives.[30] The peoples of Czechoslovakia, though alarmed by environmental degradation, seemed nevertheless more quiescent than the rest of the bloc, and the country's economic prospects were less dismal. Appearances, however, would soon prove to be deceptive.

Bulgaria's Todor Zhivkov was a slavish follower of the Soviet line, whatever it was. His only distinctive policy was "a crude and eventually disastrous campaign to force the country's ethnic Turkish minority—some

700,000 people—to abandon their Turkish characteristics."[31] In a xenophobic campaign launched in 1984, Turks were forced to take Bulgarian names (an act of impiety for Muslims), while schooling and publication in the Turkish language were banned. Hundreds of thousands of Turks were forced to flee the country in the summer of 1989, leaving their homes, bank accounts, and other assets to be pillaged by the bankrupt regime. Discrimination against the country's Roma, Macedonian, and Pomak (Bulgarian-speaking Muslims) communities was almost equally harsh. Patriotism—or more accurately vulgar nationalism—had once again proved to be the last refuge of a scoundrel.

Hungary's János Kádár had been in office since 1956 and had no desire to complement the genuine liberalization of the country's economy with political change à la glasnost. A "significant substratum of enterprise and autonomy already existed in Hungary" as private farmers, providers of services, and people doing second jobs gave the economy more dynamism than anywhere else in the bloc. Private enterprise was given an additional boost after March 1980, when the Party Congress praised market liberalization and the contribution of entrepreneurs to the national wealth. A series of measures broadening the scope for private economic activity followed.

"Goulash communism" was not without flaws, however. Overwork took a toll on the Hungarian population, with alcohol abuse and stress reaching alarm levels. Inflation ate away the workers' gains. By the mid-1980s, the Hungarians were the classic hamsters on a treadmill, running faster and faster just to stay still. A rising tide of criticism began to seep into political life. *Samizdat* publications, the most important of which was *Beszélő*, a magazine published by the philosopher János Kis from 1981, appeared and enjoyed a wide distribution. Citizens were also politicized by the Nagymáros Dam, a huge project, developed in conjunction with the Czech and Austrian governments, to harness the flow of the Danube to generate electricity. Austria, which was paying most of the costs, was slated to get 60 percent of the energy produced; Hungary only 5 percent. However, one of the most beautiful stretches of the river in Hungary would be ruined and the ancient town of Visegrád would be swamped.[32] Protesters formed the so-called Danube Circle in 1984, and though their first organized demonstrations were stifled by the police, their numbers swelled rapidly. In Czechoslovakia, by contrast, where communist rule was more authoritarian, environmental activism was suffocated at birth. From 1987 onward, Hungarians also became alarmed by the fate of their fellow Magyars in Romania, whose villages looked likely to be the main casualty of "systemization," and pressed their government to condemn a fellow communist regime. The agenda of Hungarian politics, in short, was being increasingly influenced by public opinion: anathema in a communist society.

In June 1985, general elections were held. A large number of independent candidates ran against party apparatchiks. More than forty were elected to parliament. It was a sign of things to come. Across the bloc, once people could vote relatively freely, they invariably cast their votes for reformers. The Hungarian communists heeded the signal. Regime moderates, headed by a former culture minister, Imre Poszgay, began pressing for radical economic and political change, including outright political pluralism. Another faction within the party, led by Károly Grosz, was less concerned with political pluralism, but focused on modernizing the economy to raise living standards. Grosz became premier on 26 June 1987.

By then, many Hungarians were prepared publicly to brave the wrath of the authorities. On 15 March 1988, fifteen thousand people turned out in Budapest to commemorate the traditional national day; in June 1988, on the thirtieth anniversary of the execution of Imre Nagy, baton-wielding police broke up unofficial gatherings to commemorate the 1956 revolution's heroes. By then, however, Kádár was out of power. The May 1988 meeting of the Central Committee had pushed Kádár upstairs to the party chairmanship and replaced him with Grosz.

In Poland, where communist rule had survived only because of the imposition of martial law, the regime was particularly unloved. Though Solidarity was banned, it struggled on as an underground organization and had the charismatic Lech Wałęsa, Nobel Laureate for Peace in 1983, as its figurehead. Both Solidarity and the Church retained more authority than the party leadership, especially among the young, who had given up on communism by the mid-1980s. Yet the Jaruzelski regime was unwilling to recognize the union as an interlocutor, knowing that Solidarity's legitimacy would surpass its own.

When the economic crisis bit in 1987, the regime's legitimacy deficit became a political issue. The government could not inflict another bout of hardship on the people without talking to the still illegal union. Pope John Paul II drove the point home when he made a pastoral visit in June 1987. The pope's sermons appealed to the universal value of human rights, and in Gdansk, Solidarity's birthplace, he asserted that the August 1980 Gdansk agreements permitting free trade unions had been an "expression" of the "growing consciousness of working people's responsibility for social and moral order," a responsibility that was still "unfulfilled." On 14 June 1987, before returning to the Vatican, the pope visited the grave of Jerzy Popiełuszko, a priest active in Solidarity who had been murdered by members of the security forces in 1984.[33]

This brief survey of the communist regimes of Europe in the 1980s makes understanding why so few analysts foresaw the monumental events of 1989 all the harder. There is perhaps a human propensity to assume that what is will continue to be. Yet the signs of collapse were clearly there. Oppressive regimes can survive if they fail to put butter on the table. If they are efficient at repression, or offer an enticing vision of the future to justify present sacrifices, they can even survive being identified with their own people's conquerors. But by the late 1980s, all the regimes of Central Europe could offer was continuing to live a lie that Moscow itself manifestly no longer believed.

The ice cracked first in Poland and Hungary. After Kádár's enforced "promotion," political discussion exploded in Hungary. Previously taboo subjects, above all the official depiction of the Soviet invasion in 1956, were discussed with much greater openness: an independent report by a team of historians into the events of 1956 and in January 1989 published its findings even though they contradicted the official party line on the subject. Political "clubs" were formed. Imre Poszgay was associated with the Hungarian Democratic Forum (MDF), which had twelve thousand members by the beginning of 1989. János Kis became president of the Alliance of Free Democrats (SzDSz), which openly espoused free-market economics and political pluralism. The third important club was the "Alliance of Young Democrats," (FIDESz) open only to under-35s, and politically the most radical of the three.

These clubs were destined to become the main political parties in post-communist Hungary. From January 1989 onward, the clubs, together with other bodies formed in Hungary's nascent civil society, began to press the Communist Party to proceed to multiparty democracy and to recognize that 1956 had been a national uprising against communism, not, as the official textbooks would have it, a counter-revolutionary coup. Dissent was by now becoming mainstream opinion. On 15 March 1989, unofficial national day celebrations in Budapest were attended by one hundred thousand marchers who halted their procession at locations of symbolic importance for Hungarian history.

Premier Grosz tried to buy time by making concessions. External as well as internal controls were loosened. In February 1989, the Hungarian authorities agreed to loosen border controls with Austria—which led to a bonanza for Austrian shop owners when the border was opened in May. The right to strike was enacted in March. The "Danube Circle" won a striking victory in May 1989 when construction on the Nagymáros Dam was suspended—a communist government had been forced by people power to back down.

The year 1989 was not 1956. Soviet troops were leaving Hungary, not invading it. Some sixty thousand Soviet troops were withdrawn from Eastern Europe, including Hungary, in April 1989. In June 1989, the Hungarian Communist Party agreed to open discussions with the "Opposition Round Table," an umbrella body composed of the various clubs and civil society movements, to arrange free elections and to institute a multiparty system. On 16 June, with great solemnity, the exhumed bodies of Imre Nagy and other leaders of the 1956 uprising were reburied and the events of that year were finally recognized for what they were.[34] Hungarian communism was crumbling like a sandcastle as irresistible waves of public opinion lapped against its walls and as leading members of the party, sensing the way the tide was flowing, converted opportunistically to the cause of political pluralism.

The same was true of Poland. In 1988, the ailing Polish economy tanked. Inflation surged to an annual rate of 80 percent, wiping out the savings of the poor, and the government was forced to hike the price of basic foodstuffs to levels that ordinary workers could not afford. Solidarity offered to cooperate with Jaruzelski to restore economic order if freedom of association were allowed and if the union were allowed to reform. The regime refused to countenance this offer until widespread industrial unrest compelled it. In August 1988, the Polish authorities opened discussions with Wałęsa in order to stop strikes—which the canny electrician, putting all his personal authority on the line, managed to do. In return, the Jaruzelski regime proposed to hold a "Round Table" on the country's political future with representatives of Solidarity and the Church, but did not commit itself to legalizing the union, or even recognizing it officially.

This partial opening to Solidarity was somewhat spoiled by the appointment in October 1988 of Mieczysław Rakowski as premier. Rakowski had been one of the regime's few advocates of social and political change. But he was a hard, opportunistic man whose tolerance stopped short of imagining that the ruling party could ever share power. Solidarity's intellectual advisers such as Jacek Kuron and Adam Michnik were anathema to him.

Despite the new government, Wałęsa shrewdly bolstered the union's position. At the end of November 1988, Wałęsa held an unprecedented debate with the head of the official trade unions on television and scored points by appearing witty, patriotic, and constructive. In December, he visited France and was treated with the respect accorded to a world leader. Jaruzelski bowed to the inevitable and in January 1989 urged the party's Central Committee to approve negotiations with Solidarity.

On 6 February 1989, the Round Table began. The chief communist negotiator was Interior Minister Leszek Kiszczak, who had been the target of one of Adam Michnik's most trenchant polemics during martial law.[35] Kiszczak was nevertheless far more personally acceptable to Solidarity than Rakowski would have been.[36] Given the tense circumstances, the talks were conducted in a conciliatory atmosphere and ended on 5 April 1989 with a series of accords that legalized Solidarity, guaranteed freedom of speech and the press, and made sweeping constitutional innovations. In brief, the accords created a dual chamber parliamentary system by adding a Senate to the existing *Sejm*, or Parliament. Elections to the *Sejm* would be "non-confrontational" with 65 percent of the seats reserved for the Communist Party and its allies. Elections to the Senate, which would have veto power over legislation, would be entirely open, though the *Sejm* could overturn a Senate veto by a two-thirds vote. The two chambers would together choose a powerful president of the Republic, who would enjoy absolute authority in foreign and defense policy, power to veto *Sejm* legislation and to call a state of emergency, and the right to dissolve any legislature that threatened the president's own constitutional prerogatives, or could not form a government. Elections would take place as soon as June 1989.[37]

Everybody assumed that the Round Table accords would give a gloss of democratic respectability to continued communist rule. Wałęsa and his advisers hoped to win a majority of the contested seats, but essentially regarded the new constitution as a price they had to pay to get Solidarity legalized. Ordinary citizens, however, grasped that the Round Table had given them their first chance since 1945 (elections in January 1947 were contested, but were not remotely free and fair) to say what they thought about the political system that had been foisted upon them.

When elections were held on 4 and 18 June 1989, they issued a "humiliating, definitive repudiation" of the regime.[38] Solidarity-backed candidates won all but one of the 161 contested seats in the *Sejm* election. In the Senate elections, they won 99/100, with the odd seat going to a wealthy independent, not to a Communist. Voters to the *Sejm* could also express their opinion on a special national list of thirty-five prominent Communists by crossing out the names of the candidates they did not want. Thirty-three out of the thirty-five names, including Rakowski and Kiszczak, were deleted by gleeful voters and hence were not elected. As Bronisław Geremek, a distinguished historian who was one of Wałęsa's closest advisers, subsequently acknowledged, the results of the Polish elections were a "turning point." They not only showed that the emperor "had no clothes," but provided empirical proof for a fact that was "intellectually evident": namely that only inertia and the communists' dominion over the levers of power allowed them to cling on to authority.[39]

The results, in short, were a catastrophe for the Polish authorities—but a triumph for freedom and the Polish people, as President George H. W. Bush pointed out when he visited Poland and Hungary in July 1989 and was greeted by immense crowds waving the Stars and Stripes. "It is Poland's time of destiny, a time when dreams can live again," Bush told the crowds in Gdansk.[40]

It was also a time of some confusion. It had been taken for granted that Jaruzelski would be the new president, but after the election results, his nomination was uncertain: "Solidarity found itself in the horrifying position of apparently being able to prevent Jaruzelski being elected president."[41] On 19 July, the architect of martial law in 1981 was made president only thanks to the abstentions of the men and women he had once vilified and jailed. In a last attempt to preserve some vestige of the regime's power, Jaruzelski nominated Kiszczak as premier, but it was a forlorn hope. The new mood of democratic change would not permit another communist as the head of government. On 24 August 1989, Tadeusz Mazowiecki, a Catholic philosopher who had been the "first intellectual not from Gdansk who actively supported the August 1980 strike," also became the first non-communist premier of a Central European state since 1948.[42] His government, which included both Kiszczak and Jacek Kuron, in other words, jailers and jailed, immediately launched a policy of economic "shock therapy" to combat hyperinflation. The "velvet revolution" had begun.

THE VELVET REVOLUTION

Voting the communists out was impossible in the GDR. In May 1989 local elections, the ruling SED and its allies obtained a 96 percent plurality. The figure, while lower than the usual 99 percent plebiscite, was obviously fraudulent. Civil society groups had monitored voting in selected locales and had witnessed unprecedented numbers of ordinary citizens, especially the young, registering their negative votes with the policemen stationed at the polls. The regime's poll fixing was an unsubtle way of warning that the ballot box was useless in the GDR, however powerful it might be in Budapest or Warsaw. The following month, the Honecker regime sent an even more powerful signal by applauding the Chinese government's massacre of student protesters in Tiananmen Square.

East Germans drew the conclusion, just as they had in the years prior to the construction of the Berlin Wall in August 1961, that they had no choice but to vote with their feet. Their own country's boundaries were impassable, so they went around them. In the summer of 1989, the opening of the Hungarian border with Austria encouraged growing numbers of East Germans to load their Trabants and pass into Hungary through Czechoslovakia. Once there, they tried to get into Austria across country since the Hungarian government was still enforcing passport controls. Ten of thousands of "holiday-makers" were roaming the country by mid-August. The Hungarians, who were in any case about to make the sweeping constitutional changes that would in September–October 1989 turn Hungary into a fully-fledged democracy, increasingly turned a blind eye to the escapees.

On 11 September 1989, Hungary announced that East Germans could cross freely into Austria. The exodus was on. In September 1989, more than thirty-three thousand East Germans flocked into Austria and, in most cases, proceeded to reception centers set up in West Germany by Bonn. The West German embassies in Prague and Warsaw were occupied by asylum seekers. At the end of September, Honecker agreed that the individuals camped out in Prague could leave for the Federal Republic via East German territory.[43] The operation did not go off smoothly. On 4 October, desperate would-be migrants fought a pitched battle with police when special trains carrying more than seven thousand refugees from Prague arrived in Dresden.

Civil society was raising its head within the country. Peaceful demonstrations against the regime began in Dresden on 4 September. "New Forum," a pressure group for social change, was founded by some thirty dissidents in East Berlin on 10 September 1989. Two days later, a second group, "Democracy Now," was formed. These groups were hardly right-wing nationalists. Democracy Now's program emphasized the need for ecological, sustainable living, called for an improbable alliance between "Christians and critical Marxists," and, while it rejected the command economy, plainly had Stockholm, not California, as its economic model. Its political demands were more uncompromising: free elections, freedom of association, free access to the media, an end to indoctrination in schools, the right to strike, freedom to travel and emigrate, and an end to arbitrariness in the justice system and to ideological dogma in cultural life.[44]

As the protests swelled and the refugee crisis dominated the world's front pages, the regime was poised to celebrate the fortieth anniversary of the GDR's foundation on 6–7 October 1989. The top brass of world communism, including Gorbachev, were to be in East Berlin. The Honecker regime had to decide whether to use the occasion to start a dialogue with civil society or stay in its bunker. Gorbachev privately urged the former course in his meetings with Honecker and the East German Politburo, but Honecker chose the second option. Protesters were allowed to gather in East Berlin's huge Alexanderplatz on 7 October to chant Gorbachev's name and to proclaim "we are the people" (though the police were waiting for them away from the eyes of the world's press and hundreds were badly beaten), but in the days following the anniversary celebrations Honecker ignored attempts by the youngest member of the Politburo, Egon Krenz, to adopt policies more in keeping with the rest of the bloc.[45]

On 9 October, a huge crowd gathered outside St. Nicholas's Church in Leipzig, the epicenter of the popular revolt. Had security police opened fire, October 1989 might have become a continent-wide tragedy, not a prelude to the triumph of democracy and human rights. On 17 October, the day after more than one hundred thousand people had again demonstrated in Leipzig, Honecker was compelled to step down by a unanimous Politburo vote.

Honecker was replaced by Krenz, who swiftly proved to be a miserable choice for an impossible job. Krenz fancied himself as the GDR's Gorbachev, but his wolfish looks, jargon-filled speeches, and reputation as Honecker's "narrow-minded, obedient henchman," all denied him public trust for that role.[46] Krenz lacked the moral vision of a Gorbachev, or a Dubček, or even Jaruzelski's stark realism. He spoke of restoring "socialist human rights," but until mid-November the Politburo was packed with the Honecker regime's grimmest bureaucrats. By now people wanted, at minimum, concrete legal rights to emigrate and to travel, to vote for whom they chose, and to free speech: Krenz showed few signs that he was prepared to go so far.

Throughout October, the exodus continued: more than eleven thousand citizens departed on November 8, the last day before the Wall was breached. Demonstrations, meanwhile, had reached oceanic dimensions by the first week of November. On 4 November, some six hundred thousand people gathered in East Berlin to call for democracy; in Leipzig a scarcely smaller crowd gathered on 6 November. For the first time, the crowds began to call for a united Germany, a taboo subject among intellectuals on both sides of the Wall, and speakers from the SED were not allowed to address the crowd.

On 7 November, Czechoslovakia, alarmed by the threat posed to its own internal stability by the flood of asylum seekers, threatened to close its frontiers, a proposal that was bound to lead to clashes between enraged East German citizens and Czech border troops. On the evening of 9 November, the East German government essentially acceded to the protesters' demand to permit free travel. At a crowded press conference, a harried government spokesman announced that from 8.00 a.m. the following morning, visas and passports would be issued to anybody who asked for them. The regime seemingly did not guess what the effect of its decision would be. By midnight it knew. Exultant, tearful crowds, unwilling to wait until offices opened in the morning, had breached the Wall and surged into West Berlin, which enjoyed the largest street party in history.

More than five million East Germans would visit the West in the next four days, and many of them bought all the consumer goods they could carry, a task the West German government facilitated with one hundred million marks of "welcome money." Some (affluent) commentators sneered at this materialism, but their condescension was surely misplaced. Western consumerism, for all its shallowness, is nevertheless a function of freedom. By asserting themselves as consumers, East Germans were saying, "I can choose." Communism had imploded in East Germany precisely because it denied this basic human longing to make one's own decisions.[47]

A week after the fall of the Wall, Hans Modrow, the party leader from Dresden and the only half-credible SED leader left, presented a new government, with twelve non-SED ministers, to the East German parliament. The new premier faced an economy in ruins and a breakdown in the regime's legitimacy that would prove impossible to repair once, in the new mood of democratic openness, East Germans grasped the extent to which the Stasi had monitored their lives and the way in which the party's top echelons had exploited their position for personal gain. Honecker—now public enemy number one—was expelled from the party in December and took refuge in a Soviet military base in the GDR in April 1990.[48] Modrow's neighbors, including many in West Germany, while delighted to see the back of Honecker, were less than enthusiastic about the prospect that the GDR's travails would lead to the unification of Germany as a whole. Modrow initially hoped to keep unification off the agenda, but that proved to be an impossible task. The country's best and brightest were in flight—more than 130,000 emigrated to the West in November 1989 alone—and the young and the skilled, in particular, showed no signs of wanting to remain. Even after the stirring events of November, emigration continued at the rate of two thousand per day.[49] East Germany was doomed, a fact that provoked much angst among the intelligentsia.[50] The people had more common sense: *Wir sind ein Volk* (We are One People) became the slogan of ordinary East German citizens in the new year.

While the GDR was falling apart, the rest of the communist bloc was not idle. Hungary took to democracy almost too well: its politics speedily became Italianesque in their contentiousness and complexity. Between 13 June and 18 September, Hungary held its own discussions between the government and a "Round Table" of opposition parties and associations and achieved widespread agreement on constitutional changes. On 18 October 1989, Hungary introduced a new democratic constitution. In the March 1990 parliamentary election, which was contested by some sixty parties, the ex-Communists got less than 10 percent of the vote, despite changing their name to the Hungarian Socialist Party in October 1989. The elections were won by the MDF, albeit with less than a quarter of the popular vote. The MDF's leader, József Antall, a distinguished historian of science, formed a conservative government together with the much smaller Christian Democrat and Smallholders' parties.

Bulgaria experienced a palace coup against Todor Zhivkov on 9 November 1989. Unlike elsewhere in the bloc, November 1989 was in Bulgaria the *start* of mass opposition to the political system, not a political epiphany.[51] Opposition to Zhivkov, stirred by Gorbachev, had mounted among the top leaders of the Bulgarian party since at least 1987. The enforced exodus of the Turkish minority and the suspicion that Zhivkov was planning to impose his son as his successor prompted the regime's top men to begin preparations for a coup in the summer of 1989. The chief plotters, foreign minister Petar Mladenov, the finance minister Andrei Lukanov, the defense minister Dobri Dzhurov, and the premier, Georgi Atanasov, launched their challenge to the dictator on 24 October 1989 when Mladenov wrote a letter of resignation to the Central Committee of the Bulgarian party that was fiercely critical of Zhivkov's personality and methods of ruling the party and the country. Taking as a pretext Zhivkov's personal rudeness to him during a meeting with the American ambassador, Mladenov asserted:

> I have come to the conclusion that the real reason for Comrade Zhivkov's irritation and rudeness is that he realizes that he has led our country into a deep economic, financial and political crisis. He knows that his political agenda,

which consists of deviousness and petty intrigues . . . has succeeded in isolat-
ing Bulgaria from the rest of the world. We have even reached the point where
we are estranged from the Soviet Union and we find ourselves . . . in the same
pigs' trough as the rotten dictatorial family regime of Ceaușescu. . . . I think
we all understand that the world has changed and that, if Bulgaria wants to be
in tune with the rest of the world, it will have to conduct its political affairs in a
modern way.[52]

Two days after Mladenov's resignation, Zhivkov showed exactly how "in
tune" he was with the rest of the Soviet bloc by crushing a public protest by
Ecoglasnost, one of the country's few civil society movements. Telling the
truth about the poisoning of the Black Sea was not tolerable for the regime.
On 9 November, the Politburo met, its building ringed by troops loyal to
Dzhurov, and Zhivkov was forced to give up power, in effect at gunpoint.

Mladenov became party secretary and president, and the regime began a
process of opening up to political change. An opposition group, the "Union
of Democratic Forces," was formed within days of Zhivkov's fall. It described itself, in a clear statement of position, as "anti-totalitarian, anti-
monopolist, anti-communist and pro-Western."[53] Over the next few months
the Bulgarian government was forced by public opinion—there were huge
demonstrations in Sofia in December 1989 and January 1990—to set a date
(June 1990) for free elections and to end its own monopoly on politics and
chose of its own accord to alter its name to the Bulgarian Socialist Party
(BSP).

People power was also on display in Czechoslovakia. On 21 August
1988, more than ten thousand mostly young people had marched to condemn
the twentieth anniversary of the Soviet invasion. A second protest, which this
time was crushed by the police, took place in Prague on 28 October, Czechoslovakia's national day. The following month, the Jakeš regime allowed
Alexander Dubček to emerge from obscurity and to travel to Italy to receive
an honorary degree from Bologna University. If its plan was to win kudos for
its openness, the regime's plan backfired badly. Dubček delivered a thoughtful speech that made clear that the oppression of the Prague Spring had
condemned the bloc to twenty years of "economic stagnation, sterility and
incalculable moral damage."[54]

On world human rights day, 10 December, thousands gathered to hear
leading dissidents speak of the human rights situation. French president
François Mitterrand was on an official visit to Prague at the time and so this
demonstration passed relatively unscathed. On 15 January 1989, the anniversary of Jan Palach's self-immolation, the regime's critics were not so fortunate. Riot police broke up the gathering and numerous human rights activists,
including Václav Havel, were sent to jail (Havel was released in May). For
several days afterward, however, Prague was the site of running battles between students and police.

Czechoslovakia's intellectuals responded by circulating a petition, "A Few Remarks," that was issued in June and rapidly signed by forty thousand people. The text of "A Few Remarks" illustrates what the Czechs who were "living in truth" wanted: they wanted "real social dialogue" before social tensions spilled over into violent conflict. This dialogue could take place, however, only if basic conditions were met. The regime should release political prisoners, end censorship, respect the right of people to worship freely, and permit a free discussion of the Prague Spring and the subsequent process of "normalization."[55] Such conditions were anathema for the regime. But as East German "tourists" besieged the West German embassy, it was becoming obvious to everybody except Husák, Jakeš, and the grim functionaries surrounding them that dialogue was the only alternative to explosion. The Czech regime could not ease the pressure for change by allowing the young, the skilled, and the disaffected to leave.

Students were the section of society most determined to press for reforms. On 17 November 1989, independent student organizations marched to commemorate Jan Opletal, a student killed in 1939 while protesting against the Nazification of Czech universities. Some fifteen thousand university students, wearing white carnations and carrying candles, set out along the procession's path through Prague. But the march's numbers swelled as citizens joined it: the march "seemed to take on a life of its own."[56] Soon, the procession had turned into a spontaneous anti-government rally. The chant of "free elections" was taken up by thousands of voices, and the crowd headed toward Wenceslas Square, the heart of Prague. Riot police blocked its path. The students responded by provocatively jangling key-rings in the faces of the waiting troops. This gesture, symbolizing their wish to open the door to freedom, would become the emblem of the velvet revolution.

On 17 November 1989, however, the regime still intended to keep the door shut if it could. Police attacked the protesters savagely: the youngest casualty of their assault was just eleven years old; the oldest demonstrator hospitalized by a beating was aged eighty-three.[57] For all its violence, the regime's response was a sign of weakness, not strength. Had it still possessed the will to power, it would have fired on the crowds, as the Chinese had done. The repressive action of the police was brutal enough to inflame huge numbers of people who had hitherto been prudent in their opposition to the communist system, but not ruthless enough to awe the population into obedience. The independent student organizations appealed for a general strike to take place on 27 November and were joined in their protest by the nation's actors. The Magic Lantern theater, which had produced Václav Havel's plays before he was banned, became the headquarters of Civic Forum, a coalition of opposition groups, including reformist communists, that was formed on 19 November. A similar group, called "People Against Violence," was formed the same day in Bratislava, the principal city of Slovakia. Havel became

Civic Forum's spokesman and de facto leader, although he was, despite his courageous opposition to the regime, anything but well-known to ordinary Czechs.

Seven weeks later he would be the country's president. By the end of November, communism in Czechoslovakia was all but finished. As the witticism had it, it had taken the Poles ten years to make their democratic revolution; the Hungarians had taken ten months. The Czechs needed just ten days. Crowds jingling their key-rings and chanting, "Now's the Time" occupied Saint Wenceslas Square every evening from 20 November onward. On 24 November, Dubček and Havel, tears of joy coursing down their cheeks, embraced on a balcony overlooking the great square. Three hundred thousand voices took up the cry "Dubček to the Castle"—the *Prasky hrad* being also the presidential palace and seat of government. Jakeš resigned on the same evening. On the weekend of 25–26 November, two gigantic demonstrations—a million people participated on Sunday, 26 November—heard Havel and other speakers call for a "real, pluralistic democracy." The two-hour general strike held the following day was adhered to by the vast majority of the population.[58]

Civic Forum published its program, "What We Want," on 26 November. Drafted with an important contribution from "the other Vaclav," the right-wing economist Vaclav Klaus, "What We Want" was very different in tone from the Marxist progressivism proposed by the Czech opposition's peers in the GDR. What the Civic Forum wanted was to become part of the West as fast as possible. As well as calling for the rule of law, an end to the party's leading role in the state, free elections, political pluralism and an end to censorship—by now standard demands everywhere in Central Europe—Civic Forum wanted to become "part of the process of European integration" and to "create a market un-deformed by bureaucratic intervention" that would gradually become "open to the world." As Timothy Garton Ash remarked: "After twenty years, the clocks had started again in Prague. The most western of all the so-called East European countries was resuming its proper history."[59]

It was this desire to become western as fast as possible that explains why Dubček did not become president. Dubček persisted in talking as if the communist system could be humanized. The Civic Forum wanted to start anew, though Havel was not averse to cooperating with party realists such as Ladislav Adamec, the prime minister, with whom he negotiated the transfer of power. Havel was actually elected president (Gustáv Husák having resigned on 10 December) by the former communists of the country's parliament (the Communist Party disintegrated on 22 December) just in time for the New Year. Marián Čalfa, a regime reformist, became the first premier of democratic Czechoslovakia, though his tenure would be only temporary.

Dissidents were transformed overnight into government ministers. Dubček was elected speaker, and free elections were scheduled for the spring.

The peroration of Havel's New Year Address, his first act as president, can serve as an epitaph for the whole glorious semester that had preceded his speech: "People, your government has returned to you!"[60] From Stettin on the Baltic to Trieste on the Adriatic, the iron curtain had been swept aside in six hectic months. All comment is superfluous: the scale of the events speak for themselves. The nearest historical comparison is with 1848, when liberal revolutions erupted all over Europe. Yet those revolutions ended in authoritarian reactions and left piles of dead patriots and ignorant conscripts bloody on the ground. In 1989, as Lech Wałęsa proudly told the U.S. Congress on 15 November, the revolutionaries, at any rate in Poland, did not even "break a window."[61]

It was a truer revolution for being peaceful and almost unanimous. The desire for western prosperity, the desire for political freedoms, the desire to make the history books tell the truth, fused with contempt at the system's manifold hypocrisies to create a popular will for democracy. Even the communist leaders themselves stopped "living in the lie," which is probably why they renounced power so tamely. The will to power endures so long as we think we are in power for a purpose. By making the Soviet system face up to its failings, and by insisting that the USSR would not defend stagnation and injustice in the name of socialism, Gorbachev let a powerful genie out of the bottle. His "new thinking" weakened the will of the communist bloc's leaders, by sapping their faith in the rightness of the system they administered, and stimulated the oppressed peoples of Central Europe to think the unthinkable. The unthinkable duly happened. The revolutions of 1989 are testimony to the power of ideas in politics.[62]

A POSTSCRIPT FROM BUCHAREST

There was to be one important exception to the general rule of peaceful revolutions leading to democratic change: Romania, whose change of regime in December 1989 was neither peaceful nor democratic, nor even a revolution, though it was certainly an improvement.

By 1989, the desire for change was beginning to make itself even in Bucharest. Pressure for reform was coming from both inside and outside the country. The policy of systemization, as we have seen, was arousing outrage in Hungary. An outflow of refugees from the Hungarian minority had begun: more than twenty thousand would be accommodated by Hungary in November 1989 alone; as the year wore on Romanian speakers fleeing starvation were increasingly numbered among the escapees. Romania's German speakers and Jews were also petitioning to leave: Ceaușescu, like Honecker, demanded hard currency in exchange for exit visas. On the eve of the dictator's fall, in November 1989, Nadia Comăneci, the great gymnast who was a propaganda icon for the Bucharest regime, asked for asylum in Hungary.

The West, which had buttered up the Romanian dictator with indecent zeal so long as he was a maverick within the Warsaw Pact, had finally begun to condemn the regime's human rights abuses in no uncertain terms. Britain's Prince Charles, atoning for the state visit Ceauşescu had made to Britain in June 1978, when together with Queen Elizabeth II he paraded, an honored guest, through London in a horse-drawn carriage, asserted in April 1989 that Ceauşescu had "embarked on the wholesale destruction of his country's cultural and human heritage." Under *Operation Villages Roumains*, Belgian, French, Swiss, and British villages began "adopting" Romanian villages, sending them food aid, clothing, and medicines and publicizing their plight. [63]

Within the country, the policy of paring down the national debt had lowered living standards to below the levels attained by most developing countries. Doina Cornea argued in fact that the regime's worst crime had been to "strip people of their human dignity, to reduce them to an animal state where their major daily concern was the struggle to find food." [64] By March 1989, even senior members of the Romanian elite shared such concerns. On 10 March 1989 an open letter to Ceauşescu, signed among others by Constantin Parvulescu, a once-prominent party member who had refused to vote for Ceauşescu's re-election as leader at the party conference in 1979; Silviu Brucan, a former ambassador to the United States; Gheorge Apostol, who had been Ceauşescu's rival for the leadership in 1965; and Corneliu Mănescu, foreign minister from 1961 to 1972, was broadcast in the West. The letter accused Ceauşescu's policies of threatening the "biological existence of our nation." [65] Yet this protest did not echo within the regime, at any rate in public. The top ranks of the party remained loyal to the *Conducator*, and sanctions were imposed on the letter's signatories.

There were, therefore, many good reasons for believing that Romania, too, would implode. But there were also good reasons for thinking that Ceauşescu might survive. As Tismăneanu has noted, "living in truth" was not an option for Romanian intellectuals. [66] Any would-be Lech Wałęsa or Václav Havel would have been imprisoned (or shot) instantly. Ceauşescu's madness also prolonged the regime's survival. Unlike the drab functionaries in Prague or Warsaw, the *Conducător* and his crazy wife, Elena, genuinely believed that they were presiding over a golden age in Romanian history. No Romanian could doubt that the *Securitate* would fire on any crowd brave enough to demonstrate. Any revolution could not be a velvet one.

The trigger for revolt was an inspiring Protestant pastor called Lászlo Tőkés, a member of Romania's Hungarian minority. His sermons against the "systemization" program had "won the admiration and loyalty" of his parishioners in Timişoara, a large town near the borders with Hungary and Yugoslavia.[67] The regime responded by trying to force the pastor from his church. Tőkés fought eviction through the courts, but lost his case and was notified that he was to be transferred on 15 December 1989. On that day, a crowd protesting his removal gathered around his house and church. When it was not immediately dispersed, thousands joined the protesters, chanting, "We want bread" and "Down with Ceauşescu." The pastor himself attempted to persuade the crowd to leave, but events spun out of control. On 17 December, desperate crowds ran rampage through the town. The authorities cracked down mercilessly. Tőkés was arrested and military police units killed nearly one hundred rioters and wounded more than two hundred, although rumors swiftly circulated that thousands had been shot.[68]

Ceauşescu thought the revolt had been contained and even made an official visit to Iran, which as a pariah state itself was one of the few remaining countries willing to receive him. In fact, he was wrong. Following additional violence by the army, mobs gathered in Timişoara on 20 and 21 December and the town left the regime's control. Riots also broke out in the Transylvanian town of Cluj, where troops also fired on crowds. The western and northern regions of the country were alive with rebellion by 21 December.

On 21 December, the dictator decided to hold a mass meeting of his supporters. A giant crowd was assembled in Piaţa Palatului, a huge square in the heart of Bucharest. The rally did not go off as Ceauşescu planned. Instead of the usual staged applause, he was greeted tepidly, and crucially, early in the speech his words were interrupted by shouts and screams caused by the police using tear gas outside the square on demonstrators. The dictator was visibly disconcerted. The mask fell away: Romanians realized that their tyrant was afraid. The rest of his speech was interrupted several times by grumbling from the crowd and chants of "Ti-mi-şoa-ra! Ti-mi-şoa-ra!" That afternoon, revolt came to the streets of Bucharest, as students battled with the police: nearly fifty demonstrators were killed and hundreds wounded and arrested.

On 22 December, the downfall of Europe's grimmest regime took place. The army top brass abandoned the dictator to his fate. At approximately 9.30 a.m., the defense minister, General Vasile Milea, committed suicide (or perhaps was murdered) after he refused to authorize the use of force against the demonstrators. His death, news of which was broadcast, weakened the army's resolve. Soldiers began fraternizing with the gathering protesters. Milea's successor, General Victor Stanculescu, withdrew the soldiers guarding the Central Committee building, where the Romanian Communist Party leadership was holed up in a desperate last meeting. Enormous crowds gathered outside demanding an end to the regime. At 11.30 a.m., Ceauşescu tried to address the crowd, but was jeered by 1989's *sans culottes*. His authority had evaporated. The crowd, seeing him depart, surged into the building and charged up the stairs intent on lynching him. The dictator escaped by helicopter, together with his wife and several officials, leaving from the roof with literally seconds to spare.

The Ceauşescus' pathetic flight need not be recounted in detail here. They abandoned their helicopter and hijacked a car. Increasingly desperate, they eventually made their way to a military barracks in the town of Târgovişte, not far north of Bucharest. There, the local commander kept them safe but did not permit them to leave, ostensibly for their own safety. In fact, the commander was waiting to see what the outcome of the Ceauşescus' fall would be. On 23–24 December, Bucharest lapsed into anarchy, with street fighting on a major scale as loyalist *Securitate* forces fired upon the crowds, many of whom by now were both armed and drunk, while the army tried to restore order. As Siani-Davis has put it, "everyone shot at everybody else."[69] According to official figures, 1,104 people lost their lives during the Romanian revolution, and well more than 3,000 were wounded. Two-thirds, approximately, of these casualties came after 12.00 a.m. on 22 December, and about half died in the street fighting in Bucharest in the days immediately after the dictator's flight.

A "National Salvation Front" (NSF) headed by Ion Iliescu, a former rising star of the regime who had fallen out of Ceauşescu's favor, was formed on 22 December. Iliescu was thought to be Gorbachev's favorite within the Romanian leadership, and he cut an authoritative figure in the television broadcasts that he made after the revolution. Just before midnight on 22 December, Iliescu pledged that the NSF would introduce democracy, hold free elections, respect the rights of the country's ethnic minorities, and make economic reforms, but this rhetoric was somewhat belied by the NSF's composition. In addition to Iliescu, the government was mostly composed of military officers, the most important of whom was General Stanculescu, and communists such as Silviu Brucan. Iliescu listed several leading dissidents as backers of the NSF, but this was window dressing: Most had not even been contacted, and they played no part in the decisions taken over the next few days.

The most important of these decisions was the one to execute the Ceauşescus. On 25 December, the dictator and his wife were subjected to a kangaroo court. No evidence was produced to justify the crimes of genocide with which the Ceauşescus were charged and the trial soon degenerated into a litany of insults. Defense counsel prudently made little effort to defend their clients. The couple were summarily condemned to death and were shot without compunction shortly after the trial was over. Romanian television exulted: "The Anti-Christ is dead!" said the newsreader on the evening of Christmas Day.[70]

Romania's revolution was a sinister reminder of what might have happened elsewhere in Central Europe had the communist regimes not abdicated peacefully. It was a violent end to a year that had otherwise been characterized by the peaceful affirmation of human rights. The miracle of 1989 lay in people power; in Bucharest what happened was a change of regime by men whose responsibility for the regime's crimes was hardly negligible. Nevertheless, even Iliescu and his fellow coup leaders now had to pay lip service to the language of democracy and human rights. Europe had entered a new, post-communist age.

NOTES

1. For this phrase, see http://www.margaretthatcher.org/document/105592.

2. Renzo Foa, "E così cambia tutt'il continente," *L'Unità*, 11 November 1989, 1.

3. Gale Stokes, *The Walls Came Tumbling Down* (Oxford: Oxford University Press, 1993), 167.

4. Dimitri Volkogonov, *The Rise and Fall of the Soviet Empire* (New York: HarperCollins, 1998), 436–38.

5. Archie Brown, *The Gorbachev Factor* (Oxford: Oxford University Press, 1996), 56.

6. Eduard Shevardnadze, *The Future Belongs to Freedom* (London: Sinclair-Stevenson, 1991), 37.

7. "Z" (pseud. Martin Malia), "To the Stalin Mausoleum," *Daedalus* 119 (1990): 323.

8. For a technical assessment of the damage done by the Chernobyl disaster, see Harold M. Ginzburg and Eric Reis, "Consequences of the Nuclear Power Plant Accident at Chernobyl," *Public Health Reports* 106: 32–40.

9. See Valerie Bunce, "The Empire Strikes Back: The Evolution of the Eastern Bloc from a Soviet Asset to a Soviet Liability," *International Organization* 39 (1985): 1–46, for this thesis.

10. See Mikhail S. Gorbachev, *Perestroika: New Thinking for Our Country and the World* (New York: HarperCollins, 1987). Quote from Seweryn Bialer, "Gorbachev's Program of Change: Sources, Significance, Prospects," *Political Science Quarterly* 103 (1988): 422.

11. This thesis is impressively argued in Stephen Kotkin, *Armageddon Averted: The Soviet Collapse 1970–2000* (Oxford: Oxford University Press, 2001).

12. My debt in these paragraphs on economic reform to Brown, *The Gorbachev Factor*, 130–55, will be obvious to anybody who has read the book. For greater detail, see Anders Aslund, *Gorbachev's Struggle for Economic Reform* (Ithaca, NY: Cornell University Press, 1989).

13. Bialer, "Gorbachev's Program of Change," 410.

14. Kotkin, *Armageddon*, 88 for sales figures.

15. Mikhail S. Gorbachev, opening speech to the twelfth special session of the Supreme Soviet of the USSR, *Documents and Materials* (Moscow: Novosti Press Agency, 1988), 6.

16. Andrei D. Sakharov, *Progress, Coexistence and Intellectual Freedom* (London: Pelican, 1969), 32.

17. For a summary of the European reaction, see Geir Lundestad, *The United States and Western Europe since 1945* (Oxford: Oxford University Press, 2005), 228–29.

18. George Bush and Brent Scowcroft, *A World Transformed* (New York: Knopf, 1998), 155.

19. John Van Oudenaren, *Détente in Europe: The Soviet Union and the West since 1953* (Durham, NC: Duke University Press, 1991), 367–73.

20. For Kohl's gaffe, see Hannes Adomeit, *Imperial Overstretch: Germany in Soviet Policy from Stalin to Gorbachev* (Baden-Baden: Nomos Verlagsgesellschaft, 1998), 259–63.

21. Marie-Pierre Rey, "Gorbachev's New Thinking and Europe," in *Europe and the End of the Cold War: A Reappraisal*, ed. Frédéric Bozo, Marie-Pierre Rey, N. Piers Ludlow, and Leopoldo Nuti (London: Routledge, 2008), 28–29.

22. Address by M. S. Gorbachev to the Council of Europe, 6 July 1989, Centre Virtuel del Connaissance sur l'Europe (CVCE), http://www.ena.lu.

23. See Mark Kramer, "Beyond the Brezhnev Doctrine," *International Security* 14 (1989–1990), 3: 25–67, for an article that both cites Tocqueville and concludes that "Hungary, East Germany and Czechoslovakia could easily experience periods of serious domestic turmoil within the next five to ten years." The right time frame was in fact five to ten days.

24. Statistics from Karen Dawisha, *Eastern Europe, Gorbachev and Reform: The Great Challenge* (Cambridge: Cambridge University Press, 1990), 170.

25. Dennis Deletant, *Romania under Communist Rule* (Oxford: Centre for Romanian Studies, 1999), 126.

26. Statistics from Tom Gallagher, *Romania after Ceauşescu* (Edinburgh: Edinburgh University Press, 1995), 65.

27. See Peter Siani-Davis, *The Romanian Revolution of 1989* (Ithaca, NY: Cornell University Press, 2005), 22–26.

28. Manfred Görtemaker, *Unifying Germany 1989–1990* (New York: Saint Martin's Press, 1994), 40. The irony is deliberate.

29. Joseph Rothschild and Nancy M. Wingfield, *Return to Diversity: A Political History of East Central Europe since World War II* (Oxford: Oxford University Press, 2000), 235.

30. Such petty harassment was transformed into literature in Václav Havel, "Reports on My House Arrest," *Open Letters* (London: Faber and Faber, 1991), 215–29.

31. R. J. Crampton, *The Balkans since the Second World War* (London: Longmans, 2003), 177.

32. Victor Sebesteyn, *Revolution 1989: The Fall of the Soviet Empire* (London: Weidenfeld & Nicholson, 2009), 146–48.

33. Jan B. de Weydenthal, "The Pope's Visit to Poland," RFE/RAD Background report 105, 26 June 1987.

34. The driving force behind the campaign for this act of retrospective justice was Miklós Vásárhelyi, Nagy's press secretary, the only survivor of the 1956 leadership team.

35. See "A Letter to General Kiszczak," in Adam Michnik, *Letters from Prison and Other Essays* (Berkeley: University of California Press, 1987), 64–70. Michnik calls him a "vindictive, dishonorable swine" among other choice insults.

36. Lech Wałęsa, *The Struggle and the Triumph* (New York: Arcade Publishers, 1992), 174, jokes that the Polish Round Table was twenty-nine feet wide because the world spitting record was twenty-eight feet.

37. *Keesing's*, April 1989, 36578, has a succinct account of the accords. A very useful book on the Polish transition to democracy is Marjorie Castle, *Triggering Communism's Collapse: Perceptions and Power in Poland's Transition* (Lanham, MD: Rowman & Littlefield, 2003).

38. Rothschild and Wingfield, *Return to Diversity*, 230.

39. Bronisław Geremek, *La Rupture: La Pologne du communisme à la démocratie* (Paris: Éditions du Seuil, 1991), 157.

40. Bush and Scowcroft, *A World Transformed*, 122.

41. Timothy Garton Ash, *The Magic Lantern* (New York: Random House, 1990), 37.

42. Wałęsa, *The Struggle and the Triumph*, 219.

43. The West German foreign minister, Hans-Dietrich Genscher, who played a crucial role in persuading the GDR to let the refugees leave, significantly begins his memoirs with a description of the Prague crisis. H-D. Genscher, *Rebuilding a House Divided* (New York: Broadway Books, 1998), 1–12.

44. Harold James and Marla Stone, *When the Wall Came Down: Reactions to German Unification* (London: Routledge, 1992), 119–23.

45. See Adomeit, *Imperial Overstretch*, 401–13, for a superb reconstruction of Gorbachev's visit to East Berlin. Adomeit is skeptical of claims that Gorbachev pushed Honecker hard to begin reforms.

46. Görtemaker, *Unifying Germany 1989–1990*, 83.

47. A point made by Stokes, *The Walls Came Tumbling Down*, 138.

48. Sebesteyn, *Revolution 1989*, 122, estimates that there was a Stasi informer or staff member for every sixty-three citizens. Five percent of the GDR's government budget was spent on the secret police.

49. Konrad Jarausch, *The Rush to German Unity* (Oxford: Oxford University Press, 1994), 62.

50. See, for instance, Günter Grass, "Don't Reunify Germany," *New York Times*, 7 January 1990; reprinted in James and Stone, *When the Wall Came Down*, 57–59. In German, of course, the literature is huge. Grass claimed that a "reunited Germany would be a colossus, bedevilled by complexes and blocking its own path and the path to European unity."

51. Kyril Drezov, "The Transition Comes Full Circle, 1989–1997," in *Experimenting with Democracy: Regime Change in the Balkans*, ed. Geoffrey Pridham and Tom Gallagher (London: Routledge, 2000), 200.

52. Letter from Foreign Minister Petar Mladenov to the Central Committee of the Bulgarian Communist Party, 24 October, 1989. *Cold War History Project*, http://digitalarchive.wilsoncenter.org/document/112510.

53. Crampton, *The Balkans since the Second World War*, 308.

54. Dubček's address was reprinted in *Il Mulino* 38 (1989), 1. Quotation from p. 6.

55. Quoted in Bernard Wheaton and Zdenek Kavan, *The Velvet Revolution: Czechoslovakia, 1988–1991* (Boulder, CO: Westview Press, 1992), 196–97.

56. John Keene, *Vaclav Havel: A Political Tragedy in Six Acts* (London: Bloomsbury, 1999), 341.

57. Wheaton and Kavan, *The Velvet Revolution*, 46.

58. The mood of these meetings, along with the rest of the velvet revolution, is vividly evoked in "Prague: Inside the Magic Lantern," in Ash, *The Magic Lantern*, 78–130.

59. Ash, *The Magic Lantern*, 130.

60. Václav Havel, *Open Letters*, 396.

61. Wałęsa, *The Struggle and the Triumph*, 233.

62. Jacques Levesque, "The East European Revolutions of 1989," in the *Cambridge History of the Cold War*, vol. 3: *Endings*, ed. Melvyn P. Leffler and Odd Arne Westad (Cambridge: Cambridge University Press, 2010), goes still further and contends, 332, that the "East European revolutions occurred when Gorbachev's tolerance for reform surpassed anything that his contemporaries had imagined. As his tolerance became clear, the reformers were emboldened, as were Bush and Kohl. East European peoples had long yearned for change; Gorbachev made it possible."

63. Deletant, *Romania under Communist Rule*, 154–55.

64. Deletant, *Romania under Communist Rule*, 140.

65. Quoted Siani-Davis, *The Romanian Revolution*, 28.

66. Vladimir Tismăneanu, *Stalinism for All Seasons: A Political History of Romanian Communism* (Berkeley: University of California Press, 2003), 212.

67. Siani-Davis, *The Romanian Revolution*, 57.

68. John Sweeny, *The Life and Evil Times of Nicolae Ceaușescu* (London: Hutchinson, 1991), 203.

69. Siani-Davis, *The Romanian Revolution*, 130.

70. Mark Almond, *The Rise and Fall of Nicolae and Elena Ceaușescu* (London: Chapman, 1992), xii.

Chapter Twelve

Unifications and Dissolutions

The events of 1989 presented Europeans with a new set of challenges. First and foremost, the question of what to do with Germany had to be decided. The ordinary people of the GDR wanted to be united with their fellow Germans in the West. The slogan "We are One People" stated a simple truth that policy makers had to deal with. The desire for a definitive breach with the GDR gained momentum, moreover, as democratization led to the opening of the Stasi archives and citizens learned just how many of their neighbors had been spying on them. East Germans voted with their feet throughout the winter of 1989 and the spring of the new year. Trabants loaded high with suitcases sputtered along the *Autobahnen* of West Germany, as *Ossis* headed westward in search of work, long-lost relatives, and a better life.

The prospect of a unified Germany raised all kinds of fears. Prime Minister Margaret Thatcher of Great Britain was not alone in worrying that a united Germany would become the continent's hegemon—and perhaps its ruler. Would a united Germany be neutral? Or remain in NATO? Or even be a member of both NATO and the Warsaw Pact? NATO membership was the White House's preferred solution. But how would the USSR respond to a united Germany in NATO? Would the GDR be ingested by West Germany, or would Germany unify through a treaty negotiated between two equal sovereign states? Would the new Germany's borders remain unaltered, or would the border with Poland be redrawn? Would the two Germanies be integrated in a currency union and, if so, would the economy of the GDR be able to withstand the impact of using the same money? How much would restructuring the GDR's economy cost?

As 1990 dawned, nobody had an answer to any of these questions; indeed, most of Europe's leaders still did not grasp that all these questions would be on the agenda in the next few months. Yet by October 1990,

Germany had become one nation once more. The principal architect of this achievement was Chancellor Helmut Kohl and his diplomatic aides, although Kohl needed the loyalty and cooperation of U.S. President George H. W. Bush, the pragmatism of President François Mitterrand of France, and the generosity, perhaps the overgenerosity, of Mikhail S. Gorbachev.

Kohl boasted an essential qualification for great statesmanship: luck. He was the right man in the right place at the right time. If the GDR had collapsed a year later, it would have been harder to incorporate it into the West. Conditions in the USSR were deteriorating fast, and opposition to Gorbachev was growing faster. Nevertheless, as Machiavelli advised in *The Prince*, Kohl made a friend of fortune in 1990 by acting with daring, not caution.[1] His *prowess* as a statesman was confirmed by the deftness with which he handled events.

This is not to dispute that the United States, in Frank Costigliola's words, had an "arm around the shoulder" of West Germany throughout the year (although, as Costigliola shrewdly points out, "Bonn was often able to use the arm-around-the-shoulder to steer them"), still less that 1990 was George H. W. Bush's "finest hour."[2] It is merely to underline that the end of the Cold War in Europe was not only the end of the conflict between the superpowers, but an upheaval in the European political order. Europeans, naturally enough, were its principal protagonists.

This was not least because German unity required a new conception of European unity. A second huge challenge for political leaders was whether the European Community, which had hitherto mostly occupied itself with trade and agriculture issues, could become a polity capable of encompassing a reconstituted Germany and of possessing a political identity of its own. With the exception of Margaret Thatcher, who placed herself in the path of history's chariot and was knocked over by it, the EC's leaders concluded that it could. They accordingly accelerated the pace of European integration. The Treaty on European Union, signed at Maastricht in December 1991, was a major development for the so-called European construction. Here, too, Kohl's leadership, in conjunction with French President Mitterrand, was courageous and, in the short term, successful—though whether history will be so kind to Kohl for his paternity of the EU as it has been for his role in unifying Germany is a matter over which the jury is still out.

The unification of Germany was a seismic shift in post-1989 European politics that was followed by a series of aftershocks of comparable magnitude. The USSR crumbled in 1991, and its collapse led to statehood for several European peoples—the long-oppressed Estonians, Lithuanians, and Latvians perhaps most felicitously. Yugoslavia disintegrated, and the consequences of its fall were dire: Balkan ghosts rubbed Europe's nose in its inability to pacify its own neighborhood. Czechoslovakia fell apart peacefully, though noisily. Albania, the last redoubt of Stalinism in Europe, became a failed state on Italy's doorstep—but Italy's own democracy was hardly a model of stability itself and, in fact, Italy became the most prominent western casualty of the Cold War's end.

EINHEIT

There were three principal obstacles to rapid German unification in 1990: membership of NATO, the economic disparity between the two halves of Germany, and domestic and wider European reluctance toward the idea of a united Germany. If one looks back at how events unfolded, one sees that Kohl resolved all three problems by wielding Bonn's mightiest weapon: its checkbook. By promising East Germans western standards of living, Kohl stoked the demand for unity among the GDR's citizens to the point that civil disorder would have broken out had it been denied. This presented opponents of unity elsewhere in Europe and in West Germany with a fait accompli. By extending loans and subsidies to Moscow, Kohl was subsequently able to "bribe" the Soviets into accepting all-German membership of NATO and early withdrawal of Soviet troops from German soil.[3] In short, Helmut Kohl grasped, sooner than anyone, that the early 1990s was not a moment for penny pinching, but for swift action.

Nevertheless, until February 1990, most Germans believed that a "two-state" solution was inevitable. Kohl proposed precisely this on 28 November 1989 when, speaking before the German parliament, he launched a ten-point plan intended to provide a road map toward eventual German unity. The plan, which advocated the rapid democratization of the GDR and the creation of "confederative structures" between the two states within a broader context of the process of European integration, was a harbinger of the style the German chancellor would adopt over the next year. As he said in his speech, the previous policy, begun by Willy Brandt, of taking "small steps" to encourage closeness with the GDR had been superseded by events.[4]

The chancellor might have been more diplomatic. Kohl did not communicate an advance text of his speech to President Mitterrand, and the French leader was offended by this lack of due respect.[5] The Bush administration, by contrast, was apprised of Kohl's intentions, although only at the last moment. The ten-point plan was anyway overtaken by events. The GDR imploded between December 1989 and February 1990. There were two main reasons for its collapse. First, the SED failed to democratize rapidly enough. Some measures were taken: Egon Krenz was ousted in December 1989 and replaced by a young lawyer called Gregor Grysi. Assorted criminals, including, as we have seen, Erich Honecker, were expelled from the party's ranks. But the SED leadership evaded root-and-branch reform of East German society. In January, alarmed by reports that files were being burned, protesters occupied Stasi buildings and called for its abolition. Prime Minister Hans Modrow, the former party chief in Dresden, whose leadership in November 1989 had won him widespread admiration, refused to get rid of the Stasi outright, a decision that had the effect of a "frost in springtime" on the public mood in Germany.[6]

The second reason for the GDR's implosion was economic. East Germany was bankrupt. The country could no longer service its external debt or pay for its welfare state. Its young people were fleeing the country, causing dislocation to production, and there was no way to stop them. Why live in the GDR when to live under democracy, and perhaps prosperity, all one had to do was fill the Traby with gas and head west? Bonn realized that bailing out East Berlin would be a waste of money. If it wanted to prevent "the citizens of Leipzig from moving toward the DM, it was necessary that the DM should go to them."[7] On 7 February 1990, Kohl proposed that the two Germanies should form a monetary and economic union. In effect, almost fifty years after it had benefited from the enlightened self-interest of the United States, West Germany now mooted a Marshall Plan of its own for the cousins who had drawn the short straw in 1945.

"Deutsche Marks for all" was a potent slogan in the GDR elections of 18 March 1990, which were, in effect, a referendum on *Einheit* (unity). Kohl stumped the country in support of the East German Christian Democrats (CDU) and their leader, Lothar de Maizière. "At stake is our German fatherland, at stake is a common future in Europe," the federal chancellor told cheering crowds.[8] The SPD had been the polls' favorite until Kohl played the card of unity with such vigor. Making an inept misjudgment of the national mood, the SPD warned against rapid unification throughout the campaign. The final result was a triumph for Kohl. The CDU-led alliance of center-right parties took over 48 percent of the votes, more than the 22 percent of the SPD and the 16.4 percent of Gregor Gysi's Party of Democratic Socialism (PDS), as the SED had rebranded itself. *Bündnis 90*, a party uniting the various civic groups that had played such an important role in November 1989, obtained a dismal 3 percent. De Maizière became the last premier of the GDR, although he was effectively Kohl's chamberlain. By the end of March 1990, the GDR was a sovereign state only in name.

The state treaty on economic unity, which proclaimed itself to be "a first significant step toward the achievement of political unity," was signed on 18 May 1990. From 1 July 1990, wages, salaries, welfare checks, and pensions were to be paid to East Germans in DM at a 1:1 rate. Debts were to be converted at a 2:1 rate, while savings were exchanged on a graduated scale: children under fourteen could exchange 2,000 East German marks at 1:1, while adults under sixty years of age had an allowance of 4,000 marks. Oversixties were able to exchange 6,000 marks at parity. Higher figures were exchanged at a 2:1 rate. These exchange rates bore no relationship to the free market price.

Of course, there was a catch. East Germany's subsidized foodstuffs and other necessities were phased out. Billions of DM were transported to the GDR's banks in time for 1 July, but consumers spent only part of their windfall. Just by going into their stores, which magically filled with western brands far superior to nondescript domestic products but also far dearer, East Germans realized that unification would not provide them with West German living standards. Unemployment surged at once, as the GDR's inefficient firms faced western competition: competition that the conversion of wages at the 1:1 rate made worse. To cope with the crisis, the West German government set up a state holding company called the *Treuhandanstalt* that shut down inefficient enterprises and privatized the survivors, and made cash transfers to the East to ease the pains of transition. The state treaty called for a "Germany Unity Fund" of DM 155 billion, of which DM 22 billion was earmarked for 1990 and DM 35 billion for 1991. But Kohl took care that such transfers did not imply higher taxes before the first all-German elections, which were scheduled for December 1990.

Economic unity—and the political unity that followed on from it—was only possible because of a successful parallel process of negotiations with with West Germany's partners in the EC and with the four wartime allies. For German unification to lead to full national sovereignty, Bonn needed to get the Soviets out of the GDR and united Germany into NATO and to persuade the eleven other European Community states to agree to a de facto enlargement of the Community.

The EC nations welcomed the fall of the Wall from the humanitarian point of view, but feared that a united Germany would be less committed to European integration. The EC had recently drawn up a blueprint for monetary union (the so-called Delors Report), and the EC's leaders had endorsed its conclusions at the Madrid meeting of the European Council in June 1989. Kohl backtracked on the monetary issue in November 1989. In Paris, his behavior was interpreted as a "sign of lack of interest in European integration," and as the dramatic collapse of East Germany absorbed his energies, French worries became more pronounced.[9] Would the Germans turn their back on the EC and seek to develop a special relationship with Russia and the United States?

Kohl's ten-point plan of 28 November 1989, despite its strongly pro-European tone in point seven, brought such fears to the surface. Foreign Minister Hans-Dietrich Genscher, who visited President Mitterrand on 30 November 1989, was exposed to the "full force of the president's fears and warnings."[10] Mitterrand told Genscher that if "integration in the West stood still," new "privileged alliances" would be formed. "It was not impossible that Europe would regress to the political ideas prevailing before the First

World War," the French president warned.[11] At the Strasbourg European Council on 8–9 December 1989, the German chancellor conceded that negotiations on monetary union would proceed, though not before December 1990. Had Kohl not made this concession, the summit's final communiqué would likely have been even more tepid than it actually was in welcoming events in East Germany—as it was, the EC's statement was ringed with qualifications and was merely "attached to the report on developments in Central and Eastern Europe."[12]

Kohl later recalled that he had "never participated at a European summit with such an icy atmosphere."[13] The German leader was subjected to a "cross-examination worthy of a trial." The fact that West Germany had always been one of the "warmest partisans" of European integration and that the Community benefited from Germany's "contributions to its coffers" counted for nothing. Kohl concluded that only Spain's Felipe Gonzalez and Ireland's Charles Haughey, of the twelve community leaders present, were favorable to the idea of a united Germany.[14]

A "German Europe" was a specter that disquieted most of the leaders who sat around the Strasbourg table, even Kohl's fellow Christian Democrats such as the veteran Italian leader Giulio Andreotti and Dutch Premier Ruud Lubbers, let alone Thatcher, who was in aggressive form. As *Le Monde* argued on 23 December 1989, Germany disturbed its neighbors primarily because of the "instability" that its economic prowess might create on the continent. A "single market, monetary union, a central bank" were essential, the Paris daily editorialized, if "one wishes to save Germany from the temptation of single-handedly choosing its own destiny."[15]

The German government underlined that any new German house would be "built beneath a European roof." In February–March 1990 Paris and Bonn negotiated hard to carry European integration forward. Mitterrand's role was crucial: contrary to accounts that portray the French leader as an opponent of German unification, the evidence shows that Mitterrand believed that German unification could be transformed into an opportunity for the European project as a whole.[16] The main doubter, of course, was Prime Minister Margaret Thatcher. Unlike, say, Andreotti, who was quick "to comprehend that the Bonn government would be able to attain its objective of bringing about a unified Germany in a relatively short spell of time," and adjusted foreign policy to suit, Thatcher was against both rapid German unification and further measures of European integration, which is a "fact that goes a long way to explaining her isolation on both issues."[17]

The Franco-German discussions resulted, on 19 April 1990, in Kohl and Mitterrand's sending a letter to Premier Charles Haughey, ten days before a meeting of the European Council in the Irish capital of Dublin. In this letter, the two leaders stated that it was necessary to "accelerate the political construction of the Europe of the Twelve" with the objective of signing a treaty embodying both economic and monetary union and political union within 1 January 1993. They proposed the constitution of an intergovernmental conference (IGC) on political union that would have four specific goals: strengthening the "democratic legitimacy" of the union; rendering its institutions more efficient; ensuring "unity and coherence" of the EC's "political action"; and defining and implementing a "common foreign and security policy."[18]

At Dublin, Kohl underlined that the costs of integrating East Germany would be borne by the German taxpayer. Germany would not expect other member states to reduce payouts from the EC's regional development funds or ask for cuts in farm subsidies. The GDR's integration would be "carried out without revision of the treaties."[19] Twenty million Germans would be joining the Community, but Germany would not get an immediate increase in its voting power.

The final communiqué of the Dublin summit accorded German unification a place of honor. The Community

> warmly welcomes German unification. It looks forward to the positive and fruitful contribution that all Germans can make following the forthcoming integration of the territory of the German Democratic Republic into the Community. We are confident that German unification—the result of a freely expressed wish on the part of the German people—will be a positive factor in the development of Europe as a whole and of the Community in particular.[20]

The European Commission subsequently drafted legislation that permitted the EC to absorb the GDR and worked throughout the summer of 1990 to prepare East German accession.[21] Underlying this willingness to skip the summer vacation was a determination not to derail the ongoing "1992 process" of creating a single market in goods, people, capital, and services. This had been the raison d'être of the EC since the signature of the so-called Single European Act in January 1986 and was the principal cause of the EC's rising stature in Washington.[22] As Falke has argued, "integrity of the Single Market project had preference over exceptional status for Germany as a whole or the former GDR territory."[23] On 28 August 1990 the commission approved a package of measures that ensured that 80 percent of extant EC law would be immediately effective, after unification, in the territories of the former GDR. The remainder would be enacted by 1 January 1993, with some derogations being permitted in the environmental field until 1995. It is no exaggeration to claim that the commission became "a major (if silent) actor in the unification process."[24]

After Ireland, the presidency of the EC passed to the Italians, who organized the so-called ambush in Rome on 27–28 October 1990 whereby Prime Minister Thatcher found herself faced with a fait accompli in the form of a commitment from the other eleven member states to accelerate monetary union and to negotiate on a long list of political developments, notably on the need for a common foreign policy and greater powers for the European Parliament. Thatcher rejected the Rome summit's drive to greater European unity, but her stand was politically fatal since a revolt against her leadership engineered by the Conservative Party's pro-European wing cost her the premiership in November 1990.

The rapid drive to German unity, in short, had been decisive in putting political union on the table in Brussels. Kohl, once again, was the key actor. His willingness to link the process of German unity, even if this meant potentially sacrificing the DM, to the project of constructing greater European unity was perceived as a safe way of giving the Germans the nationhood that most Europeans believed to be their right. The eventual Treaty on European Union (February 1992), which drew up the rules for the introduction of a single currency, strengthened the powers of the European Parliament, and outlined a commitment toward a common foreign policy, generated euphoria in Western Europe for this reason. The visions of the postwar advocates of a federal Europe seemed to be on the verge of coming true.

By the Rome summit in October 1990, Germany was already a unified country—the ceremony had been held on 3 October. Contemporaneously with the tumultuous events inside Germany, and the acceleration in the process of European integration described in the last paragraphs, in 1990 Kohl had also conducted a hardheaded negotiation with Soviet leader Gorbachev that ended with the German chancellor swapping hard cash for quick Soviet withdrawal from German territory.

Gorbachev privately accepted that German unification was inevitable as early as the end of January 1990 at an ad hoc meeting of a "small circle of top decision makers" (in 1987, he had said that "a hundred years" might be an appropriate time frame). The decision became a matter of public record after talks with U.S. Secretary of State James Baker on 9 February and with Kohl and Genscher in Moscow on 10 and 11 February 1990. As he told Kohl, Gorbachev now believed that "the Germans themselves have to make their own choice." *Pravda* stated that Gorbachev and Kohl agreed that "the Germans themselves have to . . . choose the forms of statehood and at what time, at what speed, and under what conditions they will realize . . . unity."[25] The Soviet blessing did not solve, however, the thorny problem of what role a united Germany would play in the new European security structure.

The United States wanted to make a strengthened NATO the cornerstone of European security in the 1990s. The only united Germany Washington was prepared to accept was one embedded in NATO and in which U.S. troops continued to be garrisoned in at least the western half. Kohl agreed. At a 24 February 1990 meeting at Camp David, the German Chancellor and President Bush affirmed that "a unified Germany should remain a full member of the North Atlantic Treaty Organization, including participation in its military structure" and that U.S. troops should be stationed in Germany and elsewhere in Europe. They recognized, however, that the "former territory of the GDR should have a special military status."[26] At the same time Washington did not want to jeopardize Gorbachev's position with hard-liners in Moscow by overemphasizing NATO. Secretary of State James Baker, indeed, had promised Gorbachev during a Moscow summit in early February that NATO would not move "one inch eastward" if Russia allowed a unified Germany to join it.[27] The Soviet Union's leaders had a more ambiguous position, but many preferred German neutrality, or a solution whereby Germany was outside the NATO command structure, even if it was linked to the West politically.

The superpowers' positions mattered, of course, since Germany could only become a united nation after the signature of a treaty of peace with the wartime allies. This, however, raised the question of which allies. Should there be a peace conference with thirty or more countries asking for reparations and guarantees? If so, no one could predict how long unification would be delayed. At a conference in Ottowa, Canada, on 12–13 February 1990, straight after the Gorbachev-Kohl meeting, the superpowers' foreign ministers decided that a treaty should be negotiated by the two Germanies plus the four occupation powers. This decision irritated the Dutch and the Italians in particular, but as German Foreign Minister Genscher cuttingly told his Italian counterpart: "You are not in this game."[28] The so-called 2+4 talks, which would lead to the signature, in Moscow, on 12 September 1990 of the treaty on the "Final Settlement with Respect to Germany," began in the spring.

In the final 2+4 treaty, the two Germanies accepted that the "external borders" of the new Germany should be the existing ones of the FRG and the GDR. This reassured Poland that its western border was safe, for during the March 1990 election in the GDR, Kohl, while making assurances that a united Germany would respect the Helsinki principle of the inviolability of borders, had not unequivocally certified the border's permanence. Now, Germany further pledged that it would sign a treaty with Poland confirming the border's status, once unification had taken place.

In Article 2 of the treaty, the two Germanies underlined that "only peace will emanate from German soil"; renounced nuclear, chemical, and biological weapons in perpetuity; and undertook to "reduce the personnel strength of the armed forces of the united Germany to 370,000 (ground, air and naval forces) within three to four years." Article 4 of the treaty specified that Soviet troops were to be removed from united Germany by the end of 1994. Troops from the other occupying powers would remain in Berlin so long as the Soviet troops remained in the GDR, and only "territorial defense units" of the German army could be stationed in the former GDR prior to that date. Non-German troops and nuclear weapons would not be deployed on the soil of the former GDR, but the "right of the united Germany to belong to alliances" was not be affected by the treaty: Germany, in other words, could adhere to NATO if it wanted.

This extraordinary outcome, which only ten months previously would have seemed like science fiction, and which even in May 1990 had been explicitly rejected by Gorbachev, was achieved through intense diplomacy that has already been analyzed many times in greater detail than is possible here.[29]

Two western moves were crucial in persuading the Soviet leadership to sign up to this pact. First, NATO, pressed hard by President Bush, who publicly declared the Cold War to be over, issued the so-called Declaration of London on 5–6 July 1990. The declaration was timed to coincide with the Congress of the Soviet Communist Party, at which Gorbachev was subjected to "bitter, vulgar and unrelenting attacks from opponents who wanted to oust him," and conveyed the idea that Gorbachev's new foreign policy had made the USSR safer, not weaker as his internal enemies alleged.[30] It did seemingly buy the Soviet leader some more time.

Stating that "Europe has entered a new, promising era," the declaration proclaimed that NATO, the "most successful defensive alliance in history," now had a new task: ensuring security and building trust between former enemies. The "Atlantic Community," the declaration intoned, "must reach out to the countries of the East which were our adversaries in the Cold War, and extend to them the hand of friendship." In concrete terms, the alliance proposed, "in return for reciprocal action by the Soviet Union," the "elimination of all its nuclear artillery shells from Europe" and promised to adopt a new strategy "making nuclear forces truly weapons of last resort" (France— shades of the General—stressed that its strategy of massive retaliation would not alter a jot).

It is hard to know what else the West's leaders could have done. They had won, but out of concern for Gorbachev were not rubbing it in. The declaration further urged that the CSCE, which was the favorite child of both German Foreign Minister Genscher and the French government, "should become more prominent in Europe's future," though as Sarotte points out, in the presummit briefing of President Bush by his senior national security advisers, it was underlined that the CSCE should not become a "risk to NATO's dominance."[31] The London Declaration's peroration, "we are determined to create enduring peace on this continent," was nevertheless much more than stale rhetoric.

The second, truly crucial, western move was made by Chancellor Kohl. The German Chancellor met Gorbachev first in Moscow and then flew to the Soviet leader's vacation home near Stavropol in the Crimea, on 16 July 1990. It was in these two encounters that Gorbachev made the key concessions on German membership of NATO and withdrawal of Soviet troops from East Germany that made the 2+4 treaty possible.[32] In exchange, Kohl had to spend big money. West Germany was already subsidizing the Soviet occupying forces, who, after the introduction of the DM on 1 July, had found themselves stranded in East Germany without hard currency. At the Crimea summit, Bonn agreed to pay the Soviets to leave. On September 7 and 10, the two principals, after their negotiators had reached a stalemate, fixed an immediate DM 3 billion credit and a further DM 12 billion to pay for the relocation of Soviet troops by 1994. In Moscow, hard-liners thought Gorbachev had given away the store and got little in return; in Bonn many paled at the sums that Kohl was spending to make the GDR part of a single, democratic nation.

Unification in 1990 in fact would have been impossible had democratic Germany been more spendthrift in the previous decades. Buying out the occupying Soviet army was only a drop in the ocean of cash poured into the former GDR over the next decade. Between 1991 and 1999, the German state invested DM 1.6 trillion in the former GDR, via welfare payments, pensions, infrastructure investments, and subsidies. The united country's eastern provinces contributed only DM 400 billion in taxes. Once the December 1990 elections were over, a 7.5 percent "solidarity tax" was imposed on German taxpayers, but a significant part of the immediate costs of reunification was paid for by a surge in public debt.[33]

This description of the costs associated with German reunification underlines a final point. The GDR was essentially annexed by its richer cousin in the West. The Treaty on the Restoration of State Unity, signed on 31 August 1990, dissolved the GDR into the five länder (provinces) of Brandenburg, Mecklenburg-Western Pomerania, Saxony, Saxony-Anhalt, and Thuringia, plus the metropolitan province of Berlin. The West German Basic Law, or constitution, would apply throughout the new provinces; Berlin was to be the capital of the German nation once again.

The costs of unity were still in the future. On 3 October 1990, along with hundreds of thousands of his fellow citizens, Helmut Kohl, his labors temporarily over, was able to enjoy the unification ceremony in front of the Reichstag in Berlin. Less than eleven months had passed since the Wall had been breached. In December 1990, the CDU, with 44 percent of the vote, and its FDP allies, with a record-breaking 11 percent that was a personal vote for the popular foreign minister, Hans-Dietrich Genscher, routed the SPD in the all-German elections. The SPD's left-wing candidate for the chancellorship, Oskar Lafontaine, who had been the victim of a near-fatal knife attack earlier in the year, fought a campaign characterized by "acerbic and petulant criticism" of Helmut Kohl for having risked the West's prosperity for the sake of rushing to unity.[34] Such rancor seemed petty to most voters, especially in the former GDR. The Cold War, which had arguably begun with Soviet troops draping a red flag on the ruins of the Reichstag in May 1945, had concluded in front of the same edifice. Helmut Kohl was a protagonist of the vast political process that had brought the conflict to an end. It was churlish to dispute his achievement, which was all the more remarkable because it aroused so little opposition from Germany's European neighbors. Voters reflected that Kohl deserved his moment of glory, which was the culmination of his predecessors' successful efforts to build trust in West Germany.

REDRAWING THE MAPS

According to Tony Judt, the end of the Cold War was accompanied by "a making and breaking of nations . . . comparable in scale to the impact of the Versailles treaties that followed World War One."[35] The Soviet Union, the last great European multinational *imperium*, dissolved into its constituent nationalities in the year following 3 October 1990. In the process, the three Baltic republics rejoined Europe by remaining aloof from the post-Soviet Commonwealth of Independent States (CIS) constructed in December 1991 by Boris Yeltsin. The two component parts of Czechoslovakia separated in a velvet divorce; Yugoslavia's breakup, even before the conflict in Bosnia became a killing field, was both bloody and confused.

The most significant of all these transformations was, of course, the collapse of the Soviet house of cards. In 1989 through 1991, the subject nations of the Soviet state began to press for greater freedom. The Baltic republics, inevitably, were in the forefront of this process. Protests over environmental issues, and over a feared new influx of Russians to staff the mining industry, began as early as 1987 especially in Estonia, where Russians already accounted for nearly a third of the population.[36] In the same year, symbolic protests took place in all three Baltic republics to commemorate the signature of the Nazi-Soviet Pact, whose so-called secret protocol had sanctioned the Soviet occupation in 1940.

In 1988 through 1989, "popular fronts" were formed to press for greater cultural and economic autonomy. Cultural events, notably festivals of traditional songs in Estonia, attracted huge crowds openly waving the three nations' long-banned flags. In Lithuania, Sajūdis, a mass movement ostensibly supporting perestroika, became an authentic force of opposition. Led by Vytautas Landsbergis, a professor of music, in March 1989 Sajūdis contested elections to the Congress of People's Deputies and won a landslide majority among Lithuanian-speaking voters. On 23 August 1989, the fiftieth anniversary of the Nazi-Soviet Pact, a million supporters of self-determination formed a human chain from the southern border of Lithuania to Tallinn, the capital of Estonia. Even by the standards of that remarkable year, it was a moving protest, one which showed that the vast majority of the people in the three republics wished to regain their freedom. In December 1989, the existence of the secret protocol was at last admitted and Moscow was robbed of any last vestiges of moral legitimacy for its rule over the Baltic peoples. A callous deal with Hitler was hardly a sound juridical basis for a claim to sovereign rights. By December 1989, even the Communist parties of these countries backed secession from Moscow. The Balts' calls for independence, however, were a red rag for an angry bear. The unstoppable drive to German unification and the democratization measures initiated by Gorbachev were unpopular among hard-liners in the Soviet leadership. Giving the Baltic States the independence they craved was a line that the hard-liners—including, on this issue, Gorbachev himself—refused to cross. They were well aware that it might have a domino effect throughout the USSR.

When, on 11 March 1990, the Lithuanian Supreme Council (as its Supreme Soviet had renamed itself), presided over by Landsbergis, voted by 124 votes to zero to declare independence, Gorbachev rejected any notion that Vilnius's action was legal. As Alex Pravda has argued, the Soviet leader "continued to underestimate the strength of popular feeling involved. He tended to attribute the protests to economic discontent, inept local officials, and the agitation of a handful of opportunistic secessionists," rather than to a genuine desire for national self-determination.[37]

Failure to understand this point led Gorbachev into intolerance. In April, Moscow announced a new law on secession from the USSR: would-be breakaways would have to hold referendums passed by a two-thirds majority and endure a five-year transition period before becoming independent. The Baltic republics naturally disputed that this law was applicable to them: so far as they were concerned, the USSR had been occupying them illegally since 1940. When the Lithuanians showed no signs of climbing down, Gorbachev cut off gas and oil supplies. The Lithuanians responded by cycling to work and keeping themselves warm with wood fires, but were nonetheless forced to suspend their claim to independence in June 1990. All attempts by Lithuanian leaders to secure support from the western democracies—almost none of whom had ever formally recognized Soviet sovereignty over the three Baltic republics—were rebuffed, especially by François Mitterrand, who feared that Gorbachev could fall over the issue. No world leader was willing to offend Gorbachev while German reunification was still at stake, and depended upon the Soviet leader's say-so for its realization.[38] By contrast, the Lithuanians' resistance met with greater approval within the USSR. Boris Yeltsin, who was elected president of the Russian Supreme Soviet at the end of May 1990, announced that he would permit trade with Vilnius, a move that made the boycott pointless. Yeltsin resigned from the Communist Party in July 1990. The previous month, the Russian Soviet Socialist Republic (SSR) had declared itself to be a sovereign republic within the USSR. Other SSRs followed suit; so-called autonomous regions *within* the various SSRs also proclaimed themselves to be sovereign entities (and hence to possess the right of ownership over the lucrative mineral resources found on their territory). By the fall of 1990, the once-mighty USSR was being transformed from a hierarchically controlled superpower into a mere space hosting competing territorial jurisdictions, only some of which were experimenting with democratic institutions. Gorbachev sought to impose order on the chaos by proposing, in November 1990, a plan for a Soviet confederation that would make control over tax, defense, foreign policy, currency reserves, and mineral rights the sole prerogative of the central government.

In the same month, Gorbachev vetoed a suggestion by the government of Iceland (which was, along with Denmark, the only western nation prepared to argue for Baltic self-determination openly) that the three Baltic states should attend the Paris meeting of the CSCE separately from the USSR. The conference's outcome was the Charter of Paris, which celebrated the fact that "the power of the ideas of the Helsinki Final Act have opened a new era of democracy, peace and unity in Europe." In Vilnius, Riga, and Tallinn, these words rang hollow. Certainly, despite the successful conclusion of German unification, no western statesman was willing in Paris to call Gorbachev's bluff on behalf of Baltic independence.

Gorbachev's shift toward the hard-liners caused a breach with his reformist foreign minister, Eduard Shevardnadze, who resigned in December 1990 to signal his preoccupation for the future of perestroika and glasnost. On 11 January 1991, world leaders discovered that Shevardnadze was not being alarmist. Gorbachev, capitalizing upon a split in the Vilnius leadership between Landsbergis and Prime Minister Kazimiera Prunskiene, and the distraction of the NATO powers in the Persian Gulf, where operation Desert Storm was looming, launched a sudden blitz against the rebels. KGB forces seized public buildings and proclaimed a puppet "Committee of National Salvation" in the place of the elected government.

The Lithuanians responded with passive resistance. Crowds surrounded public buildings and the national broadcasting tower. The latter was attacked by Russian troops on 13 January: fourteen of its civilian defenders were killed, including a young woman in her early twenties, Loreta Asanavičiūte, who was crushed beneath a tank. Hundreds were wounded. Repressive action on a smaller scale took place in Latvia. These grim events finally stirred the West to condemnation. The KGB forces were at once withdrawn—the Soviet leader was well aware that he could not risk a clash with the West over democracy and human rights. Gorbachev was, incidentally, the 1990 recipient of the Nobel Peace Prize.

In the wake of the events in Vilnius, Moscow announced that on 17 March 1991, Soviet citizens were to participate in a referendum asking whether "the preservation of the USSR as a renewed federation of equal sovereign republics, in which the rights and freedoms of an individual of any nation will be fully guaranteed" was "necessary." The objective of clamping down on national separatism was obvious. The Baltic nations were un-daunted. On 9 February, Lithuania held a referendum on independence: 90 percent voted in favor. Estonia and Latvia followed suit on 3 March 1991. Turnout was high in all three cases, and voting was free and fair. The 17 March referendum, by contrast, though it was successful in some other SSRs, was boycotted by most of the population of the Baltic republics, with only Russian speakers and Red Army troops typically casting their votes.

By the time of the March 1991 poll, the twin nemeses of the Soviet state—economic collapse and nationalism—were looming large. The Soviet economy was in freefall, with triple digit inflation and shortages of even basic necessities; the component republics of the USSR, notably Russia, where Boris Yeltsin was elected president on 12 June 1991, were acting more and more like separate nations. The USSR's transformation into a "Union of Sovereign States," in which foreign and defense policy at least remained in the hands of an elected federal president, was scheduled for 20 August 1991.

Gorbachev had been "crippled politically by his nationality crisis," although he did not yet realize by how much.[39] His opponents within the Kremlin, prompted by the head of the KGB, Vladimir Kryuchkov, were poised to turn the clock back to the days of centralized Soviet power. Their attempted coup d'état was to be a last, frightening spasm of the Cold War. On 18 August 1991, key figures in the party and state hierarchy confronted Gorbachev at his vacation home in Crimea and demanded that he either declare a state of emergency or resign and name Vice President Gennady Yanayev, a member of the plot, as acting president. Gorbachev refused and was placed under house arrest. The so-called State Committee on the State of Emergency proceeded to mobilize troops in Moscow, arrest key officials, and take over broadcasting stations.

Foolishly, however, they did not detain Boris Yeltsin. For all his subsequent exploits with the vodka bottle, and for all his encouragement of a new class of "oligarchs" who corruptly benefited from liberalization of the Russian economy, Yeltsin won a lasting place in history in August 1991 by standing on a tank in front of the "White House," the building in Moscow that hosted the elected assembly of the Russian republic, to rally the Russian people to the support of their fledgling democracy. Thousands of ordinary citizens flocked to the White House's defense; troops guarding the building got ready to fight. Faced with the prospect of carrying out a 1956-style massacre against their fellow Russians, key units mobilized by the State Committee stayed in their barracks. The coup ignominiously collapsed. Gorbachev was released and flew back to Moscow, where he resigned as general secretary of the Communist Party, which was duly banned from political activity. Effective political power now passed to Yeltsin.

The coup's failure heralded the end of the USSR. Estonia, Lithuania, and Latvia were immediately recognized by Iceland and the other Scandinavian states as independent countries. In the first week of September 1991, the three Baltic nations were admitted to the United Nations. The Soviet Union was wound up on 8 December 1991 when Russia, Ukraine, and Belarus seceded from the USSR and formed the Commonwealth of Independent States (CIS). The other constituent republics of the USSR joined the CIS (Georgia only in 1993) and embarked upon roller-coaster transitions from Soviet authoritarianism and central planning to political stability and market-based economies. More than twenty years on, most of them have not yet achieved either objective, let alone the more ambitious goals of democracy and respect for human rights. The last—and not the least—of the many catastrophes that Soviet communism bequeathed to the world was the chaos, poverty, corruption, and cynicism that have dominated the political life of the countries of the former USSR.

The epicenter of the political earthquake wrought by the end of the Cold War was in the former Soviet Union, but the tremors shaped the political landscape of Central Europe as well. The consensual separation of the Czech Republic and Slovakia was a second occasion in which nationalism and separatism thrived in the upheaval caused by the Cold War's end.

In Czechoslovakia, the nationalities issue took a high-profile role in the politics of post-communist Prague and Bratislava from the start. The spring of 1990 was dominated by a fierce debate over the country's name. Slovaks, irate at being denominated "Czechs," insisted that the country's name be changed to the "Czech and Slovak Federative Republic." At this point, however, outright secession was contemplated by only a minority of Slovaks and even fewer Czechs. What put secession on to the agenda was the politics of democratic transition. The two halves of the Czech-Slovak federation disagreed over the speed of change to the structure of the economy. Should "shock therapy" be applied, or should the transition to a market economy occur at a gentler pace? Unlike the former GDR, the Czech-Slovak federation had no rich western uncle willing to write the welfare checks for workers thrown out of a job.

This concern about the speed of the transition from communism grew in intensity after the first free elections in June 1990. These were won by the two formations that had guided the velvet revolution, the Civic Forum in Bohemia-Moravia and Public Against Violence in Slovakia. Civic Forum, in particular, took over 50 percent of the vote. Both Civic Forum and Public Against Violence were, however, "broad, umbrella organizations" whose goal had been to overthrow communism.[40] They were not cohesive political forces. Their internal conflicts—in particular between nationalists and liberals in Slovakia—soon came to the fore. Vladimir Mečiar, a would-be strongman, formed the populist-nationalist Movement for a Democratic Slovakia (MDS) in March 1991 and campaigned *against* rapid progress to a market economy.[41] In Prague, the principal conflict was between the "two Vaclavs":

Václav Havel, the president, a highly civilized liberal intellectual, and Vaclav Klaus, an abrasive right-winger with passionate free-market ideals. Klaus formed the Civic Democratic Party in early 1991, splitting away from Civic Forum, which disintegrated as a result.

Before long, Havel was practically the only leading politician in the country advocating "an authentic federation . . . based on genuine equality of both subject states and both subject nations that comprise it."[42] Elections in June 1992 provided a victory in the Czech lands for Klaus and a cluster of other center-right parties, though the Civic Democrats themselves obtained less than 30 percent of the vote. In Slovakia, Mečiar's MDS took 37 percent, openly secessionist nationalists took 8 percent, and the former communists took nearly 15 percent. None of these parties were in favor of Klaus's doctrinaire free-market radicalism.

After Havel was not reconfirmed as president by the federal parliament, he resigned before his term of office expired rather than acquiesce in the dissolution of the country. Klaus and Mečiar had no such qualms. To quote Havel: "Every night during the summer of 1992, representatives of the Czech Civic Democratic Party and the Movement for a Democratic Slovakia, two parties that had a lot in common, stood at the microphones and informed their publics about how one country would be divided into two." Havel bitterly remarked that, to him, this seemed like "the 'leading role of the party' in a new guise."[43] On 25 November 1992, the parliament of the Czech-Slovak federation approved the division of the country by a whisker more than the constitutionally required 60 percent majority. On 1 January 1993, the velvet divorce was consummated. Europe's map had to be redrawn yet again. The episode left its mark on Havel, who became skeptical about democracy's capacity to remain vital in the absence of a vigorous civil society able to prevent political parties from declining into "degenerate ghettoes whose only purpose is to elevate their members into positions of power."[44]

Atlas publishers were also forced to address the border changes provoked by the *violent* divorce of Slovenia and Croatia from Yugoslavia, a change that was itself a prelude to the catastrophic Bosnian conflict. Conflict had been latent in Yugoslavia since the late 1960s, when the leaderships of the Communist parties of Yugoslavia's component nations (Slovenia, Croatia, Serbia, Bosnia, Macedonia, and Montenegro) had opposed a policy of centralizing power in the capital, Belgrade, pressed by Tito's right-hand man Aleksandar Ranković. Drastic revisions to the constitution in 1974 devolved power to the periphery and, in effect, turned Yugoslavia into a confederation of one-party states with a collective national leader in the person of Tito. A booming economy, fuelled by remittances from Yugoslav guest workers in West Germany, hefty foreign loans, and a summertime influx of tourists kept separatist tendencies at bay. The personality cult of Tito to some extent also acted as a unifying force. In the 1970s, Yugoslavia was the freest communist state. Foreign books and magazines circulated relatively freely, and individual Yugoslavs possessed a liberty of movement beyond the dreams of an average citizen of the GDR or neighboring Romania and Albania. It was nevertheless a state where communist discipline kept order throughout the federation.

Tito died in 1980, which removed prop number one from the country's stability. The economy imploded, which removed prop number two. Loan repayments exceeded the country's ability to pay; heavy industry projects proved to be white elephants and ran up huge losses. When a desperate government resorted to the printing press, inflation took off in catastrophic form. By 1989, *monthly* inflation was in triple digits.[45]

As in Weimar Germany, inflation bred virulent nationalism, especially in Serbia. Prominent Serbian officials and intellectuals resented the fact that Belgrade had lost its centrality within the Yugoslav state since 1974. The Serbs were accordingly unwilling to accede to the demand of the Albanian-speaking minority within Serbia that the province of Kosovo should become an independent republic within the Yugoslav confederation. Kosovo was the heartland of Serbian history, even though, by the 1980s, nearly 90 percent of the population was ethnic Albanian. In April 1987, a senior Serbian official turned upheaval by the Serbian and Montenegrin minority in the Kosovo to his own advantage by promising a crowd that the state would protect them from their Albanian neighbors: nobody, he vowed, would ever beat up a Serb again.

The official's name, of course, was Slobodan Milošević. In the following two years, Milošević took over the Serbian Communist Party and inflamed public opinion with a demagogic campaign against the aspirations of the Kosovars. Hundreds of thousands took to the streets in his support. It was an ironic contrast to the vast demonstrations that contemporaneously brought down communist regimes from Riga to Sofia. The notion that there should be a greater Serbia, encompassing all those territories within Yugoslavia where Serbs were a majority of the population, as well as the territories that Belgrade already controlled, began to gain ground.

This idea of a greater Serbia implied grabbing territory from Croatia and Bosnia as well as denying the ethnic claims of the Kosovars. Even as Milošević harangued the Belgrade crowds in 1988 through 1989, nationalist tendencies were surfacing in neighboring Croatia and Slovenia. In June 1989, the leading Croatian nationalist, Franjo Tuđjman, formed the Croatian Democratic Union (HDZ), which soon captured widespread support. But this development took away the third prop holding up the edifice of the Yugoslav state. The central government in Belgrade, headed by a technocrat called Ante Marković, was striving to defeat inflation by introducing a new currency, squeezing the money supply, and freezing wages and prices. Such policies required, however, a degree of cohesion among the leaders of Yugoslavia's component republics that no longer existed. There was no single party line to follow, or enough party discipline to prevent Milošević, in particular, from spending his way to popularity. The League of Yugoslav Communists collapsed in January 1990 when the Slovenes withdrew from the organization.

In the spring of 1990, both Slovenia and Croatia held elections. In Slovenia, elections were won by DEMOS, the "democratic opposition of Slovenia," a federation of five non-communist forces. The presidency remained in the hands of a reformist communist leader, Milan Kučan, who had been the architect of democratization. In Croatia, the HDZ won at the polls by evoking the memory of the wartime Croatian state—one of Hitler's most repugnant allies. The HDZ took 60 percent of the vote and Tuđjman was elected president of the republic by the new parliament. The large Serb community in Croatia, mindful of the atrocities perpetrated against them by the Croatian state's militia, the *Ustaša*, during World War II, promptly demanded autonomous rule, which the nationalists in the Croatian capital of Zagreb rejected out of hand. Serbia and the Serbs would subsequently be demonized in Western Europe and the United States for their role in the civil war that broke out in June 1991, but their fears of Croatian extremism were comprehensible. If during the March 1990 elections in the GDR, Helmut Kohl had boasted of Germany's national history, and made use of imperial or Nazi symbolism, Israel, France, and Poland would have been rightly anxious about what the future might bring.

The truth is that by mid-1990 both Tuđjman and Milošević were consciously playing with fire. Tuđjman, by evoking the fascist epoch, was implicitly threatening the integrity of Bosnia, which had mostly been under wartime Croatian control, and was provoking the Serbs in the most reckless way imaginable. Milošević's rhetoric dangled the prospect of the inclusion within a greater Serbia of the more than two million Serbs living in the other Yugoslav republics—which could only mean civil war. His message nevertheless pushed the right buttons with Serbian voters. Milošević was elected president of Serbia in a free election by a 65 percent majority in December 1990. The candidate who came second essentially attacked the Serbian strongman for not being nationalist enough.

War duly came. Serbian enclaves inside Croatia were the site of bloody skirmishing between the Croatian police and Serbian guerrillas from the fall of 1990 onward. In February 1991, Serbian separatists proclaimed the independence of the Republic of Krajina, a long strip of territory bordering on Bosnia primarily occupied by ethnic Serbs. Thereafter, the situation in Croatia went "from bad to worse to appalling."[46] When Croatia declared independence on 25 June 1991, fighting broke out between Serb partisans, aided and abetted by the Yugoslav army, and Croatian security forces. Serbs soon controlled a third of Croatian territory and conducted a brutal policy of "ethnic cleansing" in the areas under their sway. The Serb commander, Ratko Mladić, was subsequently tried before the International Criminal Court for the atrocities his troops committed. Towns such as Vukovar became notorious across the globe for the ferocity with which civilians were treated. Gospić, a town in Croatia where more than one hundred Serbs were butchered by the Croatian National Guard in October 1991, was another terrible case of slaughter.

In Slovenia, events were less bloody. Following referendum on independence in December 1990, Slovenia announced that it would secede on 26 June 1991 unless a new constitutional arrangement for the whole of Yugoslavia that safeguarded its rights was agreed and implemented. Independence was actually declared a day early. The Yugoslav army made a half-hearted attempt to block Slovenian withdrawal, but Milošević was unwilling to press the issue to the point of war. Slovenia was the most homogeneous republic in Yugoslavia and had western friends.

Slovenia was fortunate. The conflict in Croatia illustrated that the end of the Cold War did not mean that Europe was necessarily destined to be a safe haven in a troubled world. Yet despite the fact that the breakup of Yugoslavia was taking place on their doorstep, Europeans were unable to find—let alone impose—a solution for Yugoslavia's ethnic strife. This was not for want of ambition. Jacques Poos became the best-known foreign minister of Luxembourg ever when, in a moment of hubris, he proclaimed that the Yugoslav crisis would be "the hour of Europe." Negotiations for the Treaty on European Union were in train in June 1991, and the notion that Brussels should have a foreign policy role as part of its emerging political identity was widely taken for granted. Washington itself thought that the EC's taking the lead in Yugoslavia was as "good a first test as any" of its capacity to fulfill the duties of a great power.[47]

The Europeans flunked the test. The strategy of the EC's chosen mediator, former British Foreign Secretary Peter Carrington, was to put as much of Humpty together again as possible. In the fall of 1991 Carrington advocated a revived Yugoslav confederation that guaranteed a "wide gamut of individual, cultural and political rights to the Serbs outside Serbia."[48] However, what was sauce for the goose was also sauce for the gander: Belgrade would have had to grant similar rights to the Kosovars. Milošević insisted that he would not accept such a plan unless there were border changes to include as many Serbs as possible under direct rule from Belgrade. To this, the Croats would not agree. In the meantime, the bloodshed continued unabated.

The EC had neither the clout to impose its preferred solution on the contending parties, nor the political will to put troops on the ground as peacekeepers. On 15 January 1992, Germany unilaterally recognized Croatia and Slovenia as independent nations. This action was taken despite an EC-commissioned report by an eminent French jurist that identified Macedonia and Slovenia as the only two Yugoslavian republics where there was adequate human rights protection, against U.S. advice, and against Carrington's warning that it would scupper the peace process and lead to trouble in Bosnia, which might demand independence too. Everybody knew that the Serbs of Bosnia would fight rather than accept minority status and that the other ethnic groups of Bosnia would fight rather than be minorities within a rump Yugoslavia dominated by nationalist Serbia. The subsequent Bosnian civil war is too complex a story to be recounted here, but its savagery shocked the world. Europe's long peace terminated barbarically in what news bulletins by now referred to as "the former Yugoslavia."

Geography is not just a question of maps, or even borders. It is also a question of minds. The events described in this brief section redefined Europe's conception of itself. Russia, in effect, had retreated back into Asia. A belt of independent states, the largest of which was Ukraine, now separated Central Europe from Moscow. This fact was both a threat and an opportunity for the states of the former Soviet empire. Uneasy about an eventual Russian recovery and determined, like Spain in the 1980s, to make an unambiguous statement about their own "western" identity, the former communist states, with the Czechs and Poles in the vanguard, clamored to join NATO and the European Union (EU).

Throughout the 1990s, U.S. administrations milked the Central Europeans' desire to join NATO as a way of keeping the security organization in being, even though its ostensible enemy—the Warsaw Pact—had obviously disappeared.[49] Poland, Hungary, and the Czech Republic joined NATO in 1999; a further expansion to the three Baltic republics, Slovenia, Slovakia, Romania, and Bulgaria was agreed in Prague in December 2002 and duly occurred in March 2004. A decade after the end of the Cold War, Europe was united, for security purposes, under American leadership: a fact that sowed renewed discord with Russia, especially after the demise of Boris Yeltsin.

The EU spent the 1990s "widening and deepening." By the latter, the EU meant increasing the scope of the policies decided in Brussels. By the former, the EU meant broadening membership. Negotiations for the entry of the Baltic states, Poland, the Czech Republic, Hungary, Slovakia, and Slovenia (as well as Cyprus and Malta) began in the late 1990s and these nations became member states in 2004. Romania and Bulgaria joined in 2007. Three Cold War neutrals—Austria, Finland, and Sweden—joined the EU as early as 1995. A mere decade after the end of the Cold War, the map of Europe's political organization was unrecognizably different from that of the previous decades.

ADRIATIC WHIRLPOOLS

It might seem odd to conclude a book on the Cold War in Europe with a comparative discussion of Albania and Italy. Yet the two countries, whose modern histories are indissolubly linked, were deeply shaken by the fall of communism, which brought about the implosion of their respective political systems and an interweaving of their political destinies. Albania, the last redoubt of European Stalinism, became after 1989 an authentic "failed state." One of the Cold War's grimmest legacies for Europe, surpassed only by the skin-and-bones children of Bucharest's orphanages, was the flood of desperate Albanian "boat people" who commandeered ships in 1991 to flee across the Adriatic—or drown in its waters. Albania's refugees headed toward Italy because since 1988 they had been introduced to its somewhat meretricious prosperity via television. Italy was at the zenith of its postwar wealth when the Cold War ended, with a higher GDP than Britain, and to the penniless inhabitants of the Balkan nation, it represented what the film director Gianni Amelio called "Lamerica" in the unsparing film he made about the Albanians' exodus.

Italy's enviable living standards did not, however, placate the Italians' own growing frustration at the political order that the Cold War had foisted upon them. Václav Havel's warning against the tendency of political parties, unchecked by civil society, to turn themselves into "degenerate ghettoes" concerned only with place and patronage, was sublimated in Italy in the 1980s. The DC and the PSI, the principal parties of government, having overcome the challenge of the PCI in the 1970s (see above, chapter 10), had become a byword for corruption, pork barrel politics, and wasteful public spending by 1989. Italy's national debt zoomed in the 1980s as the DC- and PSI-controlled government bought popularity with public money.

When the Wall fell, the *partitocrazia* fell, too. Italian institutions and public opinion asserted themselves with vigor. The established political order was swept away by a "landslide" of protest.[50] Italians voted at the polls for a change of regime, the judiciary struck ruthlessly against corrupt politicians of every stamp, and civil society activists organized campaigns for electoral reform and against the stifling hold of the mafia on the country's south. It was the only case of popular contestation bringing down a democratic government during the European Cold War, and it occurred only as the conflict was concluding and contestation became safe.

The PCI, long the alternative to the DC, did not benefit from the system's demise. The avatar of the Eurocommunist challenge in the 1970s was a spent force by the mid-1980s. Enrico Berlinguer died in 1984 and his successor, Alessandro Natta, was a bureaucrat unable to solve an internal conflict between the so-called *miglioristi*, who wished to woo the PSI from the DC's embrace, and the party's Brezhnevite left, whose chief figure, a Milanese boss politician called Armando Cossutta, had long been the conduit for the Kremlin's illicit funding of the party.[51] The PCI in general remained too uncritical of the USSR: "Perestroika and glasnost were seen as signs that the Soviet system, while ailing, was not yet moribund, and this led to an almost embarrassing cult of Gorbachev in the party press."[52] A poll of delegates at the seventeenth party congress of the PCI in 1986 revealed that more than 30 percent continued to believe that the USSR was the society that "most closely approaches the ideal."[53]

The PCI's internal disagreements and its inability to make a clear break with Moscow prevented it from taking advantage of the groundswell of protest against the DC-PSI "regime" in power. The PCI was seen as part of the problem, not the solution to Italy's increasingly evident political crisis. Its vote slumped to well under 30 percent in the 1987 elections, a setback that generated a debate of "unprecedented dramatic intensity" in its ranks.[54]

Natta was succeeded in June 1988 by a young reformer called Achille Occhetto. At the eighteenth party congress in March 1989, Occhetto persuaded the PCI to remove references to Marx, Lenin, and Togliatti from the party statute and abolished "democratic centralism," in other words, the obligation on members to follow without question the party line imposed by the leadership. The symbols of communism, notably the hammer and sickle on the party emblem, remained, however. In May 1989, the PCI left the Communist group within the European Parliament.

These modifications seemed daring, but they were eclipsed by the sheer speed of change in Poland and Hungary. The PCI hesitated over whether it should break decisively with its communist heritage, or else flaunt its credentials as the one communist party that had founded a democratic republic and remained loyal for nearly half a century to constitutional principles. The party of Enrico Berlinguer had no reason to be ashamed of its history and values, or so it was sustained. This argument had merit, but the PCI was also the party of Togliatti, of the cult of personality, and of grim apparatchiks like Cossutta. Occhetto grasped that the PCI had to rebrand itself as a progressive party campaigning for renewal of the Italian political system. Five days after the fall of the Wall, Occhetto crossed a personal Rubicon by contending that the PCI should transform itself into a radical leftist force "new even in name."

Constructing this new entity proved to be a *via crucis*. Resistance to changing the party's name was pronounced. The party accordingly consulted the membership about what kind of party the PCI should become. As Occhetto acknowledged, "first comes the thing [*la cosa*], then comes the name."[55] Until October 1990, when Occhetto suggested the Democratic Party of the Left (PDS) as its new name and unveiled a symbol of an oak tree with the hammer and sickle amid its roots, the PCI was known (at times contemptuously) as "the thing."

The PDS was officially born at the end of January 1991 at the twentieth congress of the PCI. A group of hard-liners headed by Cossutta split away to form *Rifondazione comunista* (Communist Refoundation). Cossutta subsequently sided with the plotters during the August 1991 coup attempt in Moscow. Occhetto was doubtless glad to see him go. He was presumably less glad that the congress initially refused to nominate him as party leader and that there was an exodus of party activists to *Rifondazione comunista*. The PDS was born in an atmosphere of controversy that robbed it of momentum.

Despite its lengthy gestation, the new party had still not made up its mind what it wanted to be. Occhetto favored a radicalized party, allied with progressive Catholics and civil society single-issue movements. The targets of its propaganda would be the malaises of the Italian political system, especially the need for electoral reform, and international imperialism, which during the twentieth congress was on show in the Gulf War against Iraq. Or so Occhetto depicted the U.S. war against Saddam Hussein. His opponents within the party, especially the *miglioristi*, wanted by contrast to ally with the PSI's leader, Bettino Craxi, and to consolidate relations with the United States and Italy's NATO allies to configure the PDS as a potential party of government.

Whatever the PDS might become, it was clearly no longer Moscow's fifth column, if indeed it ever had been. This fact had a huge impact, for two reasons. First, the Italian middle class no longer felt constrained to vote for the DC but could experiment with new options. The *Lega Nord*, a cluster of northern autonomist movements, was the principal beneficiary of this shift of mood. The second reason is less obvious. The leaders of the DC and the PSI *continued to fight the Cold War*. Rather than change a system that suited them, the leaders of the DC and the PSI sought to destroy the PDS as an electoral force by tarring it with the PCI's Stalinist past. Italy's 1992 general election campaign was drenched with Cold War rhetoric. As in 1948 and 1976, the parties of government demonized the communist peril. History was put to political use in February 1992 by the publication in the news magazine *Panorama* of a letter written by Palmiro Togliatti during World War II, when he was a senior official in Moscow. In the letter's text, Togliatti icily refused to save the lives of Italian soldiers captured by the Soviet army. The letter was subsequently shown to have been transcribed wrongly by its finder, an Italian academic historian. It was nevertheless a document, even in revised form, that starkly depicted Togliatti's fundamental cynicism. Just as cynical, however, was the use that was made of the letter. The party-controlled media blasted the PDS day after day, alleging that its unwillingness to distance itself from Togliatti's legacy was proof that it remained Stalinist at heart.[56]

Italians wanted answers to their present problems, not an inquest on the past. When voters went to the polls in April 1992, they slapped all the main traditional parties. The DC fell under 30 percent for the first time in postwar history. The PSI slipped back to 13.5 percent, 3 percent behind the PDS. The PDS and *Rifondazione*, added together, still represented a fifth of the electorate, although it was clear that communism in Italy had been definitively weakened. The threat now was from the *Lega Nord*, which took nearly 9 percent of the vote nationally and 18 percent in the north.

Bereft of a stable majority, the DC and PSI were unable to impose Prime Minister Giulio Andreotti as president of the republic. The mafia killed a national hero, the prosecutor Giovanni Falcone, provoking outrage to sweep the country. In the summer of 1992, the lira collapsed and the Italian government introduced austerity measures worth 6 percent of GDP. Judicial investigations uncovered rampant corruption, especially by the PSI, and brought to light links between politicians and organized crime in the country's south. Andreotti himself was accused of conspiracy with the mafia. Public opinion accordingly rebelled against the Cold War order. By the end of 1993, the DC, in new guise as the "Popular Party," commanded a mere tenth of the electorate. The PSI had been wiped out. Thousands of politicians had admitted guilt in corruption cases, although most plea-bargained themselves out of jail. Craxi had been hit by dozens of investigations and would eventually flee to Tunisia, protesting to the end of his life that the USSR's lavish support for the PCI had compelled him to raise money by illicit means. By December 1993, Italy had had its own velvet revolution, although that did not mean that it would henceforth enjoy political stability. The subsequent electoral success of Silvio Berlusconi, which other Europeans find so hard to explain, is incomprehensible unless one understands that the toxins produced by the Cold War have never been purged from the Italian body politic.

The implosion of Italian democracy had been *triggered* (not caused) by a class of politicians that underestimated the latent hostility toward the political system. Yet, like Watergate in the United States, the rebellion of the Italian electorate testified to the country's fundamental democratic health. Faced with scandalous abuses, Italy's democracy "threw the rascals out" without bloodshed. Albania's crisis was of a completely different order. The problems of even the worst democracy in Western Europe paled by comparison with the existential problems of a still-Stalinist society in a state of dissolution.

Since its breach with Khrushchev in the 1960s, Albania had become more and more of a hermit state. Its links with China were discontinued when Beijing deviated from pure Mao Zedong thought and permitted free enterprise. By the mid-1980s, Albania was an autarchy "in the same league as many poorer Third World countries." It was an "island of increasing poverty and demoralization, with a rapidly disintegrating infrastructure, crumbling buildings, malnourished and poorly clad workers and peasants using primitive agricultural equipment, all surrounded by slogans reminding them that *Partia mbi te gijtha* (the Party is above everything)." It was the "world's first atheist state" and a totalitarian one: its secret police, the *Sigurimi*, ensured that "organized dissent was impossible."[57] Party leader Enver Hoxha was the beneficiary of a Stalinist cult of personality; a gilded statute of the dictator disfigured the central square of the Albanian capital, Tirana. Hoxha died in 1985, but a longtime henchman, Ramiz Alia, preserved his legacy until 1990. Insofar as Albanians learned of the transformations under way in Central Europe, it was through recently unjammed Italian and Greek television and whispered conversations with the handful of compatriots who were entitled to travel abroad. For some in the regime, the velvet revolutions of 1989 were actually proof that deviations from Stalinist orthodoxy would lead to the revival of capitalism.

By the spring of 1990, however, Ramiz Alia was facing pressure for reform within the ruling Party of Labor (PLA). He belatedly began a process of liberalization. But it was too little, too late. In July 1990, protesters occupied western embassies in Tirana and fought the police in the seaport town of Durres, where they hoped to seize a ship to sail to Italy. Italy evacuated hundreds of the asylum seekers, which of course gave hope to the hundreds of thousands desperate to leave. Tirana, in the meantime, had fallen prey to mobs of protesters and to gangs of hooligans who roamed the capital damaging the relics of communist rule and stealing public property.

Political pluralism was introduced in December 1990 and elections were scheduled for March 1991. The run-up to the elections was characterized by street violence and the pulling down of Hoxha's garish statue in Tirana by a mob. Such events led the outside world to assume that the last bastion of European communism was doomed. In fact, the PLA won two-thirds of the seats in parliament. A massive turnout among voters in rural areas—97 percent of the electorate voted—and the use of a majoritarian rather than proportional system of voting ensured that the PLA defeated its only serious rival, the Democratic Party (DP), which was headed by Sali Berisha, a well-connected cardiologist who would become the politician of choice for the U.S. embassy in Tirana. The DP dominated the country's urban areas, especially Tirana.

The PLA's victory was a pyrrhic one. Its vote had relied more upon name recognition than ideology. Ramiz Alia became president of the Republic of Albania, as the country was now renamed. The new constitution, adopted in April 1991, expunged all references to Marx, Lenin, and Hoxha and affirmed liberal principles such as the right to possess private property, strike, worship freely, and emigrate.

The right to strike was, in fact, what brought closure to communism in Albania. The PLA government, led by a young modernizer called Fatos Nano, was overborne by the country's economic problems. Inflation was 250 percent per month and unemployment endemic. Food shortages were rife. GDP per head was probably less than $500. A month-long general strike by factory workers and miners compelled the Nano government to resign on 4 June 1991. It was a "final irony that a party which had so idealized the image and ethos of industrial workers was ultimately brought down by this social group."[58] A government of national unity, including the opposition DP, was formed to substitute the Nano administration. The PLA, like the SED or the PCI, at once turned itself into a post-communist party, the Socialist Party of Albania (SPA), to the disgust of Hoxha-ist true believers, who split away to form the Albanian Communist Party (ACP).

The task of feeding the country, however, was increasingly in the hands of Italy, which took charge, under constant threat from criminal gangs, of "Operation Pelican," a humanitarian mission tasked with distributing food aid donated by the West.[59] Italy had good reasons for keeping Albania provisioned. An armada of boat people embarked for Apulia (the heel of the Italian boot) in August 1991, where they were held for several days, under a hot sun and without adequate food or shelter, in a makeshift camp inside the soccer stadium of the town of Bari before armed police deported them. Greece was equally ruthless with its Albanian asylum seekers. Fear that Albania would become a sort of European Somalia, exporting refugees and criminality to its neighbors, was rife in the summer of 1991.

The government of national unity lasted until December 1991, when the DP pulled out. New elections were called for 22 March 1992. This time, the DP, lavishly funded by émigrés abroad, took 62 percent of the vote to the SPA's 25 percent. The ACP, putting the legacy of Enver Hoxha to the test of public opinion, received 0.4 percent: a fitting epitaph for the former regime. Sali Berisha became president and, encouraged by the United States, introduced free-market reforms. Some of these, notably privatization of the land, were popular; most were hated. Berisha swiftly eliminated "all vestiges" of Albania's communist past.[60] Ramiz Alia was arrested in September 1992 and, along with a number of former officials of the PLA regime, was condemned, after a show trial, to a stiff prison sentence in July 1994.

The March 1992 elections in Albania marked the ignominious end of European communism. The Balkan hermit state represented a parody of the failure of the communist experiment as a whole. An ideology that had planned to build a glorious new civilization had left half a continent economically backward, environmentally ruined, and psychologically scarred. All the post-communist states would have to endure a lengthy period of economic "shock therapy," political turmoil, and rampant corruption while they reconstituted themselves as normal societies. Romania, for instance, rivaled even Albania for the scale of its problems and the rapaciousness of its new post-communist political class.[61]

One way of characterizing the Cold War is to say that it was a clash between two superpowers in which both used military means, propaganda, and political intimidation to promote their rival belief systems and national

interests. A historian from Vietnam, Chile, Guatemala, or the Congo would hardly look upon the Cold War as a triumph for western values—or more likely would regard the principal western values as being militarism and neocolonialism. From a European perspective, however, the Cold War *was* primarily the story of the unraveling of communism as a political ideal and of the victory of the social and economic model prevalent in the continent's western half. Communism established its rule in Europe through terror, maintained its position through the power of the Soviet armed forces and/or the secret police (Berlin 1953, Budapest 1956, Prague 1968, Warsaw 1981), and prolonged its lifespan by using western loans to provide a façade of prosperity. It then went spectacularly bankrupt and its economic failure pulled away the last fig leaf covering its intellectual nakedness. The only books worth reading in the communist bloc were written by the novelists and political thinkers who told the truth about the system oppressing them.

Yet Europe's Cold War was not *only* characterized by the failure of the communist experiment. It was also a half-century in which West European elites chafed at the burden of their military obligation to the United States. The West was a sometimes contentious place. France rejected the EDC in 1954; Britain and France played gunboat diplomacy during the 1956 Suez crisis; de Gaulle and Olof Palme castigated the Vietnam War and flirted with Brezhnev; Helmut Schmidt derided the Carter administration for its weak dollar policy; the anti-nuclear movement stigmatized U.S. imperialism as the worst threat to peace, especially after the election of Ronald Reagan. Leading the West was a thankless task at times, though so was being led.

The difference between the two halves of the continent was nevertheless clear. However much European leaders contested Washington's specific policy preferences, no West European country, Italy excepted, contemplated experimenting with communism; nor did any, Italy included, reject the democratic institutions and values adopted after 1945. Political life was characterized in Western Europe by a growing conviction that a society based upon political pluralism, the welfare state, human rights, and a mixed, largely capitalist, economy was a worthwhile political goal; more worthwhile, indeed, than the ideological fantasies that had inflamed European imaginations throughout the twentieth century.[62] Such convictions can easily be characterized as materialistic, shallow, and unambitious. But they do at least allow citizens to shape their own lives, express their own opinions, and be saved from the worst consequences of personal or economic failure. Communist society did not provide these basic social and psychological needs, even the last named. Its peoples rebelled against it for that reason.

NOTES

1. Niccolò Machiavelli, *The Prince*, trans. George Bull (London: Penguin, 1961), Discourse 25, "How far human affairs are governed by fortune, and how fortune can be opposed."

2. Frank Costigliola, "An Arm around the Shoulder: The United States, NATO, and German Reunification, 1989–90," *Contemporary European History* 3 (1994): 88. Michael Cox and Stephen Hurst, "His 'Finest Hour'? George Bush and the Diplomacy of German Unification," *Diplomacy & Statecraft* 13, no. 4 (2002): 126.

3. M. E. Sarotte, "Perpetuating U.S. Preeminence: The 1990 Deals to 'Bribe the Soviets Out' and Move NATO In," *International Security* 35 (2010): 130.

4. An English translation of Kohl's speech is to be found in *When the Wall Came Down: Reactions to German Unification*, ed. Harold James and Marla Stone (London: Routledge, 1992), 33–41.

5. Mitterrand's close aide Jacques Attali records the French president as saying, "Mais il ne m'a rien dit! Rien dit! Je ne oublierai jamais!" in Attali, *Verbatim III, 1988–1991* (Paris: Fayard, 1998), 350.

6. Helmut Kohl, *Je Voulais l'Unité de l'Allemagne* (Paris: Éditions de Fallois, 1997), 205.

7. Kohl, *Je Voulais*, 216.

8. Konrad Jarausch, *The Rush to German Unity* (New York: Oxford University Press, 1994), 125.

9. Hans Stark, "Helmut Kohl and the Maastricht Process," in F. Bozo, M-P Rey, N. Piers Ludlow, and L. Nuti, eds., *Europe and the End of the Cold War: A Reappraisal* (London: Routledge, 2008), 251.

10. Kenneth Dyson and Keith Featherstone, *The Road to Maastricht* (Oxford: Oxford University Press, 1999), 364.

11. Hans-Dietrich Genscher, *Rebuilding a House Divided* (New York: Broadway Books, 1998), 308.

12. Helga Haftendorn, "German Unification and European Integration Are But Two Sides of One Coin: The FRG, Europe, and the Diplomacy of German Unification," in Bozo et al., eds., *Europe and the End of the Cold War*, 140.

13. Kohl, *Je Voulais*, 163.

14. Kohl, *Je Voulais*, 165. It is impossible not to note that these two countries were the only ones not to have been attacked and/or occupied by Germany between 1939 and 1945.

15. "Le défi allemand," *Le Monde*, 23 December 1989, 1.

16. See Frédéric Bozo, *Mitterrand, the End of the Cold War, and German Unification* (New York, Berghahn Books, 2009), for this argument. Bozo insists, p. xxii, that "at no moment did French diplomacy seek to slow down, let alone impede, German unification."

17. Quotations from Antonio Varsori, *L'Italia e la fine della guerra fredda* (Bologna: Mulino, 2013), 44, and N. Piers Ludlow, "A Naturally Supportive Environment? The European Institutions and German Unification," in Bozo et al., eds., *Europe and the End of the Cold War*, 167.

18. See Bozo, *Mitterrand, The End of the Cold War, and German Unification*, 237–38, for background to this letter.

19. *Bulletin of the European Communities*, 4/90, 8.

20. *Bulletin of the European Communities*, 4/90, 8.

21. For a warm tribute to the commission's efforts to make the absorption of the GDR happen, see Jacques Delors, *Mémoires* (Paris: Plon, 2004), 368.

22. See Mark Gilbert, "A Shift in Mood: The 1992 Initiative and Changing U.S. Perceptions of the European Community, 1988–89," in Kiran Klaus Patel and Ken Weisbrode, eds., *European Integration and The Atlantic Community in the 1980s* (New York: Cambridge University Press, 2013), 243–64.

23. Andreas Falke, "An Unwelcome Enlargement? The European Community and German Unification," in M. Donald Hancock and Helga Walsh, eds., *German Unification: Process and Outcomes* (Boulder, CO: Westview Press, 1996), 183.

24. Falke, "An Unwelcome Enlargement," 176.

25. For more particulars about Gorbachev's acceptance of German unity, see Hannes Adomeit, *Imperial Overstretch: Germany in Soviet Policy from Stalin to Gorbachev* (Baden-Baden: Nomos Verlagsgesellschaft, 1998), 478–90; quotes at 478, 487, 489.

26. The text of the Bush–Kohl press conference can be found at http://www.presidency. ucsb.edu/ws/index.php?pid=18188.

27. M. E. Sarotte, "Not One Inch Eastward? Bush, Baker, Kohl, Genscher, Gorbachev, and the Origin of Russian Resentment toward NATO Enlargement in February 1990," *Diplomatic History* 34 (2010): 119–40.

28. The phrase was regarded as a "slap in the face" by some Italian politicians. Kohl soothed ruffled Italian feelings at a meeting of Christian Democratic leaders held in Pisa on 18 February 1990. See Varsori, *L'Italia e la fine della guerra fredda*, 34–35.

29. See, for example, in English, Philip Zelikow and Condoleezza Rice, *Germany Unified and Europe Transformed* (Cambridge MA: Harvard University Press, 1997); George Bush and Brent Scowcroft, *A World Transformed* (New York: Knopf, 1998); Helga Haftendorn, *Coming of Age: German Foreign Policy since 1945* (Lanham, MD: Rowman & Littlefield, 2006), 275–310; M. E. Sarotte, *1989: The Struggle to Create Post Cold War Europe* (Princeton, NJ: Princeton University Press, 2009).

30. Sarotte, "Perpetuating U.S. Preeminence," 130.

31. Sarotte, "Perpetuating U.S. Preeminence," 129.

32. See Hanns Jürgen Küsters, "The Kohl-Gorbachev Meetings in Moscow and the Caucasus, 1990," *Cold War History* 2 (2002): 195–235 for transcripts; Kohl, *Je Voulais*, 360–68.

33. Michael Munter and Roland Sturm, "Economic Consequences of German Unification," *German Politics* 11, no. 3 (2002): 183-86.

34. Dennis L. Bark and David R. Gress, *A History of West Germany*, vol. 2: *Democracy and Its Discontents, 1963–1991* (Oxford: Blackwell's, 1993), 742.

35. Tony Judt, *Postwar: A History of Europe since 1945* (New York: Penguin, 2006), 637.

36. Kristian Gerner and Stefan Hedlund, *The Baltic States and the End of the Soviet Empire* (London, Routledge, 1993), 74.

37. Alex Pravda, "The Collapse of the Soviet Union, 1990–91," in the *Cambridge History of the Cold War*, vol. 3: *Endings*, ed. Melvyn P. Leffler and Odd Arne Westad (Cambridge: Cambridge University Press, 2010), 359.

38. See Kristina Spohr Readman, "Between Political Rhetoric and Realpolitik Calculations: Western Diplomacy and the Baltic Independence Struggle in the Cold War Endgame," *Cold War History* 6 (2006): 1–42, for an exhaustive analysis of the diplomacy of the Baltic crisis.

39. Martha Brill Ollcott, "The Soviet (Dis) Union," *Foreign Policy*, no. 82 (Spring 1991): 136.

40. Joseph Rothschild and Nancy M. Wingfield, *Return to Diversity: A Political History of East Central Europe since World War II* (Oxford: Oxford University Press, 2000), 272.

41. Paal Sigurd Hilde, "Slovak Nationalism and the Break-Up of Czechoslovakia." *Europe-Asia Studies* 51 (1999): 647–65.

42. Václav Havel, *To the Castle and Back* (London: Portobello, 2006), 98.

43. Havel, *To the Castle*, 99.

44. Havel, *To the Castle*, 120.

45. Gale Stokes, *The Walls Came Tumbling Down* (Oxford: Oxford University Press, 1993), 239.

46. Stokes, *The Walls Came Tumbling Down*, 249.

47. James Baker, *The Politics of Diplomacy* (New York: G.P. Putnam's, 1995), 637.

48. Laura Silber and Allan Little, *Yugoslavia: Death of a Nation* (New York: Penguin, 1997), 193.

49. The last meeting of the pact was in Prague on 1 July 1991. Havel, *To the Castle and Back*, 293–94, has some interesting reflections about the "absurdity" of its final two years and the difficulty of dissolving it.

50. The metaphor is Luciano Cafagna's: *La Slavina* (Venice: Marsilio), 1993.

51. The best book on the subject is Valerio Riva, *Oro da Mosca. I finanziamenti sovietici al PCI dalla Rivoluzione di Ottobre al crollo dell'URSS* (Milan: Mondadori, 2002). Berlinguer renounced the USSR's money in 1981.

52. Mark Gilbert, *The Italian Revolution: The End of Politics, Italian-Style?* (Boulder, CO: Westview Press, 1995), 67.

53. Piero Ignazi, *Dal PCI al PDS* (Bologna: Il Mulino, 1992), 59.

54. Ignazi, *Dal PCI al PDS*, 61.

55. Achille Occhetto, *Una costituente per aprire una nuova prospettiva a sinistra* (Rome: PCI, 1989), 17.

56. Giampaolo Pansa, *I bugiardi* (Milan: Sperling & Kupfer 1992), 76–92 *passim* for the episode; see also Gilbert, *The Italian Revolution*, 114–16.

57. Miranda Vickers and James Pettifer, *Albania from Anarchy to Balkan Identity* (London: Hurst & Co, 1997), 2, 12, 16.

58. Vickers and Pettifer, *Albania*, 66.

59. For Italy's role, see Varsori, *L'Italia e la fine della guerra fredda*, 159–87.

60. Vickers and Pettifer, *Albania*, 83.

61. The first six chapters of Tom Gallagher, *Theft of a Nation: Romania since Communism* (London: Hurst & Co., 2005) are depressing but invaluable reading.

62. Francis Fukuyama, *The End of History and the Last Man* (New York: The Free Press, 1992), so often depicted as a celebration of the universality and superiority of American values, was in reality making precisely this, surely uncontroversial, point.

Select Bibliography

The following books and articles were particularly helpful to me when I was writing this volume. They are not necessarily the most recent works; simply, they provoked me to think and shaped the interpretations that I have advanced in this narrative.

GENERAL NARRATIVES

Brown, Archie. *The Rise and Fall of Communism*. London: Harper Collins, 2009.

Fejto, François. *A History of the People's Democracies*. London: Pall Mall, 1971.

Gaddis, John Lewis. *The Cold War: A New History*. New York: Penguin, 2006.

Harper, John Lamberton. *The Cold War*. Oxford: Oxford University Press, 2012.

Hitchcock, William I. *The Struggle for Europe*. London: Profile, 2004.

Hobsbawm, Eric. *The Age of Extremes: The Short Twentieth Century*. London: Michael Joseph, 1994.

Judt, Tony. *Postwar: A History of Europe since 1945*. New York: Penguin, 2006.

Lundestad, Geir. *The United States and Western Europe since 1945*. Oxford: Oxford University Press, 2003.

Mazower, Mark. *Dark Continent: Europe's Twentieth Century*. London: Penguin, 1998.

Romero, Federico. *Storia della guerra fredda: L'ultimo conflitto per L'Europa*. Turin: Einaudi, 2009.

Rothschild, Joseph, and Nancy M. Wingfield. *Return to Diversity: A Political History of East Central Europe since World War II*, 4th ed. Oxford: Oxford University Press, 2008.

Stokes, Gale. *The Walls Came Tumbling Down: The Collapse of Communism in Eastern Europe*, 2nd ed. Oxford: Oxford University Press, 2008.

Westad, Odd Arne. *Global Cold War*. Cambridge: Cambridge University Press, 2006.

Young, John. *Cold War Europe: A Political History*, 2nd ed. London: Arnold, 1996.

MONOGRAPHS

Adomeit, Hannes. *Imperial Overstretch: Germany in Soviet Policy from Stalin to Gorbachev*. Baden-Baden: Nomos Verlagsgesellschaft, 1998.

Aga-Rossi, Elena, and Victor Zaslavsky. *Togliatti e Stalin: Il PCI e la politica estera staliniana negli archivi di Mosca*. Bologna: Il Mulino, 2007.

Aldcroft, Derek H., and Stephen Morewood. *Economic Change in Eastern Europe since 1918*. Aldershot, UK: Edward Elgar, 1995.

Applebaum, Anne. *Iron Curtain: The Crushing of Eastern Europe 1944–1956*. London: Allen Lane, 2012.

Arendt, Hannah. *The Origins of Totalitarianism*. Cleveland: The World Publishing Company, 1951.

Aron, Raymond. "The Imperial Republic." In Raymond Aron, *The Dawn of Universal History*. New York: Basic Books, 2002.

Ashby Turner, Henry. *Germany from Partition to Reunification*. New Haven, CT: Yale University Press, 1992.

Brandt, Willy. *The Ordeal of Coexistence*. Cambridge, MA: Harvard University Press, 1963.

Brown, Archie. *The Gorbachev Factor*. Oxford: Oxford University Press, 1996.

Calleo, David. *Rethinking Europe's Future*. Princeton, NJ: Princeton University Press, 2001.

Charlton, Michael. *The Eagle and the Small Birds: Crisis in the Soviet Empire: From Yalta to Solidarity*. Chicago: Chicago University Press, 1984.

Clogg, Richard. *A Concise History of Greece*. Cambridge: Cambridge University Press, 1995.

Courteois, Stéphane, ed. *Il libro nero del comunismo europeo*. Milan: Mondadori, 2007.

de Gaulle, Charles. *Memoirs of Hope: Renewal and Endeavor*, (New York: Simon and Schuster, 1971).

Deighton, Anne. *The Impossible Peace: Britain, the Division of Germany and the Origins of the Cold War*. Oxford: Clarendon Press, 1994.

Deletant, Dennis. *Communist Terror in Romania*. London: Hurst, 1999.

Djilas, Milovan. *Conversations with Stalin*. London: Penguin, 1962.

Friedman, Max Paul. *Rethinking Anti-Americanism: The History of an Exceptional Concept in American Foreign Relations*. New York: Cambridge University Press, 2012.

Furet, François. *The Passing of an Illusion: The Idea of Communism in the Twentieth Century*. Chicago: Chicago University Press, 1999.

Gaddis, John Lewis. *The Long Peace: Inquiries into the History of the Cold War*. Oxford: Oxford University Press, 1987.

Gati, Charles. *Failed Illusions: Moscow, Washington, Budapest, and the 1956 Hungarian Revolt*. Palo Alto, CA: Stanford University Press, 2006.

Garton Ash, Timothy. *The Polish Revolution: Solidarity*, 3rd ed. New Haven, CT: Yale University Press, 2002.

———. *The Magic Lantern*. New York: Random House, 1990.

Gleason, Abbott. *Totalitarianism: The Inner History of the Cold War*. New York: Oxford University Press, 1995.

Hanreider, Wolfram. *Germany, America, Europe: Forty Years of German Foreign Policy*. New Haven, CT: Yale University Press, 1989.

Haslam, Jonathan. *Russia's Cold War: From the October Revolution to the Fall of the Wall*. New Haven CT: Yale University Press, 2011.

Havel, Václav. *Open Letters*. London: Faber and Faber, 1991.

Hodos, George H. *Show Trials: Stalinist Purges in Eastern Europe, 1948–1954*. New York: Praeger, 1987.

Horne, Alistair. *Macmillan 1957–1986*. London: Macmillan, 1989.

Ionescu, Ghita. *The Break-Up of the Soviet Empire in Eastern Europe*. London: Penguin, 1965.

Judt, Tony. *Past Imperfect: French Intellectuals 1944–1956*. Berkeley: University of California Press, 1992.

Kemp-Walsh, Anthony. *Poland under Communism: A Cold War History*. Cambridge: Cambridge University Press, 2008.

London, Artur. *The Confession*. New York: Morrow, 1970.

Leffler, Melvyn P., and Odd Arne Westad, eds. *The Cambridge History of the Cold War*, 3 vols. Cambridge: Cambridge University Press, 2010.

Levy, Robert. *Ana Pauker: The Rise and Fall of a Jewish Communist*. Berkeley: University of California Press, 2001.

Louis, Wm Roger, and Roger Owen, eds. *Suez 1956: The Crisis and Its Consequences*. Oxford: Clarendon Press, 1991.

Margolius-Kovály, Heda. *Under a Cruel Star: A Life in Prague 1941–1968*. Cambridge, MA: Plunkett Lake Press, 1986.

Marsh, David. *Germany and Europe: The Crisis of Unity*. London: Heinemann, 1994.

Mastny, Vojtech. *The Cold War and Soviet Insecurity*. Oxford: Oxford University Press, 1996.

McCarthy, Patrick. *The Crisis of the Italian State*. New York: St. Martin's, 1995.

Miller, David. *The Cold War: A Military History*. New York: St. Martin's, 1998.

Miłosz, Czeslaw. *The Captive Mind*. London: Penguin, 1980.

Naimark, Norman. *The Russians in Germany: A History of the Soviet Zone of Occupation 1945–1949*. Cambridge, MA: Harvard University Press, 1995.

Navratil, Jaramir, ed. *The Prague Spring 1968*. Budapest: Central European University Press, 1999.

Papandreou, Andreas. *Democracy at Gunpoint: The Greek Front*. London: Pelican, 1973.

Rainer, János M. *Imre Nagy: A Biography*. New York: I.B. Tauris, 2009.

Revel, Jean-François. *The Totalitarian Temptation*. London: Secker & Warburg, 1976.

Sarotte, M. E. *1989: The Struggle to Create Post-Cold War Europe*. Princeton, NJ: Princeton University Press, 2011.

Servan-Schreiber, Jean-Jacques. *The American Challenge*. London: Pelican, 1968.

Seton-Watson, Hugh. *The East European Revolution*. London: Methuen, 1952.

Skidelsky, Robert. *The World after Communism: A Polemic for Our Times*. London: Macmillan, 1995.

Snyder, Timothy. *Bloodlands: Europe between Hitler and Stalin*. London: Random House, 2011.

Solzenhitsyn, Alexander. *The Gulag Archipelago*. London: Fontana, 1973–1978.

Taubman, William. *Khrushchev: The Man, His Era*. London: The Free Press, 2006.

Thomas, Daniel C., *The Helsinki Effect: International Norms, Human Rights, and the Demise of Communism* (Princeton, N.J.: Princeton University Press, 2001).

Tismăneanu, Vladimir. *Stalinism for All Seasons: A Political History of Romanian Communism*. Berkeley: University of California Press, 2003.

Trachtenberg, Marc. "The United States and Eastern Europe in 1945: A Reassessment." In *The Cold War and After: History, Theory and the Logic of International Politics*. Princeton, NJ: Princeton University Press, 2012.

———. *A Constructed Peace: The Making of the European Settlement*. Princeton NJ: Princeton University Press, 1999.

Vaisse, Maurice. *La grandeur: Politique étrangère du general de Gaulle 1958–1969* . Paris: Fayard, 1998.

Varsori, Antonio. *L' Italia e la fine della guerra fredda: la politica estera dei governi Andreotti (1989–1992)*. Bologna: Il Mulino, 2013.

Wałęsa, Lech. *A Path of Hope*. London: Collins Harvill, 1987.

"Z." "To the Stalin Mausoleum." *Daedalus* 119, no. 1 (1990): 295–344.

OTHER SOURCES

I have also hugely benefited—as even a glance at the endnotes shows—from the scholarly literature published in specialist journals of contemporary political history and international politics. *Cold War History* and the *Journal of Cold War Studies* are predictably the two most cited journals, but helpful articles have also been found in *The American Journal of International Law*, *Ayer*, *Canadian Slavonic Papers*, *Contemporary European History*, *Cold War History Project Bulletin*, *Current History*, *Daedalus*, *Diplomatic History*, *Diplomacy and Statecraft*, the *Economist*, *English Historical Review*,

Europe-Asia Studies, European History Quarterly, Foreign Affairs, Foreign Policy, Geopolitics, German Politics, German Studies Review, Government and Opposition, History and Memory, International Affairs, International History Review, International Organization, International Political Science Review, International Security, Journal of Contemporary History, Journal of European Integration History, Journal of European Studies, Journal of Farm Economics, Journal of Modern European History, Journal of Modern Italian Studies, Journal of Peace Research, Mediterranean Quarterly, Il Mulino, New Statesman and Nation, Political Science Quarterly, Il Ponte, Presidential Studies Quarterly, Problems of Communism, Public Health Reports, Relations Internationales, Revue d'histoire moderne et contemporaine, Slavonic and East European Review, Soviet Studies, Studi Storici, Survey, Survival, Les Temps Modernes, The Times, L'Unità, Vingtième Siècle, World Politics, World Today.

There are a large number of online sources for contemporary European and Cold War history. The two I used most frequently are the Cold War History Project, http://digitalarchive.wilsoncenter.org/theme/cold-war-history, and the Centre Virtuel de la Connaissance sur l'Europe, http://www.cvce.eu. This is a website maintained by the government of Luxembourg that gives an unequaled panorama of the principal developments in postwar European history.

Index

About the Author

Mark Gilbert is resident professor of history and international studies at SAIS Europe, the Bologna Center of the Paul H. Nitze School of Advanced International Studies of the Johns Hopkins University. His previous books include *European Integration: A Concise History* (Rowman & Littlefield, 2011).